THE SPIRIT OF VENICE

THE SPIRIT OF VENICE

From Marco Polo to Casanova

Paul Strathern

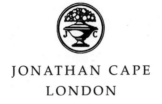

JONATHAN CAPE
LONDON

Published by Jonathan Cape 2012

2 4 6 8 10 9 7 5 3 1

First published in Great Britain in 2012 by
Jonathan Cape
Random House, 20 Vauxhall Bridge Road
London SW1V 2SA

www.vintage-books.co.uk

Addresses for companies within The Random House Group Limited
can be found at: www.randomhouse.co.uk/offices.htm

The Random House Group Limited Reg. No. 954009

A CIP catalogue record for this book is available from the British Library

ISBN 9780224089791

The Random House Group Limited supports The Forest Stewardship Council (FSC®), the leading
international forest certification organisation. Our books carrying the FSC label are printed on FSC®
certified paper. FSC is the only forest certification scheme endorsed by the leading environmental
organisations, including Greenpeace. Our paper procurement policy can be found at
www.randomhouse.co.uk/environment

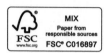

Typeset in Centaur MT by Palimpsest Book Production Limited
Falkirk, Stirlingshire

Printed and bound in Great Britain by Clays Ltd, St Ives PLC

To Oona

Contents

List of Illustrations

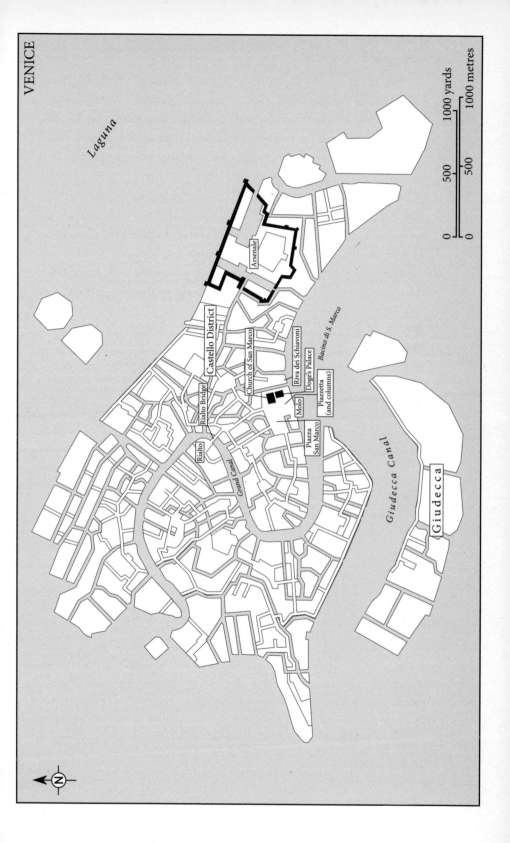

VENICE

Laguna

Castello District

Rialto Bridge

Rialto

Grand Canal

Church of San Marco

Riva dei Schiavoni

Doge's Palace

Molo

Piazzetta
(and columns)

Piazza
San Marco

Arsenale

Bacino di S. Marco

Giudecca Canal

Giudecca

| 0 | 500 | 1000 yards |
| 0 | 500 | 1000 metres |

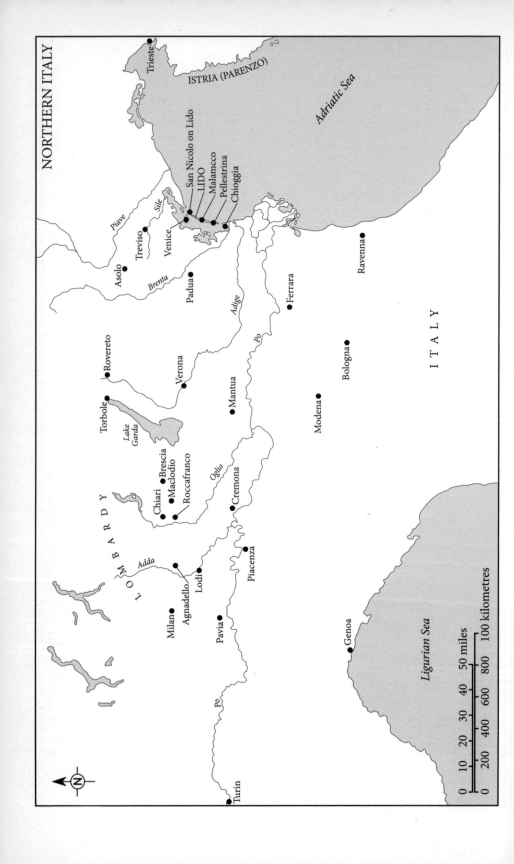

NORTHERN ITALY

Trieste

ISTRIA (PARENZO)

Adriatic Sea

San Nicolo on Lido
LIDO
Malamcco
Pellestrina
Chioggia

Piave

Sile

Treviso

Venice

Asolo

Brenta

Padua

Adige

Ferrara

Po

Ravenna

Rovereto

Verona

Mantua

Bologna

Torbole

Lake
Garda

Modena

L O M B A R D Y

Chiari
Brescia
Maclodio
Roccafranco

Oglio

Cremona

Adda

Piacenza

Milan
Agnadello
Lodi

Pavia

Po

Genoa

Ligurian Sea

Turin

I T A L Y

0   10   20   30   40   50 miles
0   200   400   600   800   100 kilometres

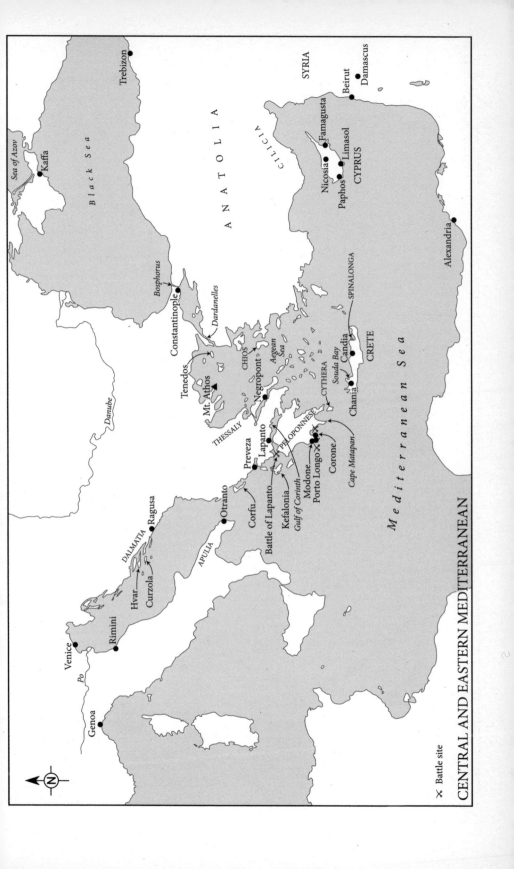

CENTRAL AND EASTERN MEDITERRANEAN

✕ Battle site

Venice
Genoa
Po
Rimini
Hvar
Curzola
DALMATIA Ragusa
APULIA
Otranto
Corfu
Battle of Lapanto
Kefalonia
Gulf of Corinth
Modone
Porto Longo
Corone
Cape Matapan
Preveza
Lapanto
THESSALY
Mt. Athos
Tenedos
Negropont
CHIOS
Aegean Sea
PELOPONNESE
CYTHERA
Souda Bay
Chania
Candia
SPINALONGA
CRETE
Danube
Constantinople
Bosphorus
Dardanelles
ANATOLIA
Black Sea
Sea of Azov
Kaffa
Trebizon
CILICIA
SYRIA
Beirut
Damascus
Famagusta
Nicosia
Limasol
Paphos CYPRUS
Alexandria
Mediterranean Sea

N

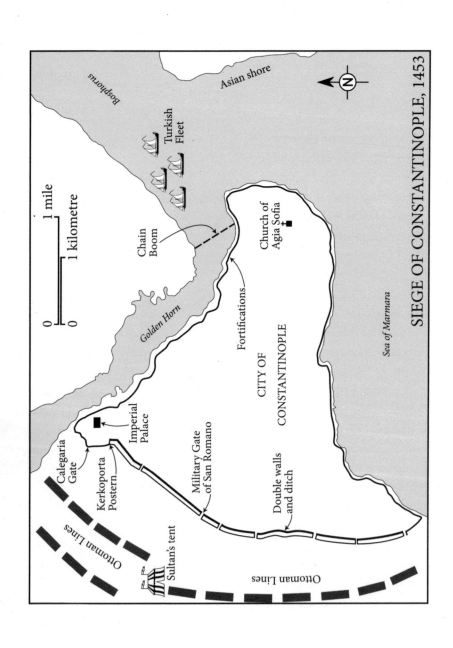

SIEGE OF CONSTANTINOPLE, 1453

Bosphorus

Asian shore

N

Turkish Fleet

1 mile

1 kilometre

0

0

Chain Boom

Church of Agia Sofia

Golden Horn

Fortifications

CITY OF CONSTANTINOPLE

Sea of Marmara

Imperial Palace

Calegaria Gate

Kerkoporta Postern

Military Gate of San Romano

Double walls and ditch

Ottoman Lines

Sultan's tent

Ottoman Lines

Prologue

IN THE WORDS of the renowned historian John Julius Norwich, 'One of the most intractable problems with which the historian of Venice has to contend is that which stems from the instinctive horror, amounting at times to a phobia, shown by the Republic to the faintest suggestion of the cult of personality.' Indeed, he goes on to say, 'it is hard to find much human interest in the decrees and deliberations of the faceless Council of Ten'. My intention is not to write another history of Venice, but to show that – despite pursuing this policy – the city not only produced, and attracted to its shores, a succession of outstanding characters, but also that these characters (ranging from Marco Polo to Casanova) often embodied the spirit of Venice, which in its turn frequently took on a distinctly individual character of its own. They will be described against the background of events that over the centuries forged and finally destroyed the most powerful of all Mediterranean cities. Venice came to see itself as *La Serenissima* ('the Most Serene Republic'), yet here its self-identification was as faulty as its attempt to suppress all individuality. Far from being so tranquil and clearly aloof from everyday concerns, its behaviour could be dark and obfuscating, proud and avaricious, efficient or incompetent, devious, vengeful, glorious even, and certainly, towards the end, eaten away by a self-destructive paranoia so embodied by that very Council of Ten, the committee of public safety, spies and secret police.

The Venetians, like the British, were a seagoing island race, who laid claim to an extensive empire out of all proportion to the size of their homeland, whose influence at times extended to the reaches of the known globe. Yet like America, Venice's empire was more concerned with trade domination than with actual territorial possession. And, like both empires, it was not afraid of isolationism: of turning its back on the large land mass that began just across the water, or of ignoring the larger continental worlds beyond – in the form of Europe, America and Asia.

Venice was ruled over by a doge, an elected position held for life, whose holder initially held great power, which was gradually diminished over the centuries until he became little more than a figurehead, his sovereignty similar to that of the British monarch today. Although nominally a democratic republic, Venice was in reality an oligarchy ruled by an extensive class of wealthy 'noble' families. Only members of these families could sit on the parliamentary-style Great Council and vote, a jealously guarded right handed down from generation to generation, and they alone could be elected to senior administrative positions, such as membership of the many interlocking councils that ensured the checks and balances of ordered daily governance, or become members of the supreme Council of Ten, or become doge.

We have much to learn from the historical parade of varied characters who so reflected Venice's rise and long, long decline. Venice was a city state like no other, in that it was surrounded by no extensive rural hinterland. In consequence, it was forced to rely upon entrepreneurial trade and ingenuity, essentially individual characteristics. This meant that the city developed several of the traits of an industrial revolution some centuries before the actual Industrial Revolution began in eighteenth-century Britain. In the great ship-building yard at the Arsenale, Venice pioneered the manufacturing technology of the assembly line, and its glass-manufacturing factories on the island of Murano saw the beginnings of industrial urbanisation. In order to facilitate their import and export business, the Venetians all but invented banking, established much of the mechanism of overseas trade (bills of lading and so forth) and made financial manipulation an art of their own. At the same time it is hardly by chance that this urban concentration of skills and imaginative thinking not only pioneered printing in Italy, but also nurtured some of the finest artists, musicians and scientists that Europe had seen. Venice nurtured genius and wastrel alike, inspiring tragedy, triumph and all in between, forever reflecting on itself in the mirror of its own enclosed lagoon. Yet this was also the city whose ambitions, as it approached its zenith, drove its citizens to seek out the furthest ends of the Earth.

Part One
Expansion

I

'Il Milione'

IN 1295 MARCO POLO, accompanied by his father and his uncle, arrived back in Venice having travelled 'from the Polar Sea to Java, from Zanzibar to Japan'. According to the man to whom Polo would one day dictate the story of his travels:

> from the time when Our Lord formed Adam our first parent with His hands down to this day there has been no man, Christian or Pagan, Tartar or Indian, or of any race whatsoever, who has known or explored so many of the various parts of the world and of its great wonders as this same Messer Marco Polo.

There is no reason to doubt this claim. Marco had left Venice at the age of seventeen, and had been away travelling for twenty-four years. By the time he returned to Venice he was unrecognisable. Just over two centuries later the scholar Giovanni Battista Ramusio, drawing on stories passed down from father to son by Venetian families who were close to the Polos, described their appearance on their return: 'They looked just like Tartars, and they even spoke with an odd accent, having all but forgotten how to speak in the Venetian tongue.' In 1295, the Republic of Venice was more than eight centuries old, and the Council of Ten had over the years imposed very precise sumptuary laws prescribing for its citizens appropriate dress for different classes, commending modest attire, decreeing short hair and prohibiting extravagant or colourful clothes except on special occasions. But Venice was also a busy port, and its citizens would have been accustomed to seeing visitors in rather more exotic attire than their own – ranging from mainland farmers in their traditional peasant dress, their dark faces all but obscured beneath wide-brimmed straw hats, to Arab merchants wearing turbans and djellabas; Slavs and Albanians in tribal baggy trousers; and local Jews in their long dark gaberdine cloaks. Even so, the long hair and long beards of the returning Polos, with their weather-beaten skin deeply tanned and wrinkled by long exposure to tropical sun and desert winds, together with their heavy tattered kaftans, which appeared more like carpets than civilised Venetian cloth, must have stood out. Heads would have turned as they walked from the landing stage across the rickety old wooden Rialto Bridge and through the narrow alleyways of the Castello district to the Ca' Polo, the family mansion, where no one at the gate even recognised them.

The Polos were a minor family of the ruling patrician class, and their fluctuating commercial fortunes had driven them eventually to undertake the bold and ambitious trading journey into the unknown Orient. (In Venice, unlike the kingdoms and dukedoms of the rest of Europe, upper-class families were deeply involved in trade: this was the ethos of the mercantile republic.) The late thirteenth century marked an age of expanding Venetian enterprise; spurred on by competition with their Genoese rivals, Venetian explorers began searching out new markets by sea as well as by land. The Polo family was the embodiment of this adventurous spirit.

Upon their arrival back in Venice, however, word soon spread that the Polos had been reduced to rags, that after twenty-four years of trading they had returned with no more than a Tartar slave bearing a trunk containing their few remaining possessions. As a result, the good name of the Polo family, long respected for their business acumen, suffered severe damage. Without a sound reputation, ventures now undertaken by any of the Polos were liable to attract few — if any — backers or investors. If such rumours were allowed to spread, the family faced the prospect of ruin.

In order to restore their good name, soon after their return the Polos decided to throw a banquet, inviting all members of their family and including as many influential people as they knew. When the guests were seated, Marco Polo, together with his father Niccolò and uncle Maffeo, appeared before the company dressed in flowing robes of the finest silk.

They then proceeded to remove these garments and began tearing them into strips, distributing the colourful tatters amongst the servants, before retiring and returning in yet more fine robes, this time made of red velvet. In the midst of the meal the Polos rose once more and began tearing their expensive robes into strips, again distributing these amongst the servants. They then retired and returned once more clad in the finest robes; at the end of the meal, these too were torn to shreds and given away. By now, all understood: the Polos could hardly be poor if they could afford such extravagant gestures. But Marco, Niccolò and Maffeo had one more sensational demonstration, which was to be the finale of their performance. They returned clad in the ragged Mongol attire they had worn on their return to Venice. Ramusio describes how the three of them produced knives and began cutting through the inner seams of their thick garments, 'causing a cascade of precious gems to spill out. These rubies, sapphires, carbuncles, diamonds and emeralds had all been concealed within the garments in such a cunning fashion that no one could have guessed what they contained.' This story has the flavour of an oriental tale, and could indeed be straight out of *Scheherazade*, though Polo's biographer Laurence Bergreen is of the opinion that here Ramusio 'was probably embellishing but not inventing'. At any rate, this or some similar act certainly seemed to restore the Polo name as successful traders.

However, as we now know with the benefit of hindsight, the three Polos were indeed enacting something of an oriental charade – for they were withholding a disastrous secret. They may have returned with a stock of precious gems, but they had in fact been robbed of the major fortune they had made in the course of their twenty-four years of trading. During their travels throughout the Mongol Empire their safety and that of their goods had been under the protection of the Mongol emperor Kublai Khan, who had taken them into his service and issued them with a *paiza* (a privileged diplomatic pass). This consisted of a gold tablet one foot long and three inches wide, on which was inscribed: 'By the power of Eternal Heaven, holy be the Great Khan's name. Any one not giving reverence to the bearer of this evidence of the Khan's power will be slain.' This had guaranteed them complete protection and gracious hospitality on all their travels.

However, towards the end of their voyage home they had arrived at the empire of Trebizond, a remote Byzantine outpost on the south-eastern Black Sea coast. Here for the first time they were venturing outside the Pax Mongolica, beyond the western jurisdiction of the khan's *paiza*. Trebizond was nominally a Christian ally of Venice, but its very remoteness, some 500 miles east of Constantinople, meant that it was to all intents and purposes a law unto itself. When the Polos had arrived here, instead of receiving a welcome from their fellow Europeans, they had watched powerless as their trunks of gold had been confiscated by corrupt local authorities. The sum of their losses would seem to have represented a considerable fortune, and might even have been enough to elevate the Polos to a place amongst the richer noble families of Venice, had they retained it. Needless to say, Marco glossed over the distressing events at Trebizond in his account of his travels, and neither his father nor his uncle ever made mention of their huge loss – not until after the death of Uncle Maffeo was reference to this incident found in his will, when accounting for the paucity of inheritance and certain debts that the family owed.

The loss of this fortune probably also accounts for the three Polos arriving back in Venice dressed in such outlandish garb. They could easily have purchased more suitable Venetian clothing when they passed through Constantinople, which had a large, established Venetian trading community. Yet at the time they arrived there the Polos would have been decidedly short of spending money, as well as being wary of risking the secret of their Mongol clothing by exchanging jewellery.

Apart from this episode, Marco Polo soon began regaling all who would listen with tales of his travels in the East, including exotic descriptions of China and Kublai Khan. Ramusio described how:

> He kept repeating these stories, always emphasising the magnificence of the Great Khan, claiming that his revenue was between ten and fifteen millions in gold. Likewise, when speaking of the fabulous nature of the other countries he visited, he always spoke in terms of millions. As a result, he soon acquired the nickname Messer Marco Milione, and was even mentioned in the records under this name, while his house became known as the Corte Milione.

And the name persists to this day, having been given to the remaining arches of the Ca' Polo that can still be seen on the façade of the Teatro Malibran in the midst of the Castello district of Venice.

By now Genoa posed a serious threat to the expansion of Venetian trade, especially in the eastern Mediterranean, the Levant and the Black Sea. On his return journey from the Orient, Polo himself was surprised to notice as he passed along the shores of the Caspian Sea how 'Genoese merchants have taken to launching ships on this sea and sailing on it'. Already the Genoese had well-established colonies and trading partners at points all around the coast of the Black Sea; now they appeared to be expanding far beyond the confines of Europe. (Indeed, Genoese influence in Trebizond may even have played a part in the seizure of the Polos' treasure.) In 1296, just a year after the Polos had passed through Constantinople, the Genoese launched an attack on the Venetian colony there, seizing all its assets and putting its traders to the sword. The Genoese trading colony in Constantinople would soon be accruing a massive revenue, three times greater than the entire income arriving at the capital city from all over the Byzantine Empire.

The sacking of the Venetian colony in Constantinople set the stage for outright war. After a number of increasingly serious skirmishes between ships of the two rivals, in August 1298 news reached Venice that a Genoese fleet of eighty-eight ships under the command of Admiral Lamba Doria was stationed at the entrance to the Adriatic – posing a direct threat to Venice's trading routes. Doria was keen to draw out the Venetian fleet and engage them in battle, but for some reason the Venetians refused to be drawn. Doria, mindful of his reputation as the greatest naval tactician of his age, suspected that the Venetians were afraid of him. In an attempt at further provocation, he decided to sail into the Adriatic itself – a move that finally forced the Venetians into action.

In the heat of the last days of August, a fleet of ninety-six Venetian galleys – including one under the command of the forty-four-year-old Marco Polo – disembarked from Venice led by Admiral Andrea Dandolo. On assembling outside the lagoon, the fleet began rowing and sailing its way down past the islands of the Dalmatian coast. Impatiently awaiting the appearance of the enemy, the Genoese fleet anchored 300 miles south in the lee of the Venetian island of Curzola (modern Korčula). Here a sudden storm blew up, sinking six of their ships. Exasperated by this development, Doria ordered Genoese forces ashore, where they proceeded to inflict rape and pillage on the local settlements, a move intended to draw the Venetians to the scene as soon as possible. While the Genoese waited, a calm descended and banks of mist began to drift over the glassy sea. Early on the morning of 6 September the sharp black prows of the Venetian galleys appeared out of the mist, as if ready for battle. Then, for no accountable reason, they disappeared back into the mist once more.

Doria suspected that the Venetians, despite their superior numbers, were still afraid of taking on the might of the Genoese fleet. But this was not the case. Dandolo had been informed of the position of the Genoese fleet by boats in flight from Curzola, and now sailed to the other side of the island. Here he put ashore a contingent of soldiers who covertly began making their way over the barren rocky mountains to the far shore. On the morning of Sunday 8 September, in a coordinated attack, the Venetian soldiers stormed the Genoese encampment while the Venetian fleet rounded the island on a following wind and launched into the Genoese galleys. Owing to the element of surprise, the Venetians were able to gain the upper hand, ramming and setting on fire a number of Genoese galleys. On land, a hail of Venetian arrows rained on the Genoese camp and the Venetians charged. At sea, Dandolo managed to capture ten Genoese galleys, but in the midst of this operation a number of his own galleys ran aground in shallow water. Doria immediately seized upon this mishap. As the sea battle continued, he surreptitiously manoeuvred the Genoese ships around the Venetian galleys, until at last he had them surrounded. As Doria began forcing the Venetian galleys into an ever tighter concentration, rendering them unable to manoeuvre, the Genoese began firing burning arrows into their midst. Fire began to spread through the Venetian fleet, yet still they continued to fight. However, after almost nine hours of continuous fighting the Genoese finally overwhelmed the Venetian fleet, eventually capturing or destroying eighty-four of their original ninety-six galleys, and taking prisoner no fewer than 8,000 men. This represented a staggering blow to Venice's ability to fight; at the time the entire population of the city was just under 100,000, and these

prisoners accounted for almost one-third of the able-bodied male population of the city.

Faced with the prospect of disgrace and capture by the Genoese, the
humiliated Dandolo took his fate into his own hands. It is said that he
gave orders that he be lashed to his flagship's mast, and then proceeded
to smash his head against it until his skull split open. However, his defeat
had not been quite as devastating as he perhaps imagined. Dandolo's fleet
had managed to inflict sufficient damage on the galleys under Doria's
command that the Genoese admiral decided not to risk consolidating his
victory by sailing to attack Venice itself.

Amongst the Venetians taken prisoner was Marco Polo. Since returning
to Venice he had continued to trade, and had done so with such success
that he soon had sufficient funds to sponsor the building and equipping
of a galley, which he himself captained in the campaign. Along with his
thousands of fellow captives, Marco Polo was now transported back to
Genoa in triumph aboard the captured galleys. Within a month of the
battle he found himself confined inside the grim Palazzo di San Giorgio;
adding insult to injury, this prison had been constructed out of stones
taken more than thirty years previously from the sacked Venetian embassy
in Constantinople. Polo and his fellow Venetians now faced the prospect
of being confined for many years.

In the manner of the period, the prisoners were allowed to range freely
within the castle, and 'nobles' such as commander Marco Polo were
permitted large cells that could be decorated with furniture – carpets, bed,
hangings and so forth – sent from home. Although many of the poorer
ordinary sailors were all but starving, the 'nobles' were permitted to purchase
extra rations to ensure their survival. As the months passed, Marco Polo
reverted to character, keeping his fellow prisoners entertained with the
fabulous tales of his travels through the East. Word of the exploits of 'Il
Milione' began to spread through Genoa and, according to Ramusio, 'he was
visited by the most noble gentlemen of the city, who bestowed upon him
presents to alleviate his confinement'.

Polo now attracted the attention of another prisoner, who had already
been in San Giorgio for fourteen years by the time of Polo's arrival. This
was the writer known as Rustichello of Pisa, who had in his day been

something of a storyteller himself, having penned numerous tales of courtly love and knightly valour, specialising in Arthurian romances. These latter had earned him such renown that he had been invited by the future King Edward I of England to join his court and entertain him during his crusade to the Holy Land some twenty-five years earlier. There is some speculation that Rustichello may even have met, or at least heard of, Polo during this period, which coincided with the Polos' outward journey through Palestine. At any rate, Polo and Rustichello were to make an ideal partnership: the compulsive storyteller and the writer of legendary tales would combine to produce what would become one of the best-known works in Europe. This might not have been a great work of literature, but its content more than made up for its lack of style. Here was the first description of an exotic civilisation whose existence had lain all but unknown on the other side of the world. We were not alone in the universe: here was another world. Little wonder that an early title given to Polo's work was simply *Il Mondo*.

It is no exaggeration to say that in many ways Polo had visited the future. While for the most part Europe languished in medieval stasis, China had seen the invention of gunpowder, paper money, printing, and the burning of coal as a fuel. According to some sources, Polo brought to Venice in his remaining luggage examples of another Chinese invention, namely ground lenses, which he is said to have used as a form of spectacles to boost his failing eyesight in old age. These could have been used to make a microscope or a telescope, but no mention is made of this, and it would be another 300 years before these instruments were 'invented' in Europe. And beside these innovations China could also boast such futuristic wonders as Kinsai, the 'City of Heaven', which in Polo's description sounds almost like a utopian vision of Venice. What he saw was:

> the finest and most splendid city in all the world, filled with wide and spacious waterways. On one side of the city is a lake of crystal clear fresh water. Its shores are thirty miles long and are filled with stately palaces and mansions of such splendour that it is impossible to imagine anything more beautiful. These are the abodes of nobles and magnates. At the same time there are also cathedrals and monasteries. The surface of the lake is covered with all manner of barges

filled with pleasure-seekers. Once they have finished their work the people of this city like nothing better than to spend their time enjoying themselves with their womenfolk or with hired women.

Polo describes such 'hired women' in revealing detail:

They are found throughout the city, attired in the highest fashion, smelling of sensual fragrances, waited on by attendants, and living in richly decorated accommodation. These ladies are exquisitely practised and accomplished in the use of endearments and caresses, using words perfectly suited to the occasion and the person who is with them. Those who have enjoyed their company remain utterly beside themselves and so captivated by their delicacy and sweet charms that they can never forget them. As a result, when any foreigner returns home, he boasts that he has been to 'Kinsai', in other words to Heaven, and can hardly abide the time before he returns.

Marco Polo, by then in his early twenties, would seem to have experienced these qualities at first hand. He also describes the delights of the table. China not only had its own, entirely original cuisine, but also had foodstuffs such as rice and rice pasta, which were as yet unknown to Europe. In Kinsai:

because the fish in its lakes are so well-fed, they are plump and delicious. When you see all the different varieties of fish on display in the streets, you wonder how on earth they will all be sold. Yet in just a few hours they have all been bought. Because so many of the citizens have grown accustomed to the highest cuisine, they are used to eating both fish and meat at the same meal.

Little wonder that so few believed the tales told by *Il Milione*. Yet surprisingly, Polo's Kinsai has been identified as modern Hangzhou, and his descriptions would seem to be true, apart from a few minor exaggerations (the lake had a shoreline of ten rather than thirty miles). His account is confirmed by that of the contemporary Persian historian Vassaf, as well as by the words of a travelling Franciscan friar named Odoric of Pordenone,* who passed through Kinsai some forty years later and also claimed that it was 'the greatest city in all the world, and the most noble'.

There is no denying that Rustichello's written version of Polo's travels contains the occasional exaggeration or even plain falsehood. He was, after all, a romance writer by profession, and as such saw no harm in including entire passages lifted verbatim from his own works. For example, Polo's description of his second meeting with Kublai Khan is recognisable as Rustichello's earlier written account of the legendary Tristan's arrival at King Arthur's court at Camelot. Other reasons for questioning the veracity of Polo's account include the very obvious things that he missed out, such as tea-drinking, chopsticks, printing and the Great Wall of China.† It is possible that Polo did mention these items, and Rustichello simply found them too incredible to include in the finished version. However, despite Rustichello's 'assistance', most of what Polo described was to be confirmed by later writers. Such confirmation would take time – indeed, certain remote parts of south-east Asia and Burma that he passed through would not see a European face for over 600 years (until the Second World War). And as for the wonders that he left out, Polo would have had a ready explanation for these. On his deathbed, in 1324, he would inform his listeners, 'I did not tell a half of all I saw.'

The presence of Odoric of Pordenone in Kinsai during the early 1300s confirms that the Polos were not the only Venetians venturing beyond the horizon of the known world during this period. Just half a century after the death of Marco Polo, the Zeno brothers, Nicolò and Antonio, members of the distinguished family that produced doges and famous admirals, were reported to have sailed beyond the British Isles and reached an icy land called Engronland. It has been suggested that this was Greenland, but their

* A small city north of Venice.
† It has recently been claimed that the Great Wall was not yet built at this time, and it is true that the final version we know today was only completed during the Ming Dynasty, which lasted from the mid-fourteenth to the mid-seventeenth century. However, previous similar constructions, sections of which were incorporated into the present structure, date from as far back as the Qin Dynasty in the third century BC. As some of these early walls were more than 1,000 miles long, they would have proved a spectacular sight, which Polo would surely have remembered, or at least heard about.

description of a monastery heated by boiling water which gushed from the earth makes it sound more like Iceland. The Zeno brothers are then said to have travelled on to a country called Estotiland, where they describe recognisable Native Americans and Inuit with kayaks and igloos, as well as the Norse settlement in Labrador, which only died out at the end of the fourteenth century (all this, well over a century before the arrival of the Genoese-born Columbus).*

Early in the same century, the Venetian geographer Marino Sanuto (known as 'the Elder' to distinguish him from the well-known diarist who lived 200 years later) travelled throughout the Levant and as far north as the Baltic. On his return to Venice he began creating a five-sheet atlas of the known world, incorporating previous maps and his own first-hand experience. This atlas covered territory from Flanders to the Sea of Azov, from Scandinavia to Africa. However, although Sanuto is said to have incorporated information from Marco Polo's *Travels*, his atlas gives little detail of China or India. In fact, its most impressive cartography is focused upon Palestine and Egypt. Like so many maps, then and now, this had a hidden purpose. Sanuto was advocating a vast crusade that would invade the Nile delta, conquer Egypt and then move on to Palestine. This would be followed by a blockade of trade along the entire swathe of Moslem territory from Syria through North Africa as far as Granada in Spain. The consequent ruin of the Arab world would be followed by the launching in the Persian Gulf of a Christian fleet, which would sail into the Indian Ocean and take over the spice trade. Such world ambition was symptomatic of Venice during the early fourteenth century. If they could but defeat the Genoese, with whom they continued to do battle, the world was theirs.†

---

* Many scholars now dispute this story about the Zeno brothers. Yet there is no denying that as early as 1291 a Venetian translation was made of the legendary voyage by the sixth-century Irish monk St Brendan the Navigator, who was said to have sailed west from Ireland until he reached the 'Isle of Promise and Saints'. This was almost certainly a legend. Even so, it is known that Columbus read of St Brendan with great interest, as well as possessing a well-annotated copy of Polo's *Travels*. Before setting out he is said to have declared that he was going in search of the 'Island of St Brendan'.

† Sanuto's maps, if not their intention, were for the most part grounded in reality and contained a revolutionary innovation. His detailed map of Palestine was the first to use a network of straight lines similar to longitude and latitude, intended to delineate relative distances and

Despite Sanuto's bold plans, intended to thwart the Genoese as well as the Arabs, it was in reality the Genoese who proved more bold. Not only had they inflicted a humiliating defeat on the Venetians at Curzola in 1298, but they had proved to be more courageous in their trade-inspired expeditions and would continue to be so. As early as 1277 the first Genoese trading galleys had arrived in the North Sea off Sluys, the port of Bruges; it would be 1314 before the first Venetian galleys arrived here. And while the Venetians were merely reading about the legendary expedition of St Brendan the Navigator, in 1291 the Genoese brothers Ugolino and Vandino Vivaldi sailed beyond the Straits of Gibraltar west into the open Atlantic in search of a direct sea passage to India. Though nothing was ever heard from them again, there are suggestions that they may have made landfall on the Canary Islands before passing westward, encouraged by two priests on the expedition who had brought with them the work of their fellow Franciscan, Roger Bacon. According to another persistent myth, the Vivaldi brothers are said to have rounded Africa and been taken captive by the mythical Christian king Prester John.

By 1306 the Genoese had certainly reached Poland; and in 1374 the Genoese Luchino Tarigo sailed from the Black Sea up the River Don and transported his ship overland some thirty miles or so to the Volga, whence he sailed down to the Caspian Sea. This was certainly a first for Genoese traders;* the intrepid Genoese whom Polo had observed sailing on this sea almost a century previously had not brought their ships overland, but had simply hired local vessels, which then traded under the Genoese flag. Alas, on reaching the Caspian, Tarigo abandoned all pretence of a trading expedition and launched into a campaign of piracy, which

---

territorial area with greater accuracy than hitherto. It has been argued that had he extended this technique to a map of China, his geography of the world might have persuaded Columbus that his landfall in 1492 could not have been China, as he believed. However, this is unlikely, as Columbus ignored the correct Ancient Greek calculations of the circumference of the Earth, convinced by the writings of the thirteenth-century English Franciscan monk and pioneer scientist Roger Bacon that the distance west from Spain to China was much less than had previously been supposed.

* Though as with Columbus in America, here too the Genoese had been preceded some 500 years earlier by the Vikings, whose far-flung expeditions had by this time passed into the mists of myth and oblivion.

enabled him to seize a fortune from the defenceless shipping on this inland sea.

As with trading, so with the currency of trade: here too the Genoese were ahead of the Venetians. In order to facilitate trade, and marginalise their main trading rivals, the Genoese had realised the advantage of having an identifiable and trustworthy currency of their own. In 1252 they issued a gold coin known as the genoin.* It was more than twenty years before the Venetians understood the importance of having a distinctive inter-nationally recognised currency of one's own, and in 1284 they minted their own golden ducats. These gleaming small coins were produced at the old Zecca (the Mint), and hence became known locally as *zecchini* (the origin of our word 'sequin'). In the same year, Venice's other main trading rival of Florence issued its own gold florin. Yet in the commercial world it is often not the pioneers who make the most out of their discoveries and innovations. While the Genoese were more adventurous traders, both the Florentines and the Venetians were superior as bankers. The Florentines had a banking network that stretched over Europe from Geneva to Bruges and as far afield as London. Venice too had a network of banks in Europe reaching as far north as Bruges. The Republic even ran a regular postal service overland between the two cities, a distance of some 700 miles, which was covered by messengers riding post-haste between staging posts to ensure delivery in seven days. Yet where the Florentines had a network of banks in Europe, this was only a part of the Venetian operation, which had established banking agencies around the Levant as well – ensuring them access to the vast market of Asia. And it was this network of small state-backed banks in the eastern Mediterranean, together with the efficient bureaucracy in Venice that administered them, which would eventually enable Venice to outwit its rivals.

Unlike the cities and countries of Europe, island Venice had virtually no home-based industry or production apart from its highly efficient naval yards and its glass-works on the island of Murano. Whereas the banking cities of Florence and Siena flourished in the wool trade, and even Genoa had an

---

* An indication of the primitive state into which trade had lapsed since the classical era can be seen in the fact that this was the first gold coin minted in Europe since Roman times.

agricultural hinterland with connections to Milan and northern Europe, Venice relied largely upon the import–export business carried by its shipping. And, increasingly, a good part of this business came to be devoted to bullion.

During this period gold was the most valued currency, but there was also a practical need for lesser-valued silver coins. Indeed, much of the Byzantine Empire and the northern-European Holy Roman Empire maintained a currency based on a silver standard. However, the exchange rate between gold and silver varied considerably across Europe and the Levant. By the beginning of the thirteenth century Venice had begun importing ever larger quantities of silver from the main European mines of Hungary, Germany and Bohemia. This soon accounted for around 25 per cent of European-produced silver, which was then exported to the eastern Mediterranean. And it was here that the Venetian administration revealed its banking acumen.

Twice a year, under heavy protection from the Venetian navy, a fleet of some two dozen or so merchant galleys laden with silver would sail for Egypt or the Levant. Silver was in short supply throughout Asia, and its price against gold was correspondingly high, resulting in huge profits for the Venetian bullion-traders. Moreover, in the early decades of the thirteenth century the Asian need for silver became acute. Marco Polo, during his travels in China, had noticed the use of paper money notes, which were 'as formal and authoritative as if they were made of pure silver or gold'. This innovation had yet to reach Europe, and even in China the implications of its use were not fully understood. To begin with, it had been backed by silver (as well as precious stones and gold). However, as the emperor's need for money increased, so (according to Polo) he 'had as much quantity of this paper money made that with it he could have bought all the treasures in the world'. The result was inevitable inflation and a decline in the value of paper money; at the same time, although the emperor insisted that merchants should trade in this form of currency, many came increasingly to favour the more solid and reliable currency of silver as a form of capital savings. Despite China's vast empire, it had little access to silver, which soon began pouring in along the silk and spice routes from the Levant. Regular supplies from Venice increased, while the Venetian bullion fleet returned with cheaper gold from India and the mines of Sudan, Ghana, Mali and as far afield as the legendary Great Zimbabwe.

By judicious hoarding of its large gold imports, Venice was thus able to maintain a high rate of exchange for the gold Venetian ducat. However, by the 1330s it was becoming clear that this policy was also favouring the gold Florentine florin. As a result the florin, and the Florentine banks, were now achieving ascendancy on the Italian mainland and throughout Europe. In response to this development, in 1335 Venice surreptitiously began to reverse its policy, releasing larger quantities of its gold, whilst at the same time keeping back its supply of silver, causing the price of gold to fall against the dwindling supplies of silver all over Europe. This policy came to a climax in 1345, when the overstretched Florentine and Sienese banks were caught with large quantities of loans and investments in gold, whose price was now rapidly deteriorating. Even so, the Florentine banks had access to considerable assets, and might well have weathered this storm. But at this point the English king, Edward III, rendered penniless by his persistence in waging the Hundred Years War against France, reneged on his debts to the Florentines. This would contribute to the collapse in 1345 of the two largest Florentine-Sienese banks, run by the Bardi and the Peruzzi families, followed a year later by the third great Florentine bank, that of the Acciaiuoli family. The repercussions of these collapses, combined with widespread harvest failures in 1346 and 1347, left the European economy reeling. Banks throughout the continent found themselves short on funds, and without investment mainland trade slumped – whereas offshore Venice continued to prosper.

With its wealth bolstered by the increasing value of its large silver reserves, Venice could now afford to buy up supplies of grain from the eastern Mediterranean, as well as continuing to finance its other merchant ventures. The Republic's growing eastern empire, which by this time included the large Greek islands of Negropont (Euboea) and Crete, as well as preferential trading rights with Cyprus, provided for its material needs such as corn supplies at a considerably reduced price, while its bullion trade continued apace. Moreover, Venetian currency manipulations had directly undermined the Genoese, and the slump in transalpine trade had also hit them particularly hard. Since Genoa's high point after the Battle of Curzola in 1298, its trade had slumped by more than 50 per cent, while during this same period Venetian trade had increased by almost 40 per cent.

It is difficult not to see behind Venice's policy of financial manipulation the guiding hand of an individual pioneer economist of some brilliance. This was so much more than simply a theoretical idea: it required the constant surreptitious and incremental pursuit of marginal exchange adjustments, whilst at the same time maintaining both balance and confidence in the very financial system being undermined. Yet the identity of this financial genius remains buried for ever amongst the anonymity of the city's councils and their supporting hierarchy of civil servants.

As Venice was in fact ruled by a number of councils, with the doge a mere figurehead, it had a bureaucracy second to none. Indeed, the Venetian civil service was so efficient, meticulous and far-reaching that everything – from the population to the movement of shipping and the price of flowers – was duly recorded. Not for nothing did the great Swiss Renaissance scholar Jacob Burckhardt state that Venice 'had a strong claim to be the birthplace of statistics'.

What had been achieved during this skilful financial manipulation had been no less than shifts in the foundations on which the entire edifice of commercial value had been built: one false move, and the whole pan-European system of money – tied to belief in the value of the precious metals that supported it – could have collapsed. Unlike Polo's real 'millions', which had been dismissed as nothing, here were real millions that had been conjured up out of nothing. And as a result *La Serenissima* now reigned supreme.* Adventure, daring and chance – such were the characteristics of this early Venetian period, and such too were the characteristics of its

---

* There was then, just as there is now, no necessary and indissoluble link between the value of all-but-useless precious metals and the value of the functional commodities they purchase. Economists define such a contingent link as fiduciary – that is, dependent entirely upon confidence. The accelerating fluctuations caused by Venice in the value of coinage and precious metals (against each other, as well as against commodities) could easily, in inexperienced hands, have caused such inflation that faith in gold and silver prices simply collapsed. This would have precipitated a flight from precious metals and coinage into more tangible and evidently useful land and commodities. These valuables may have been unwieldy, and thus may have destroyed the efficiency of international trading, but their very unwieldiness and solidity were what inspired confidence. Such loss of faith in investable currency would occasionally be precipitated, in one form or another, with catastrophic effects over the coming centuries. Indeed, more 'experienced' hands than those of that unknown fourteenth-century Venetian financial genius continue to this day more or less deftly to undermine the very system they seek to exploit.

guiding spirits, in both the fields of exploration and of finance. Yet this success could only have been built upon the solid base of the city's stable and reliable institutions, which normally sought to efface such individuality. Here we see the creative tension that drove *La Serenissima*.

2

Survivors and Losers

T HE VENETIANS DID not have long to enjoy the fruits of their financial chicanery. It was as if the wrath of God himself had been incurred, prompting Him to awesome retribution. All who witnessed the events of the ensuing years would come to see them in such biblical terms. In the beginning came the first rumblings. Just a year or so after the collapse of banks across Europe in the middle of the fourteenth century, Venice would suffer a serious earthquake, which caused the bells of St Mark's to toll and clang in discordant fashion, while chunks of masonry fell from other chiming church towers into the canals. This was followed by another earthquake the following year, when there were such low tides that the Grand Canal was barely navigable and the citizens watched fearfully as the mainland mudflats crept closer and closer to their naked, wall-less defenceless city.

Meanwhile, far away in the northern Black Sea, the Golden Horde of the advancing Mongol army that had swept into Russia began laying siege to the Genoan trading outpost of Kaffa (modern Feodosiya) on the coast of the Crimea. By now many of the Golden Horde had begun to suffer from a mysterious and hideous disease, which according to information gathered from merchants by the contemporary Arab writer Ibn al-Wardi had originated in the 'Land of Darkness' (now thought to have been central Asia). The contemporary Italian chronicler Gabriele de Mussis, piecing together first-hand reports, recorded how in 1347:

the Tartars, worn out by this pestilential disease, and falling on all sides as if thunderstruck, and seeing that they were perishing hopelessly, ordered the corpses to be placed on their engines and thrown into the city of Kaffa.

Some historians have seen this as the first recorded instance of germ warfare. The disease was soon so rampant within the city walls of Kaffa that the inhabitants:

were not able to hide or protect themselves from this danger, although they carried away as many dead as possible and threw them into the sea. But soon the whole air became infected, and the water poisoned, and such a pestilence grew up that scarcely one out of a thousand was able to escape.

Those lucky enough to escape set sail for home. Yet by the time they had crossed the Black Sea and reached Constantinople symptoms of the illness had begun to appear. These were recorded by the Byzantine emperor himself, John VI Cantacuzenus:

Sputum suffused with blood was brought up, and disgusting and stinking breath from within. The throat and tongue, parched from the heat, were black and congested with blood. It made no difference if they drank much or little. Sleeplessness and weakness were established forever.

Abscesses formed on the upper and lower arms, a few also in the maxillae [upper jawbone], and in other parts of the body. In some they were large and in others small. Black blisters appeared. Some people broke out with black spots all over their bodies.

Little wonder this pandemic would later be christened the Black Death. Cantacuzenus recognised it as the Athenian plague that had been described by Thucydides in 300 BC, and most medical historians now agree that this medieval outbreak was a virulent and extremely contagious strain of the bubonic plague (so called because it gave rise to buboes or boils). All Cantacuzenus could do was describe its symptoms, and the course it took: 'some died the same day, a few even within the hour. Those who could resist for two or three days had a very violent fever'; those who survived 'were no longer possessed by the same evil, but were safe. The disease did not attack twice in order to kill them.' Yet despite the emperor's meticulous attention to detail, no physician could discover a cure: 'There was no help from anywhere.' Only now do we know that this pandemic almost certainly arose from a bacillus passed on by the bite of a flea (*Xenopsylla cheopis*) carried by the black rat (*Rattus rattus*). And as the Venetian merchants fled Constantinople in the ensuing panic, their galleys carried with them some of these black rats. On their voyage home during the latter months of 1347 these galleys called at various Venetian trading ports on the way, spreading the plague to Negropont (Euboea), Crete, Corfu and up the Adriatic islands, to Trieste.

The first recorded death from plague in Venice occurred on 25 January 1348. The putrid waterways provided an ideal breeding ground for the black rats, which quickly spread. By the coming of the heat and stink of spring, officially designated barges had begun plying the canals crying out for '*Corpi morti*' (dead bodies). Corpses were transported to be buried on remote islands of the lagoon. Soon there were so many that they were simply tossed ashore to rot. By the height of summer it has been estimated that there were 600 people dying each day. The streets were littered with suppurating bodies, the canals bobbed with bloated corpses; the stench was almost unendurable. Commercial activity, and even the city's renowned bureaucracy, had come to a virtual standstill. The prisons were thrown open in an attempt to replace municipal manpower, but as many as could simply fled to the mainland. This belatedly included most of the city's physicians, who had suffered disproportionate losses whilst vainly attempting to treat the disease.

Within months the disease had swept across the Alps and by the summer of 1348 it had even reached England. An anonymous monk in Austria recorded, 'And in this year a pestilence struck that was so great and universal that it stretched from sea to sea, causing many cities, towns and other places to become almost totally desolated of human beings.' At the same time bands of frenzied survivors, maddened with grief and terror, sought out scapegoats. Jews throughout Europe soon became targets, and the Jews of Venice were no exception. They lived on the island of Spinalunga (now known, after its former inhabitants, as Giudecca), which made them easy targets. When news reached Italy from Switzerland that two Jews had been tortured into confessing that they had poisoned the local wells with a plague powder concocted from 'Christians' hearts, spiders, frogs, lizards, human flesh and sacred hosts', the situation became further inflamed. During the course of 1348 Pope Clement VI was forced to issue two papal bulls instructing the clergy to protect the Jews, and condemning those who blamed the Jews for the Black Death as having been 'seduced by that liar, the Devil'.

In Venice all citizens lived cheek-by-jowl, its population being the most concentrated and urbanised in Europe. As a result, no class of citizens was to be spared the scourge of this pandemic. By October 1348 as many as fifty noble families had been completely wiped out, their centuries-old names vanishing into history. Such losses were reflected several times over amongst the poor. To make up for this depletion, many exiles were encouraged to return, and even debtors who had fled or been imprisoned were absolved on payment of a token amount of their debt. Formerly Venice had guarded its citizenship with jealous pride; rarely were any other than those born in the city permitted to become Venetians. Yet within nine months of the plague arriving, the government was even advertising for citizens, promising that anyone who settled in Venice within the year would be guaranteed citizenship. A crucial aspect of the Republic's character was now showing itself — the belief in pragmatism rather than ideals, no matter how long these ideals may have been held.

It is impossible to tell how many died. Most experts concur that the toll across Europe probably amounted to around one-third of the population, with other estimates varying between 20 per cent and 80 per cent mortality. The involvement of Venice and Genoa in the lucrative Black Sea and Levantine trade had made them amongst the richest, and probably the most populous, cities of the Western world — inspiring the contemporary poet Petrarch to refer to them as 'the twin torches of Europe'. Yet they would pay dreadfully for their involvement with the Orient, suffering much higher mortality rates than other trading cities. According to the historian Christopher Hibbert, writing of Venice, 'In all there were some seventy-two thousand deaths in a population of about a hundred and sixty thousand.' Genoa is said to have suffered a 60 per cent loss of population.

If this were not bad enough, Venice would be stricken by lesser outbreaks of the plague at least once a decade throughout the last half of the four-teenth century. Despite this, the city's trade quickly revived in the wake of the Black Death. The main engine behind this revival was the Arsenale, the city's ship-building centre. This formidable enterprise had been founded as early as 1104 by the city authorities, its name deriving from the Arabic *dar sina'a*, meaning 'place of construction', strongly suggesting that, like several European innovations of the medieval period (such as negative numbers and double-entry bookkeeping), this was based on an Arab original. The Arsenale was soon producing galleys of the highest standard, which were leased to private merchants for commercial enterprises. It also began producing armed galleys for the city's defensive fleet and to protect the bullion convoys to the eastern Mediterranean. The industry and efficiency of the Arsenale would soon become legendary. Here, for the first time, assembly-line production was introduced (nearly 600 years before Henry Ford adopted this method for his car-building plants). Once the bare hull was complete, it would be launched, then towed up a canal overlooked by a wall. As the ship passed along the canal, through windows in the wall would be passed in succession equipment, sails, armaments and dry-goods supplies (culminating in barrels of hard tack), until the ship emerged at the other end of the canal, entering the lagoon fully constructed, rigged and stored-up, ready for manning by a crew of sailors and oarsmen. Utilising sail-power, and disciplined rowers at close quarters, meant that these galleys were highly manoeuvrable (prior to the sixteenth century Venetian galley-oars were powered by highly motivated, well-fed young Venetians). Besides rapid production, this assembly-line manufacture would also enable stand-ardised ships' parts to be transported to Venetian depots throughout the Mediterranean, available for immediate replacement of faulty or damaged equipment as soon as a ship put into port.

This massive state-run enterprise also enabled the introduction of neces-sary modifications across the fleet, such as powerful rudders, streamlined hulls and compasses to assist in the reading of charts. Soon merchant ships – formerly cumbersome vessels powered by sail alone – had evolved into massive galleys, capable of transporting 150 tons of cargo. These were powered by 200 oarsmen, so that they could keep up with the naval galleys that protected them against pirates on the increasingly large convoys to the Levant. These would soon be leaving Venice at the rate of one every two months and consisted of as many as 200 ships. At its height, the Venetian fleet would have 36,000 sailors manning 3,300 ships.

The *Arsenalotti*, as the workers became known, would over the coming centuries hone their assembly-line production to a fine art. When the young Henry III of France visited Venice in 1574, he was shown the *Arsenalotti* laying down the keel of a galley, and was then taken for a meal. When he had finished his dinner, he marvelled to see that an entire galley had been assembled, rigged out and armed in just two hours. Conditions in the Arsenale were more like those in a factory of the Industrial Revolution than a craftsman's workshop of the medieval era. During the early years of the fourteenth century the Arsenale was visited by Dante Alighieri, who was so struck by what he saw that he incorporated it into a scene in his *Inferno*:

> As in the Arsenale at Venice
> They boil in winter bubbling pitch . . .
> One man hammers at the prow, another at the stern,
> This one shaves oars, that one rigging twists,
> Still others make the mainsail and the mizzen . . .
> Fire . . . thick boiling pitch with great bubbles black as ink,
> Rising and bursting in a seething tide . . .

Working in the heat of the forges, and assembling the galleys beneath the burning sun, proved thirsty work for the industrious *Arsenalotti*, and a free wine fountain was provided for them to slake their thirst. At the height of the Arsenale's productivity this fountain accounted for more than 13,000 gallons of wine in a year, with individual workers consuming as much as a gallon a day. Even though the wine would certainly have been watered down, this nonetheless marked a prodigious consumption. The *Arsenalotti* were a proud breed, who were recruited exclusively from the three neighbouring parishes of the Castello district. They regarded themselves as superior to other workers of the city, and certain privileged employment was restricted to their number. Only *Arsenalotti* were permitted to form the bodyguard of the doge, or make up the force of rowers required for the doge's barge, the large golden ceremonial *Bucintoro* (from *bucio in oro*, or 'barque in gold'). Likewise, only *Arsenalotti* were considered sufficiently skilled and trusted to be employed in the city's Mint, or to be retained by the corps of city fire-fighters.

The setting of the Arsenale at the eastern end of Venice overlooking the lagoon is both formidable and spectacular. Its high pink-brick walls look down over open water and surrounding inland canals, which combine to give it the appearance and defensive strength of a vast moated castle. Its architecture includes ancient and modern in characteristic Venetian fashion: the magnificent landside gateway to the Arsenale was one of the first examples in Venice of Renaissance architecture, whilst two of the nearby stone lions represent spoils of war dating from earlier centuries. One was seized from amongst the sacred sixth-century BC ruins on the island of Delos, while the other, captured from Piraeus (the port of Athens) is marked with graffiti of runes carved by eleventh-century Viking mercenaries employed by the Byzantine emperor.

In the aftermath of the plague all Europe suffered from a huge depletion in manpower. Household servants, manual labour in the fields and the cities – all were in short supply. Venice found itself ideally placed to remedy the gap in the market. From as early as the eleventh century the Venetians and the Genoese had shipped slaves from the Black Sea to the markets of the Levant and Egypt, with a number ending up back in Europe. Now they were able to utilise these trading contacts to purchase larger numbers for transport to Europe. Although several papal edicts had been issued against slavery over the centuries, these were ignored during the post-plague years. Venice soon led the lucrative trade in importing Slav, Caucasian, Armenian and Georgian slaves, purchased from Tartar merchants at outposts on the Black Sea, such as Sinope and Trebizond, as well as Nubians purchased from Egyptian caravaners in Alexandria (although these black slaves seldom reached Europe, as they were mostly sold for work in the sugar plantations of Cyprus and Crete). This pitiful trade had originally relied upon a regular supply from Tartar merchants buying up young men and girls sold by their impoverished families in mountain villages of the Caucasus and other remote eastern regions. Now, such was the demand for slaves in depleted Italy that the young men, women and children on the market often represented the entire able-bodied population of mountain villages, who had simply been rounded up by the Tartars. This trade proved hugely profitable for the Venetian traders, who could realise as much as 1000 per cent on the purchase price of each slave. Whereas the changes to citizenship laws during the plague saw the Republic jettisoning long-held ideals in the name of pragmatism, the opportunistic acceleration of their participation in the slave trade represented a colder element in the Republic's character – the willingness to jettison morality for the sake of profit.

In Venice, slaves had originally been sold at what is still known as Riva degli Schiavoni (literally 'landing stage of the Slavs', the word 'slave' being derived from the Slav name). Once purchased, slaves were deemed to be the property of their owners, and were listed on tax returns as chattels along with domestic animals and furniture. Despite such callous disregard for human dignity, slaves were for the most part treated with a degree of humanity by their Italian masters. Many slaves from Venice were exported to cities such as Florence and Rome, where they entered households and undertook domestic duties like any other servant. As such, they would often dine at the family table and suffered no more or less than the usual affection or maltreatment meted out to the vulnerable country girls who made up the lower retinue of servants. When the banker Cosimo de' Medici was working in Rome he impregnated his slave girl, whereupon she was sent home to the family mansion to give birth, and her son was treated in much the same way as any other illegitimate offspring of a well-to-do family in Italy; he was educated and then sent to a nearby city to take up a position that had been secured for him in the Church. Such consideration was certainly not the norm, but it was not exceptional. Slaves who had served a family loyally over the years would sometimes be set free in their master's will, just as Marco Polo had done with the Tartar slave he brought back with him from the East. On the other hand, the Venetian authorities did on occasion purchase slaves to make up numbers in the galleys, though this was only as a last resort. Youths from artisan families traditionally volunteered for a term in the galleys, where (if they were lucky) they could become rich through a share in the spoils of war. The men who manned the oars were also expected to fight in naval engagements, which made the authorities wary of seconding to the galleys slaves whose patriotism was liable to be suspect.

After a post-plague truce lasting barely two years, Venice soon found its galleys becoming involved in an increasing number of naval skirmishes with its Genoese counterparts. By 1352 the situation had escalated to outright war. Leading adversaries in this lengthy war would emerge from two distinguished families – the Pisani of Venice and the celebrated Doria of Genoa (who had already provided Lamba Doria, the victor of Curzola).

The kingdom of Aragon in south-east Spain, wishing to drive the Genoese from the western Mediterranean, chose to ally itself with Venice, and in February 1352 Nicolò Pisani led their combined fleets north up the Aegean Sea to confront the Genoese fleet in the Bosphorus under the command of Paganino Doria. Here Pisani was provided with further Greek naval assistance by the Byzantine emperor John VI Cantacuzenus, who felt threatened by the fortified Genoese colony just north of Constantinople on the other side of the Golden Horn, the narrow stretch of water leading off the Bosphorus. Making full use of his home-port advantage, Doria withdrew his fleet into a line across the narrow mouth of the Golden Horn, thus ensuring that he could not be outflanked and attacked from the rear, breaking his line. By now a winter storm was raging, and the wind and waves rendered Doria's position all but impregnable. But to Pisani's dismay the Aragonese admiral Ponzio di Santa Paola then proceeded to launch his ships into a frontal attack on the Genoese, which soon resulted in catastrophic losses. Pisani realised that he had no alternative but to advance in support of his foolhardy ally; meanwhile his Greek allies hastily retired from the battle. As the storm continued and night fell, the Venetian and Genoese fleets battled it out. Incendiary arrows and missiles had set alight fires in both fleets, and these quickly passed from ship to ship in the high wind. Chaos ensued, with ships grappling and men fighting in the garish glare, often unaware who was friend or foe. As dawn broke, the remnants of the Venetian fleet found themselves battling against wind and current and were forced to flee. By now Paolo was dead, while Pisani had lost most of his galleys and 1,500 men – a colossal loss given the recent predations of the Black Death.

Technically, the Genoese had won the Battle of the Bosphorus, but in terms of men and galleys their losses were on a par with those of the Venetians. On the other hand, they were now in a position to force the Byzantine emperor Cantacuzenus to grant them certain exclusive trading rights, especially in the Crimea and the Sea of Azov – the termination of lucrative trading routes to the Orient. Venice had now lost all access to the Black Sea as well as access to Byzantine ports in the Aegean. Venetian ascendancy in the eastern Mediterranean looked to be under threat. Many in Venice wished to see Pisani summoned home and put on trial for his life. Instead he was merely subjected to the interrogation of an official inquiry, which eventually exonerated him. Desperate to regain his honour, in the summer of 1353 Pisani switched his tactics, leading a Venetian fleet into the western Mediterranean. The Aragonese were bent on wresting Sardinia from the control of Genoa and had begun to blockade the port of Alghero on the north-western coast of the island. As luck would have it, Pisani turned up just as the Aragonese were expecting the arrival of the Genoese fleet and they immediately handed overall command of the new joint fleet to Pisani. By the time the Genoese arrived, Pisani was ready for them, and on 29 August 1353 – just eighteen months after his humiliating loss at the Battle of the Bosphorus – he redeemed himself by inflicting an overwhelming defeat on the Genoese fleet. Of sixty galleys, only nineteen managed to limp back to Genoa.

This was a blow from which the Genoese were unable to recover: they had now suffered catastrophic destruction of manpower and galleys in two successive major battles, and Venice controlled the Mediterranean, thus cutting off the city of Genoa from its lucrative trade with the Black Sea and the Levant. Notably in this instance it had been the ambition of an individual, rather than the calculated will of the Venetian authorities, that had reversed the Republic's fortunes. Just months earlier Venice had stood on the precipice of disaster, and now its bitter rival was crushed.

This defeat was not only disastrous in terms of commerce, but threatened the very lives of the Genoese themselves. The city had by now spread over much of the thin strip of agricultural land between the mountains and the sea, forcing it to rely upon outside trade for its grain supplies. These were usually obtained from the Levant and from the fertile Lombardy plains in the territory of Milan to the north. But now even Milan had turned against Genoa. Giovanni Visconti, the Lord and Archbishop of Milan, saw this as his chance to overcome Genoa, and in return for supplies the Genoese were forced to sign a humiliating 'treaty' with Milan, which virtually made the city a vassal of its powerful northern neighbour. This was a strategic masterstroke by Visconti, who thus denied the Venetians the chance of destroying Genoese power once and for all and threatening Milan in the process. Instead it was now Milan that became the overwhelming major power in northern Italy, and in doing so threatened Venice.

Venice realised this danger and quickly organised a defensive league of inland cities between it and Milanese territory. Gerona, Mantua, Verona and Padua were all bribed to sign up, with Charles IV of Bohemia agreeing to be paid as commander of the league's forces. According to the Venetian historian Lorenzo de Monacis, writing some sixty years later with access to the relevant documents, all this was accomplished 'at almost incredible cost'. However, the Venetians underestimated Visconti of Milan, whose even greater financial inducements soon dissolved the league, allowing Charles IV to retire from his command with a further 100,000 ducats in his pocket. Even so, Visconti was not yet ready to take on Venice and despatched a peace mission to the city.

This mission was led by the forty-nine-year-old poet and scholar Francesco Petrarca (now known as Petrarch), who would later develop a special relationship with Venice. At this time, he was the most celebrated intellectual figure in Italy since Dante. Twenty years previously he had been crowned 'poet laureate', complete with laurel wreath, in a ceremony at the Capitol in Rome that had not been performed since ancient classical times. He was an early champion of the new humanism, which sought a rebirth of classical learning, with its emphasis on human enquiry and action, rather than the religious authority and spiritual aspirations of the medieval era, which he referred to as the 'Dark Ages'. For this reason Petrarch is often regarded as the father of the Renaissance.

He had a wide circle of humanist friends, which included Guidone da Settimo, the Archbishop of Genoa, as well as the Doge of Venice, the scholarly Andrea Dandolo.* Indeed, as early as 1351 Petrarch had written to the Genoese and to Doge Dandolo suggesting that the Venetians and the Genoese should desist from waging war against one another, join forces and sail to the Canaries, the Orkneys, Thule (in Greenland) and the regions of the extreme north and south. But this remarkably prescient advice had fallen on deaf ears — not until two centuries later would gold be discovered in West Africa and serious exploration would reveal the New World and a passage around Africa. And despite Petrarch's close friendship with Doge Dandolo, his peace mission to Venice would be met with equally deaf ears. Petrarch blamed himself for what happened, but there is no denying the anger he felt at his rejection:

When many words had been wasted, I returned as full of sorrow, shame, and terror as I had come full of hope. To open to reason ears that were stopped and hearts that were obstinate was a task beyond my eloquence, as it would have been beyond that of Cicero.

Yet Venice had good reason to reject Petrarch's offer from Archbishop Visconti. Despite Genoa's apparent submission to Milan, it had unexpectedly decided to revive the war of its own accord, carrying the fight right into Venice's back yard. Early in 1354 Genoese galleys made a lightning strike into the Adriatic, laying waste the Venetian islands of Curzola and Lesina (modern Hvar), before disappearing back into the Mediterranean as swiftly as they had appeared. Venice at once decided to pursue the war with renewed vigour. Over the winter, their depleted fleet had been restored by the production line at the Arsenale, enabling them to mount two separate naval expeditions. The first was a squadron ordered to seal off the mouth of the Adriatic by mounting a constant patrol across the sixty-mile channel between Otranto on the Italian mainland and the island of Corfu, to prevent any repeat of this incident. The second was a fleet of fourteen galleys under the command of Pisani, which were ordered to liaise with nineteen further galleys from Venetian ports along the Dalmatian coast

---

* Not to be confused with his relative Admiral Andrea Dandolo, who killed himself after his defeat at Curzola.

and as far afield as Crete. Pisani was then to hunt down and destroy the Genoese squadron responsible for the attack, as well as any other Genoese shipping it came across on the open sea. Having picked up his reinforcements, Pisani at once set sail for Sardinia, the scene of his former triumph. He knew that the Aragonese were still blockading Alghero, and surmised that Genoa would soon rally all its available naval forces to relieve the port.

This proved to be a fatal blunder. The arch-tactician Paganino Doria, who had sailed from Genoa with the remnants of the city's fleet, eluded his rival and completely outmanoeuvred both Venetian fleets. In a superb piece of seamanship, he managed to slip past the Venetian patrol at the mouth of the Adriatic without his ships being detected, and then headed north up the Adriatic towards Venice. In August 1354 he made landfall on the Istrian peninsula, attacking the Venetian port of Parenzo (modern Poreč) less than forty miles south of Venice itself. Here he set fire to buildings and added insult to injury by desecrating the great sixth-century Euphrasian Basilica, carrying off the bodies of St Maurus and St Cyrillus.*

When news of this outrage reached Venice it caused consternation. Yet, as ever, the authorities refused to panic. A skilled captain-general was designated to take charge of the city's defences, and twelve men of noble family were appointed as his deputies, with each charged to raise 300 men. At the same time the citizens were mobilised, all galleys in the Arsenale were commissioned and, contrary to tradition, even Doge Dandolo donned armour in readiness to defend the city. At the same time, a large boom constructed of galleys and massive tree-trunks linked together by chains was strung across the narrow 300-yard channel between San Nicolò on the Lido and the Sant'Andrea fort, the main entrance from the sea into the lagoon.

Doria now sailed for Venice, where he arrived off the Lido. Onshore,

---

* These were much-revered saints of some importance. St Maurus was a sixth-century Italian monk whose many miracles, whilst alive and dead, included healing the sick and bringing sight to the blind. In 1985 his remains were spectacularly rediscovered beneath the floorboards of a Czech castle, where they are now considered to be 'the second most important historical artefact . . . after the Czech crown jewels'. St Cyrillus was the ninth-century Greek who introduced the written word to the Slavs, after whom is named the quasi-Greek Cyrillic script now used in Russia, Bulgaria and Serbia.

Venetians lining the beach watched in horror as the Genoese galleys hunted down a defenceless merchantman, capturing it and setting fire to it less than a mile from where they stood. Thus Doria demonstrated that Genoa now had control of the Adriatic, yet he quickly saw that he would be unable to pass the boom and attack Venice itself. And such an attack would have been largely symbolic, for he did not have the manpower to take the city. He also realised that the Venetian navy was bound to return soon, and decided to set sail for the safer waters of the open Mediterranean.

Sure enough, Pisani soon returned from his fruitless searching in the eastern Mediterranean. Upon being told what had happened, he tried to deduce what Doria's next move would be. By now autumn was approaching, and Pisani guessed that Doria would most likely put in for the winter at the Genoese island stronghold of Chios, which lay off the Aegean coast of Anatolia (modern Turkey). He knew that here Doria would be able to stock up on provisions and repair his ships in a safe, protected harbour. Pisani duly sailed east into the Aegean and eventually spied Doria's ships at Chios.

Yet Doria would not be drawn to leave harbour; he was expecting a reinforcement squadron of twelve galleys, and it seemed likely that he would sit out the winter in Chios. The notorious October storms were now sweeping down the Aegean, and Pisani decided to retire for the winter himself. He embarked for the south-western tip of the Peloponnese, calling in at the Venetian fortress of Corone to pick up fresh despatches from Venice. These warned him not to launch any precipitate attack on the Genoese, as peace negotiations were to be renewed. He then rowed his galleys to the nearby small harbour of Porto Lungo.

By now Doria's reinforcements had arrived, and he decided against sitting out the winter at Chios. He and his fleet, which at this point consisted of twenty-five galleys, would be needed at Genoa. In the last week of October he embarked on a southerly course, hoping to round the Peloponnese before the worst of the winter storms. But this time his luck did not hold, and he was forced to take shelter in the south-west Peloponnese. By chance, the bay in which his ships anchored lay just over a mile down the coast from the place where Pisani's fleet was wintering. As the storm abated, Doria despatched his nephew Giovanni in a light trireme to reconnoitre. Giovanni returned to report that the Venetian fleet was ripe for the taking, with just fourteen galleys guarding the bay and the other smaller ships, together with twenty-one galleys all lashed together by the shore. Despite having fewer galleys at his disposal, Admiral Doria seized his opportunity and on 4 November 1354 launched his fleet into the attack. In the ensuing surprise his nephew Giovanni succeeded in eluding the protective line of Venetian galleys, leading a further dozen galleys into Porto Lungo, where the tied-up Venetian galleys were soon captured and their crews taken prisoner. Reflecting patriotic bitterness and the prejudice of his age, the Venetian historian de Monacis remarked of Doria's victory, 'He routed them without a struggle, and overcame them without a victory. You would have thought that one side was made up of armed men, while the others were unarmed women.'

In all, the Genoese finally captured more than thirty galleys, and took 5,000 prisoners. The remaining Venetians, together with Pisani, managed to escape ashore and made their way five miles along the coast to Corone. This time Pisani would be granted no leniency. As a result of his humiliating defeat, when he arrived back in Venice he was sentenced to pay a heavy fine and stripped of any further command for life.

On 7 September 1354, in the midst of the renewed hostility with the Genoese, the venerable doge Andrea Dandolo had died. Although his eleven-year reign had witnessed disasters ranging from earthquakes to the plague and the two wars with Genoa, he remained a highly respected figure throughout. Dandolo came from a distinguished family, which had already provided the city with doges and an admiral. As a young man he had shown such marked legal talent that he had been elected to a senior post within the administration in his early twenties, and this had led to him being elected doge at the exceptionally young age of thirty-six. Previous doges had often been elected from the city's leading families on account of their military achievements, but it was felt that Dandolo's legal preoccupations would enable him to avoid becoming embroiled in the increasing disputes between the city's leading families. And this proved to be the case. Dandolo instituted a review of the city's legal system, which resulted in the ironing out of many potentially conflicting anachronisms, and he played a similar role with regard to the city's external affairs, rationalising Venice's treaty obligations towards foreign powers both within Italy and beyond. He also found time to write a history of Venice, but in the words of the distinguished Renaissance historian Frederic C. Lane, this further task was unfortunately undertaken 'in the same lawyer-like spirit. His chronicle contained a mass of documents selected to prove that Venice was always right.' As Dandolo's friend Petrarch wrote: 'Death was kind to him, in sparing him the sight of his country's bitter sorrow [after the defeat of Porto Longo], and the still more bitter letters I would have written him.' Although Petrarch referred to Dandolo as 'a good man, beyond any corruption', he remained angry at Dandolo's rejection of his peace mission.

The doge was traditionally chosen by a specially selected council of forty-one nobles, and the cautious policy of this council ensured the choosing of a man who was both old and wise (the average age of a doge on election was seventy). Dandolo's successor, the sixty-nine-year-old Marin Falier, was chosen for office on the first ballot by a resounding thirty-five votes. During a long and distinguished career Falier had served as commander of the Black Sea fleet and had led an army in the city's service, as well as being the Republic's *podestà* (provincial governor) in both Chioggia and Treviso. Back home, he had frequently been elected a member of the Council of Ten. Despite his age, he remained vigorous and was deemed the ideal man to lead the city during this dark time of war.

At the time of his election Marin Falier had been on a diplomatic mission to Pope Innocent IV in Avignon, petitioning him to mediate in the conflict between Venice and Milan (and, by extension, Genoa). When Falier returned to Venice, the lagoon was shrouded in a thick October fog, causing his boat to miss the official jetty and put in at the stone quay known as the Molo. When Falier stepped ashore and walked between the two columns, which to this day stand between the landing stage and the Doge's Palace, many saw this as an evil omen – here was the site where public executions were held. The story of what ensued is equally enshrouded in fog, but this time the fog of legend.

Falier is said to have been a headstrong man, who not only bore long-term grudges, but had a quick temper (whilst *podestà* of Treviso, he had publicly slapped the local bishop for arriving late at a ceremony). When he had been recalled to become doge, he had expected to take on the role of forceful wartime leader. Instead he was forced to sign a *promissione* (a solemnly sworn, legally binding document) containing restrictions on the doge's power, which had recently been voted into law.

Falier's chagrin had been reinforced when news of the defeat at Porto Lungo reached Venice just a month after he had taken office. There was a widespread feeling in the city that the catastrophe of Porto Lungo had been the culmination of bad leadership by the nobles, whose arrogance was becoming intolerable to the wider section of the populace. Falier decided that in this time of need the city required leaders who had expertise rather than breeding, and ordered the commissioning of four armed galleys under the command of experienced sea captains who were commoners. This appointment was greeted with some consternation by the nobles, and matters are said to have come to a head at the pre-Lenten Carnival banquet, a boisterous occasion that was traditionally hosted by the doge in his palace. When a young noble called Michele Steno began drunkenly molesting one of the dogaressa's female attendants, Falier ordered him to be removed.

Several years earlier Falier had married a second wife, who was some decades his junior, and Steno now avenged himself by placing a placard on the doge's throne in the council chamber, on which was written the following scurrilous verse:

Marin Falier has a wife who's a cracker,
While he keeps her, others fuck her.

Falier immediately reported this insult to the Forty, the council ultimately responsible for justice, expecting them to give Steno an exemplary punishment. However, in the light of Steno's youth and previous good character, the Forty chose to treat the matter as little more than a Carnival jape, instead passing a light sentence. Falier was outraged at what he saw as an insult to himself, his wife and his office – and at the connivance of nobles who had turned against him.

Around this time another incident was to aggravate the tensions between the nobility and the new doge. A popular ship's captain called Bertucci Isarello, who was a commoner, had been approached by the noble Giovanni

Dandolo, a naval administrator, and instructed to take on a family friend as a member of his crew. When Isarello refused, Dandolo struck him. This dispute took place in the Camera dell'Armamento, the armoury in the Doge's Palace (of which the doge's personal quarters formed only a small part; this building also contained the government offices, such as the Great Council chamber, as well as those of other councils and administrative departments, the law courts and prison). Incensed at his treatment, Isarello stormed out of the palace onto the quayside, where he soon gathered together a gang of sympathetic sailors who proceeded to pace menacingly back and forth outside the palace, waiting for Dandolo to come out. Realising the danger he was in, Dandolo fled to the doge, who summoned Isarello and sternly reprimanded him, yet in such a manner that Isarello understood he had the doge's sympathy. The sailors dispersed from the Piazzetta, but this indication of where the doge's sympathies lay soon reached the ears of the nobility.*

A similar incident involved the noble Marco Barbaro, an important member of the city legislature known as the Great Council, and the commoner Stefano Ghiazza, the commander of the Arsenale. In the course of an altercation between them, Barbaro struck Ghiazza in the face – a very public humiliation for a senior commoner who was also a well-respected man throughout the city. When Ghiazza later complained to the doge, Falier once again privately indicated his sympathy – whereupon Ghiazza is said to have muttered, 'Wild animals should be chained up; either that, or you should get rid of them by bashing them on the head.'

Falier quickly understood that he could trust Ghiazza, and that in him he had a considerable ally. As commander of the Arsenale, Ghiazza had the loyalty of the powerful *Arsenalotti*, who were also by tradition the doge's bodyguards. Falier saw this as an opportunity to liberate himself from the

---

* The Piazzetta is the extension of the Piazza San Marco leading down to the waterfront of the Molo. Under normal circumstances this was a popular gathering place for members of the administration in San Marco, where between business they would gather in groups scheming, soliciting votes or attempting to ingratiate themselves with leading council members. In former times it had been in the grounds of the San Zaccaria convent, forming the garden (*il brolo*); consequently the complex ebb and flow of political activities that took place here gave rise to our word 'imbroglio'.

humiliating restraints imposed on him by the nobles who on his accession had made him sign the *promissione*. Between them, Falier and Ghiazza set in motion a plot. On 15 April 1355 rumours were to be spread throughout the city that the Genoese fleet was about to attack. This would draw a crowd of citizens, commoners and nobles alike, to the Piazzetta in front of the Doge's Palace. Here, armed *Arsenalotti* would mingle with the crowd, ostensibly protecting the palace. At a signal, they would seal off the exits and begin murdering all the nobles they could identify. Falier would then appear on the balcony of the Doge's Palace and offer himself to the people as Prince of Venice, their saviour in this time of turmoil. Encouraged by the *Arsenalotti*, the people would then confirm Falier as *Principe* by popular acclaim.

Such a plan involved considerable organisation, as well as the strictest secrecy, especially amongst the *Arsenalotti*. Yet word leaked out, and on 14 April a furrier from Bergamo by the name of Beltrami happened to warn his noble friend and customer Nicolò Lioni not to venture onto the streets the next day. Lioni immediately began questioning him, and Beltrami soon revealed all he knew: there was to be an uprising against the government. He let drop the names of a few nobles, but not that of Falier. Lioni then hurried to Doge Falier to inform him that he had uncovered a plot to overthrow the government. Lioni became suspicious when Falier dismissed this as mere tittle-tattle and at once called on a member of the Council of Ten to report his suspicions. The Council of Ten had meanwhile been informed of a rumour about an uprising by the *Arsenalotti*. The reliable source of this rumour had been a sailor called Marco Nigro, who lived amongst *Arsenalotti* residents in the Castello district, and his rumour was confirmed after enquiries by other informants. The Council of Ten imme-diately came to the obvious conclusion: the doge himself was intending to overthrow the noble government and set himself up as a dictator. A secret meeting of the Council of Ten was held, away from the Doge's Palace at the monastery of San Salvatore, where those present decided to summon an emergency meeting of all members of the leading councils, with the exception of any members of the Falier family. This meeting took place in the Doge's Palace that night, presumably under circumstances of the utmost secrecy. On the morning of 15 April, the entire militia of around 7,000 men was ordered into the Piazzetta, and at the same time 100 cavalry were assembled ready to put down any disturbances that broke out elsewhere in the city. Simultaneously, the arrest was ordered of all the major suspects now known to be taking part in the conspiracy. Ten of the principal conspirators were quickly condemned to death and pushed from the windows of the Doge's Palace with a rope around their neck, where their bodies were left dangling in a row as a public example. Others were given lengthy prison sentences. However, according to a contemporary chronicler, 'Many were acquitted and set free.'

The fate of Marin Falier was not so easily decided. In order to try him, the Council of Ten called for the formation of a *zonta*,* seconding twenty respected senior nobles to their number, a measure that was allowed by the constitution in times of extreme danger to the Republic. When confronted by his accusers, Marin Falier immediately confessed to his leadership of the plot, and on 17 April was condemned to death. He would be executed early on the morning of the following day. According to Petrarch (relying upon inside information from his friends in Venice), Falier was 'dragged in servile fashion' from his chambers to the top of the grand staircase leading down to the inner courtyard of the palace (the very place where just six months earlier he had been proclaimed doge). Here he was stripped of his insignia, in particular the *corno*, the distinctive hat worn by the doge as his symbol of office, with its characteristic single round horn (*corno*) at the back. He was then beheaded with a single blow of the executioner's sword, whereupon he 'fell down a headless corpse, and stained with his blood the doors of the church and the entrance of his palace, and the marble stairs often made glorious by solemn feasts or the spoils of enemies'.

Petrarch was in no doubt as to the significance of what had happened:

The sensation caused by this event is so great that, if one considers the form of government and the customs of that city, and what a revolutionary change the death of one man portends, a greater has hardly shown itself in our days in Italy.

* Venetian dialect version of the Italian *giunta*, the origin of the modern term 'junta'.

The failure of the plot, and Falier's execution, were in fact significant in affirming the strength of the nobility's well-established grip on the Republic's system of government, a reminder that the oligarchy and its councils could be threatened by no individual, no matter how strong they might seem.

After Falier's beheading, the doors of the Doge's Palace were thrown open, so that all those gathered outside could see for themselves what had taken place, and his body was then 'displayed to the people'. Falier's remains were then carried off, to be placed in an unmarked grave. In a later frieze that depicted portraits of the historical succession of doges, the place occupied by Falier was ordered to be painted over with a black veil bearing the inscription in Latin: 'Here is the place of Marin Falier, beheaded for his crimes.'

Such is the legend that has come down to us, many parts of which are undeniably true. However, certain elements of this story remain open to question. For instance, there is little evidence to support the veracity of the incident at the Carnival banquet, and Steno's subsequent insulting verse. Records indicate that dogaressa Aloica (née Gradenigo – like the Dandolo, one of the most distinguished families of the era) was probably over fifty years old at the time, making her a matronly figure hardly appropriate for Steno's ribald verse, which only surfaces in written records more than a century later. Michele Steno would in fact one day become doge himself – an unlikely circumstance if he had made enemies of the Gradenigo family. Others, such as Petrarch, have questioned why a man of Falier's undoubted popularity and advanced years should have sought to establish himself as a supreme ruler so late in life, especially when he had no children to succeed him.

The indications are that this was a time of extreme social tension in the city. The arrogance of the nobles had made them detested by the common people, who were not afraid to show this – as attested by the behaviour of the gang of sailors who quickly gathered to support Isarello, marching up and down in such menacing fashion outside the Doge's Palace. The nobles certainly felt threatened, and it has been suggested that there was widespread support amongst them for a monarchist party, which sought a strong leader, untrammelled by quasi-democratic restraints, during this nadir in Venice's fortunes. Support for such leadership may even have existed amongst certain groups of commoners – the *Arsenalotti* being the most obvious candidates. If such was the case, Doge Falier, far from being consumed with ambition, may only have become privy to any plot when it was already well advanced. This would explain why the initial uncovering of the plot did not implicate him. In the end, his taking full blame may have been an act of noble self-sacrifice rather than ignominious confession – he had no wish for the Republic to fall victim to hopeless divisions and reprisals in the aftermath of the plot's failure. Such an explanation would clarify why afterwards so 'many were acquitted and set free'; and the mysterious fact that Falier's name did not appear on the list of those condemned for the plot, which is set down in the usual meticulous records. And, tellingly, why the furrier Beltrami did not receive the full reward he expected for his part in revealing the plot; as well as the mysterious fact that some years later he would be stabbed to death by one of the conspirators. Indeed, there are indications that much of the 'story' concerning Falier was nothing more or less than a vast cover-up. If this is the case, it certainly reaffirms the power of the nobility, as well as their ruthlessness when faced with a challenge to their authority. The success of such a cover-up would also indicate the conspiratorial secrecy that was now increasingly adopted by the authorities.

3

The Saviours of Venice

W ITHIN JUST THREE days of Falier's execution a new doge had been elected — this was the seventy-year-old Giovanni Gradenigo, who interestingly was a close relative of the former dogaressa Aloica. The first major achievement of his reign was the signing on 1 June 1355 of a peace treaty with Genoa, under the auspices of the three Visconti brothers — Matteo II, Bernabo and Galeazzo — who now jointly ruled Milan after the death of their uncle, Archbishop Giovanni Visconti. Although by any reckoning Venice had come off second-best in the war, the treaty imposed by Milan was surprisingly even-handed. Both signatories undertook to return all prisoners and to stay out of each other's home waters — which for Venice was deemed to be the entire Adriatic, while for Genoa this was limited to the stretch of the Mediterranean between Marseilles and Pisa. And both sides were required to suspend for three years all trading in the contested region of the Sea of Azov; and to ensure adherence to the treaty, both cities were required to deposit 100,000 gold florins in a neutral city.

Despite this favourable treaty, Venice (and its trade) would suffer during the ensuing years from another enemy, as the powerful and expansionist King Louis of Hungary laid claim to Dalmatia. Venice had neither the money nor the stomach for another prolonged war, and in 1358 ceded the entire territory to Hungary — a great loss of face as well as a dangerous strategic setback. The fact is that the long wars against Genoa and the subsequent loss of trading revenue had reduced the city to the verge of bankruptcy. The public debt was consolidated in the fund known as the *Monte Vecchio*, to which all property-owning citizens were obliged to contribute by buying bonds proportionate to their wealth (and which paid out 5 per cent). This debt had mushroomed alarmingly from 432,000 ducats in 1343 to around 1,500,000 ducats by 1363. And now higher taxes were needed to make up for the loss of income from Dalmatia, which resulted in the other colonies being forced to contribute even more than previously to the Venetian exchequer.

In 1363 this led to a revolt in Venice's largest colony, the island of Crete, which contained many feudal estates owned by Venetian landlords. The spark for this revolt was the Venetian demand that the capital city of Candia (now Heraklion) pay a tax for extra repairs needed to the harbour, which was in fact mainly used not by the Cretans or the local Venetians, but by passing shipping en route from Venice to Cyprus and the Levant. This tax was proclaimed by the city's heralds in Candia Cathedral on 8 August 1363, with the warning that anyone refusing to pay faced confiscation of their property or the death penalty. The following day a large angry procession of local Greeks led by Venetian feudal landlords, many of whom were members of noble families, marched into the main square and stormed over the rooftops into the palace of the Venetian governor, Leonardo Dandolo, son of the late venerated doge. With cries of 'Death to the traitor!', the rebels, led by the hotheaded Venetian landlord Tito Venier (who was also of a noble family), were only prevented from murdering governor Dandolo because he was hustled away to the safety of a prison cell by some of the Venetian landlords.

The Cretans had rebelled against Venice before, but this was the first time the local Greeks had been joined by the feudal Venetian landlords. A sizeable proportion of them had now lived on their estates on the island for two or three generations and had adopted many aspects of the indigenous Greek culture. They resented the increasingly burdensome taxes being imposed upon them by what they had come to regard as a foreign and autocratic regime. An indication of the widespread and deep nature of this pan-Cretan resentment can be seen from the fact that over the next few days Venetian rule in the cities of Rethimno and Chania (now Xania) was toppled, and by the end of the week the entire 150-mile length of the island was effectively in the hands of the rebels.

Symbolically, the Venetian flag of the Catholic San Marco was hauled down, and in its place was run up the flag of St Titus, the Byzantine Orthodox patron saint of the island. The rebels elected the Venetian land-lord Marco Gradenigo as the new governor of Crete, along with two councillors, while Tito Venier was rewarded with the governorship of the city of Chania. Amongst governor Gradenigo's first measures was recruiting an army to defend the island. As there was no money to pay soldiers, they were recruited from amongst the pirates, brigands, murderers and assorted desperadoes detained in the local prisons, who were willing to serve without pay for the first six months in return for their freedom. Over the month of August governor Gradenigo issued a series of proclamations, aimed at establishing the new Cretan nation. Amongst the most radical was one that proclaimed equal rights between the Catholic Church (which answered to the pope in Rome and ministered to the Venetian colonists) and the previ-ously discriminated-against Greek Byzantine Church (whose loyalties were to Constantinople and the indigenous population). In consequence, a Catholic monk named Leonardo Gradenigo would even go so far as to abrogate his vows and become a Byzantine Orthodox monk. Another proclamation decreed that from now on Cretan vessels were to fly the flag of St Titus, instead of that of San Marco, both at home and especially when visiting foreign ports. This was intended to demonstrate the perma-nence of the new regime, as well as to broadcast its existence to ports throughout the Mediterranean.

Not until September did news of the revolt reach Venice, and even then it hardly created a stir. Evidence of the Venetian regard for their colony can be seen in their earlier reaction to the Venetian landlords' petition to send a delegation of twenty *savi* (wise men) to Venice to put their case, to which the Great Council had replied, 'We were not aware that there were twenty wise men in Candia.' In response to the revolt, Venice despatched three commissioners to sort out what they evidently regarded as a little local difficulty. When they were greeted by jeers and insults as they made their way through the streets, and a second delegation was chased by an angry mob back to their galley, it was belatedly decided that more serious measures should be taken.

This would demonstrate the full might and efficiency of the Venetian administrative machine, once it had committed itself to action. First, a precautionary diplomatic campaign was launched, with letters seeking support against the revolt being despatched to Pope Urban V, Queen Giovanna of Sicily and Jerusalem, the kings of Cyprus, Hungary and Naples, the Grand Master of the Knights Hospitaller of Rhodes and even the Doge of Genoa. This was an astute move: none of these rulers wished to see such a revolt succeed, in case it set an example to their own subdued populations or remote provinces. In their replies, not one of these rulers actually went so far as to pledge forces to help suppress the revolt, but most declared support for Venice and agreed to bar their subjects from trading with Crete.

Venice now hired the powerful Veronese *condottiere* (mercenary commander) Luchino dal Verme, and his mercenary army consisting of 1,000 cavalry and 2,000 infantry, to be transported by a fleet of thirty galleys to Crete to crush the revolt. This force included the usual assortment of Italian soldiers, as well as freebooters from as far afield as Albania, Switzerland, England and Turkey, together with a contingent of Bohemian mine-layers with specialist siege engines. When news of the size of this invading army reached Crete, many Venetian colonials began to desert the rebels' cause. In a move to contain this, the apostate monk Leonardo Gradenigo formed an alliance with a Greek priest called Milletos (who was promised a bishopric for his support), and together with an armed band of peasants, Venetians and Greek priests they roamed the countryside murdering all the Venetian landlords who did not support the revolt. Leonardo Gradenigo then decided to carry this campaign into Candia, where he gathered up a mob with the intention of breaking into the prison and murdering arrested Venetian landlords who had turned against the new regime, but their efforts were thwarted. Meanwhile, in the countryside, Milletos and his gang had launched into an indiscriminate campaign of slaughter against any Venetian landlords they could find, as well as their families. The authorities became alarmed, and even Leonardo Gradenigo began to have misgivings about his friend. He set out into the countryside, where he persuaded Milletos to put up in a monastery. Leonardo and his men then raided the monastery and took Milletos prisoner, whereupon he was delivered to the governor's palace in Candia. The actions of Milletos, intended to make the Greeks turn on the Venetians, had in fact angered Greeks and Venetians alike, and a vengeful crowd gathered in the square outside the palace, baying for his blood. They watched as Milletos was led onto the roof and then pushed off into the square below, where his broken body was set upon by the angry mob.

News now reached Candia that the disembarkation of the Venetian mercenary invasion fleet was imminent. In the spring of 1364 governor Gradenigo despatched his relative Leonardo on a mission to Genoa, in a desperate attempt to win over Venice's old enemy. Around 6 May, dal Verme's army landed at the small port of Fraschia, seven miles west of Candia, and began their march on the capital. Upon hearing this news, the Cretan brigand army melted away into the countryside, allowing dal Verme to occupy Candia virtually unopposed. Governor Marco Gradenigo and his two councillors were captured and immediately beheaded, where-upon the citizens of Chania, and then Rethimno, quickly surrendered without opposition, their rebel Venetian landlords fleeing for the mountains.

It was at this point that the rebel delegation to Genoa, whose mission had been unsuccessful, sailed back into Cretan waters. Leonardo Gradenigo was warned by Greek fishermen of what had happened in his absence, and the galleys of the flotilla immediately changed course. Leonardo sailed for south-eastern Crete, attempting to take refuge on the remote island of Gaidouronisi, but was soon tracked down and hauled back to Candia to be executed. Others managed to put ashore in western Crete and make their escape. Greek peasants soon directed them to the location where the rebels were hiding out on the estate of a Greek landlord called Ioannes Calergi. Although dal Verme and his army held the cities, subduing the countryside and the mountains proved another matter altogether. Calergi and the rebels, who now included some fifty rebel Venetian landlords, began conducting a guerrilla campaign to drive the invading Venetians from the island, and soon the entire west of the island was in rebel hands. In response, Venice mounted a coordinated military operation to rid the island of rebels.

In the end, this operation would last for four long years, with one military delegation after another being despatched from Venice to subdue the island. The last of these was issued with explicit orders to track down and take prisoner 'all the Calergi and Tito Venier and a great many other Greek and

Latin rebels and traitors and bring the entire island to peace and submission to the Doge's Venetian domination'. Finally, in 1368, with all other rebel bands captured or killed, the by-now-legendary Ioannes Calergi and his Venetian cohort Tito Venier, along with their last faithful supporters, were hunted down and trapped in a mountain cave, where they fought to the last man.

Back in Venice, the visiting Petrarch in his palazzo on the Riva degli Schiavoni had witnessed the arrival of the first news of dal Verme's invasion of Crete:

At around the sixth hour on the fourth of June 1364, I happened to be standing at my window looking out over the lagoon . . . when of a sudden I saw one of those long ships they call a galley. This was garlanded with green bows and rowing fast towards the shore . . . As it sped closer, its sails billowing in the wind, I saw the joyful faces of the sailors, and a band of smiling youths crowned with green leaves waving banners above their heads . . . As the ship came in, we saw the enemy flags trailing astern in the water . . . When the messengers came ashore, we soon learned what had happened . . . a great victory had been won in Crete, the enemy slain or captured, the loyal citizens of the republic rescued, the cities captured, and the island once more belonged to Venice!

For years now there had been little to celebrate in Venice and, despite the somewhat premature nature of this news, the city launched into three days of enthusiastic celebration, with jousting, displays of horsemanship and mock-battles staged in the Piazza San Marco before the doge on his throne, with Petrarch sitting at his right hand.

The sixty-year-old Petrarch was a guest in the city, having fled there two years earlier to escape from an outbreak of plague in nearby Padua. He had arrived with his extensive library, in the form of bales of manuscripts strapped to the backs of a lengthy string of packhorses. The city was honoured to receive such a celebrated guest, and Petrarch was offered the free use of the Ca' Molina delle due Torri (Palazzo of the Two Towers) overlooking the main harbour, in return for which he promised that on his death he would donate to the city his library, which is known to have contained some 200 codices of priceless manuscripts and books that he had collected during the long years of his travels through Europe.* His fervent wish was that his collection should form the core of a great library used by visiting scholars, in conscious echo of the ancient Library of Alexandria, which had been used by the likes of Euclid, Archimedes and Plutarch.

Petrarch enjoyed the company of many friends in high places in Venice, most notably Benintendi dei Ravignani, the Grand Chancellor of the city,† 'who would arrive on his gondola at dusk, after his fatiguing day's work, and we would relax together in scholarly conversation as we were rowed across the night-bound lagoon'. We know from Petrarch's many letters to his friends elsewhere that he admired Venice for its just government and its citizens' sense of adventure; he is also known to have enjoyed its 'foaming wine' and to have passed many happy hours gazing down at the busy port below his window, where:

> even amidst the gloom of winter and the violent springtime storms the water was crammed with ships, one turning its prow to the east, the other to the west; some carrying off our wine to foam in British cups, our fruits to flatter the palates of the Scythians . . . others to the Aegean and the Achaian isles, some to Syria, others to Armenia, some to the Arabs, others to the Persians, carrying oil and linen and saffron, and bringing back all their many wonderful goods.

Yet the Florentine-born poet's relationship with the city remained essentially ambivalent. He admired Venice for being 'strong in power, and even stronger in virtue', but paradoxically found its 'foul language and excessive

---

* Many of these codices contained more than one manuscript, such that the entire library probably contained more than a thousand items, some of which are known to have been the sole surviving copies of Ancient Roman works. Petrarch's collection of his beloved Cicero and Virgil was unsurpassed in his lifetime.
† The Grand Chancellor was head of Chancery, the all-important public record office. Though selected by the Great Council, this was the highest office in the administration to be occupied by a man who was not a member of a noble family.

licence' offensive. Similarly he admired its cosmopolitanism, but was repelled by 'encountering in the alleyways filthy slaves with Scythian features'. Likewise it seems that the 'father of humanism', for all his great learning, was not fully appreciated by the more advanced local intellectuals, who tended to favour scientific knowledge over humanist studies. And apart from these, most of the local thinkers clung to the rigid medieval authority of Aristotle, which Petrarch's humanism sought to overcome. When some-time during 1367 he heard that behind his back 'four friends . . . had called him ignorant and illiterate' because he did not read Aristotle, he decided this was the last straw and determined to leave Venice. The following year he crossed to the mainland, taking his library with him, regardless of his promise, and settled once more in the territory of Padua, whose ruler Francesco da Carrara was no friend of Venice. Deep in the countryside by the village of Arquà,* on a hillside above the distant Venice lagoon, he built himself a house beside a vineyard and an olive grove and here he lived out his last years. He died peacefully whilst reading in his library on the warm summer night of 19 July 1374, on the eve of his seventieth birthday.

Petrarch's will made no mention of his precious library, or of his promise to Venice. As a result, the manuscripts and books were sold off piecemeal, and can now be found scattered in collections ranging from the Bodleian Library in Oxford to the Vatican Library in Rome, as well as in London, Paris and even Venice. Indeed, it appears that when Petrarch departed in high dudgeon from Venice he may even have left a part of his library behind in the Ca' Molina. These manuscripts would become, in the words of the modern Italian scholar Manlio Stocchi, the 'subject of an uncertain and veiled tradition . . . halfway between history and legend'. In 1635, the antiquary Giacomo Tomasini discovered a long-forgotten cache of Petrarch's manuscripts hidden away in a small dark room behind the four horses of San Marco, above the great entrance doorway. According to the nineteenth-century historians Charles and Mart Elton, 'Some had crumbled into powder, and others had been glued into shapeless masses by the damp. The survivors were placed in the Libraria [*sic*] Vecchia.' Many historians

* Now called Arqua Petrarca in his honour.

now dispute that these were left behind by Petrarch, claiming that the abandoned 'survivors' in fact came from Petrarch's dispersed collection. Either way, neither Petrarch nor Venice fared well from this 'veiled tradition' of broken promises, ingratitude and neglect.

While the Venetians had celebrated their crushing of the Cretans, the early 1370s saw familiar anxieties return, with another increase in tension between the Republic and Genoa. This would come to a head in Cyprus at the coronation of the fifteen-year-old King Peter II, which took place in October 1372 at Famagusta. Afterwards a grand banquet was held at the royal palace. The festivities were attended by a variety of local nobles, church dignitaries, visiting foreign aristocracy, as well as the resident Venetians and Genoese, who were segregated at separate long tables. After the consumption of much strong local wine, the Venetians and Genoese began boisterously pelting each other with bread. This quickly turned nasty when the Genoese drew back their robes to reveal that they were armed with swords and daggers – an unforgivable breach of etiquette as well as a threatening insult to the king. Amidst widespread outrage a riot ensued, with the Genoese coming under violent attack from both angry Cypriots and Venetians (who appear to have found miraculous access to arms of their own, with no recorded breach of etiquette). A number of Genoese were thrown to their death from the palace balcony, and others were rounded up outside and summarily executed, while a mob began to rampage through the Genoese quarter, setting fire to buildings. Scores of Genoese managed to board two ships in the harbour, eventually making it back to their home city, where their arrival caused a sensation.

The Genoese bided their time, assembling two fleets, which set sail for Cyprus the following summer. The first, consisting of seven galleys, landed raiding parties at several spots along the coast, with armed men conducting a campaign of rape, plunder and hostage-taking. Meanwhile the other fleet of thirty-six ships, carrying some 14,000 men as well as cavalry and artillery, landed at Famagusta. Within days the Genoese had virtual control of most of Cyprus. At a stroke, the balance of power in the Mediterranean had taken a decisive shift. Holding Cyprus meant that the Genoese had command over the lucrative trade routes to the Levant. Such were the origins of the Fourth Genoese War (also known as the War of Chioggia), by far the most vicious and dangerous conflict to erupt between the two maritime republics. Both sensed that this would be a fight to the death, and reacted accordingly.

Venice appointed to take charge of its fleet two exceptional admirals. The first of these was Carlo Zeno, a brother to Nicolò and Antonio, the explorers who may have sailed to Greenland and America earlier in this period – indeed, according to some sources, Carlo accompanied his brothers on this legendary pioneer voyage. The Zeno family was amongst the more distinguished Venetian nobility, but Carlo was one of ten brothers and was forced by financial circumstances to take up holy orders at an early age. Seldom would a vocation prove more inappropriate. However, all began well enough and the young priest was despatched to France, to serve in the papal court of Clement V at Avignon. The pope eventually rewarded the teenage Venetian with the post of canon of the cathedral of Patras in the distant Greek Peloponnese. This benefice provided him with a sizeable income, and after sixteen months at Avignon Carlo set off back to Italy, where he decided to study law at the University of Padua. Here, despite his priestly vows, he threw himself wholeheartedly into student life, especially the pursuit of women, gambling and revelry – to such an extent that he was eventually forced to sell everything he had, including his books, and enlist as a mercenary to escape his creditors. And it was now that his true character emerged.

Carlo would prove to be an embodiment of that Venetian adventurousness so admired by Petrarch. He was a natural soldier, and he spent the next five years honing his military skills, travelling as far afield as France, Germany and England in the service of the Holy Roman Emperor, Charles IV.* Surprisingly, he then arrived at Patras to take up his post as canon of the cathedral; he was now a battle-hardened warrior of twenty-two. At this time the Ottoman Turks were advancing into the Peloponnese, and once again Zeno took up arms. However, although the Bishop of Patras saw nothing remiss in one of his canons leading a troop of cavalry, he drew the line at undisciplined behaviour. When the hotheaded Carlo

---

* Charles IV of Bohemia had been crowned Holy Roman Emperor in Rome in April 1355.

challenged one of his fellow officers to a duel, the archbishop stripped him of both his military rank and his post as canon. Considering himself to be absolved of his priestly vows, Carlo immediately married a local Greek lady, who soon died – whereupon he returned to Venice and married a Venetian lady belonging to the noble Giustinian family. According to his grandson, Japopo Zeno, Bishop of Padua, who wrote his biography drawing on family papers, Carlo now:

> made up his mind to adopt the life of a merchant; and leaving Venice with this intention, remained seven years absent, living partly in a castle called Tanai on the banks of the river Tania [at the head of the Sea of Azov], and partly in Constantinople.

The other admiral appointed by the Venetians to take charge of their fleet at the start of the War of Chioggia was Vettore Pisani, nephew of the celebrated Nicolò, who during the previous hostilities had led the Venetian fleet to its great victory over the Genoese off the coast of Sardinia, and had later been lucky to escape with his life in the catastrophic defeat by his rival, Paganino Doria, at Porto Lungo.

The young Vettore Pisani is said to have been present at Porto Lungo, and to have escaped with his uncle. Though he was charged with cowardice on his return to Venice, his case was overwhelmingly dismissed. He was a courageous, flamboyant character and became a popular naval captain, commanding the loyalty and admiration of his crews. Such regard was unusual during this period, when nobles were still much despised for their arrogant behaviour. On one occasion Pisani stood up for a galley master wrongly accused of smuggling for his own gain, a serious offence. One of the accusers was the noble Pietro Cornaro, who during the proceedings sarcastically implied that Pisani was lying. Outraged at this affront to his honour, Pisani afterwards went up to Cornaro in the street and demanded to know if he was armed. When Cornaro replied that he was not, Pisani knew that he could not challenge him, so he warned him that next time they encountered each other Cornaro should make sure he was armed. That night Pisani stood waiting for Cornaro to return to his palazzo, so that he could challenge him. But as soon as Cornaro saw Pisani he fled into a nearby house. For this serious breach of public order Pisani was fined 200 ducats, and was stripped of a public office in Crete to which he had recently been elected. However, such was his popularity that he was quickly elected to another Cretan post, and would become one of the few to serve the Republic with honour and bravery during the Cretan revolt. The choice of Vettore Pisani to lead the Venetian fleet, along with the redoubtable Carlo Zeno, was popular with citizens of all ranks throughout the city.

The official outbreak of the War of Chioggia came in 1378, a good six years after the riot at the coronation of King Peter II in Famagusta. The Venetians held an early advantage thanks to the adventurous escapades of the irresponsible Zeno. In 1376 he had found himself in Constantinople when the Byzantine emperor John V Palaeologus was deposed by his son Andronicus, who imprisoned him and two of his sons in the Tower of Anema, at the same time declaring himself emperor. The former emperor John V had spent some time in Venice (where he had suffered the indignity of being confined in a debtors' gaol); nevertheless he remained a friend of Venice, while his son – the new emperor Andronicus IV – favoured Genoa. According to the papers consulted by Zeno's biographer-grandson, which contain Carlo's not-always-reliable version of events, he now became involved in a spectacular adventure that would change the course of Venetian history no less. Seemingly, John V managed to smuggle a message from his cell in the Tower of Anema to Carlo Zeno, imploring the Venetian to rescue him. Under cover of darkness, Zeno and some companions rowed across the Golden Horn in a small boat, putting ashore beneath the Tower of Anema, where John V let down a rope-ladder from the window of his cell. Zeno climbed up the ladder, but John V refused to escape unless he could take his two sons with him. As there was no room for his sons on the boat, Zeno was eventually forced to leave empty-handed. Making his getaway as best he could, Zeno raised sail and made for the Sea of Marmara. Here he was eventually picked up by a Venetian squadron, which happened to be under the command of his father-in-law, Mario Giustinian. In recompense for Zeno's brave attempt to rescue him, John V had handed Zeno an imperial decree granting possession of the Aegean island of Tenedos (modern Bozcaada) to the Venetian Republic. This island was of great strategic importance, guarding the entrance to the Hellespont (Dardanelles). When Giustinian landed and showed the imperial decree to the Byzantine-Greek commander of Tenedos, he immediately handed over the island, making no attempt to defend it.

However, it so happened that the new emperor, Andronicus IV, had just promised Tenedos to the Genoese, and the following year a Genoese-Byzantine fleet arrived off Tenedos to enforce this claim, but was soon repulsed by the resident Venetian forces. Although the Genoese continued to hold Cyprus and command the trade routes to the Levant, Venice now commanded the trade routes running through the Hellespont into the Black Sea and the ports in the Sea of Azov that lay at the western end of the Silk Route from the Orient.

Despite this early advantage, guaranteeing Venice an important source of income from the Orient, which should have enabled it to compete with Genoa, it proved of little avail, as the Republic now found itself under severe threat at home. Hungary remained in possession of much of Dalmatia, and Francesco da Carrara appeared to be marshalling troops in Padua. With Venice all but surrounded on the mainland side, it was likely that Genoa – allied to the Hungarians – would attempt to mount a direct attack on Venice from the sea, much as Paganino Doria had done in the previous war, only this time they would bring the full might of their fleet. Consequently Pisani was ordered to use his fleet to protect the Adriatic and its approaches against any direct Genoese threat, whilst Zeno was given a more general brief to patrol the Mediterranean, attacking Genoese colonies and any enemy convoys that he came across on the trade routes.

The extent to which Venice remained economically and militarily depleted can be seen from the fact that Pisani had command of just fourteen galleys, and even these were undermanned. The loss of Dalmatia had cut off not only an important source of grain, but also a recruiting ground for galley oarsmen. Several of Pisani's galleys were manned by Cretans, and a few were even reduced to skeleton crews, with just one man to some oarsmen's benches. As a result, these galleys were almost totally reliant upon sails for propulsion, and could not manoeuvre at close quarters – the one great military advantage of rowed galleys.

The first serious naval encounter of the war took place in late May 1378, when Pisani spotted a convoy of ten Genoese galleys moving down the south-western coast of Italy near the mouth of the Tiber. Pisani set off in pursuit, catching up with the Genoese off the cape at Anzio on 30 May. By this stage a storm had blown up, with heavy seas and darkened skies, but Pisani ordered his galleys to attack nonetheless. As a result of the weather, and undermanning, four of Pisani's galleys were unable to engage with the enemy, and while the others closed in on the Genoese, grappling proved extremely hazardous. Despite this, only four of the Genoese galleys managed to escape, one was driven onto the rocks and the other five were captured, together with the Genoese commander, Luigi de' Fieschi.*

Pisani had hardly won a great naval victory, but its effect would prove as such. At the time the citizens of Genoa were much in need of reassurance with regard to this latest war with Venice. Encouraged by Venice, Genoa's neighbour, Francesco, Marchese dal Carretto, had risen up and seized Albenga just forty miles west along the coast, laying waste to Genoese territory in the process. Now, with Genoa's naval defences down to a minimum, came news of a threatening Venetian victory, quickly followed by rumours that the enemy fleet was assembling in the Bay of Spezia, just over a day's sailing distance to the east. Overcome with fear, the population of Genoa rose up on 17 June and stormed the palace of the aged, long-serving doge, Domenico di Campofregoso, causing him to be deposed. When order was restored, the younger and more popular Niccolò Guarco was elected in his place.

In fact, the victorious but undermanned Venetian galleys were nowhere near Spezia. Pisani realised that he had insufficient strength to take Genoa, no matter how ill-defended it might have been. Instead, he sailed east to keep a rendezvous off the south-western Peloponnese with six galleys from Crete. After a fruitless search for Genoese shipping he set off back for the

---

* De' Fieschi and the other captured Genoese nobles were duly shipped back to Venice, where they appear to have proved something of an attraction. According to the Victorian historian F.C. Hodgson, delicately paraphrasing a contemporary source, the Genoese captives 'were treated with humanity, Venetian ladies of rank being zealous in their care of them'. He added, in case of misinterpretation, 'Many, no doubt, were wounded.'

Adriatic, where he attacked the strategic Hungarian-held ports of Cattaro (modern Kotor) and Sebenico (Šibenik), returning them to Venetian control. He then set sail for Venice, intending to winter his ships in the lagoon, where they could be refurbished at the Arsenale, and many of the sailors could spend some well-earned time with their families.

To Pisani's surprise, his request to enter Venice was denied by the authorities. He was instead expected to winter almost 100 miles to the south at Pola, in readiness to escort and protect an expected convoy of grain ships from Apulia in the heel of Italy. This decision by the Venetian authorities has been called 'a serious error of judgement', resulting as it did in an unnecessary collapse of morale amongst the crews, who would spend the winter in damp, cramped conditions aboard ship, rather than at home where they felt they deserved to be after six months of risking their lives and fighting for their country. Likewise, this decision also affected the readiness and seaworthiness of the ships, which could not be so easily overhauled with the lesser facilities available at Pola. On the other hand, what Pisani could not have realised was that by now the city of Venice was down to its last supplies, with virtually all its sources of food cut off.

After a winter of storms, and disease amongst his crews, in February 1379 Pisani duly despatched a flotilla to escort the grain fleet up the Adriatic to Venice. In the course of this two of his ships were driven ashore and lost at Ancona. Then, on the morning of 7 May, the Venetians in the harbour at Pola were shocked when they awoke to the sight of a large Genoese fleet hove-to in the nearby waters. The Genoese admiral, Luciano Doria, had wintered his twenty-five ships 100 miles down the coast at the Hungarian-held port of Zara (Zadar). Intelligence from local travellers and fishermen had led him to suspect that Pisani was at Pola, and his hunch had paid off.

The Genoese now challenged the Venetians in the traditional manner by hauling aloft their battle ensigns depicting a raised sword; but Pisani realised that his ill-readied ships were in no fit state to take on such superior numbers, even though his depleted crews had now been supplemented by a large number of locally recruited Slavs. Pisani refused to allow his ships to put to sea, ordering them to remain within the safety of Pola's protected harbour in the well-founded hope that Carlo Zeno and his fleet would soon return. But Pisani's captains were dissatisfied at such orders, seeing them as cowardice; after much wrangling Pisani caved in, against his better judgement. Gathering his ships together, he delivered a rousing speech to the assembled crews: 'Brave men, now is the time to prove your valour . . .' He then ordered the trumpets to sound the call to attack and led his ships into battle. Pisani was no coward, and could not tolerate the fact that his men might see him as one. Indeed, his initial sortie resulted in such success that he personally was responsible for the death of Luciano Doria. However, although the Genoese were initially surprised by the speed of Pisani's sudden attack, they quickly regrouped, proceeding to inflict a heavy defeat on the Venetians, capturing fifteen galleys and no fewer than 2,407 prisoners, described by the chronicler Daniele di Chinazzo as 'the flower of seamen of Venice'. Pisani decided to cut his losses and managed to flee, along with six heavily damaged galleys, which limped up the coast to the safety of the port of Parenza (Poreč). From here he was eventually summoned to Venice, where he suffered the fate of any Venetian commander defeated in battle – he was put on trial. Regardless of his bravery, it was charged that he 'led the fleet into battle in disorderly fashion' and that 'he had quit the fight while the battle was still going on'. The guilty verdict left him disgraced, sentenced to six months in prison and banned from all public office for five years. Had he not been so popular, he might well have suffered a more severe punishment (an admiral on such charges was liable to suffer execution).

Venice now faced extreme danger. Its fleet was destroyed, the Hungarians had cut off the trade routes to the north, while the Paduans held the mainland to the west. And the Genoese fleet was evidently poised to attack from the sea. All the authorities could do was strengthen the defences of their wall-less city. The fortifications in San Nicolò di Lido at the main entrance to the lagoon were reinforced with artillery, and a chain-boom with two hulks was strung across the channel. In case the invaders broke through this defence, the posts marking the navigable channels through the treacherous shallow waters of the lagoon to the city itself were uprooted. Meanwhile the citizens gathered in the churches praying for a miracle – the return of Carlo Zeno and his fleet. But no word of him was forthcoming: throughout the Adriatic, from Pola to the Peloponnese, no report of his whereabouts in the Mediterranean had been received. He could have been anywhere from Cyprus to Constantinople, from Crete to Sardinia.

Meanwhile a relative of the slain Luciano Doria, Pietro Doria, had now taken command of the Genoese fleet and was awaiting reinforcements. In view of the situation, Pietro Doria decided against the customary exchange of the many Venetian and mercenary prisoners taken at the Battle of Pola, and instead 800 of them were summarily beheaded, their bodies thrown into the sea. Having signalled his intentions, he then set off to liberate the Dalmatian ports of Cattaro and Sebenico, before joining up with his reinforcements and burning to the ground various Venetian ports at the head of the Adriatic.

At the same time, reports were coming in that Francesco da Carrara's Paduan forces had been joined by 5,000 militia despatched by the Hungarians; these were now said to be ranged along the mainland shore of the Venetian lagoon. During the first days of August a flotilla of small Genoese ships appeared some way off the Lido. Pisani's replacement as naval commander, Taddeo Giustinian, had just six serviceable ships at his disposal in the Arsenale, but decided to embark and investigate nonetheless. Voyaging out into open sea off the Lido, he came across a lone man swimming. This turned out to be a Venetian who had been captured by the Genoese at the Battle of Pola and had dived overboard as soon as he saw the approaching Venetian ships; he now informed Giustinian that a large Genoese fleet was waiting just over the horizon. Giustinian rapidly returned to the safety of the lagoon.

On 6 August 1379 Pietro Doria appeared off the Lido with forty-seven galleys and launched an attack on San Nicolò. Unable to breach the main entrance into the lagoon, he proceeded east along the Lido, landing soldiers who burned everything in their path, as well as attacking the towns of Malamocco and Pellestrina. Within a few days Doria's fleet had reached the fortified island-town of Chioggia at the southernmost entrance to the lagoon. Here, aided by 24,000 Paduan and Hungarian land forces, the Genoese laid siege to the 3,000 Venetian troops in the garrison. On 16 August Chioggia fell in a bloody slaughter, leaving Venice all but surrounded. Never before in its history had it faced such an overwhelming threat.

When news of the fall of Chioggia reached Venice, all semblance of commercial activity on the Rialto petered to a halt. The bells rang out from the Campanile and the citizens flocked, silent and fearful, into the Piazza San Marco. Meanwhile Doge Andrea Contarini and the sixty members of the Senate (responsible for foreign affairs) met in emergency session. Seeing no alternative, the Venetians decided to open negotiations with the Genoese. But these came to no avail when Pietro Doria scornfully dismissed the Venetian peace envoy, famously declaring that the Genoese would not cease fighting 'until after they had bridled the horses of San Marco' – a fitting metaphor for Venice's defeat and utter humiliation.

Some members of the Senate now came to the conclusion that all was lost. The most radically innovative action was required: it was time for the Venetians to abandon Venice altogether and shift the capital of their empire to Candia or Constantinople (despite the fact that this was not even Venetian territory). The city had always looked east, where its empire lay. The island-city in the lagoon was merely a historical anomaly, a vulnerable trading port at the western limit of the empire. The heart of the Venetian Empire no longer lay in Europe, in any sense – strategic or commercial. Such arguments held considerable force. Indeed, they had been seriously considered in the past, especially during times of expansionist ambition. One only had to look at the city's architecture to see this oriental inclination expressed in solid form – the basilica of San Marco, the church of the city's patron saint, was unmistakably Byzantine, while the famous four horses also came from Constantinople. And the symbol of San Marco, the winged lion on its pedestal overlooking the Molo, originated from even further east – from Syria, Persia or perhaps China. More than a thousand years previously the Roman Empire had divided between East and West, between Rome and Constantinople: Venice now surely belonged with the eastern Empire, not with Italian Rome. Indeed, in what sense was the Venetian Empire really European at all? Such self-questioning had long remained beneath the surface, but arising as it did now, this was nothing less than defeatist talk. Although well into his seventies, Doge Andrea Contarini, along with the majority of his ageing senators, vigorously dismissed any such mutterings. On the contrary, they made it clear that, despite their age, they would be volunteering to fight for their city.

Meanwhile extreme measures were implemented: the salary of all civil servants was withheld, and a forced loan imposed on all nobles and merchants in order to raise the equivalent of 400,000 ducats to finance an emergency programme to defend the city as well as to launch a major programme of refurbishment and ship-building at the Arsenale. However, much of this money would be placed at the disposal of envoys despatched on clandestine missions to the mainland to hire mercenary commanders and all the soldiers they could muster. At the same time, in view of the crippling food shortages, all wealthy houses were ordered to open their doors to provide free meals for the poor.

By this time Contarini had been doge for more than ten years, yet he remained an energetic man and an able politician who quickly sensed the mood of the public. According to the chronicler Chinazzo, the imprisoned Pisani remained disliked by the nobles, but 'all the people loved him, and were disappointed at his punishment'. Contarini was well aware of this, and in the face of popular agitation ordered Pisani's release. The result was a wave of popular feeling for the only man whom the people believed could save the city. On his release, Pisani was cheered through the Piazza San Marco by a horde of seamen – and, indeed, 'half of Venice' – shouting, 'Viva Messer Vettoe.'

New galleys were now leaving the Arsenale production line at a prodigious rate, and citizens from all walks of life were lining up to volunteer as crews. At the same time, hundreds of fishermen from Murano, Burano and the outlying islands of the lagoon had rowed in to sign up, waving their banners before the Doge's Palace and pledging their allegiance to serve under Pisani. However, in the face of opposition from the nobles, Contarini had been forced to make a concession. Pisani had not been given command of the fleet, but instead had been appointed to a lesser post under his succesor, Taddeo Giustinian. When the fishermen from the islands heard this they threw down their banners in disgust and headed back home, 'uttering words the chronicler thought too indecent to record'.

Venice could hardly afford internal dissent at such a time, and Doge Contarini quickly moved to resolve the situation diplomatically, in order to eliminate the very real possibility of a civil war between the arrogant nobles and the despairing citizenry. He appointed himself Captain-General of the Sea, while Pisani was appointed his chief deputy, to whom he effectively delegated command of the navy. As soon as Pisani set up tables at the Molo to enlist crews for his galleys, the recruiting clerks were at once besieged by volunteers. Some of these were experienced oarsmen, others were practised naval archers, but most were inexperienced as seamen. And once again the aged Doge Contarini demonstrated his abilities to the full. In all, thirty-four galleys had by now emerged fully equipped from the Arsenale, and Contarini in his capacity as captain-general was determined to ensure that these crews were properly trained. Each day he was up first thing overseeing the raw recruits rowing their galleys, directing them to row them from the naval yard on Giudecca to the Lido and back, a good five-mile haul. As each day passed, the new sailors – teenage boys, craftsmen, middle-aged servants, stall-holders and the like – under the supervision of experienced oarsmen, gradually gained greater cohesion, learning how to manoeuvre their craft and follow battle orders.

After the capture of Chioggia, the Genoese had sat back expecting to starve the Venetians into submission. Instead the city was given precious time to organize its defences, transform its citizens into a fighting force and, most importantly of all, rally their flagging morale. Crucially, it also gave Pisani time to plan his campaign.

In line with the mood of his men, Pisani decided that instead of waiting for the enemy to make a move, he would strike first with a bold counter-move on Chioggia. He bided his time until the night of 21–22 December, the longest night of the year, before launching his attack. Under cover of darkness, a flotilla of towed stone-laden barges guarded by galleys and long boats set off south into the lagoon under the joint command of Pisani and Contarini. As dawn came up, the Genoese look-outs on the ramparts of Chioggia raised the alarm at the sight of the approaching Venetians. Soldiers were put ashore south of Chioggia, and the Genoese immediately launched an attack, forcing them to retreat. But this was simply a diversionary move. While the Genoese were thus distracted, the stone-laden barges were sunk, blocking the main supply channels to Chioggia from both the Paduan-held mainland and the Genoese fleet out in the Adriatic. The besiegers were now the besieged in Chioggia. While Pisani harassed the Genoese galleys that were attempting to clear the channel from the sea, Contarini manoeuvred his galleys along the narrow channels through the mudflats, preventing Carrara's forces from clearing the channels so that they could supply Chioggia from the mainland. However, Contarini's ragtag volunteer soldiers – from shopkeepers to ageing senators – soon became disillusioned with the wet, cold misery of living amidst the fringes of the lagoon. Although spurred on by the constant encouragement and example of their venerable leader, it was evident that they could not last out much longer; and Pisani knew that he could not keep up his raiding tactics indefinitely without suffering more losses than the city's depleted defensive fleet could bear.

In the words of the chronicler:

The galleys were so riddled with the arrows of the enemy that the sailors in desperation cried with one voice that the siege must be relinquished, that otherwise all that were in the galleys round Chioggia were dead men. Those also who held the banks, fearing that the squadrons of Carrara would fall upon them from behind, demanded anxiously to be liberated, and that the defence of the coast should be abandoned. Pisani besought them to endure a little longer . . .

What Pisani and Contarini were doing was little better than a desperate holding operation. The Genoese in Chioggia may well have been faced with starvation, but so too were the people of Venice.

Then the miracle that all Venetians had been praying for came to pass. On 1 January 1380 Carlo Zeno sailed back to Venice with fourteen galleys manned by battle-hardened Venetian sailors who had spent the last year or so hunting down Genoese shipping all over the Mediterranean. Off Sicily he had destroyed two convoys bringing supplies to the Genoese fleet in the Adriatic, which was consequently beginning to run short of essential supplies. True to form, he had then ignored orders and set off booty-hunting in the eastern Mediterranean, ranging as far afield as Constantinople, Rhodes and even Beirut. The success of this escapade had netted him and his crews so much booty that he had been forced to put all his treasures ashore in the safe-keeping of the governor of Crete, assuring his crews that they would return later to divide up the spoils. Ignoring a despatch requesting him to return to Venice, Zeno had then set off with his galleys in pursuit of the greatest prize of all, the treasure-ship *Richignona*, said to have been the largest ship afloat at the time, which he had heard was making its way home that autumn from Syria to Genoa with a cargo of unimaginable riches. Zeno caught up with the *Richignona* at Rhodes, where he immobilised it by setting fire to its sails before overwhelming its protective vessels. The *Richignona* was found to be carrying a cargo worth 500,000 ducats, as well as nearly 200 merchants and nobles who, as prisoners, would fetch a huge ransom. When this treasure was divided up in customary fashion amongst his crews, even the lowliest oarsmen in the galleys received twenty ducats each (easily enough to keep an entire family for well over a year).

Carlo Zeno and his fanatically loyal fleet of sailors arrived back in Venice to a heroes' welcome. Given the pressing needs of the hour, the matter of his ignored despatch was tactfully shelved and Zeno prepared for the greatest action of his life. He was now fifty-four years old, yet according to his biographer-grandson (who as a boy had known his illustrious relative) he still cut quite a figure:

> He was square-shouldered, broad-chested, solidly and strongly made, with large and speaking* eyes, and a manly, great and full countenance . . . Nothing was wanting in his appearance which strength, health, decorum, and gravity demanded.

(According to the American historian Margaret Oliphant, the etched portrait of Zeno that serves as the frontispiece to Francesco Quirino's 1544 translation of this biography – from the original Latin into Italian – displays a 'bold pirate-like countenance'. In fact, despite his splendidly bushy, full black beard his features present a distinctly bland, somewhat pop-eyed appearance. However, Oliphant's description is certainly truer to the character of the man.)

Zeno was immediately despatched to prevent a determined effort by the Genoese fleet to relieve Chioggia. This resulted in fierce fighting, in

* *sic*: possibly a misprint for sparkling

the course of which Zeno added to the many wounds he had received in battle, but the Venetians managed to prevail. Even so, when Zeno returned to Venice, he and Pisani stuck to their strategy of avoiding direct large-scale engagement with the sizeable Genoese fleet anchored provocatively off the Lido. Instead, they continued to patrol the entrances to the lagoon, whilst at the same time seeking to extend Venetian control around the lagoon, which remained the city's main protection.

According to the naval historian Frederic Lane:

> Although cannon had been used in the West since very early in the fourteenth century, the War of Chioggia was the first in which cannon were used on Venetian ships. Cannons were mounted on the forecastles of the galleys and they were placed also on the smaller long boats much used in the fighting around Chioggia.

These cannon fired stone cannonballs, which could weigh anything up to 200 pounds. However, these weapons were highly unpredictable and inaccurate – liable to blow up, or rain cannonballs on adjacent friendly troops. They were much better at battering down defensive walls than inflicting losses on the enemy. On 6 January a Venetian cannon secured a vital double-blow when a direct hit caused the Brandolo campanile in Chioggia to collapse. Pietro Doria, who had been appointed Genoese commander of the city, had been overseeing troop movements from the top of the campanile, and was crushed amidst the rubble when it crumbled beneath him.

Meanwhile in Venice conditions continued to deteriorate, with all sections of the population now living hand-to-mouth. During April, in a desperate attempt to relieve the situation, Taddeo Giustinian was despatched with twelve galleys to pick up grain in Sicily. However, having eluded the Genoese fleet off the Lido, he then encountered a newly arrived Genoese fleet under Marco Maruffo further down the Adriatic. In the consequent battle Giustinian and all his ships were captured.

By the spring of 1380, both sides in the conflict were employing mercenaries. The Genoese ally, Francesco da Carrara of Padua, launched German mercenaries across the mudflats and sandbars in several attempts to relieve Chioggia. These were repulsed by Venetian troops reinforced by 6,000 mercenaries that the city envoys had managed to hire. This was a mixed force of Italian and English freelance soldiers, which was based on the island of Pellestrina, the southern extension of the Lido littoral, just north of Chioggia. This contingent was notionally under the command of the renowned English *condottiere* John Hawkwood.* Unfortunately, Hawkwood never turned up to take command of this force, and consequently the notoriously belligerent English mercenaries soon fell to fighting their Italian colleagues rather than the enemy. Disaster was averted only by the intervention of Zeno, whose naval experience had taught him all too well how to deal with such mutinous elements. Fortunately, his rallying of these mercenaries to the Venetian cause came in the nick of time, for the Genoese besieged in Chioggia had just begun covert negotiations with the senior mercenary captains in this force, with the aim of bribing them to defect. Zeno's intervention brought a swift end to these moves, and shortly afterwards the 4,000-strong Genoese garrison ran out of supplies and ammunition, causing them to surrender on 24 June, with the Venetians taking possession of nineteen galleys into the bargain.

This victory was greeted with jubilation in Venice, resulting in one of the greatest celebrations in the city's history. Doge Contarini, who had remained at the head of his troops on the lagoon outside Chioggia, was received with huge acclaim on his return. The doge's great ceremonial gold barge, the *Bucintoro*, sailed out to meet him, accompanied by a vast flotilla of boats of all shapes and sizes. It is said that almost the entire population of Venice was waiting to cheer him as he stepped ashore at the Molo, accompanied by a triumphal procession, which led in its tow the lines of grim, humiliated Genoese prisoners. A painting of Contarini's triumphant arrival by Paolo Veronese now adorns the west wall of the Great Council Chamber in the Doge's Palace.

The outpouring of emotion by the citizens of Venice was in fact more an expression of immense relief, rather than joy at victory. The taking of

---

* Also known by Italian versions of his name, such as Giovanni Aguto, Acko, Acuto, and so forth, while the French called him Haccoude. Born in 1320, the son of an Essex tanner, Hawkwood operated for some thirty years in Italy as the head of a powerful mercenary army, which was variously employed by Florence, Milan, Perugia and other cities, as well as for and against several popes of the period.

Chioggia may have enforced the city's mastery of the lagoon, and thus re-established its impregnability, but it was hardly the end of the war. Despite this, events would soon demonstate that this was the beginning of the end for Genoa: it had thrown everything into its attempt to destroy Venice once and for all, and the defeat of Chioggia left it overstretched and demoralised.

Pisani now set off into the Adriatic with the aim of hunting down and destroying the newly arrived Genoese fleet under Maruffo, and then bringing grain back to Venice. In the second week of August he came across twelve Genoese galleys off the coast of Apulia. In the subsequent engagement the Genoese managed to escape, but Pisani himself was severely wounded in the fighting. He was put ashore at the nearby port of Manfredia, but nothing could be done to save him and he died on 13 August 1380. The funeral of the man who has gone down in history as the 'saviour of Venice' was conducted with all due pomp on the arrival of his body at the Arsenale.

Carlo Zeno succeeded Pisani as commander of the fleet and immediately set off around Sicily in his pursuit of Genoese shipping. But these hostilities were desultory, and diplomatic feelers were soon put out. Consequently in the summer of 1381 a peace conference was called at Turin under the auspices of Count Amadeus VI of Savoy. Although it was generally accepted that the Venetians were the victors, the ultimate terms of the treaty were hardly favourable to them. Venice was required to give up Tenedos, accept the prevailing Genoese control of Cyprus and pay an indemnity to the King of Hungary, who nonetheless retained Dalmatia. However, in the event it marked the end of the Genoese as an equal maritime and trading power. The civil strife in Genoa that had seen a doge deposed during the war now led to the overthrow of no fewer than ten doges in five years, before the city eventually fell to the French in 1394.

Venice, on the other hand, showed considerable resilience. Aided to a great extent by the strength and effectiveness of its institutions of government, the city soon began regaining its confidence and commercial supremacy. As all classes had been depleted by years of plague and war, thirty new names were now entered into *Libro d'oro* (the Golden Book), which contained the list of hereditary nobles who could attend the Great Council and become candidates for high office. This measure was popular with the citizenry as a number of these new nobles were merchants, tradesmen and commoners like themselves. It also served to temper the arrogance of the nobles, which had caused such divisions in the past. However, it did not signal a change in the administration's already firmly established policy towards those who demonstrated dangerous individuality. When the venerated Doge Andrea Contarini finally died on 5 June 1382, the obvious successor was Carlo Zeno – a choice that would have been popular throughout the city. Yet precisely because he was so popular, the Council of Forty put forward instead the wealthy Michele Morosoni, who had the dubious distinction of having made a fortune by buying up properties at rock-bottom prices during the economic collapse brought on by the War of Chioggia. Morosini was duly elected, and Zeno did not even come second in the ballot. Indeed, lest he should get above himself, he was even charged for his failure to take the small and isolated Genoese fort of Marano, some fifty miles east up the coast from Venice, during the final days of the war. Zeno was so contemptuous of this charge that he made it known he would not even deign to defend himself. But bureaucracy will have its way: he was ordered to undergo the indignity of defending himself, and the court eventually subjected him to an official censure.

Zeno's encounters with Venetian justice were not to end there. In 1405 Venice finally turned on Padua and overthrew the ruling Carrara family. During the course of this attack, the seventy-two-year-old Zeno heroically led his men across a river through water up to his neck. But on his return to Venice he was in for a shock. When the Venetian bureaucracy began poring through the Paduan account ledgers, they discovered an entry apparently recording a payment to Zeno. Charged with treason, he was hauled before the Council of Ten, which stripped him of all his offices and sentenced him to a year in prison. Twelve years later, when he died at the age of eighty-five, the authorities hypocritically accorded him a public funeral, which was attended in large numbers by the genuinely distressed and grateful people.

As the ascendancy of the Republic continued, its horror of instability, coupled with its deep fear that a charismatic leader might emerge and one day establish himself as a dictator, remained as strong as ever. Indeed, many of the individual leaders who played such a large role in this growing

Part Two

The Imperial Age

4

Innocents and Empire-Builders

ALTHOUGH GENOA'S THREAT to the Venetian Empire had been largely overcome, a new threat now arose. As the Byzantine Empire remained riven with internal conflict, the Ottoman Turks continued their expansion through Greece and Anatolia (modern Turkey), posing a threat to Venetian trading outposts. Meanwhile the War of Chioggia had impressed upon Venice its vulnerability from the hinterland beyond the lagoon. Partly owing to these developments, Venice now adopted a new policy of expansion on the mainland: 1405 saw the defeat of Carrara and the absorption of Padua into the Venetian Republic. Three years beforehand, the powerful ruler of Milan, Gian Galeazzo Visconti, had died leaving a power vacuum as his heirs squabbled over their inheritance. Seizing the opportunity, Venice occupied the Milanese-held territories of Vicenza and Verona, establishing its territory as far west as the banks of Lake Garda. Venice had now become a major power, not just on the high seas, but in mainland Italy, ranking alongside Naples, Rome, Florence and Milan.

This would mark the beginning of an imperial age for Venice. Its population had begun to recover from the depredations of plagues and warfare, and had once again exceeded 100,000 (considerably larger than London and Paris at the time). Instead of concentrating so exclusively upon its maritime empire, and the import–export trade, it now encouraged various other indigenous trades to flourish in the city, such as dyeing, silk-working and especially glass-making. The last-named industry had a long history in Venice and the lagoon islands, with finds dating as far back as the Roman era, though more recent Venetian expertise had almost certainly come from Byzantine and Levantine sources. These included various stained-glass processes, which added luminous radiance to medieval church windows all over Europe, as well as the use of manganese oxide to produce clear and transparent glass, a technique that had been lost to Europe since classical times. As early as 1291 glass furnaces had been moved out of the city for safety reasons and relocated on the island of Murano. During the following century or so Venetian glass-blowing had achieved such renown that an awed visitor declared, 'in the whole world there are no such craftsmen as here'. In order to protect the skills and secrets of the trade, master glass-workers were forbidden on pain of death from leaving the island, but in compensation were granted considerable social privileges. Murano glass-workers were accorded the singular honour of being allowed to wear swords, and the son of a glass-worker's daughter who had married into one of the noble families automatically became a noble himself (which was certainly not the case with other 'outside' marriages).

The opening up of mainland trade soon saw an influx of German and other foreign merchants, as well as skilled craftsmen. There had long been a transalpine trade, and as early as 1228 foreign merchants had been permitted to lease a building on the Grand Canal beside the Rialto Bridge in which to live, store and exchange their merchandise. This building was called Fondaco dei Tedeschi (literally 'Warehouse of the Germans'), though it in fact housed many different foreign merchants and their cargoes. In Venice, 'Tedeschi' became a blanket term for many 'foreigners' from beyond the Alps, including north and south Germans, Bohemians and people from the Low Countries.* The residence of all such traders was strictly controlled by the Venetian authorities, and according to regulations later approved by the Senate, which dealt with foreign relations: 'no German merchant may on any pretext take lodgings in any place outside the exchange house'. At the end of the fourteenth century Murano saw an influx of German looking-glass makers, with a consequent transformation of the Venetian expertise in making mirrors.

An indication of Venice's new-found importance in mainland Italy came

---

* The original Fondaco dei Tedeschi burned down in 1550, and its successor, on the same site, is now the city's main post office.

in 1406 with the election as pope in Rome of the Venetian cardinal Angelo Correr, who took on the name Gregory XII. The first Venetian pope, Gregory XII was already into his eightieth year. During his long period in the priesthood he had gained a reputation for piety and wisdom, living an ascetic life to the point where, according to one commentator, he resembled 'only a spirit appearing through skin and bone'. Twenty-eight years prior to his election the Church had been riven by the Great Schism, and as a result there were now two popes – one in Rome and one in Avignon. Gregory XII had been elected unanimously by the conclave of fifteen cardinals in the Vatican on the understanding that he would do his utmost to bring an end to this schism, and was even willing to step down in favour of any new pope who would unite the Church. Gregory was as good as his word, and within a week of his election he wrote to his opposite number Benedict XIII suggesting that they meet to resolve the schism – declaring that if Benedict XIII was willing to resign, he would do the same. He assured Benedict XIII that he was willing to travel to meet him by any means possible, even on a humble fishing boat if no galley was available, even on foot if no horse was available. Intermediaries arranged a meeting, to be held on 29 September 1407 at Savona in northern Italy. However, as the Catholic scholar Micheline Soenen points out, there was a side to Gregory XII's character that is often overlooked: 'Gregory XII's moral virtues were darkened by corresponding defects: stubbornness, indecision, dependence on his entourage, and a senile weakness of mental acuity, with a tendency toward vanity and flagrant nepotism.'

Gregory XII became suspicious: Savona was in Genoese territory, and Genoa was now subject to France, which favoured the Avignon pope. On 9 August Gregory XII finally set out from Rome. His progress was slow indeed: by 4 September he had only reached Siena, just over 100 miles to the north. He was said to be ageing fast; others detected the malign influence of his two spendthrift nephews, who were in no mood to relinquish their access to lavish papal funds, now that these had at last fallen within their grasp. They had formed a tactical alliance with Giovanni Dominici, Archbishop of Ragusa (modern Dubrovnik), who over the years had insinuated himself into the affections of the aged ascetic figure who had now become pope. Gregory XII's flaws evidently included gullibility, for

Giovanni Dominici was a figure of some notoriety who would later become the subject of an infamous satirical letter, purportedly addressed to him by Satan, which was full of 'ironical illusions to personal peculiarities, to various occurrences, and some revolting practices and manners'.

With such friends concerned about his health, it came as no surprise that Gregory was persuaded to rest in Siena. On 27 September, Benedict XIII arrived early at Savona, but there was still no sign of Gregory leaving Siena. Days passed, weeks passed, then months passed, while Gregory XII continued to rest in Siena. Finally, on 22 January 1408, it was deemed that the pope was well enough to travel, covering the fifty or so miles to Lucca in just six days, where once again it was decided that he needed to rest.

Matters were now complicated by the intervention of King Ladislas of Naples, who had an agenda of his own. In April he marched north with 12,000 infantry and 12,000 cavalry and laid siege to Rome, quickly achieving his object by bribing the papal commander and occupying the city. It had long been clear that the dashing thirty-two-year-old Ladislas of Naples had overweening territorial ambitions. He had already claimed the kingdom of Hungary, on disputed hereditary grounds, and had also occupied a number of the papal territories, which at the time controlled the band of central Italy stretching from the Adriatic coast south of Venice to the west coast north of Naples. King Ladislas had no wish for a strong united papacy in Rome with allies capable of evicting him from the papal territories and even threatening his hold on the kingship of Naples, to which there was a strong French claim. In occupying Rome, Ladislas was signalling his determination that, whatever else happened, Gregory XII should remain pope in Rome.

With Gregory supine in Lucca, the patience of the loyal cardinals accompanying the pope on his mission to meet Benedict XIII was now close to breaking point. Many of them had residences in Rome, and it seemed unlikely that King Ladislas would return these to their rightful owners. Sensing that all was not well amongst his delegates, on 9 May Gregory was persuaded to reinforce his delegation by appointing four new cardinals, including his two nephews. When the other cardinals heard this news, nine of them under the leadership of the powerful Cardinal Cossa departed in high dudgeon to confer with the cardinals accompanying Benedict XIII.

This resulted in another time-consuming hiatus, but after lengthy negotiations the cardinals of the respective papal camps agreed to a general council, which would open at Pisa on 25 March 1409. It now became transparently clear that neither Gregory XII nor Benedict XIII was in fact in favour of surrendering his papacy. Both independently responded to the news about Pisa by pointing out that the cardinals had no right to call such a council, which could only be summoned by the supreme ruler of the Church – namely the pope. Consequently both vowed they would not attend the council, which went ahead without them on 25 June, when the 500 delegates at the Council of Pisa came to their self-justifying conclusion. In the words of the papal historian Ludwig Pastor:

> No one seriously believed the assertion by which the council supported its actions. It was declared to be a matter of public notoriety that Benedict XIII and Gregory XII were not merely promoters of the Schism, but actually heretics in the fullest sense of the word, because by their conduct they had attacked and overturned the article of faith regarding the One, Holy, Catholic and Apostolic Church. Having thus invented a basis of operations, the Synod of Pisa proceeded with feverish haste to the most extreme measures . . . Without further negotiations with the two Popes, neither of whom had appeared at Pisa, their deposition was decreed, and a new election ordered.

No sooner were both popes 'deposed' than the very next day the Cardinal Bishop of Milan, Petros Philargos, was elected the new pope, taking on the name Alexander V. As his name suggests, he was of Greek origin, having been born seventy years previously at Candia in Crete. According to one source, his family was so poor that as a child he ended up surviving on the streets as a beggar, before being taken in by the Franciscan order, where his exceptional intellectual ability soon became apparent. At the age of eighteen he was sent to study at Padua and Oxford, before being appointed a professor at the University of Paris, then regarded as the intellectual centre of Europe.

Far from ending the schism, the election of Alexander V only made matters worse. As Gregory XII and Benedict XIII both adamantly refused to resign, the One, Holy, Catholic and Apostolic Church now had three popes. Though Gregory XII still considered himself to be pope, he now found himself to all intents and purposes homeless, forced to accept hospitality as he roamed northern Italy with his 'court' of remnant cardinals and family hangers-on. In order to gain access to much-needed funds, he took the drastic step of simply selling off the Papal States to King Ladislas of Naples for a mere 25,000 florins. This act reeks of desperation, to say nothing of illegality, and was in all likelihood arranged by the Bishop of Ragusa and Gregory XII's nephews. Many were outraged at this disposal of what was after all the papal inheritance, rather than Gregory's personal possession. On the other hand, it could be argued that Gregory XII (or his 'intermediaries') were doing nothing more than making the best of an impossible situation. Ladislas of Naples had already occupied many of the Papal States, and would probably have occupied the rest regardless. However, many were not prepared to see the balance of power in Italy shifted in such a dramatic fashion, and by the end of 1409 Florence and Siena had forced Ladislas to relinquish his gift from Gregory XII.

The reaction of Venice to the deposing of its first pope was naturally unfavourable. Despite Venice's new position as the major power in northern Italy, supposedly eclipsing the likes of Milan and Florence, its political influence appeared as nothing amidst the expert machinations of the Italian scene. It was an open secret, for example, that Florence had played a major role in engineering the election of Alexander V. Within weeks of his election, a delegation of ambassadors from England, France and Burgundy arrived in Venice with the intention of persuading the authorities to accept the dubious legality of the Council of Pisa and recognise Alexander V as pope. It was evident that Venice was now regarded as a power far beyond mainland Italy, and was in a position to use its new European influence to cement some important alliances. Here was a chance not to be missed: Venice's pragmatism would now blossom into opportunism.

Many in Venice were coming round to the view that Gregory XII's behaviour as pope, especially with regard to the papal territories, hardly reflected well on the Republic. Consequently delicate negotiations were opened with the visiting ambassadors pressing the case for Benedict XIII. However, in August 1409, in the midst of these discussions, the authorities found themselves embarrassed by the arrival of the itinerant Gregory XII at the border of their territory, requesting permission to enter what was undeniably his home city. The authorities faced a choice of either refusing their famous son or offending the visiting European ambassadors. Confronted with this dilemma, they decided to exercise their fledgling diplomatic skills by granting Gregory permission to travel through Venetian territory, while at the same time refusing him permission to cross the lagoon and set foot in the city itself.

Meanwhile the Senate continued to debate, in increasingly heated terms, the question of whether the Republic should recognise Alexander V. Supporters of Gregory XII insisted that Venice should remain loyal to one of its own citizens; their opponents ingeniously argued that this applied equally to Alexander V, whose birth in the Venetian colony of Crete also made him technically a Venetian citizen. After a stormy debate, the senators decided by sixty-nine to forty-eight in favour of recognising Alexander V. This confirmed Venice's alliance with Florence, as well as causing France, England and Burgundy to remain favourably disposed towards the Republic. After years of being outmanoeuvred during negotiations prior to peace treaties, Venice was at last becoming more adept at mainland politics.

Yet in May 1410 the situation was once again thrown into confusion when Alexander V died, whilst on a visit to Cardinal Cossa in Bologna. Despite widespread suspicion that Cossa had poisoned Alexander, the Council of Pisa quickly elected him the new pope and he took on the title of John XXIII. Many felt that he alone had sufficient expertise to resolve the papal situation, though there was no denying that the new pope was an unscrupulous character. John XXIII had been born forty years previously in Naples of impoverished nobility, but as a young man he had remedied the family's impecuniousness by making a fortune as a pirate, preying on merchant shipping in the Mediterranean. Consequently he had taken a degree in law at Bologna, and then used his fortune to buy himself increasingly powerful posts within the Church. In 1403 he had succeeded in getting himself appointed as cardinal and papal legate of Bologna, whose citizens he proceeded to tyrannise in unrestrained fashion. According to the contemporary chronicler Theodoric of Niem, 'an eyewitness to many of these events', Cardinal Cossa's spiritual qualities were 'zero, or minus zero'. He immediately proceeded to recoup from the citizens of Bologna the large fortune that he had spent rising up the Church hierarchy. His position as the pope's representative also gave him free reign to debauch 'hundreds of wives, widows and maidens, as well as a vast number of nuns'. Extraordinarily, despite being a cardinal, he had not in fact been ordained, though this oversight was remedied on 24 May 1410, a week after he was elected pope.

In an attempt to resolve the ongoing anomalous papal situation the Holy Roman Emperor Sigismund persuaded John XXIII to call the Council of Constance in 1414. All three popes were expected to attend, but to the surprise of John when he arrived in Constance he was imprisoned and charged with heresy, poisoning Alexander V and no fewer than seventy further misdemeanours. As the eighteenth-century historian Edward Gibbon put it, when it came to John XXIII's trial, 'The most scandalous charges were suppressed; the Vicar of Christ was only accused of piracy, murder, rape, sodomy and incest.' Left with little alternative, John promised to resign, on condition that his two fellow popes followed suit. Gregory XII, now in his ninetieth year, was persuaded to abdicate in July 1415. Benedict XIII proved less malleable, so the Emperor Sigismund ordered him to be deposed. Consequently the Great Schism was finally healed with the election of Martin V as the sole pope in 1417.

To appease the dignity of Venice, which did not take kindly to the demotion of its first pope, the Council of Constance decreed that the former Gregory XII should be made senior cardinal bishop in the Church, ranking second only to the new pope himself. He then retired to Recanati near the coast some 150 miles south of Venice, where he died in October 1417, declaring, 'I have not understood the world, and the world has not understood me.'

Such an aggrieved sense of isolation might well have been felt by the Republic itself when it came to its complex and dangerous relations with the other powers of Italy over the next few years. After King Ladislas of Naples had claimed the throne of Hungary, along with its Balkan possession Dalmatia, he had eventually found himself with no money to maintain the large army that was necessary for him to fulfil his ambitions in Italy. In 1409 he made a drastic move to remedy this situation, offering to sell the whole of Dalmatia back to Venice. Though still very much beginners in the field of political negotiation, the Venetians were masters of financial negotiation, and managed to secure Dalmatia for the bargain price of just 100,000 florins. Unfortunately, five years later Ladislas died and the Emperor Sigismund inherited the throne of Hungary. He then abrogated the treaty signed by Ladislas and claimed back Dalmatia. When the Venetians refused to recognise this claim, the Emperor Sigismund began orchestrating a political and military campaign against Venice. Covert moves were made to induce the citizens of Padua and Verona to rebel against their new Venetian overlords, and when these failed Sigismund assembled an army of 20,000 men under the flamboyant young Florentine *condottiere* known as Pippo Spano, who was already gaining a reputation as a dashing military genius. In an attempt to avoid a disastrous war it could ill afford, Venice sent a delegation including its most accomplished ambassador, Tommaso Mocenigo, to negotiate with Sigismund. Mocenigo stressed that Hungary had virtually no naval power, and would thus be unable to control the pirates who infested the Adriatic islands and preyed upon shipping. Sigismund was well aware that most of this shipping consisted of Venetian merchant ships, a source of great wealth and power to the Republic, and refused to withdraw his claims. Even when Mocenigo made it clear that Venice was willing to concede Hungarian sovereignty over Dalmatia, as long as Venice was permitted to pay a handsome sum to rent the territory as a vassal state, Sigismund still refused. He had dreams of making Hungary a Mediterranean power, which meant that he needed access to the sea; at the same time he knew that he would have to destroy Venice if he was to achieve such an ambition. Mocenigo and his delegation were dismissed, and Sigismund ordered Pippo Spano to prepare to march on Venice. As a counter-measure the Republic quickly began conscripting an army from its Italian territories on the western mainland, such as the formerly independent city states of Verona and Padua. This army was then placed under the command of the brothers Carlo and Pandolfo Malatesta, experienced *condottieri* from Rimini.

Hostilities of one form or another would continue for some years, with

Spano and the Malatesta brothers campaigning sporadically over Venice's mainland territory to the north and west of the lagoon. At one point, Pippo Spano launched a characteristically daring raid on the Lido, near the fort of San Nicolò, but his limited force was quickly beaten back. Later Pandolfo Malatesta sailed inland up the mouth of the River Livenza, some twenty miles west of Venice, with a fleet of three galleys and seventy lesser craft to inflict a surprise defeat on Spano. But in truth, as the historian Horatio F. Brown put it, this had become 'the contest of the dog and the shark'. Neither side could win. Spano realised that he would never be able to take Venice itself, thus giving Sigismund access to the sea, while Venice realised that it could not hope to retain control over wide stretches of the Lombardy plain.

Yet still the war dragged on. Soon it was costing Venice a ruinous 50,000 ducats a month to keep its army in the field, and in 1413 Tommaso Mocenigo managed to negotiate a five-year truce. However, no sooner had this expired than once again Sigismund invaded the Venetian mainland territory from the north; but this time he proved to have overplayed his hand, and Venice prevailed to such an extent that by 1420 the Republic held the vital trade routes across the Alps to the north, and Dalmatia was once again fully under its control.

The risks and draining effort involved in landward expansion should by this stage have been evident to the Venetian authorities. Despite this, the Republic's politics now became increasingly polarised between the 'Party of the Sea' and the 'Party of the Land'. The latter favoured looking west, to the mainland, seeking to extend Venice's role in Italian politics by making an alliance with Florence, the cultural hub of Italy, where the Renaissance was by now beginning to flourish. This policy was favoured by an unlikely alliance of the few Venetian humanists, who sought to introduce Renaissance art and thought to Venice, and those who covertly sought to reinstate Venice as the major power in northern Italy. The 'Party of the Sea', on the other hand, sought to consolidate Venice's empire to the east, where its network of trading colonies throughout the eastern Mediterranean was responsible for the lucrative trade that brought the city so much of its wealth. This empire would not simply continue of its own accord, for it was now coming under increasing threat from the expanding Ottoman

Empire, which besides its seemingly unstoppable land advance through the Balkan, Anatolian and Greek territories of the Byzantine Empire was also beginning to clash at sea with the Venetian navy.

By 1423 the former negotiator Tommaso Mocenigo was doge, a position he had occupied for almost ten years. He was deeply in favour of the 'Party of the Sea', and had used his considerable influence to ensure that their policy prevailed. But by now he was eighty years old, and it was evident to all that he was dying. Summoning to his bedside the Signoria, his six-man committee of senior advisers, Mocenigo delivered a stark warning:

Be sure to take great care in the choice of my successor, for he will have in his power the ability to do Venice much good or much evil. I know that many wish to select Messer Francesco Foscari, not fully realising what an arrogant windbag he is – an impetuous rabble-rouser, no less.

If he becomes doge we will be continually at war and our citizens will be ruined. He who now has a fortune of 10,000 ducats will have it reduced to 1,000; he who owns two houses will lose them both. You will all lose your gold and silver, your honour and your respect. Though at present masters of your fate, you will be reduced to slaves, condemned to follow the decisions of foreign mercenary generals and their soldiers.

Tommaso Mocenigo died on 4 April 1423, the date on which, according to the historian W.R. Thayer, 'Medieval Venice is commonly said to have passed away.' Despite his warnings, in less than a fortnight Francesco Foscari had been elected to succeed him. However, to the surprise of many, one of his first actions was to accept the request from the Greek city of Salonica for Venetian protection against the Turks. This was the second city of the Byzantine Empire, and in accepting its defence it appeared that Foscari was making an unmistakable statement of intent to the Turks. Venice would not tolerate the defeat of the Byzantine Empire. Yet many now accepted the inevitability of this defeat, and Foscari was in fact manoeuvering in the hope of obtaining a favourable peace treaty from the

Ottoman sultan, thus allowing Venice's eastern-Mediterranean trade to continue unmolested. And having made his tactical move in the east, Foscari now devoted his attention all but exclusively to the west, fulfilling Mocenigo's worst fears by declaring war on Milan in 1426. As Frederic Lane succinctly put it: 'Within a few years Venice was sending a bigger navy up the Po River . . . than to the Aegean Sea, and Salonica was lost.'

The days of the young Visconti brothers squabbling over their inheritance were now over, and a new tyrant of Milan had emerged in the form of Filippo Maria Visconti. From this time on, for almost twenty years, Foscari's policy would ensure that Venice was engaged in war against Milan and its allies. And just as Mocenigo had so ominously predicted, Venice was forced to hire mercenary generals who would gain increasing sway over the decisions taken by the Republic. The first of these powerful *condottieri* was Francesco Bussone, better known as Carmagnola.

Carmagnola was said to have been born the son of a swineherd on the banks of the Po south of Turin sometime before 1382. At the age of twelve he ran off to join, or was sold into, the mercenary army in the service of the previous tyrant of Milan, Gian Galeazzo Visconti. Demonstrating precocious ruthlessness and skill in battle, he quickly rose through the ranks. When Gian Galeazzo died in 1402, Milan became divided amongst his squabbling heirs, and his son Filippo Maria realised that he would have to go to war if he was to secure what he considered to be his rightful claim to the duchy and its entire territories. But he did not immediately achieve his aim, and the struggle against his brothers dragged on. It was now that the military skill of the thirty-year-old Carmagnola came to the notice of Filippo Maria, who took him under his wing and appointed him commander of his mercenary army. Carmagnola more than fulfilled his expectations, and in 1412 Filippo Maria was able to claim the entire Duchy of Milan as his own.

Filippo Maria had further territorial ambitions for Milan, and over the ensuing years Carmagnola enabled him to begin realising them, executing a number of brilliant victories, most notably defeating a force of Swiss infantry, generally reckoned to be the toughest fighting men in Europe at the time. Consequently Carmagnola was soon regarded as the finest general in Italy, his army feared by all others. Filippo Maria rewarded him handsomely; he was aware that, as Carmagnola was now such a renowned soldier-of-fortune, he was liable to receive other offers for his services, and he wished to bind him as closely as possible to the cause of Milan. As a result, Carmagnola was given a magnificent palazzo, a tax-free income of 40,000 florins a year, and the hand in marriage of Filippo Maria's cousin, Antonia Visconti. Filippo Maria made it clear that Carmagnola was now much more than a mere *condottiere*: he bestowed on him a title, acknowledging him as the second most powerful man in Milan, and as such his close personal friend.

Even the more flattering portraits of Filippo Maria Visconti cannot disguise the curious squashed ugliness of his bulging features, an unattractive appearance which was more than echoed in his paranoid and unpredictable personality. He had already demonstrated the characteristic Visconti ruthlessness by having his wife beheaded. It was soon clear that, despite all the favour that he had bestowed upon Carmagnola, Filippo Maria did not trust him – suspecting that, as the power of his mercenary army increased, and with it Carmagnola's popularity amongst his men, he might one day seek to take the Duchy of Milan for himself. Consequently in 1422 Filippo Maria appointed Carmagnola governor of Genoa. At a stroke, this removed him from the centre of power in Milan, and separated him from his troops who were now campaigning against Florence. At the same time, it also gave Carmagnola's many jealous enemies at the court in Milan the chance to feed Filippo Maria's paranoia with poisonous rumours.

No doubt prompted by such whisperings, in 1424 Filippo Maria suddenly stripped Carmagnola of his post in Genoa, without offering his 'friend' a word of justification. Carmagnola at once set out for Milan to demand the reason for his dismissal. On his arrival at court, he was refused an audience with the duke. Carmagnola felt deeply betrayed by the man who had even gone so far as to take him into his own family. At the same time, he also realised the danger of his situation, and immediately fled with his wife and children across the border to Savoy, where he sought the protection of the ruler, Duke Amadeus VIII. Carmagnola was now bent on seeking revenge for what he saw as his betrayal, and began attempting to turn Amadeus VIII against Filippo Maria. But the court of Amadeus in Turin was not like the court of Filippo Maria in Milan had once been.

Here Carmagnola was no longer treated by the ruler as a friend, but as a mere peasant boy who had risen to become an uncouth *condottiere*. Owing to his lack of sophistication and diplomatic skill, Carmagnola had severely misjudged the political situation. Amadeus VIII reacted by seizing Carmagnola's wife and daughters, although Carmagnola himself managed to escape. This was the man who arrived in Venice on 23 February 1425, accompanied by eighty of his most loyal men-at-arms, offering his services to the Republic.

Carmagnola had arrived in Venice at an opportune moment: Foscari had begun negotiations with Florence, with the aim of forming a northern Italian league against Milan. Although Carmagnola found the social graces of Foscari and his Signoria somewhat intimidating, he did his best to convince them of his invaluable worth by revealing his inside knowledge of Milan's military strengths and weaknesses. Foscari then assured Carmagnola that, if all went well in the negotiations between Venice and Florence, he would be appointed commander-in-chief of the league's forces, although for the time being it would be diplomatic if he retired to Treviso on the other side of the lagoon while negotiations continued. However, even at this early stage in Carmagnola's relationship with Venice he may well have been considering the possibility of treachery, or maybe he did not feel fully reassured by Foscari, for during his stay in Treviso he was willing to receive secret messengers from Filippo Maria in Milan. He appears to have been hoping for a reconciliation, but this was not the messengers' true intention; instead they had been ordered to poison Carmagnola. Their purpose was quickly detected and Carmagnola handed them over to Venice, where they were publicy tried for attempted murder and then hanged – all without mention being made of Filippo Maria, for the secret negotiations with Florence had not yet been concluded.

In February 1426, Venice and Florence finally signed an agreement, with each side promising to contribute 8,000 cavalry and 3,000 infantry, and Venice supplying a fleet of ships for campaiging along the navigable channels of the Po river system, which run right across the Lombardy plain. Carmagnola was recalled to Venice, where he was formally invested by Doge Foscari as commander of the Venetian forces and handed the standard of St Mark at a ceremony in the basilica of San Marco attended by all the great and good of the city. Spurred on by the generous salary of 1,000 ducats a month, Carmagnola launched his army across the border into Milanese territory, where he laid siege to the strategic city of Brescia. After this initial success he requested permission from the Venetian authorities to retire to the thermal baths at Abano just outside Padua, claiming that he had suffered an awkward fall from his horse. Although this was some 100 miles behind the lines, the authorities reluctantly agreed, as long as his therapeutic visit was a short one. Carmagnola had made his point to his Venetian superiors: even a former peasant boy was entitled to take the waters like a Roman general.

The siege of Brescia dragged on through the long hot summer months, and in October Carmagnola once again felt the need to retire to the baths at Abano, even though the Venetian authorities remonstrated that they knew there was nothing wrong with him. In his absence Brescia surrendered to the Venetian forces. The authorities in Venice were overjoyed; while Filippo Maria, sensing his vulnerability, agreed to sign a peace treaty. However, this was only intended to give Filippo Maria time to regroup his forces, and within weeks Milan had launched a spring offensive. Despite orders from Venice, Carmagnola could not be induced to budge from his winter headquarters, citing insufficient forage for his cavalry, then insufficient money to pay his troops, and finally claiming that his army would be heavily outnumbered. The Venetian authorities knew that by now he had 36,000 men under his command, the strongest army yet seen in northern Italy, in every way superior to the Milanese forces, but despite constant urgings he still showed himself reluctant to engage the enemy, even after his army belatedly emerged from their winter quarters in April 1427. This only came about when he appeared to be stung into action by an ambush. Despite being caught off guard by the Milanese forces under the new young *condottiere* who had succeeded him, Carmagnola demonstrated his tactical genius by turning the tables on them and gaining a comprehensive victory at Casalmaggiore. As he well knew, this victory was doubly to his advantage: not only did it demonstrate to his paymasters in Venice the wisdom of continuing to employ him, but it also demonstrated to Filippo Maria his incontestable superiority in the field, and thus the wisdom of re-employing Carmagnola if he wished to achieve his objectives.

When news of the victory at Casalmaggiore reached Venice, the city was overjoyed. However, this joy was soured by the consequent news that the following day Carmagnola had released all the prisoners he had taken at Casalmaggiore so that they could return to the opposing army, ready to do battle once more. At the time this was in fact common practice in Italy amongst mercenary armies, which knew that it was in their interests to keep wars going for as long as possible and well understood that today's enemy could easily become tomorrow's ally. The Venetian authorities, still somewhat inexperienced in the ways of the mainland, realised there was little they could do, short of dismissing Carmagnola. And that was a course of action that by this stage they were reluctant to take. News had now come in that Carmagnola was openly in contact with Filippo Maria, who had regained Carmagnola's naive trust by persuading Amadeus VIII of Savoy to free the *condottiere*'s wife and children, so that they could return to him. Filippo Maria judged correctly that Carmagnola had begun to long for a return to the old days when he was the 'family friend' in Milan. Carmagnola, for his part, excused his contact with Filippo Maria by explaining to Doge Foscari that he was sure he would be able to succeed, where previously the Venetians had failed, in negotiating a lasting peace with Milan.

The Venetian citizenry, whose increasingly burdensome taxes were paying for Carmagnola and his army, were beginning to express their dissatisfaction with their *condottiere*, demanding that he should be recalled and put on trial for treason. The Venetian authorities now found themselves in a quandary. Although they faced civil unrest within the city, they knew that if they moved against Carmagnola he would in all likelihood simply offer his services to his old master Filippo Maria, and all the money they had invested in him and his army would come to nothing. The Council of Ten debated long and hard on the matter, before coming up with a feeble compromise. A carefully worded despatch was conveyed to Carmagnola suggesting that he should leave any peace negotiations to his employers.

At this stage, Carmagnola received word of the volatile situation in Venice, which he realised could easily turn against him. Not willing to have his hand forced, for he still did not fully trust Filippo Maria, he knew that his only recourse was to immediate action. Once again demonstrating his supreme tactical ability, he advanced his army to within seven miles of the River Oglio, where he took up a position at the village of Maclodio. Here, on 11 October 1427, he was confronted by the Milanese army under the command of the distinguished *condottiere* Francesco Sforza and Carlo Malatesta (who, after serving Venice so well in the war against Hungary, had offered his services elsewhere as soon as peace was declared).

Carmagnola knew that the land in front of Maclodio was treacherous terrain, and when he appeared to withdraw, the hotheaded Malatesta immediately charged forward, leading his troops into a marsh where they quickly became bogged down. This time Carmagnola secured an even greater victory than he had achieved at Casalmaggiore, further consolidating his reputation as the greatest general of his era, though it must be emphasised that this was a typical *condottiere* battle. Rather than actual fighting, such engagements usually aimed at a tactical victory, consisting largely in manoeuvering the enemy into a position where they had no option but to fight to the last man or surrender (or, if possible, flee the field). Mercenaries on both sides had no appetite for the first option, whereas the other options enabled them to continue practising their profession on another day. Contemporary sources concur that around 30,000 men took part in the Battle of Maclodio, during the course of which most of the village was destroyed and many horses were slaughtered. However, according to the fifteenth-century Venetian historian Marcantonio Sabellico, 'Those who were there affirm that they heard of no one being killed, extraordinary to relate, though it was a great battle.'

Once again, when news of this great victory reached Venice there was much rejoicing, and once again this was tempered by Carmagnola's consequent actions. So comprehensive had been his victory that he had succeeded in capturing Malatesta himself, as well as 8,000 of his mercenaries, before the others had managed to make good their escape. The following day Malatesta and the prisoners were allowed to return to the service of Milan. Worse still, Carmagnola refused to act on his victory. All he had to do was march twenty miles south, crossing the River Oglio, and he could have taken the undefended city of Cremona. This would have protected his rear, allowing him to make a rapid advance on Milan itself, which would almost certainly have fallen, thus bringing the war to an end. Instead, he once again did nothing, preferring to withdraw to his quarters, where his army sat out the winter while he retired once more to the baths at Abano. Meanwhile, the frightened Filippo Maria desperately sought to sign a more lasting peace treaty with Venice, which was eventually signed in May 1428.

Desperate to retain Carmagnola's services, the Venetian authorities invited him to return to Venice to discuss his terms of future employment. Here, despite being given his own palazzo, the rough-and-ready Carmagnola found himself distinctly uncomfortable amidst the comparative sophistication and luxuries of Venetian life. The charm and courtly manners of the Venetians only had the effect of making him retreat even further into his recalcitrant ways as he negotiated with Foscari and the venerable members of his Signoria ranged around the table in all their finery. Carmagnola struck a hard bargain, and in the event the Venetian authorities agreed to continue paying him 1,000 ducats a month, even during peacetime, at the same time binding him even further to their cause by awarding him the fiefdom of Chiari and Roccafranca, which he would be allowed to pass on to his heirs, making them a hereditary dynasty.

Nonetheless, with the advent of peace, Carmagnola reopened contact with Filippo Maria, taking the precaution of passing on to Doge Foscari copies of any letters that he sent and received. As it happened, Foscari was already aware of this development as Filippo Maria had been sending him copies of the letters he had been receiving from Carmagnola. Unfortunately, these were different from the letters that Foscari was receiving from Carmagnola himself – a fact that was duly noted in the archives.

Seen in this light, Carmagnola's 'treachery' becomes more understandable. While seeking to obtain the maximum gain from his employment as a mercenary, he knew that he was essentially on his own. He did not trust Venice any more than he trusted Milan, because he knew that neither of them trusted him. Such was the complex web of mistrust in which the Republic now found itself embroiled. Yet who else could Carmagnola turn to? The plight of a *condottiere*, especially a powerful one, could be as dangerous as it was lucrative.

Despite Filippo Maria's friendly gesture to Venice in passing on useful information regarding Carmagnola, intelligence reaching Foscari and the

Signoria gave them to understand that Milan was once more preparing for war. Ironically, in the light of its attitude towards powerful individuals, Venice now found itself utterly reliant upon just such a man. The need to retain Carmagnola became tantamount, and in August 1430 Foscari went so far as to promise him the dukedom of Milan if he managed to win the coming war by actually taking the enemy capital.* At the same time a large Venetian fleet of thirty-eight galleys and forty-eight lesser craft, manned by 10,000 fighting men, was assembled ready for a naval campaign in the Po river system. Although nominally under the overall control of Carmagnola, the fleet was placed under the immediate command of admiral Nicolò Trevisano, who had already distinguished himself in action on the Po. It was felt that such a command structure would enable this powerful fleet, manned by Venetians, to be more reliable when it came to following orders from Venice.

In early 1431 Filippo Maria duly reopened hostilities, but this time the Venetians were more fully prepared. Carmagnola and Admiral Trevisano were ordered to strike deep into the heart of enemy territory, launching a daring land and river coordinated attack on the city of Lodi, beside the River Adda just fifteen miles south-east of Milan. Trevisano and the Venetian fleet quickly reached Lodi, but owing to insufficient support from Carmagnola's slow-moving land troops they were unable to take the city. Forced to retreat downriver, Trevisano decided to mount an attack on Cremona instead. But here he was caught by surprise on 22 May by the Milanese fleet, whose ships were manned by experienced sailors from Genoa. The swift Milanese fleet quickly began outmanoeuvring the more unwieldy seagoing Venetian craft. Trevisano sent messages appealing to Carmagnola for land support, but he replied that he was unable to move from his position, owing to the fact that Sforza's forces were encamped in a threatening position nearby. Meanwhile on the river the two fleets engaged in earnest, with the fighting continuing through the day and into dusk, with the Venetian fleet hemmed in against the shore. Under cover of darkness,

---

* Some sources suggest that Carmagnola was merely promised rule over 'a city within the territory of Milan', though it is likely that by this stage he may well have harboured a secret ambition to rule Milan itself (as indeed did the young *condottiere* Francesco Sforza, who would in fact wrest the dukedom from the Visconti family some twenty years later).

Sforza withdrew his men from the vicinity of Carmagnola's encampment and marched to Cremona, where they embarked on a flotilla of waiting Milanese craft. As the dawn rose, Trevisano was shocked to see this flotilla making its way downstream towards him, the decks of its ships filled with armed men, their armour glinting in the morning sun, their colourful banners unfurled and signifying their readiness for battle. Once again the two sides engaged, with the Venetians doing their best to mount a rearguard action as heavy fighting continued through the morning. Carmagnola and his men did not arrive until later in the day, when they could only watch powerless from the opposite bank as the Milanese overwhelmed the Venetian ships. This was no mercenary land battle, but was fought by Venetian and Genoese sailors who were used to more bloody seaborne encounters and bore a long-established enmity towards one another. When the battle was over, Venice had lost as many as twenty-eight galleys and more than forty smaller craft, and according to the contemporary Venetian chronicler Bigli, 'The slaughter was greater than any that was ever known in Italy, more than two thousand men being said to have perished, in witness of which the Po ran red, a great stream of blood, for many miles.'

Of the few who managed to make it ashore, many were slain by local peasants only too keen to avenge themselves on the invaders. However, Trevisano himself managed to escape. When news reached Venice of what had happened, the outrage of Foscari, the Signoria, the Ten and all the citizens was such that Trevisano was immediately tried and sentenced to prison in his absence, then banished and outlawed when he chose not to return to Venice and surrender himself. Someone had to be the scapegoat for such a disastrous loss (which certainly eclipsed the great victory at Maclodio). But why was Carmagnola not blamed for what had taken place? He did in fact put on a big public display of remorse for what had happened, appearing to take the defeat personally. At the same time, however, he wrote to Venice informing Foscari that Trevisano had disobeyed orders in attacking Cremona. There was some truth in this, and for the time being many amongst the Venetian authorities were in favour of overlooking Carmagnola's late arrival on the scene. Others were less forgiving and insisted on a public debate. According to Sabellico:

There were not a few, who, from the beginning had suspected Carmagnola. These now openly in the Senate declared that this suspicion not only had not ceased but increased, and was increasing every day; and that, except his title of commander, they knew nothing in him that was not hostile to the Venetian name. The others would not believe this, nor consent to hold him in such suspicion until some manifest signs of his treachery were placed before them.

Such open debate in the Senate reflected the essentially democratic style of Venice, even if this remained an effective force only among the city's noble families.

While the debate raged back in Venice, Carmagnola lay low in his tent in the field. In the autumn of 1431 despatches arrived from Venice ordering him to attack Cremona and establish a bridgehead on the far side of the Adda; but although he was camped only three miles from the city he chose not to move. However, seemingly on their own initiative, several young officers, including Ugolino Cavalcabò, the son of the murdered Lord of Cremona, launched a surprise attack under cover of darkness, seizing the fortress of San Luca, the key to the city's defences. If this had been followed by swift action from Carmagnola the city would have fallen by dawn; but he remained in his encampment and the attempt failed.

By a quirk of fate which Carmagnola could not have foreseen, this was to be the final act that inadvertently precipitated his downfall. In the expectation that Cremona would fall by morning, a messenger had been despatched that night to Venice announcing a great victory. The news was greeted by public rejoicing, which was transformed into disgust and anger when a further messenger revealed the truth of what had happened.

The Senate expressed its outrage, and demanded an immediate explanation of Carmagnola's behaviour. But in the end more patient, and more devious, counsel prevailed. Carmagnola was now resting a hundred miles away in his winter quarters at Brescia, and was all but unassailable. He was unlikely to expect, or indeed obey, any orders from his employers: despatches from Venice were only liable to raise his suspicions. It was decided to see the winter out.

Finally, on 27 March 1432, the Council of Ten met to discuss the situation, and summoned a *zonta*: an extraordinary meeting to be attended by the thirty-seven senior members of the administration. A secret pact was taken, on pain of death for anyone present divulging what had been discussed. Two days later, the secretary of the Council of Ten, Giovanni da Impero, a man 'with a face as pale as a ghost', left for Carmagnola's winter quarters at Brescia. He carried a message saying that the doge wished Carmagnola to return to Venice so that he could seek his advice 'on the best means for carrying out the summer campaign . . . for much difference of opinion exists amongst the city councillors'. At the same time, secret messages were despatched to the commandant of the Brescia garrison and captains of the Republic in the field: they were to give their support to da Impero, no matter what order he gave.

In the event, da Impero had no need to order the detention of Carmagnola, for he unwittingly agreed to accompany him at once to Venice. As arranged, when he arrived at Padua that evening having completed the first stage of his journey, Carmagnola was greeted with all the pomp and ceremony due to the commander-in-chief of the Venetian forces. That night, in accordance with the prevailing custom of the time for such celebrated guests, he shared the bed of 'his good friend' Federigo Contarini, the Captain of Padua.*

On 7 April, Carmagnola crossed the lagoon to Venice, where he was met at the landing stage by a guard of honour and escorted to the Doge's Palace. Here, according to well-documented descriptions of the ensuing events (which disagree only on minor points), his personal bodyguard was dismissed with the words, 'The master will dine with the Doge, and will come home after dinner.' He was then led up the grand staircase and shown into the Salle delle Quattro Porte (Hall of the Four Doors), the official chamber where visitors waited before seeing the doge. After kicking his heels impatiently for some time, Carmagnola was informed by a member of the Council of Ten that the doge had suffered a minor accident and would be unable to receive him. Visibly irritated by the delay, Carmagnola

---

* As the historian W. Carew Hazlitt explained: 'It was common practice for the most exalted personages to become bedfellows. We find Charles VIII of France and the Duke of Orleans so resting together.' In similar medieval fashion, the servants of the bedchamber and the master's dogs would have slept at the foot of the bed.

declared, 'The hour is late and it is time for me to go home' and left the room.

But as he was on the point of leaving the building for his waiting gondola, one of the attendant nobles stepped in front of him, saying, 'This way, my lord' and indicated the corridor that led away to the Orba prison.

'But that is not the right way,' he replied.

'Indeed it is,' replied the noble, and Carmagnola was hustled down the corridor towards the cells.

Only then did it dawn on him what was happening. He is said to have exclaimed, '*Son perduto*' (I am lost) as they locked him in his cell.

For the next two days he refused all food in protest, but to no avail. His trial for treason began on 9 April. As was the Venetian custom of the period in such cases, he was 'examined by torture before the secret council' (that is, the *giunta*, who were to act as his judges). The actual physical process was carried out by 'a master torturer from Padua'. One source has it that Carmagnola was 'put to the brazier and confessed'. According to Sabellico, the main evidence produced against him was 'in letters which he could not deny were in his own hand'. All his private documents in Brescia had been commandeered by da Impero, so that copies of all the letters he had sent to Filippo Maria of Milan could now be compared with the doctored versions he had sent to the Venetian authorities, as well as the versions passed on by Filippo Maria himself.

The trial continued, with a ten-day break for Holy Week and the Easter celebrations, until 5 May, when Carmagnola was pronounced guilty by a twenty-six to one majority (with the rest of the judges abstaining). Doge Foscari then recommended a sentence of life imprisonment, but this was overturned by the *giunta* and Carmagnola was sentenced to death. At the same time, his fortune was ordered to be confiscated by the state, apart from a moderate pension to provide for his wife and sons. Late in the afternoon of the same day he was dressed for his execution: clad in ceremonial scarlet, his hands tied behind his back, a gag stuffed in his mouth – the traditional method to prevent the victim when in front of the crowd from insulting the Republic, spreading seditious ideas or revealing state secrets. Carmagnola was then led out of the Doge's Palace onto the Piazzetta between the two columns, where it took three strokes of the axe to sever his head from his body.

With this, Venice sent out a message that reverberated through Italy: any *condottiere* who volunteered his service to the Republic would be well rewarded, but would also be expected to commit entirely to his masters. *Condottieri* were not used to accepting such terms of employment, but the message was duly noted. As for Carmagnola, on balance he appears to have sinned only slightly more than he was sinned against. His position became untenable the more his hopes relied upon returning to the man he naively believed to be his only friend, Filippo Maria. In the end, he was on his own and had nowhere to go.

Venice was learning important lessons on how politics was conducted in Italy. Yet it would continue to interpret these lessons in its own distinctive fashion. In order to maintain its imperial power, it would need to be as ruthless with its apparent friends as it had always been with its own individual citizens.

5

'We are Venetians, then Christians'

WHILE VENICE CONTINUED with its war in mainland Italy, events at the very eastern limit of mainland Europe were moving towards a climax. Here, arguably the most significant event in Venetian history was taking place nearly 1,500 miles sailing distance from the lagoon. This was an event that would transform Europe, putting an end to an era which had lasted for more than a thousand years. In doing so, it would reveal to the world (and perhaps even to the Venetians themselves) the basic motive and driving force of their Republic, a motive that would eventually permeate the entire continent of Europe, and arguably continues to do so to this day.

By the early decades of the fifteenth century the Ottoman Empire had overrun much of the territory of the Byzantine Empire (which less than two centuries previously had covered most of the Balkans and much of Anatolia). Any minor hindrance to the advance of the Ottoman forces was treated with the utmost severity. The conquest of Salonica in 1430 had, according to the few survivors, seen the Turks 'destroy the place to its foundations', the soldiers behaving 'like wild animals' and the city 'filled with wailing and despair' as 'men, women, children, people of all ages, bound like animals' were marched off into slavery.

Less than twenty years later, the nineteen-year-old Mehmet II had become sultan of the Ottoman empire, and had publicly declared his intention to make Constantinople his capital. The Byzantine emperor Constantine XI immediately sent out a desperate appeal to Venice for help; but Venice was too involved in its mainland war with Milan – which was proving a huge drain on its finances, manpower and navy – and declined the invitation to act on its own. Instead, Venice intimated that it would contribute to the defence of Constantinople if other Christian forces joined together in a Holy League against the Moslems. However, given the weakness and disarray of the pope, the Holy Roman Emperor and other European rulers, this could only have been achieved with any speed if Venice had directed all its powers to stressing the utmost urgency of the situation for all concerned, which it refused to do. Despite Venice's parlous finances, its attitude to Emperor Constantine's plea was all but suicidally short-sighted, as Venice relied crucially upon its trade with the Black Sea and the eastern Mediterranean, both of which would stand under serious threat if Constantinople should fall to the Ottomans.

Step-by-step Mehmet II now set about achieving his declared aim. According to the Venetian doctor Nicolò Barbaro, who kept a diary of events in Constantinople during this time:

> During the month of March 1452, Mehmet II began building a superb castle six miles north of Constantinople towards the mouth of the Black Sea. It had fourteen towers, with the five main towers lined with lead and built with thick walls.

This massive castle was completed in just five months, and overlooked the Bosphorus at its narrowest point, where it is just over 600 yards wide. All were aware of what was happening, and as Barbaro recorded, 'It was made with the express purpose of taking Constantinople.' Mehmet named it Bogazkesen, meaning 'strait cutter' (more ominously, *bogaz* also meant 'throat')',* and:

> He issued a decree that all ships sailing from the Black Sea into these Straits must haul down their sails and send a boat to make contact with the officer in charge of the castle. Only he could give permission for them to pass, otherwise they would be sunk . . . Every ship would have to pay the officer a toll.

---

* It is now known as Rumeli Hisari, meaning Roman castle, as it was built on the site of an ancient Roman fort; its impressive ruins still stand on the hillside overlooking the Bosphorus.

On 26 November, a Venetian merchant ship captained by Antonio Rizzo laden with provisions from the Black Sea for depleted Constantinople attempted to run the blockade, but was holed by a cannonball fired from the walls of Bogazkesen, and its crew were taken prisoner. Most of these were summarily beheaded, though some were permitted to go free so that they could spread word of the fate that had befallen their crewmates. And in two instances this had indeed been exemplary: Mehmet II had ordered Captain Rizzo to suffer death by impalement on a stake, while the young son of the ship's clerk had been despatched to serve as a member of the sultan's harem.

This was an act of war, and when news of the incident reached Venice the Council of Ten belatedly stirred into action. A squadron of five galleys under the command of Gabriele Trevisano was despatched to Constantinople, though even these did not carry their full compliment of fighting men, owing to the war with Milan. And when they arrived in Constantinople in December, the emperor was disconcerted to learn that Trevisano intended to leave after just ten days – his orders were to take on board as many Venetian merchants as wished to leave, and then carry out patrols protecting Venetian merchant shipping. The resident Venetian merchants were so disgusted at this that they refused to leave, at the same time boarding the galleys, to prevent them from leaving too. A message was despatched back to Venice explaining, in Trevisano's defence, that he had not disobeyed orders, but had simply been prevented from carrying them out by outraged Venetian citizens.

By this time Constantinople was already in a desperate state. Yet not everyone appeared to care. Indicative of this is the reaction of a Hungarian named Orban, the greatest cannon-founder of his time, who arrived to offer his services in defence of the city. When Constantine XI was unable to employ him, pleading that he had neither the raw materials to build a cannon nor sufficient funds to pay him, Orban simply offered his services to Mehmet II. The grateful sultan sent Orban to the foundry at Adrianople, where he cast an enormous twenty-seven-foot cannon capable of firing 1,200-pound cannon balls over a distance of half a mile. This was named the 'basilic' (king), and was the most powerful cannon the world had yet seen. It would take three months to build, and would then set out on the

150-mile journey towards Constantinople, hauled by sixty oxen. Even so, it remained to be seen whether it would be capable of breaching the formidable walls, which stretched for more than fourteen miles, encircling the city by land and sea. The walls lining the three sides of the city surrounded by water were considered unassailable. The walls on the landward side to the west of the city contained both an inner and outer ring of defences, were more than twenty feet thick in places and were reinforced by scores of vast towers nearly forty feet high. These defences had withstood all attempts to breach them for almost a thousand years.

On 29 January 1453 a welcome relief squadron arrived at Constantinople under the command of the Genoese Giovanni Longo, a relative of the distinguished Doria family. With him he brought 700 soldiers recruited in Rhodes and Chios. Owing to Longo's renown as a commander of cities under siege, the grateful Constantine XI placed him in charge of the four miles of walls, including no fewer than sixteen turreted gates, which constituted the city's landward defences. Mindful of the ever-increasing emergency of the situation, Girolamo Minotto, the Venetian *bailo* (chief representative of the permanent colony of Venetian merchants in Constantinople), now despatched a desperate letter to Venice. This was swiftly followed by similar letters to the pope, the kings of Hungary and Naples and the Holy Roman Emperor, begging them to send reinforcements before it was too late. No action was forthcoming from these leaders of Western Christendom. Minotto's letter to Venice arrived on 19 February and demanded immediate action, 'in view of the immense peril which now threatens Constantinople'. The Senate swiftly voted to send a second fleet consisting of fifteen galleys, each carrying 400 men. There was just one snag: the city had neither the men nor the available galleys. Nothing could be done without raising further taxes, which would be required before the galleys could even be fitted out in the Arsenale and men trained or seconded from the mainland war. It would be almost three months before this fleet finally embarked from Venice under the command of Giacomo Loredan.

Meanwhile, many in Constantinople were becoming tired of waiting for assistance from the West, and less than a month after Minotto had sent his letters appealing to the Western leaders, seven Venetian ships under the command of Pietro Davanzo carrying 700 passengers sneaked out of the Golden Horn under cover of darkness and made their way to freedom. Despite the morale-sapping effect of this flight, none of the Greeks and Italians remaining in the city made any attempt to follow them.

Things soon took a turn for the worse. These were described by the Venetian physician Nicolò Barbaro, who was in Constantinople at the time and kept a diary of events as they unfolded: 'On the fifth of April, an hour after daybreak Mehmet II arrived before the walls of Constantinople with an army of around a hundred and sixty thousand men, which encamped about two and a half miles from the city.' The long-expected siege of Constantinople had begun. The following day, in a well-drilled exercise, 'the Turkish Emperor marched with half his army to within a mile of the walls of the city'. Then a day later 'he advanced with most of his army to within a quarter of a mile of the walls, and they then spread in a long line encompassing the whole length of the city walls on the landward side'.

Mehmet II issued the traditional call to Constantine promising that he and all the inhabitants of the city would be spared if they surrendered at once. Constantine XI rejected this offer and watched from the western walls as Mehmet had his tent pitched outside the Military Gate of San Romano.* The city's defenders lining the castellated walls peered down as the Turkish soldiers began digging in, erecting earthworks to protect their positions. Then, in a gruesome reminder of what fate they could expect at Turkish hands, now that they had turned down the offer of surrender, the Sultan ordered thirty-six Byzantine soldiers who had been captured at a nearby fort to be impaled before the walls, their pitiful shrieks and cries all too audible up on the ramparts during the long hours of agony that they endured before dying.

After this, the siege began in earnest, as Barboro related:

On the eleventh of April, Mehmet II placed his line of cannon opposite the walls, especially at their weakest part of the city, seemingly intent upon a swift victory. He placed these cannon in four strategic places . . . One of the cannons which he stationed opposite

* Often known simply as the 5th Military Gate. Confusingly, there was also a Civil Gate of San Romano half a mile or so to the south.

the Gate of San Romano was capable of firing a ball that weighed around twelve hundred pounds and was thirteen *quarte* [around twelve feet] in circumference, which gives some idea of the terrible damage which it inflicted where it landed.

In all there were a dozen Turkish cannon of various sizes, and the next day they launched into their bombardment of the city walls, a deafening thunder that would continue 'with ceaseless monotony' throughout the coming weeks. Simultaneously the next stage of the Ottoman strategy was put into place:

In the early afternoon of the twelth of April, the Turkish fleet moved towards the harbour of Constantinople, their oars rowing with great purpose. Finally, they dropped anchor at the anchorage known as 'The Columns', the sailors on their ships letting out blood-curdling cries, sounding drums and trumpets so as to fill our soldiers on the city walls with great fear, and cause consternation amongst the men of our fleet in harbour in the Golden Horn. Their entire fleet consisted of over 145 ships, and when they anchored we Christians began wondering what they were going to do. For the rest of the day and into the night they went silent, and their ships made no movement, while our soldiers on the walls were placed on alert.

As the defenders watched anxiously from the walls, it gradually became clear that the Ottoman fleet was not poised to attack, but had begun a blockade of the Golden Horn, cutting off the city's harbour from access to the Bosphorus, and thence the Black Sea to the north and the Sea of Marmara to the south.

Just four days later this blockade was put to the test:

During the afternoon of the twentieth day of April, four large ships hove in sight to the south on the sea of Marmara. They had evidently come from the West by way of the Dardanelles, and looked as if they had come from Genoa with the aim of bringing supplies to Constantinople.

Looking down from the walls of Constantinople, Barbaro described the ensuing scene:

The four Genoese ships approached the city walls aided by a fresh southerly breeze, but no sooner were they close to the walls than the wind suddenly dropped and they found themselves helplessly becalmed. No sooner were they becalmed than the Ottoman fleet stirred into activity, with shouts and the sounding of drums as they rowed towards them at full speed.

The Genoese ships did their best to elude the attackers, but in the end were forced to confront them, as more and more citizens of Constantinople lined the walls looking down at the Bosphorus. Owing to the inept tactics of the Turkish admiral Baltoghlu, the Genoese ships eventually managed to outwit the Turkish fleet, pouring 'Greek Fire'* onto the surface of the sea so that it drifted downstream and engulfed the pursuing Turkish triremes in flames.

Later, under cover of darkness, the Genoese ships raised sail and reached the safety of the chain-boom stretched across the Gold Horn. This was quickly lowered, allowing them to reach the sanctuary of the harbour. The captains of the four Genoese ships were immediately led to Constantine XI, who proceeded to question them about the situation in the West, but they had no meaningful news. They brought no reply to the letters he had despatched in the last days of January to the pope, the kings of Hungary and Naples and the Holy Roman Emperor. And there was no news from Venice. Nonetheless, Constantine still placed great hopes in the letter that his *bailo* Minotto had despatched to the Republic. Surely this would have reached one of the fortified Venetian trading posts in the Aegean, which formed a chain of communication through to the Adriatic and thence to Venice itself. The Venetians must have been stirred into action by now.

* What we know as 'Greek Fire' was probably first concocted by alchemists in Constantinople in the seventh century. It was a particularly effective naval weapon and was used with great effect in the waters of the Bosphorus. Thought to have been a mixture of bitumen, petroleum and other inflammables, the liquid floated on the surface of the sea, could be ignited and remained alight even in fairly choppy seas, setting fire to any ships it came up against.

After all, the plight of Constantinople mattered almost as much to the Republic as it did to the Byzantines. On 3 May, Constantine XI summoned the Venetian commanders to his presence, addressing them:

> My Lords and Captains, so far it is not possible for us to tell whether your Signory has sent any assistance to protect our unhappy city in its hour of need. I beseech you to despatch some small vessel into the Aegean, in the direction of your colony at the Negropont, where it can make contact with any Venetian fleet and instruct it on the need to make speed towards Constantinople with the greatest urgency.

The Venetians were as baffled as Constantine by the lack of response from the Republic, and readily agreed to his plan. In the early hours of that night, under cover of darkness, the boom across the Golden Horn was briefly lowered, and a small Venetian brigantine flying the Turkish flag and manned by twelve volunteer sailors in Turkish dress slipped unnoticed into the Bosphorus, where it swiftly sailed south into the Sea of Marmara, heading for the Aegean.

Meanwhile, the Turks set about tightening their grip upon the city in spectacular fashion:

> On the night of the eighteenth of May the Turks built a tower on the edge of the ditch which surrounds the city walls. This tower reached higher than the ramparts and was just ten paces distant from the main city walls . . . The Turks built this tower so quickly that the soldiers patrolling on the ramparts did not even realise that it was being built, except when they saw it in the first light of day, a looming sight which filled them with terror.

Mehmet's forces began shooting flaming arrows and bolts onto the roofs of Constantinople below. The following day, on the other side of the city:

> The wretched Turks, filled with evil schemes, now began constructing a bridge, made of large barrels strapped together, with long wooden

planks placed across them, and fastened together to make a roadway for their army to cross from the Pera shore to Constantinople.

The defenders realised that as soon as the Turks began to drag this into place, it could easily be destroyed by a single direct hit from a cannon; but it eventually dawned on them that this was in fact part of a more devious strategy – its intention 'was to make sure that our soldiers were spread around the entire walls, so that they could not concentrate at the weaker spots'.

Meanwhile the very walls themselves remained under constant threat. Each day the cannon barrage continued, and each night the citizens frantically worked to shore up the damaged sections:

Men and women, children and their grandparents, and even the priests, all came out to work together to make good the necessary repairs. This was a matter of the greatest urgency, as the walls had to be kept strong and intact. The cannon used by the Turks were very powerful, but one was exceptionally so. Whenever it fired, the explosion made all the walls of the city shake, as well as the ground inside the walls, and even the ships in the harbour shuddered under its power. The tremendous noise of its detonation kept causing women in the city to faint.

Fortunately for the Byzantines, such was the sheer magnitude of Orban's great 'basilic' cannon that it took the Ottoman artillerymen three hours to reload it, and by now, after almost seven weeks of siege, there were very few of its massive cannonballs remaining.

At noon on 21 May, Barbaro recorded:

We discovered a mine under the north-western walls by the Calegaria gate. The evil Turks had dug under the foundations of the walls and up towards the inside of the city. Their intention was to explode the mine at night and launch a surprise attack. But the whole thing was not quite so dangerous as it at first appeared, and as soon as the tunnel was discovered we destroyed it by pouring fire into it.

The following day they discovered another tunnel close by 'and once again our soldiers poured fire into it, burning alive the Turks who were inside'. The same day yet another tunnel was discovered at Calegaria. 'This tunnel was much better hidden, but by the grace of God it simply collapsed of its own accord, killing all the Turks inside.'

Then, during the afternoon of 23 May, the lookouts on the walls over-looking the Sea of Marmara spied a brigantine tacking against the wind towards them, pursued by a number of Turkish galleys. The lookouts eventually recognised it as the brigantine that had sailed to the Aegean earlier that month in search of the Venetian fleet. As the news spread through the city, many speculated that the brigantine might be the vanguard of the Venetian fleet on its way to rescue the city. The brigantine finally managed to elude its pursuers, and under cover of darkness slipped over the boom into the Golden Horn. But the news conveyed by the Venetian captain of the brigantine to Constantine XI was dire. After searching for almost three weeks around the Aegean, they had discovered no evidence of any Venetian fleet, and no news that one had even set sail. When the emperor heard this, he is said to have muttered that the city could now only place its faith in Christ and His mother, and in St Constantine, its founder.

By now, all hope amongst the besieged citizens of Constantinople was fading fast. The constant bombardment, the proliferation of tunnels under-mining the walls, the blockading Turkish fleet reducing the city to starvation – an atmosphere of doom and despair pervaded the houses lining the eerily empty, rubble-strewn streets. Yet curiously, and unknown to the besieged citizens, morale in the Turkish encampments below the walls was little better. Constantinople seemed to be resisting all that the great Ottoman army could throw at it, and still the infidels refused to surrender. The Ottoman officers felt humiliated; and to their soldiery, unused to long spells of inaction in the trenches, it began to seem as if the order to attack was never going to come. Although they were set to work at night filling in the ditches at the foot of the walls, in evident preparation for a final assault, discipline amongst the ranks had begun to deteriorate, with internecine fighting and even desertions.

Then news reached Mehmet II of alarming developments. There were rumours that the King of Hungary had gathered an army for the relief of Constantinople and had already crossed the Danube. And reports from the Aegean suggested that a Venetian fleet had already reached the island of Chios, just 200 miles sailing distance south of Constantinople. The twenty-one-year-old Mehmet summoned his council to his tent; whereupon the venerable and experienced Grand Vizier (chief minister) Halil Pasha, who had from the start warned the headstrong young sultan against embarking upon such an ambitious enterprise, insisted that the time had come to abandon the siege. Surprisingly, Mehmet agreed to a compromise, and a peace envoy was sent to Constantine XI, promising that the siege would be raised if the emperor agreed to pay the sultan an annual tribute of 100,000 gold bezants (the equivalent of around 50,000 gold ducats*). Constantine simply did not have 100,000 gold bezants, but nonetheless summoned his Byzantine Council to deliberate upon an answer to the sultan's ultimatum. The councillors could do nothing but dither and bicker, their arguments suitably embodying the name of their council. The envoy returned with a devious, prevaricating reply, to which Mehmet reacted in anger: 'the only choice left to the Greeks lay between surrender of the city, death by the sword, or conversion to Islam'. At the ensuing council meeting on 25 May, Halil Pasha still insisted upon lifting the siege, but was overcome by more passionate advocates who supported what they knew to be the sultan's view.†

On 28 May, the Byzantine soldiers on the battlements reported that overnight the Ottoman soldiers had largely completed filling in the ditch at the foot of the walls, and now many of them appeared to be resting in their tents, whilst others could be seen constructing ladders for scaling the walls. Late that afternoon Constantine XI led a long procession of hymn-singing patriarchs of the Orthodox Church bearing icons and holy relics,

---

* At this time a modest Venetian merchant could maintain his house, his family and his servants for around 200 ducats a year.

† Some contemporary sources suggested that Halil Pasha, a man known for his tolerance of Christians, may in fact have been bribed by the Byzantines. Although this seems unlikely, such a story was soon being circulated by Halil Pasha's enemies. In fact, his family had become inordinately powerful and rich in the service of the sultans, to the point where Halil Pasha was said to have been richer than the sultan himself. At any rate, a week after this council meeting Mehmet II had Halil Pasha executed and ordered his possessions to be seized.

followed by representatives of the Roman Church and other nobles, around the city to the walls on each side, and finally to the cathedral of Hagia Sophia, where a solemn ceremony was held. This was said to have been attended by all the citizens except the soldiers lining the walls. As the chanting voices echoed beneath the great 100-foot-diameter dome, a structure unrivalled since classical times, Constantine gave his blessing to those present, urging them to be prepared to die for their religion and reassuring them that, with the help of God, their cause might yet prove victorious. Few were convinced – sources alluded to the sense of apocalyptic foreboding that prevailed, as many sensed they were partaking in the final act of Christian worship in the church that had been the centre of Eastern Christianity for a thousand years.

A few hours later, just after midnight on 29 May 1453, Mehmet II gave the order for the assault to begin. Suddenly the silence of the night was filled with the screaming battle-cries of the Turks, urged on by drums and blaring trumpets, as they rushed over the filled-in ditch towards the foot of the walls. Immediately the lookouts on the ramparts sounded the alarm, and the churches near the walls began ringing their bells, their peals chiming out over the rooftops of the entire city, summoning every able-bodied man, priest and youth to hurry to his post in defence of Constantinople. Meanwhile the townswomen and nuns began loading carts of stones with which to repair the walls, as well as bringing pails of water to assuage the thirst of the defenders as they fought during the heat of the day. The older women carried the children into the churches, where they began to pray for their lives and the salvation of Christendom.

The main attack was concentrated on the walls just south of the Military Gate of San Romano. The first wave of the assault consisted of 50,000 conscripted irregulars, a motley horde that included ill-trained Turks, Slavonic mercenaries, even Christians press-ganged from the conquered Balkan territories. Barbaro describes how they:

> were ordered to carry the ladders to the walls and lay these against them so that they could climb up to the battlements. But as soon as they raised the ladders, our soldiers quickly managed to throw them back, so that they fell to the ground, killing those who were already trying to

climb the ladders. We then threw huge stones down from the battlements onto the heads of those who were waiting to climb the ladders, so that most of them were killed. And even their replacements were squashed. When those who were trying to raise the ladders saw how many were being killed, they began fleeing back towards their camp, trying to escape the hail of stones. But when the rest of the Turks who were behind them saw that they were running away, they drew their scimitars and began cutting them to pieces, driving them back towards the walls, so that they only had the choice of being crushed or being sliced to pieces.

Many of the defenders still believed this was no more than an isolated night attack, intended to wear down the city's defences prior to the major assault that would come hours, or even days, later and probably at a different point in the walls. Then came a second attack, consisting of waves of fully trained Anatolian troops, who 'leapt forward like lions unchained' towards the foot of the great walls:

They too launched a concerted attempt to raise scaling ladders up against the walls, but once again our soldiers on the ramparts bravely hurled them to the ground, killing many Turks. At the same time, our crossbows and cannons on the battlements continued firing down onto the enemy camp, killing a huge number of Turks.

For a moment there was a lull, as the sounds of fighting faded into the darkness. Then Mehmet II ordered in a third wave of attackers, consisting of the crack regiments of his personal guard, the feared Janissaries:

These charged like men possessed, with such screams and shouts, banging of drums and blaring of trumpets, that they could be heard throughout the city. This third wave of Turkish soldiers was confronted by our soldiers on the walls, who were already tired out from repulsing the first two waves.

All this took place in the moonlit hours before dawn, and when the clouds obscured the moon the scene was illuminated by the garish light of flares. At the foot of the outer walls the Janissaries clambered over each other, perching on each other's shoulders as they attempted to press ladders up against the ramparts, but to little avail. Yet just as this third wave too appeared to falter, the pre-dawn darkness was filled with the unmistakable boom of the great 'basilic' cannon, and a vast cannonball scored a direct hit on the outer wall beside the Military Gate of San Romano, causing a wide section of the ramparts to collapse. Amidst the clouds of dust, the Janissaries charged forward over the rubble.

With dawn rising over this scene of chaos, the defenders desperately sought to contain the breach in the outer walls. But now the Genoese troops began retreating through the Kerkoporta postern, a small gate in the northern part of the walls. Amidst the confusion the gate was left unlocked, and the Janissaries began streaming after them into the city itself. By now Constantine XI had personally entered the fray, taking command of a company of Byzantine soldiers at the breach by the Military Gate of San Romano. At first the emperor and his men stood their ground, but soon it became clear they were being overwhelmed. The emperor, sensing that all was lost, determined to fight to the last. According to a contemporary source, 'He rushed into the mêlée with his sword drawn, fell, rose again, fell once more, and so died.' (This account was later confirmed by the discovery, amidst the bodies of the slain defenders, of a headless corpse wearing Constantine XI's insignia of golden Byzantine eagles, its legs wrapped in the imperial purple buskins.)

After fifty-two days the siege of Constantinople was over, and the Ottoman troops poured into the city in their tens of thousands, hell-bent on looting, rape and pillage. When the hordes reached the precincts of Hagia Sophia, they broke down its great bronze gates and surged into the cathedral itself, where numerous old men, women and children had fled for sanctuary. Amidst scenes of mayhem, many were slaughtered, women were stripped of their valuables and maidens were carried off. Others were fought over, before being roped together and led off into slavery.*

---

* According to the prevailing rules of war, such behaviour by the soldiery was condoned at the end of any siege in Europe and further afield. Customarily it was allowed to continue for three days — though in this case Mehmet II ordered an end to the looting after just one day.

Few come well out of this historic day. The remnant Venetian and Genoese soldiers simply fled for the harbour, scrambling aboard their ships; when these were full and had cast off, others swam out into the Golden Horn after them, their beseeching voices crying out in vain across the water. Alviso Diedo, commander of the Venetian fleet in the Golden Horn, led his flotilla towards the boom followed by seven Genoese ships. At the boom, Diedo ordered his sailors to hack through its wooden floats, so that the boom drifted open in the current.

By this time there was no threat from the Turkish fleet, which had been anchored in the Bosphorus, as it had made its way to Constantinople:

where all the sailors had disembarked, leaving their ships beached on the shore without even anyone to guard them, as they were all running like dogs into the city in the hope of seizing gold, jewels and treasure, or to capture some rich merchant for ransom. They particularly sought out the monasteries, where all the nuns were carried off and ravished, prior to being sold off as slaves for the markets of Anatolia. Likewise all the young women they could capture were also ravished and then sold off for whatever price they would fetch, although some of these women, and also some married women, preferred to throw themselves down wells and drown rather than fall into the hands of the Turks.

Taking advantage of a northerly breeze, Diedo led his Venetian ships, together with the following Genoese, down towards the mouth of the Bosphorus and the open sea. His flotilla had by now been joined by all the other Venetian warships in the harbour. As the straggling fleet of escaping ships sailed away from the doomed city, Barbaro (who had made it onto one of Diedo's ships) described the last of Constantinople:

According to the practice of the Turks, once their soldiers had taken a house or a church or a monastery they raised a flag with their emblem on it, so that no one else would come and pillage it. However, some houses flew as many as ten flags, because the Turks were so excited at their great victory. As far as I could estimate, there were over 200,000 Turkish flags flying from the rooftops and the towers all over the city . . . whilst it was evident that the great slaughter of Christians continued as we had seen it before, with blood flowing through the gutters like rainwater after a summer storm. Meanwhile the corpses of Turks and Christians alike had been thrown into the water, where they floated out to sea like melons bobbing along a canal.

So the Venetians made good their escape. But what had become of Giacomo Loredan and the Venetian fleet that had supposedly been sent to relieve the city – the fleet that the searching brigantine from Constantinople had been unable to find?

Loredan had set sail with fifteen galleys sometime before 9 May, accompanied by Bartolomeo Marcello, who had been appointed as Venice's ambassador to Mehmet II. But far from being instructed to proceed with full speed, even at this late stage, Loredan had in fact been ordered to put in at Corfu to collect another galley and then to proceed to Negropont, where he would rendezvous with two further galleys. Only then was he to sail for Tenedos, at the mouth of the Dardanelles, where he would link up with a Venetian flotilla under Admiral Alvise Longo, which had been sent ahead to gather intelligence on the strength and disposition of the Ottoman fleet. Loredan was then to sail for Constantinople, taking great care not to engage any Ottoman ships on the way.

It is at this point that the duplicity of Venetian policy becomes evident. Plainly the Senate hoped that the Venetian fleet would arrive too late. In this event, ambassador Marcello was instructed to present himself before Mehmet II and explain that Venice had only peaceful intentions towards the Ottomans, and that the purpose of Loredan's fleet was merely to protect Venetian trading interests and escort any of the city's merchantmen out of harm's way. If, on the other hand, Constantinople had not fallen, Marcello had instructions to advise Mehmet to agree to peace talks, while Loredan pressed similar advice upon Constantine XI, urging him to accept any offer made by Mehmet II, regardless of the conditions. In either case, Venice's immediate and short-sighted aim was simply to ensure continuance of the Republic's trade.

News of the fall of Constantinople reached Venice precisely a month after the event, on 29 June, when trading on the Rialto immediately came to a halt. The merchants in the market place were well aware of the momentous significance of this event, even if their legislators (many of whom were also merchants) chose not to be. The progress of Admiral Loredan, ambassador Marcello and their accompanying fleet had been so slow that by this date they were still making their long way towards Constantinople. On 9 July further directions reached them from Venice. In the light of the definite news that Constantinople had fallen, there was to be a change of plan. Loredan was to make sure that any remnant Venetian shipping bound from the Levant for Constantinople was diverted to Modane in the Peleponnese, whilst he himself was to proceed at once to secure the defence of Negropont and order the reinforcement of all Venetian trading posts in the Aegean. At the same time Marcello was to continue on to Constantinople, where he was to negotiate an agreement with Mehmet II aimed at re-establishing the Venetian colony in the city and ensuring the continuance of the Republic's trading privileges. Marcello was also author-ised to spend 1,500 golden ducats on 'presents' to the sultan and any of his officials who might assist in the signing of such an agreement. All this, regardless of the fact that many hundreds of Venetians including several dozen from amongst the most distinguished noble families had lost their lives at the fall of Constantinople, after which, to add insult to injury, Mehmet had personally ordered the public beheading of the Venetian *bailo*, Minotto, and his son. And as if this was not enough, Venice had also lost property in the city worth more than 300,000 ducats, a loss that resulted in several of the Republic's most distinguished merchants going bankrupt.

The Venetian Senate's justification for this betrayal of an empire, of their religion and even of their own countrymen was summed up in an infamous public declaration of their present policy: '*Siamo Veneziani, poi Cristiani*' ('We are Venetians, then Christians'). From now on the Republic would pursue a foreign policy guided by commercial principles alone. In the Venetian imperial age, conscience would be utterly overruled by expediency.

Despite Mehmet II's contempt for such self-serving hypocrisy, he consented to open negotiations with ambassador Marcello, which dragged on for months on end. After a long process of cat-and-mouse, Mehmet

6

Father and Son

THE FALL OF Constantinople in 1453 emphasised the split between East and West, which had first come into being more than a thousand years previously when the Roman Empire had split in two, leading to the establishment of the (Byzantine) Orthodox Church and the (Roman) Catholic Church. Now this was to be replaced by the division between the Moslem East and the Christian West, which roughly followed the same tectonic fault-line through the Balkans, a feature that has continued to this day. Although it had been a long time coming, the final demise of Constantinople can be blamed on Venetian short-sightedness, prompted by what it saw as its own self-interest.

Indicative of Venice's moral malaise was the fact that Doge Francesco Foscari, elected despite Tomasso Mocenigo's deathbed warning, had now been in office for thirty years, the longest any man had ever held this post. The administration was in a rut, and the Republic had now been at war almost continuously on the mainland since Foscari had become doge; financially the city's coffers were drained, and its commerce with the eastern Mediterranean was severely reduced. From the very inception of Foscari's rule, things had not augured well. He was the first doge to have secured his election by deception and widespread bribery. Such practices were not unknown in gaining the city's highest office, but the choice of Foscari in 1423 was generally reckoned to have been the first in which fraudulence proved crucial. During his previous occupancy of the post of procurator, in charge of the city's charitable fund for impoverished nobles, his scrutiny of the neglected accounts had uncovered an overlooked surplus of 30,000 ducats. This he had judiciously distributed amongst various noble families, thus ensuring their support when it came to the election. Even so, it was generally assumed that the popular Pietro Loredan would quickly emerge as victor amongst the list of candidates. However, Foscari's supporters amongst the forty-one noble electors had secretly decided upon a deceptive strategy. During the early ballots they voted for a candidate whom they knew to be detested by Loredan's supporters, causing them to vote for Loredan in order to exclude their bête noire. Then, on the tenth ballot, Foscari's supporters suddenly switched their votes to their genuine choice, enabling him to secure more than the necessary twenty-five votes.

The newly elected fifty-year-old Foscari was in fact a man of considerable intellect and ability – he had been a leader of the Council of Ten no fewer than three times. Mocenigo's characterisation of him as an 'arrogant windbag' and an 'impetuous rabble-rouser' was mainly directed at his declared intention to pursue the ruinous war against Milan. Indeed, Foscari had soon fulfilled Mocenigo's worst forebodings, launching into a long and expensive campaign in Lombardy. Meanwhile the Loredan family had not forgiven him for his deception, and swore to do all they could to oppose him.

Foscari eventually attempted to heal this breach in the time-honoured fashion, by arranging a marriage between the two families. But during the engagement a dispute led to this being broken off, such that it only ended up making matters worse. Foscari was well aware of Pietro Loredan's continuing popularity, which grew considerably after he led the Republic's army to a crucial victory in the Po delta during the war. However, in 1439 Pietro fell ill and died under circumstances that were never fully explained. Opposition to Foscari had now lost its able and popular leader; and although there was no proof of Foscari's involvement in Loredan's death, many suspected that he had been poisoned at the doge's behest.

Foscari was now able to consolidate his position, and two years later arranged for his son Jacopo to be married to Lucrezia Contarini. This cemented an alliance with one of the most prestigious noble families: Foscari was the first of his family to become doge, whereas the Contarinis had already produced three doges. Foscari was determined that the marriage of his son should be remembered as a historic event, and despite the city's straitened circumstances his extravagance ensured this would be so. His son Jacopo was also noted for his extravagance. Unlike the sons of most noble families of the period, Jacopo had not received a practical education in mercantile trading, but had been privately tutored in the new humanism by the Renaissance scholar Francesco Barbaro (a relative of Nicolò, the physician who would record the fall of Constantinople). Jacopo had studied Greek and Latin texts intended to instil in him an understanding of the nobility of the ancient philosophers and legislators. However, his education appears instead to have given him something of a superiority complex, and he soon joined a number of like-minded young nobles in a recently formed exclusive society known as the Campagna della Calza, whose members disported themselves in a uniform that consisted of *calza* (multicoloured stockings) and crimson velvet robes lined with silver brocade, and who rode horses clad in similar fashion attended by six liveried grooms.

Whereas most sons of the nobility did not marry until they were around thirty, Jacopo was probably little more than twenty at the time of his marriage, and the indications are that his bride was barely a teenager. Jacopo was Foscari's sole surviving son, and the doge was determined to consolidate his family's future prospects with the birth of grandsons during the course of his reign. No expense was to be spared on Jacopo's wedding, and contemporary sources as well as Foscari's own accounts indicate that he must have spent more than 20,000 ducats on gifts, jewellery and gowns for Lucrezia, which would have graced 'any great queen'. The celebrations began on the last days of January 1441 and appear to have continued for well over a week of officially declared public holidays, during which widows were even forbidden to wear mourning dress.

The festivities began with a grand procession around the Piazza San Marco, in which Jacopo rode on horseback escorted by a resplendent guard of his fellow members of the Compagna della Calza, followed by 200 men-at-arms and attendants. This proceeded through the streets to the Grand Canal near the church of San Samuele, where a bridge of boats had been built across the water to the San Barnaba district, where Lucrezia resided at the palazzo of her father, Leonardo Contarini.*

---

* This temporary bridge was some 300 yards north of the present Accademia bridge and crossed almost a hundred yards of open water. The palazzo of Leonardo Contarini was just one of

This parade was followed by an itinerary of events, morning, noon and night, throughout the following week – the festivities often not coming to an end until three in the morning. On one notable occasion, after a grand midday banquet at the Doge's Palace, 150 ladies-in-waiting accompanied by a band of musicians embarked upon the doge's great golden barge, the *Bucintoro*, which was escorted down the Grand Canal by a host of smaller craft to San Barnaba, where Lucrezia made her way on board up the ceremonial gangway, accompanied by a further 200 ladies-in-waiting. Not a day passed without some grand ball, masque or musical serenade. Banquets were conspicuous for their extravagance – some were even held in the Great Council Chamber, lit with 120 torches (double the usual amount), and with 'tables laden with only such fine delicacies as oyster, capons, partridges and peacocks, all served in such abundance that afterwards much of it was thrown away'.

During the afternoons jousting contests between colourfully clad contestants were held in the Piazza San Marco; on one occasion no fewer than forty contestants competed for a prize of 120 ducats before a crowd of 30,000 spectators. Afterwards, at dusk, the piazza would be lit by hundreds of torches as the noble ladies in their finest gowns were serenaded on their way to yet another masked ball. The bride's brother, Giacomo Contarini, proudly described Lucrezia's various ballgowns and dresses, of which one was:

> a dress of gold brocade, whose long open sleeves lined with squirrel fur trailed behind her along the ground, as did the dress itself, which cost almost five thousand ducats. She also had a superb collection of jewellery including a particularly fine precious stone which she wore in her hair, a ruby, an emerald, a valuable diamond, as well as a diamond shoulder clasp, a pearl and a Balas-ruby worth 3,500 ducats. Besides this, she had a necklace which had been worn by the Queen of Cyprus, which was worth around 2,000 ducats, and many rings, amongst which were four with large rubies worth another 2,000 ducats.

---

several contemporary Contarini residences, of which the superb Ca' d'Oro on the east side of the Grand Canal remains the best known.

The insistence upon such items was typically Venetian: a commercial republic had no false modesty with regard to monetary value. On the contrary, Giacomo Contarini considered this a matter of pride, all the more honourable because these valuables were provided by the Contarini family, 'who had no need to look to Monsignor il Doge for any assistance in that sort of way'. Likewise, he stressed that, as the bride's family, the Contarini family hosted at least as many banquets as the doge, at which an abundance of nothing but the most fashionable dishes was served.

All this took place in the middle of the long war with Milan – hence the marriage and its celebrations were held in January and early February, during the winter lull in the campaigning season. And despite the city's near-bankruptcy, all the indications are that these celebrations were popular. They were certainly well attended: 30,000 spectators at a jousting competition represented almost one-third of the city's entire population, and that on a chilly winter's afternoon. Indeed, the daytime temperature is unlikely to have risen much above 45°F (7°C), while it may well have fallen below freezing at night; and contemporary sources mention some events being postponed because of heavy rain. Yet the Venetian poor and artisan classes would for the most part have delighted in such a prolonged holiday of free entertainments, with tables of free food and wine customarily laid out in front of the major palazzi (to say nothing of leftovers from the feasts at the Doge's Palace); and even the merchants and all but a few of the noble families are known to have taken pride in these events, which reflected well upon the Republic. This was a matter of patriotism: no other city in Italy, or even Europe, could have staged such a display at this time. And the doge took much of the credit. Despite his enemies, Francesco Foscari had by this point been doge for eighteen years, achieving a venerable stature approaching that of the nineteen-year reign of his predecessor, Tommaso Mocenigo.

Yet his son was another matter. During the years following his marriage Jacopo's extravagance plunged him deep into debt. As a result he began trading on his father's position, covertly accepting bribes in order to use his influence in the awarding of well-paid public appointments. On 17 February 1445, word of this finally reached the Council of Ten, one of whose leaders happened to be a close relative of the late Pietro Loredan.

The Council of Ten moved swiftly, secretly apprehending Jacopo's manservant Gasparo and taking him into custody for questioning. As a result of evidence gained from Gasparo, a warrant was issued the next day for Jacopo's arrest. But by now he had got wind of what was happening, quickly gathered up all the loose money he had to hand and fled aboard a fast galley fifty miles up the coast to the port of Trieste, which lay beyond the jurisdiction of Venice.

In view of the seriousness of the matter, the Council of Ten augmented itself with senior nobles to form a *zonta*, from which the doge was excluded, however, on account of his evident family interest. This created a significant precedent limiting the doge's power and influence, and acted as a crucial counterbalance to the increasing autonomy that Foscari had begun to exercise as doge. Jacopo Foscari was duly tried in his absence, and when his servants were questioned they revealed the existence of a chest that he kept in the Doge's Palace, in which were gifts that he had been given as bribes, as well as incriminating documents. Jacopo was found guilty of corruption and duly sentenced in his absence to banishment for life to the Venetian colony of Nauplia in the eastern Peloponnese. Whereupon a galley under the command of Marco Trevisano was despatched to Trieste to serve an arrest warrant on Jacopo and escort him to Greece. But Trevisano was obliged to report back to Venice: 'I went to see my Lord Jacopo, but he rejected the warrant with disrespectful contempt, refusing point blank to allow me to convey him into exile.' There was little the authorities in Venice could do, other than seize what remained of Jacopo's possessions and declare him an outlaw.

And so the stand-off continued, with seemingly no prospect of resolution. Then in the autumn of 1446 news reached Venice that Jacopo had fallen seriously ill. Distressed at this turn of events, his mother the dogaressa begged to' be allowed to visit him, but this was refused. It soon became clear that the seventy-four-year-old doge had been extremely upset by these developments, to the point where he was having great difficulty in fulfilling his duties. Out of respect for Foscari senior, Jacopo's sentence was rescinded by the Council of Ten in November 1446 and he was allowed to return to the Republic, on condition that he lived on the mainland at Treviso and returned anything left of the bribes he had taken.

Jacopo duly returned and took up residence at his country home on the outskirts of Treviso. But the enemies of the Foscari family were none too pleased at this leniency, and it is probably no coincidence that some months later further incriminating evidence against Jacopo 'accidentally' came to light. A chest containing some 2,040 ducats, along with silver plate and other valuables, was discovered in an obscure closet at the Doge's Palace. It was soon confirmed that this constituted a bribe given to Jacopo by the Tuscan-born *condottiere* Francesco Sforza, who had been lured by Venice to command its forces on the mainland against his former employer, Milan. This represented a serious development: acceptance of gifts from foreign nationals, even if they were in the employ of the Republic, was a treasonable offence. And it now became clear that the doge himself must have known of the existence of this hidden cache. After prolonged discussions, in April 1447 the Council of Ten narrowly voted that the chest should be impounded by the authorities, but that no further action should be taken against either Jacopo or his ailing father. For the good of the Republic, the venerable doge was to be permitted to serve out his term free from disgrace.

Yet such sentiments did not take into account Jacopo's bitterness at his fall from grace. On the night of 5 December 1450, Ermolao Donato, a member of the Council of Ten, was waylaid in an alleyway and stabbed by an unknown assailant as he was returning to his home from a meeting of the Senate. Two days later he died from his wounds. Donato had been one of the leaders of the Council of Ten at the time of Jacopo Foscari's trial; yet it was known that he had also recently made other enemies and these were soon hunted down. Despite persistent interrogation, none of these suspects confessed, and all were released. Consequently a reward was offered for information leading to the apprehension of the true culprit.

On 5 January 1451 the Council of Ten received a denunciation of Jacopo Foscari by one Antonio Vernier, claiming that Jacopo had hired his servant Oliviero to murder Donato. The evidence for Vernier's claim was flimsy: Oliviero was said to have been seen hanging around the Doge's Palace the night Donato had been murdered. And, according to hearsay evidence, Oliviero had also been seen arriving by boat early the next morning at Mestre on the mainland, where he had spoken of the murder to a boatman. Jacopo was taken into custody and interrogated; yet even under torture he refused to confess, and he did not reveal the slightest bit of incriminating evidence. Even so, the Council of Ten decided he was guilty. As contemporary evidence indicates, this could not have been the result of machinations by the Loredan faction, as none of them occupied a position on the Council of Ten at the time. It seems more likely that Jacopo's behaviour had made him highly unpopular throughout the city, and the authorities wished to be rid of this embarrassment to their long-standing doge. Jacopo was duly sentenced for the second time to banishment for life, this time to the island of Crete, to which he was transported in March 1453, leaving behind his wife and family, as required by the terms of his exile.

Two months later Constantinople had fallen and the political situation in the eastern Mediterranean was transformed; despite Venice's commercial arrangement with Mehmet II, it was evident that the Ottomans now posed a real threat to their eastern trading empire. So it was understandable that Jacopo's next move provoked outrage in Venice. In the summer of 1456 a number of coded letters between Jacopo and Mehmet came into the hands of the Cretan authorities. In these, Jacopo asked the sultan to send a ship to help him escape from Crete. Surprisingly, this sensational news divided the Council of Ten: one side proposed that 'in consideration of his foolishness and the remoteness of his place of banishment', Jacopo should simply be brought before the governor of Crete and given a severe reprimand, together with a warning of the serious consequences of any further breaches of his terms of exile. Others were less inclined to leniency, and on 21 July Jacopo was brought to Venice to answer the charges against him. This time there was no need for interrogation or torture, as Jacopo confessed at once. By now Jacopo Loredan, a leader of the anti-Foscari faction, had been elected as a leader of the Council of Ten, and he immediately demanded that Jacopo Foscari should be sentenced to death and beheaded between the pillars of the Piazzetta. However, there were strong feelings of sympathy for the eighty-three-year-old doge, who had been deeply conflicted by his son's behaviour, which had caused him to age considerably. Once more, the pro-Foscari faction won the day, and Jacopo was sentenced to return and serve out his exile in Crete, with the proviso that this time he would serve the first year in gaol at Candia.

Like his father, Jacopo was now in poor health. Although he was only in his early thirties, he had never fully recovered from the illness that had led to his recall from exile in the Peloponnese, and it was this frailty that had prompted his desperate plea to Mehmet II. Indeed, according to the evidence of his relative, the contemporary chronicler Giovanni Dolfin, Jacopo's sole purpose in writing to Mehmet II was so that he would be charged and brought back to Venice to face trial, because he wished more than anything to see his 'father, mother, wife and children before he should die'. At any rate, the ailing Jacopo was permitted one final visit to see his father before being sent back into exile. Both sensed this was the last time they would set eyes on each other, and according to Dolfin, who was present at this meeting, the frail Jacopo broke down weeping at the sight of his father and pleaded, 'I beg you to use your power so that I can be allowed to return home.' Whereupon Doge Foscari rebuked him, 'My son, obey the orders of the Republic and do not ask for anything more.' Yet when Jacopo had been escorted back to his cell, Foscari collapsed back in his chair, sobbing, 'O pietà grande' ('What a terrible pity!'). The end was quicker than either of them could have foreseen: Jacopo was transported back to Crete, where he began his year in gaol; this was never to be completed, for he died on 12 January 1457.

This was too much for Doge Foscari. His enemies had at last triumphed and he withdrew into his chambers at the Doge's Palace, where he took no further part in 'the governance of the Republic'. His absence at the various committee meetings over which the doge was required to preside left the Republic leaderless. Faced with a dangerous power vacuum, the Loredan faction decided to act, and when Jacopo Loredan was once again elected a leader of the Council of Ten in October 1457, they voted for the creation of a zonta, with twenty-five selected members added to their number to form an emergency committee. Without informing the zonta of the reason why it had been called, Loredan had its members sworn to secrecy, on pain of a 1,000-ducat fine and exclusion from public office for life. On 21 October, Loredan then proposed a resolution requiring the now-ineffective doge to resign, which after three votes eventually secured the requisite majority.

Despite Foscari's frailty and near-despair, he refused to obey this resolution, pointing out that according to the statutes of the Republic only a vote by the Great Council, supported by the members of the Signoria, could demand such action. This proved a setback, but by nightfall of the following day Loredan had managed to persuade the *zonta* of the necessity to go ahead, regardless of such legal niceties. Speed was of the essence if they were to succeed in ousting Foscari. However, when the delegation from the *zonta* arrived at the doge's apartments to inform him of these developments, they were told that he had already retired to bed, so no further action could be taken that day.

Consequently, on the morning of Sunday 23 October, a delegation from the *zonta* demanded an audience with the doge, at which he was issued with an ultimatum: either he resigned and vacated the Doge's Palace within eight days or he would be removed by force, stripped of his possessions and all his family properties would be confiscated. Faced with the prospect of eking out his last days abandoned as a disgraced pauper, Foscari caved in. There followed a humiliating ceremony in which he was stripped of his symbols of office. This too was witnessed by Dolfin, who saw the doge's ring pulled from Foscari's finger and ritually destroyed; then the *corno* was lifted from his head, its horn and gold braid symbolically cut off. The following day Francesco Foscari was escorted from the Doge's Palace, insisting upon using his walking stick as his sole support to descend the main stairway. He still retained his pride: when it was suggested that he turn off and descend by the smaller stairway leading to the side entrance, he replied, 'I shall descend by the same stairway as that which I ascended to take up my office.' When he stepped onto the boat waiting at the quayside, he is said to have remarked, 'The malice of my enemies has driven me from the office to which I was raised by my own talents.' He was then rowed down the Grand Canal to take up residence in the Ca' Foscari, the palace that he had built some years previously in the hope that his son Jacopo would one day be permitted to take up residence again in Venice. After Jacopo's death the building had remained incomplete, in a state of some disrepair, devoid of furnishings, without even any glass in the windows. And it was here that Foscari was to live out the last days of his life.

When news that Foscari had been deposed spread through Venice it caused a sensation. The people, the artisans, the merchants and many of the nobles from all factions were shocked. Foscari's previous misdemeanours were now overlooked; he was venerated as a result of his years in office, and many empathised with the hapless father of a son gone to the bad. According to Dolfin: 'the grumblings amongst the citizens rose as if from amongst the very stones of the city's foundations.' But just as Loredan and his accomplices had intended, Venice had been confronted with a fait accompli: it was too late for anything to be done now, given the state of Foscari's health. Any attempt to reinstate him would probably have killed him. And with crude haste the victors were soon making sure that history, and their part in it, was being rewritten. When the Great Council was summoned for the election of a new doge, the official proclamation declared that Foscari had merely been 'absolved' from office on account of his 'inability to exercise his powers because of his old age'.

Nine days after taking up residence in his derelict mansion Francesco Foscari died at the age of eighty-four, on 1 November 1457. The hurriedly elected new doge, Pasquale Malipiero, and his Signoria, were informed of Foscari's death while they were attending the All Saints' Day service in San Marco, and according to the ever-present Dolfin they were visibly stricken with guilt, exchanging cowed glances with one another, 'for they were fully aware that they were the ones who had brought his life to an end'. To allay their conscience, Doge Malipiero ordered that Foscari's body should be laid out in the Doge's Palace dressed in his doge's robes, with his restored *corno* placed on his head, 'so that he could lie in state and the burial rites could be carried out as if he had died in office'. The hypocrisy that had characterised Venice's imperial foreign policy had now spread to the very heart of the Republic.

7

Colleoni

URING FOSCARI'S LONG reign Venice had been almost continuously at war with Milan for nearly thirty years. Despite the difficulties encountered with Carmagnola, the Republic had continued to hire *condottieri* to conduct this war. The last of these was Bartolomeo Colleoni, who was born the son of local squire Paolo Colleoni in around 1400 in Bergamo, the foothills of the Alps some twenty miles east of Milan.

During the chaotic years following the death of Gian Galeazzo Visconti of Milan in 1402, when his sons fought for the duchy, Paolo took the opportunity to seize the large nearby castle of Trezzo, inviting four of his exiled cousins to come and help him defend this newly acquired family possession. Not long after this, whilst Paolo was playing draughts, his cousins burst in and murdered him. The young Bartolomeo managed to escape to the mountains, and after spending a brief period in prison he entered service as a pageboy at the fortified palazzo of Arcelli, lord of Piacenza, just south of Milan – until once more disaster struck. By now Filippo Maria Visconti and his *condottiere* Carmagnola had begun reuniting Milanese territory, and Piacenza soon fell to their forces, with Arcelli forced to witness his sons and brothers being impaled on the battlements by the vengeful Visconti. Once again Batolomeo Colleoni was forced to flee for his life.

By now around sixteen, Colleoni decided to journey south to Naples, where he sought employment as a mercenary soldier with the *condottiere* Jacopo Caldora. During these years the kingdom of Naples was in even greater disarray than the duchy of Milan. The titular ruler, the forty-three-year-old Queen Johanna II, had named her heir as the Spanish king, Alfonso of Aragon, but this was disputed by the French king Louis III of

[126]

Anjou, who had the backing of Pope Martin V. Later, she would switch her allegiance to Louis III, further complicating matters as the French and Spanish attempted to establish their hold on Naples. This all made for rich pickings for the *condottieri* leading the various armies, who were themselves liable to switch sides if offered sufficient inducement in terms of money or some minor title with its own territory.

Colleoni's commander, Caldora, remained for the most part in the service of Queen Johanna II, and over the next decade or so Colleoni served with such distinction that he was given charge of twenty cavalry, and later of another dozen. His daring exploits also seem to have brought him to the attention of Johanna II herself, who may well have been attracted to more than his military prowess, for she awarded him a badge bearing her personal insignia, which he would continue to wear into battle for the rest of his life.

Finally, at the age of twenty-four Colleoni was given effective charge of the army that Caldora had entrusted to his young son, so that he could seize territory for himself in the north-eastern province of the Romagna. For five years Colleoni campaigned in northern Italy, but in 1429 decided against returning to Naples. Instead, leading a squadron of forty cavalry, he enlisted with Carmagnola, who was by now established as the commander of the Venetian forces fighting against Milan.

Once again Colleoni soon came to prominence. In October 1431, when Carmagnola was camped outside Cremona, Colleoni was one of the young officers who – together with Ugolino Cavalcabo, son of the murdered lord of Cremona – took the initiative and attempted under cover of darkness to seize the tower of San Luca, the key to the city's defences. According to Colleoni's near-contemporary biographer Pietro Spino, Colleoni 'showed conspicuous heroism in this assault. After being the first to climb the battlements, he then killed the soldiers and the commander guarding the tower.' Colleoni and his intrepid fellow raiders not only took the tower, but managed to hold on to it for two days, facing the full brunt of the Cremonese defenders. Only then did it become evident to them that Carmagnola had no intention of taking the city, and they were forced to withdraw at further risk to their lives.

After Carmagnola was put to death, Colleoni continued to serve as a senior commander of the Venetian forces, distinguishing himself on a number of occasions. One of these involved his birthplace Bergamo. Although at the time Bergamo remained unarmed and quasi-independent, the celebrated Milanese *condottiere* Niccolò Piccinino had decided to seize the city and use it as his winter quarters. In preparation for this, Piccinino unleashed thousands of his mercenaries over the surrounding countryside, ordering them to raze any threatening fortresses, as well as to seize all the grain, wine and supplies they could find to provide victuals for their long winter months holed up in Bergamo. 'All that could not be carried away was destroyed, the villages robbed and burned, the castles pillaged, so that the valleys were emptied and the entire land reduced to a hideous desolation.' Hearing of this, Colleoni decided on a daring plan to thwart Piccinino, whom he knew had not yet taken Bergamo. Although Colleoni only had 300 infantry at his disposal, he marched quickly under cover of darkness through the burning and ravaged countryside, aware that at any moment he might be overwhelmed by a superior force of Piccinino's mercenaries. On reaching Bergamo, he slammed closed the gates and mounted the battlement, his small force supported by eager volunteers from amongst the local citizens. By the time Piccinino arrived, the weather had broken, with rain and snow rendering any possibility of a siege out of the question. Piccinino was forced to order his men on an ignominious retreat to Milan, where Duke Filippo Maria Visconti was not pleased at the prospect of having to provide for an unruly mercenary army that was expected to fend for itself.

However, perhaps the greatest of Colleoni's accomplishments was not, strictly speaking, a military victory at all, but more an engineering feat – namely, the relief of Brescia by launching the Venetian fleet on Lake Garda. This has often been ascribed to the Venetian military engineer Sorbolo of Candia, but was in fact Colleoni's idea, just as it was his urging that convinced the Council of Ten to go ahead with it. He also closely oversaw the project, in much the same way that Hannibal organised the passage of the Carthaginian army and its elephants across the Alps. Indeed, in its own minor way Colleoni's feat stands some comparison with that of Hannibal.

In the autumn of 1438, Piccinino launched the Milanese forces in a surprise advance east of Venetian-held Brescia, cutting off the city's supply lines around the southern shore of Lake Garda from Venice. This meant that the strategic city of Brescia faced the prospect of an entire winter under siege, which it was unlikely to survive. The only way for Venice to have attempted to relieve the siege would have been to march an army around the mountainous northern tip of the lake, but this was soon found to be out of the question now that the autumn rains had flooded the rivers, turning them into raging torrents, and the snow had begun falling in the mountains. In no time the city of Brescia was starving, its people reduced to eating the cats and dogs, even grazing on weeds. The population of 30,000 would soon be halved, and at night the wolves began coming down from the mountains to scavenge the dead.

It was now that Colleoni proposed his daring plan. Venice should sail a fleet of ships up the River Adige north as far as Rovereto. Here they could be lifted ashore, dragged over the mountain and relaunched from the northern shore of Lake Garda, from where provisions could be shipped across the lake, whence they could be transported to Brescia. Although Rovereto lay less than ten miles from the northern end of Lake Garda, the mountains in between the river and the lake rose to around 6,000 feet. Despite such difficulties, Colleoni's engineer, Sabalo, was soon persuaded that this plan was feasible and, even more surprisingly, Colleoni managed to persuade the Council of Ten to finance the undertaking. Despite the administration's malaise, it was still on occasion capable of that same bold and adventurous spirit that had characterised the age of Marco Polo and the Zeno brothers.

A fleet of twenty-five transport craft and six galleys were rowed and sailed up the River Adige to Rovereto, where they were lifted from the river and placed on rollers. An artificial causeway was then cleared up the slope, and the flotilla was hauled up the mountain by teams totalling more than 20,000 oxen. At the summit the process was reversed, and the entire flotilla was gradually lowered down towards the harbour of Torbole at the head of the lake. The cost was prodigious – some 16,000 ducats – but the entire operation was completed in just fifteen days without a single craft being lost. During the last days of February 1439 all the craft were loaded with supplies and readied for sailing.

Contemporary sources differ as to precisely how much of these supplies managed to cross the lake and make it overland to Brescia. The Milanese are known to have launched a flotilla of local craft in order to try and prevent the Venetians from sailing, but this does not appear to have been entirely successful. The Venetians erected a line of stakes to protect their fleet, and many may have got through. However, the actual effectiveness of this mission was far outweighed by its propaganda value. This exploit became the talking point of Italy and beyond. From now on, it was understood that even on the mainland Venice's fabled naval power knew no bounds. Any city under Venice's protection could rely upon the Republic coming to its rescue, no matter how impossible this task might seem.

For its part, Venice was certainly grateful to Colleoni and promoted him to governor of Verona, one of the Republic's most important mainland cities. At the same time his military rank in the field was enhanced by increasing his command to 3,000 lances, in effect almost a thousand men.*

In 1441 Venice signed yet another uneasy peace with Milan. Francesco Sforza, who was *condottiere* of the Venetian forces, now found himself with no prospect of lucrative engagements, so chose to take up employment with Milan. Colleoni decided to remain in Venice; however, a year later he became involved in a dispute with the Venetian authorities; he and his men were owed 34,000 ducats, which Venice would not, or could not, pay them. As a result, he too offered his services to Filippo Maria Visconti of Milan, and once again under Sforza he soon proved his worth. However, four years later Colleoni was suddenly seized and flung into prison at the castle in Monza, almost certainly at the behest of the paranoid Filippo Maria. A year later, in 1447, Filippo Maria died and Colleoni sensed that his life was in danger. Simulating a sweating fever, he convinced the physician at Monza to wrap his entire body in water-soaked bandages to cool him down. As soon as he was left alone he unravelled the bandages and used them to lower himself from his cell into the dry ditch of the castle moat.

As Filippo Maria had died without a male heir, the duchy of Milan was once again thrown into turmoil. The authorities declared the Ambrosian Republic (named after St Ambrose, the patron saint of the city), but after

---

* At this time a 'lance' in fact consisted of three or more men: the main *cavallo* on his charger, along with his mounted attendant and his page or servant, who rode behind on a packhorse or donkey carrying their equipment.

four years this had descended into chaos, with riots breaking out in the streets of Milan and large numbers of the population reduced to starvation. In 1450 Sforza accepted the authorities' offer to take over as Duke of Milan, an ambition that he had been harbouring for some time. Colleoni was once again drafted to serve under Sforza as the Milanese war against Venice recommenced.

All Italy had come to realise the futility of this decades-long war, which had continued to draw in all its states in a series of ever-switching alliances. In April 1454 the Peace of Lodi was signed, with Milan, Venice and Florence agreeing to an unprecedented twenty-five-year truce, which was soon joined by Naples and blessed by Pope Nicholas V. A year later, Colleoni was pleased to accept the offer of commander of the forces of Venice, a position he had long coveted. The post not only involved great honour in the Republic, but was also extremely well rewarded, both in terms of salary and gifts of estates and castles on the mainland. Despite the fact that Colleoni had switched sides to fight for the highest bidder when the occasion arose, Venice recognised that for the most part he had been a loyal, brave and talented servant of the Republic and was determined that he should remain so. His services entailed little military action and the Peace of Lodi remained on the whole honoured, apart from sporadic outbreaks of low-key hostilities over territorial disputes. Indeed, such was the lack of military employment for Colleoni and his mercenaries that he was on occasion even allowed to offer his services elsewhere, when requested, to settle military disputes that did not involve the Republic. Venice was more than pleased with its loyal *condottiere*, who would now command the Republic's army for more than twenty years.

Colleoni never showed himself to be the most talented *condottiere* hired by Venice. Carmagnola, Sforza and Piccinino – all of whom commanded the Venetian army at certain periods during the long decades of the war with Milan, and under all of whom Colleoni served – had the opportunity to demonstrate that they were military leaders of the highest quality. Despite this, Colleoni would show himself capable of outwitting each one of them when the opportunity presented itself. And although he was a *condottiere*, and thus could not be expected to display unreserved loyalty, he never proved downright treacherous – something that certainly could not have been said of Carmagnola, Sforza or Piccinino, each of whom had their own reasons for owing a deeper loyalty to Milan than to Venice, even when they were in the service of the Republic.

In a way, Colleoni was unlucky: he was a generation younger than his great contemporaries (apart from the lucky opportunist Sforza), and thus never had full command of an army at any of the decisive engagements that took place during the long Lombardy War. Consequently he won no major battle, as Carmagnola did at Maclodio, yet his skill and imagination in many minor engagements indicated that he might (given the opportunity and luck so necessary for any military commander) have shown himself to be at least the equal of his illustrious peers.

During his later years Colleoni grew to love his time in Venice, softening his rough-and-ready military ways and adapting to the more sophisticated social life of the city. He maintained a fine residence in Venice itself, but also spent much of his time out at his estate at Malpaga, on the banks of the River Serio, just south of his birthplace, Bergamo. It was as if his life had come full circle. Finally, in his seventies, he retired permanently to his estate at Malpaga, regarded by all as a respected Venetian figure. (Now that Bergamo had become part of Venetian mainland territory he could even claim to be a Venetian citizen.) When he eventually died at Malpaga on 3 November 1475 his body was carried back to Venice, where it lay in state. At his funeral the people of Venice lined the streets watching the procession, which was led by 200 men bearing torches; Colleoni's coffin was followed by his favourite charger draped in black cloth emblazoned in gold with his personal device.

Colleoni had been popular with the people of Venice, and their adopted son would reward this with gratitude. He had died without a male heir to inherit his possessions, and in his will he bequeathed his considerable fortune of 216,000 ducats, as well as the equivalent of three times this amount in properties and estates, to the Republic. There was but one stipulation: in return for his generous gift he wished to have a statue of himself mounted on his favourite charger erected in the Piazza San Marco. This caused consternation: no one in the long history of Venice had yet received the honour of having a statue erected in the Piazza San Marco, which did not even contain a statue of Christ, or even San Marco himself, let alone any of the city's most illustrious doges. And here was a mere *condottiere*, who strictly speaking was not even a Venetian by birth, requesting this ultimate accolade. On the other hand, his request was very difficult to refuse, especially after the Council of Ten had replenished the city's empty exchequer with Colleoni's timely bequest, which in the final count had contained assets and holdings equivalent to almost 700,000 ducats.

In 1479 a large bronze equestrian statue of Colleoni was duly commissioned from the most accomplished sculptor of the early Renaissance, the Florentine Andrea del Verrocchio, who would in time prove a major influence on both Leonardo da Vinci and Michelangelo. The forty-four-year-old Verrochio was at the height of his powers, and excelled himself by producing a thirteen-foot-high model of Colleoni astride his horse, the like of which none had seen before. The fact that the horse had its right foreleg imperiously raised, which meant that the weighty bronze bulk of the horse and his rider would be supported by just the three narrow points of the horse's hooves, presented a problem of balance and casting such as had never before been attempted on such a scale. Yet the horse's raised foreleg was more than just a feat of technical bravado. The pose struck by the horse, combined with the magnificent pride and power of its armoured rider, was topped by Colleoni's helmeted head with its daunting expression of ferocity and hauteur. Here indeed was the very image of a man who had fearlessly served and protected the Republic, a public monument exemplary of Venice's pride and standing throughout Italy and beyond. Ironically such a monument to individuality would have been anathema to the very authorities who were commissioning it, had its subject been alive. As it was, the statue would come to be seen as an unmistakable manifestation that the Renaissance spirit had now arrived in Venice; here was a work of art that was the very embodiment of humanist pride.

Once the statue was completed, the Council of Ten was then faced with the vexed question of where to place it. Colleoni had quite plainly stated that he wished his statue to be erected in the Piazza San Marco, but this was ruled out of the question. However, after much debate the Council came up with a characteristically devious solution. Instead of placing the statue in the piazza opposite the Basilica di San Marco, it could be erected in more unobtrusive surroundings some 500 yards to the north, opposite the *Scuola* di San Marco – where it stands to this day. Once again, a version of honour had been satisfied; and the Council of Ten could feel justified in accepting Colleoni's munificent gift replenishing the Republic's empty exchequer.

The Republic's finances had never fully recovered from the expenses of the mainland war, but meanwhile the decline in eastern trade following the fall of Constantinople continued. Although the mainland provinces now contributed around 50,000 ducats to the exchequer, this did not even cover its running expenses, to say nothing of the interest rates it was meant to be paying on its debts, in the form of government bonds at 5 per cent. Meanwhile administrative expenses were severely cut back: all civil servants with salaries of more than twenty-five ducats had their salaries slashed by between 50 and 60 per cent. Senators, members of committees and the Council of Ten and even the doge himself were not immune from such measures. Further funds were raised by 'anticipating' taxes, often calculated by means of exaggerated 'estimates', which wealthier citizens had no alternative but to pay.

Yet ironically, although the municipality's finances were in a parlous state, and several well-known noble families had suffered bankruptcy through the decline in trade, many other nobles and merchants had continued to prosper. Trade may have declined, but it had done so from a position of considerable strength. In the eastern Mediterranean, despite its difficulties Venice still had a virtual monopoly on trade to Europe, with transalpine commerce and shipping to the North Sea continuing to prove lucrative for those involved. Central Venice – from the Rialto down the Grand Canal to San Marco and the Riva degli Schiavoni – still had all the bustle and appearance of one of the most prosperous cities in Europe, while the behaviour and attire of its private citizens only seemed to confirm this picture. Once again, this image of Venice echoed its physical contradictions: here was a city that appeared to float on water.

Colleoni's bequest had proved a godsend to the administration, even though he himself had not been fully aware of how much it had meant to the Republic's finances. Not being a member of the civil administration, he was not cognisant with its innermost economic secrets. Indeed, he had in fact suggested that his assets be used to finance a full-scale war against the Ottoman Empire. Despite Venice's attempts to come to a commercial modus vivendi with Mehmet II, the policy of appeasement was proving a very one-sided affair. For the time being, it was in Ottoman interests to allow the Venetians to trade with both their own expanding Ottoman empire in the eastern Mediterranean as well as with the further ports of the Levant. The Venetians may have had the commercial expertise, but it was the Ottomans who could sever such trade links whenever they chose. Furthermore, all the indications seemed to suggest that one of the central ambitions of Mehmet II's policy was no less than the conquest of Venice itself.

In fact, by the time of Colleoni's death in 1475, the Ottoman army was advancing rapidly north through Dalmatia, to such an extent that the following year Venice itself did indeed stand in peril. At night, from the top of the Campanile, the camp fires of the advanced scouting patrols of the Ottoman army could be seen burning in the darkness from the nearby hills. Even with Colleoni's gift, Venice could not afford a full-scale war. Things were so bad that by now even the patriotic *Arsenalotti* were becoming restless because they were owed so much in back-wages. So Venice sued for peace, and in 1479 a treaty was signed in which Venice submitted to the most humiliating terms. The Republic would be permitted to continue trading in the eastern Mediterranean, but it would be forced to surrender Negropont, its major trading colony in the Aegean, as well as all its remaining ports on the Greek mainland. In return, Mehmet II surprisingly allowed Venice to re-establish the merchant colony in Constantinople that it had lost during the war, thus enabling it to continue trading links with certain Ottoman ports in the Black Sea and on the Anatolian mainland. But the cost of this privilege was to be an annual payment of 10,000 ducats.

During such periods of peace between the Ottoman Empire and Venice in the latter half of the fifteenth century relations between the two powers extended much further than trade. After the signing of the peace treaty in 1479, Sultan Mehmet II went so far as to send a high-ranking Turkish delegation to Venice with the intention of negotiating a wide-ranging cultural exchange. Despite the Islamic ban on painted images, Mehmet had developed a deep interest in European art, dating back to his early encounter with Byzantine icons and the mosaics of Hagia Sophia after the fall of

Constantinople. In the past, Mehmet had been introduced to Florentine examples of Renaissance art, which had so entranced him that he determined to import Italian artists to his court. As a consequence, the high-ranking delegation to Venice in 1479 specifically asked for the services of *'un bon pytor'* ('a good painter'). Whereupon the Great Council voted to send to the sultan the painter Gentile Bellini, who was ordered to fulfil the role of both painter and cultural ambassador. Bellini was not only regarded as the finest painter in Venice at this time, but had also long cultivated a deep interest in all things Eastern. A quarter of a century previously, when in his twenties, he had followed the work of the Byzantine artists who had taken up residence in the city after the fall of Constantinople.*

On arrival at the sultan's court in the newly built palace of Topkapi, overlooking the Bosphorus, Bellini appears to have established an immediate rapport with Mehmet II. The Venetian artist and the sultan seem to have recognised each other as kindred souls, at least with regard to their interest in foreign cultures. Bellini's interest in the East had almost certainly led him to learn Greek, and his friends amongst the Byzantine scholars may even have passed on to him a smattering of Turkish and Arabic. Mehmet II, for his part, is known to have mastered eight languages before the age of twenty-one; these included Persian, Hebrew, Arabic and even French. Bellini eagerly immersed himself in his exotic new surroundings and was soon producing a succession of meticulously observed drawings of the figures he encountered – including soldiers from the sultan's personal guard of Janissaries, men in kaftans and cloaks, court officials with their heads swathed in enormous turbans (the size of turban was an indication of rank), and even depicting exotically clad, but unveiled local women (though many experts are of the opinion that these must have been indigenous Greeks). His other works are said to have included a meticulous map of

* The city was now officially known by the Turks as Kostantiniyye, but was still for the most part widely called Constantinople (in Greek *Constantinopolis*). Its present name of Istanbul derives from the Greek *eis stin poli* (meaning 'to the city'), which was used well before the fall of Constantinople, and was in fact a current Greek term for an urban centre throughout the Aegean region, originating as a reply to the greeting 'Where are you going?' The name Istanbul gradually grew in popular usage during the centuries of Ottoman rule, but was not officially designated as the name of the city until after the founding of the present Turkish Republic in 1923.

Constantinople, as well as a panorama of Venice drawn from memory for Mehmet II himself. Other demands by the sultan included a series of erotic drawings, as well as Christian scenes from the Bible. One of these was said to have depicted the beheaded St John the Baptist, though when Mehmet saw it he objected that St John's executed head was in fact faulty, as the severed neck simply did not expose the innards the way Bellini had painted it. Mehmet then demonstrated this to Bellini by beckoning for a slave and having him summarily beheaded before them.

This incident doubtless focused Bellini's concentration when he came to paint Mehmet II's portrait, which he is said to have done several times, though only one of these has survived and today hangs in the National Gallery in London. According to its inscription, it was completed on 25 November 1480,* and shows the fearsome 'Mehmet the Conqueror' to have possessed a surprisingly mild-mannered appearance, though the fixed distant gaze of his eyes gives an indication of his determination.

According to the contemporary Italian historian Giovanni Angiolello, who was attached to the sultan's court, Bellini's relationship with Mehmet II was 'unique in its intimacy'; no Islamic ruler of the period had such a close friendship with anyone working in his employ. Indeed, during the late years of Mehmet's reign a law was passed which expressly decreed that any intimacy between the sultan and his subjects was to be regarded as derogatory to the majesty of their ruler, and was to be punished as such. As a result of their closeness, Mehmet offered to grant Bellini any wish he desired. Possibly on account of his fear of the sultan, after his arbitrary slaughter of the slave, Bellini asked to be allowed to return to his native Venice. Mehmet II graciously consented to this wish, and before Bellini departed he was elevated to the nobility and presented with a solid gold chain inscribed with the sultan's name, his honorific and all his titles (according to Giorgio Vasari, writing just over half a century later, this chain 'weighed the equivalent of 250 golden ducats'). Mehmet also gave Bellini an effusive letter of recommendation, bestowing upon him further honours, including that of 'golden knight' and 'palace companion', going

---

* Sic; this must have been dated by the artist, rather than his prestigious sultan, who would have used the Islamic calendar.

on to praise his 'miraculous' artistic abilities and referring to him as 'one of the most select and intimate members of the household' – praise indeed from a man who had eight wives and maintained an extensive harem.

This letter was dated 15 January 1481, and it appears that Bellini departed for Venice soon after this. Just a few months later, in early May, Mehmet II, in his late fifties and suffering from gout, succumbed to his ailment. Despite all that Mehmet the Conqueror had achieved for the Ottoman Empire – his expansion in the Balkans, Anatolia and the Crimea, as well as his administrative reforms – many amongst the religious faction were outraged by his close relationship with Western Christians such as Bellini, his glorification of his hero Alexander the Great, and his cavalier attitude towards such Islamic strictures as the ban on images.

Mehmet was succeeded by his son, Bejazit II, who immediately reined in Mehmet II's expansionist military policy and instituted a more strict observance of Islamic law. Bejazit ordered many of his father's imagistic treasures, including his portrait by Bellini, to be removed from the Topkapi Palace and sold off in the bazaar. Resident Venetian merchants were quick to snap up these bargains, whereupon they were shipped back to Europe – which accounts for Bellini's portrait of one of the greatest Ottoman sultans being now on display in London rather than Istanbul.

Meanwhile the Ottomans continued to advance. In the very year that Mehmet signed the peace treaty with Venice, the Ottoman army simply occupied all the major Ionian islands except Corfu. This left the Turks in virtual control of the entrance to the Adriatic. Yet the true purpose behind this move remained unforeseen. Early in 1480 Turkish troops landed unopposed in the heel of Italy, laying waste to the countryside of Apulia and seizing the city of Otranto in the kingdom of Naples. Amidst scenes of mayhem the citizens of Otranto were either slaughtered or shipped back across the Adriatic into slavery. Spectacular acts of savagery included the building of a pyramid of skulls in the main square, and a public spectacle in which the Bishop of Otranto and the local commander were sawn in half.

During the quarter-century since the Peace of Lodi, Venice had remained for the most part unpopular throughout Italy, with its fellow states jealous of its power and perceived riches. Besides occupying the largest territory in northern Italy, it also had a trading empire in the eastern Mediterranean, commercial links across the Alps, galley trading routes to the North Sea, and its explorer Alvise Cadamosto had recently discovered the Cape Verde Islands and sailed as far round West Africa as the River Gambia. Even in the face of a Turkish invasion of the Italian mainland, initially it was only hatred of Venice that united the states of Italy. The ludicrous extent of this anti-Venetian sentiment can be seen from the response of King Ferrante I of Naples to the invasion of Otranto, which was in fact part of his territory. Upon hearing of the invasion, he immediately claimed that this was an aggressive act against Naples by Venice, whose recent peace talks with the Turks had in reality been nothing more than an act of treachery against his kingdom.

The Ottoman occupation of Otranto was nothing less than a beachhead for a more serious march on Rome, where the sultan intended to declare himself emperor, and then set about reconquering the entire European region that had once constituted the western half of the Roman Empire. Pope Sixtus IV himself surmised this, but he was hardly in a position to inspire Italy to attempt another holy-league crusade. Since his accession to the papal throne nine years previously he had ceaselessly intrigued with various Italian states in the furtherance of nepotistic ambitions for his nephews. Just two years previously there had been a plot to assassinate Lorenzo de' Medici, the ruler of Florence; in the aftermath of the plot's failure, Sixtus IV's leading role in the affair had become evident to all. Few Italian rulers now trusted him, and he knew that democratic Venice would certainly not break the peace treaty that it had signed with the Ottomans just a year before. With good reason, Sixtus IV knew himself to be perilously exposed if Mehmet II decided on a rapid march to Rome, and even made arrangements for the papal court to withdraw from the city.

Fortunately, Sixtus was spared by the death of Mehmet, and by his successor Sultan Bejazit II's decision against continuing a policy of rapid and reckless expansion, preferring instead a period of consolidation and coexistence (especially with Venice). The majority of the Turkish garrison was withdrawn from Otranto, and the Neapolitan army soon retook the city. For the time being, it appeared that the Italian mainland was safe.

8

The Venetian Queen of Cyprus

D
ESPITE OTTOMAN ENCROACHMENT eastwards along the Anatolian coast towards Cilicia and Syria, the key to commerce between Europe and the eastern Mediterranean remained Cyprus. This strategically located island provided protection for shipping seeking access to the lucrative trade routes in spices and luxury goods that extended from China and India to Damascus, Beirut, up the Red Sea and across the Suez isthmus, and to Alexandria. Venice had long retained trading bases in the major ports of Cyprus, and several noble Venetian families even owned large estates on the island, though there still remained a rivalry with the Genoese, who also owned sizeable estates. Cyprus was ruled by the Frankish Lusignan dynasty, whose ancestor Guy de Lusignan had been sold the island by Richard I of England in 1192 and immediately declared himself king. Since then several powers, including the Genoese, the Venetians and the Mamelukes (rulers of Syria and Egypt), had sought at various times to assert a controlling influence over the island, but with little lasting success – though Cyprus did in fact remain a tributary state of the Mamelukes. Over the centuries the Lusignan kings of Cyprus had also briefly become king of Jerusalem and then, even more briefly, ruler of the Armenian kingdom of Cilicia, which occupied the north-eastern shore of the Mediterranean opposite Cyprus. As a result, the Lusignan kings of Cyprus continued to refer to themselves as the 'King of Cyprus, Jerusalem and Armenia' – despite the redundancy of the last two titles.

By the latter half of the fifteenth century the King of Cyprus (and of Jerusalem and Armenia) was the young James II, an illegitimate member of the Lusignan line who in 1460 had ousted the rightful heir, his sister

Charlotte. Together with her husband, Louis of Savoy, she had fled to take refuge in the Genoese-held castle of Kyrenia, on the north coast, which was then subjected to a siege by James. However, after three years Charlotte and Louis had managed to escape, finally reaching Rome, where they had begun trying to recruit allies willing to invade the island and reinstate them on the throne. James II, or James the Bastard as he became widely known (both on factual and pejorative grounds), was in his early twenties and was hardly a popular monarch, on account of his wilfulness of character and his philandering amongst the wives and daughters of the island's rich landowners. Yet this behaviour was grudgingly tolerated, largely because the landowners knew that without the Lusignan monarchy the island was liable to fall into the hands of an international power, which would quickly dispossess them of their large estates.

James II, for his part, was also well aware of the vulnerability of Cyprus to foreign invasion and decided to turn to Venice for support. The Republic had welcomed this opportunity to gain influence over the island, which they had long sought to absorb into their empire. An alliance was quickly agreed and reinforced by persuading the twenty-eight-year-old James to accept as his queen the fourteen-year-old Caterina, daughter of the noble Venetian Marco Cornaro.* The Cornaro family had long had close associations with Cyprus – Caterina's uncle, Andrea Cornaro, being one of the island's largest landowners, with extensive sugar-cane estates. At the same time, Caterina's mother was of Greek descent, being the granddaughter of Emperor John Comnenos of Trebizond. Thus, as the Venetians were at pains to point out, Caterina was technically speaking of imperial blood, rather than merely royal blood.

Overjoyed by this diplomatic coup, the Venetians were determined to ensure that it was confirmed as soon as possible. As Caterina lived in Venice, the Signoria insisted that the union with James II should be sealed by an immediate marriage by proxy, which took place at Venice on 13 July 1468. The marriage may have been hurriedly arranged for purely political

---

* This family name often appears as 'Corner', as for instance in the several family dwellings in the city named Palazzo Corner (one of which is now the Palazzo Corner-Mocenigo, on the Campo di San Polo).

reasons, but its celebration showed no signs of haste or lack of feeling. This was to be one of those great state occasions at which Venice so excelled. Caterina was led in procession by forty wives of the city's noblest families from the Palazzo Corner to the nearby landing stage. Here she embarked upon the magnificent *Bucintoro* and was accompanied down the Grand Canal by a flotilla of gondolas, whilst musicians serenaded her and heralds proclaimed the passage of the doge's barge through the centre of the city to the watching crowds along the shore. On arrival at the Molo, Caterina was escorted to the Doge's Palace to the cheers of the onlookers (who had witnessed nothing like this: republican Venice had never before staged a coronation, by proxy or otherwise). She was led up the steps to the Great Council Chamber where, before the gathered representatives of the Republic, the actual ceremony took place. Doge Cristoforo Moro presented a gold wedding ring to the Cypriot ambassador, Philip Mistachiel, who as representative of James II slid this onto Caterina's finger in an act of symbolic marriage.

Although Caterina was now formally married, and thus officially 'Queen of Cyprus', the Venetian authorities were so overwhelmed by what was taking place that they took the unprecedented step of bestowing upon her the unique honour of a purely Venetian title concocted for the occasion, that of 'Daughter of San Marco'. (According to a contemporary anecdote this prompted the Bishop of Turin to point out that, according to the Bible, St Mark had not taken a wife and that, had he done so, fathering a daughter aged fourteen at his great age would indeed have been a miraculous feat, even if one quite worthy of a saint.)

Marriage by proxy was not uncommon at the time, especially between members of powerful families, and was in many ways analogous to an engagement – though such was its binding power that to break off such a 'marriage' could cause sufficient offence to provoke a declaration of war. Consequently it was not unusual that Caterina continued living in Venice for the next four years, whilst her husband remained in Cyprus.

As was the custom for a daughter of one of the most prestigious Venetian noble familes (who had already provided one doge, and would go on to provide three more), Caterina had lived a privileged and highly protected life. From birth, she would seldom have left the confines of the Palazzo Corner, and would have been heavily chaperoned whenever she did so.

Caterina's seclusion throughout her childhood precluded the possibility of any private tutor and any real education. Thus, apart from learning the graces and manners of aristocratic family life, she would have acquired few other skills: there was no possibility of instruction in dancing, or the playing of a musical instrument, or even instruction in a language (although she may well have acquired some Greek from her mother). Despite this, according to her biographer, Leto Severis: 'While still a child, Caterina gave signs of a dynamic character, a well-balanced mind and great intelligence.' Although it is difficult to assess the precise meaning of such qualities, given the historical context, there can be no doubt that she did stand out as in some way exceptional – for she was only the third daughter of the family. At the age of ten she was escorted to the strictly closed convent of St Ursula, at nearby Padua on the mainland, where she was boarded with the nuns, who would have given her a rudimentary religious-based instruction. But most importantly, they would belatedly have taught her to read and write.

When Caterina Cornaro emerged at the age of fourteen for the great public procession in the *Bucintoro* down the Grand Canal for her proxy marriage at the Doge's Palace, she would have been stepping onto the stage of a public world she could only have known about from tales and gossip – a world she had barely seen, let alone experienced in any social sense. Even her clothes would have been a novelty: at home and in the convent, like girls of all classes, she would have been plainly dressed, whereas for such a ceremony she would have been decked out in all the finery her family (and the Republic) could provide. A drawing of this event, done many years later by the artist G.L. Gatteri, who would certainly have been cognisant with the customary adornment for such an occasion, depicts the bride in a sumptuous full-length wedding dress whose resplendent train is supported by two pageboys. Although she would undoubtedly have been rehearsed for this event, all are said to have marvelled at Caterina's poise and beauty. The Cypriot ambassador, acting as proxy for James II, wrote back to his king, 'Her beautiful wide dark eyes shone like stars, her long blond, abundant hair seemed to be made of gold, and her handsome features and noble stature easily betrayed her noble origins.'

Back in Cyprus, James the Bastard showed no great enthusiasm for having his bride brought home to him. Months passed, and then years, and still he despatched no bridal flotilla; meanwhile the Venetian authorities bided their time patiently. The prize was too great to lose. However, James was in fact still engaged in widespread diplomatic activity, in the hope of attracting a more powerful ally, or combination of allies, to ensure his continued rule. Envoys with inviting offers had been despatched to all available sources: these included the Emir of Karamania (which occupied the Anatolian coast north of Cyprus), and later Mehmet II when his Ottoman army had overthrown the emir. Other offers had been sent to the Mameluke Sultan of Egypt, to the Genoese and to King Ferrante I of Naples (who had replied suggesting a proxy marriage to one of his illegitimate daughters, who was nonetheless a princess of the royal house of Naples).

Venetian diplomats had soon overheard rumours of these negotiations, reports of which were duly carried back to the Council of Ten, which remained wary, but nonetheless recognised them for what they were – the frantic and feeble attempts of a weak ruler to play any potential conquerors off against each other. Eventually the Senate conveyed to James II an official letter, whose contents demonstrated just how far their diplomatic expertise had advanced since the inept blunders of its early forays into Europe just over a century previously.

The letter opened by assuring the king how pleased and honoured the Republic was to be so closely linked with his royal highness and his island kingdom. This link was made all the more precise by the fact that it had been celebrated in such a solemn marriage ceremony, in the presence of representatives of all the noble families of Venice. In consequence, the Republic regarded this as so much more than the union between a single Venetian family (be it ever so noble) and the royal house of Lusignan – it was a union that involved the entire aristocracy of Venice. Indeed, to emphasise this point Caterina herself had been elevated to the unique rank of 'Daughter of San Marco', thus becoming a child of the city itself.

However, the Senate wished to inform his majesty that rumours had been reaching Venice that he might be contemplating a marriage contract with some other princess. In all likelihood this was the usual sort of idle gossip that frequently circulated amongst the courts of Italy. Yet should such a contract be signed, it would not only be taken as a gross insult to Caterina and all the noble families who had partaken in her marriage ceremony, but would also be seen as an aggressive act against the Republic itself. Such empty gossip should not be allowed to persist, and in order to preserve the honour and dignity of his majesty and his bride Caterina, as well as all others concerned, it was behoven upon the king to despatch with the utmost haste a flotilla of his ships to Venice to collect his bride and take her to her rightful home in Cyprus.

By now the people of Cyprus were becoming increasingly fearful of the political situation in the eastern Mediterranean. As well as advancing east along the southern Anatolian coastline, the Turkish army had completed the conquest of Greece by overrunning the Peloponnese, causing the indigenous Greek population of Cyprus to feel increasingly encircled by the menacing Ottoman presence. In consequence, they were keen for their foreign rulers and landlords to take action. Threatened by the withdrawal of Venetian support, James had no alternative but to send at once for his queen, and Caterina once more emerged from her family palace to be transported on the *Bucintoro* in a grand procession down the Grand Canal to the awaiting flotilla of four Venetian war galleys and three lesser galleys from the Cypriot navy. The doge conducted a formal farewell ceremony at the Molo, and contemporary sources describe the onlookers as being awed by Caterina's appearance. During her four years of seclusion the fourteen-year-old girl had grown into a mature eighteen-year-old woman of apparently striking attractiveness. Such fulsome descriptions of her beauty have a note of sycophancy, to say nothing of the authors being carried away by the grandeur of the spectacle and the importance it held for Venice.

The portraits painted of Caterina at this time have been lost. However, the finest portrait we have of the young Caterina was painted some thirty years after her death by Titian, who almost certainly drew on at least one contemporary portrait and possibly some lost drawings made from life. The image he conveys of her is striking indeed, a portrayal of character worthy of his imaginative genius. What we see is the portrait of a young, powerfully built woman, her robust proportions cunningly softened by her sidelong stance. She is dressed in a ruby-red velveteen gown, worn beneath a sumptuously embroidered over-garment whose long, open front collar consists of two twin lines of pearls on gold. On her head she wears a golden coronet studded with jewels and tipped with pearls, her hair modestly drawn back under a diaphanous veil, apart from the formal ringlets of red hair that hang over her forehead from beneath her coronet. Yet none of this magnificence is allowed to distract from the exceptional clarity of her features and overall expression. Caterina was not beautiful; her features appear unblemished, yet distinctly plain. But it is her sideways glance, gazing directly out of the picture, that is most revealing. Her expression is wary, uncertain almost, yet somehow manages to convey an inner strength that sits well with her powerful build. Mutely she is expressing the apprehensive feelings that must have been experienced by so many brides of the time, and of years to come. She is at once demure and determined. Here is a brave young woman of sufficient character not to be cowed by the absolutely unknown future that awaits her. And what a future this would prove to be.

On 10 November 1472, under the command of the Venetian captain General Pietro Mocenigo, Caterina's combined flotilla sailed for Cyprus, arriving at Famagusta some weeks later. Owing to its strategic position on the main trade routes still operating between Europe and the Levant, Famagusta was on its way to becoming the wealthiest city in the entire eastern Mediterranean (a fact that would prompt Shakespeare to make it the setting for *Othello*). In December a truly royal marriage ceremony was held at the Cathedral of St Nicholas in Famagusta. Surprisingly, James II and Caterina seem to have taken to each other at first sight and it was soon obvious to all that theirs was a love-match. Queen Caterina was welcomed by the Venetian gentry, and her Greek ancestry ensured that she was also popular with the indigenous population. However, despite the royal palace being home to the new lovers, not all was sweetness and light there, for it was also home to three of James's illegitimate children, Eugene, John and Carla, as well as his mother Marietta of Patras, who had been his father's mistress. All of these incumbents resented Caterina, regarding her as a foreign intruder. Marietta refused to be replaced as ruler of the royal household and presented a fearsome figure: the previous king's wife had bitten off her nose in a fit of jealousy prompted by the affair that had produced James the Bastard, causing her to be nicknamed Marietta *comomutena* (crop-nosed).

As a major landowner, Caterina's uncle Andrea Cornaro had long been a leading counsellor and close friend of James II – indeed, to such an extent that the young king's extravagant behaviour had left him deeply in debt to Cornaro, who had been instrumental in arranging the king's marriage to his niece. Despite this, Cornaro's advice had proved of little effect during the four long years after the proxy wedding in Venice, for James had also listened to counsellors representing Neapolitan, papal, Genoese and other interests, all of whom had encouraged him to send emissaries far and wide in the search for powerful protective allies. But now that Caterina had arrived and been crowned as queen, Andrea Cornaro's influence took on a more significant aspect. It was he who persuaded James to allow Captain-General Mocenigo to conduct his fleet on an extended tour of the island's coastline, repairing its defences and building up the castles that guarded its main harbours.

This task also had a hidden pretext, for news soon spread over the Mediterranean that no less than the Captain-General of Venice had a fleet patrolling the coast of Cyprus, causing all rivals to be apprehensive about attempting any surprise invasion with the intention of taking over the island during this period of uncertainty. On the other hand, the local Venetian landowners also became apprehensive concerning the presence of Mocenigo's fleet. They had long wished for an independent Cyprus, loosely allied to Venice, which would guarantee their protection in time of need. It now became clear to them that Venice had no such loose alliance in mind; it wished to impose its own direct rule upon the island – a move that would have deprived the local Venetian gentry of their considerable autonomy. At the same time, despite the reassurances of his counsellor, Andrea Cornaro, James II also became aware of what was happening. Taking matters into his own hands, in April 1473 he impetuously ordered all Venetian galleys to disembark from the port of Famagusta within two hours or they would be destroyed by the cannon lining the ramparts of the harbour fortress. From now on Venetian warships would only be permitted to put in at the minor port of Paphos, some seventy miles away at the western end of the island. For the time being, it appeared that the covert Venetian strategy had been thwarted.

Meanwhile James and Caterina remained happily in love, and there was great rejoicing in the spring of 1473 when it became known that she was pregnant. Even so, despite being enamoured of his queen, James II was loath to abandon his bachelor habits for a life of daily government business and domestic routine in the royal palace at Nicosia. He continued his philandering ways, and frequently departed for lengthy hunting expeditions in the wooded countryside outside Famagusta. In late June 1473, James and his companions, accompanied as usual by his friend Andrea Cornaro, set out on yet another hunting trip to Famagusta. Days later a royal messsenger galloped into the palace courtyard and went immediately to inform the queen that her husband had taken ill and was dying. Despite being at least six months pregnant, Caterina insisted upon setting out at once on the thirty-mile trip to see her husband. By the time she arrived in Famagusta, her husband was fading fast – his physicians announced that he had contracted a severe bout of dysentery, but some were secretly convinced that he had been poisoned. Also at his bedside were Andrea Cornaro and the Venetian Captain-General Mocenigo, who by fortuitous coincidence had been sailing nearby and had immediately put ashore, ostensibly to offer his protection to the ailing king and his queen. However, James II had already delegated the official role of protector of himself, his queen and their future offspring to the two friends he trusted above all others – namely, Cornaro and his old schoolfriend and fellow hunter, the Sicilian Rizzo di Marino, who had also become his close political adviser. With his last energies James now dictated his will: this decreed that Queen Caterina was to be the legal heir to the throne of Cyprus. If their child was male, he would be the next in line. Should both mother and child die in childbirth, the next in line to the throne would be James' three illegitimate children, Eugene, John and Carla. Just nine days after being struck down by his mysterious illness James II died in the early hours of 7 July.

The suspicion that he had been poisoned was widespread. But who was to blame? He certainly had enemies, especially amongst the cuckolded Venetian gentry and several noble fathers whose daughters' virginity he had violated. But in this case there appeared to be a deeper purpose unfolding. The obvious culprits were the Venetians, and even Caterina was not sure how far she could now trust her compatriots. She had become involved in she knew not what. There were two other serious suspects. Some months before James had died he had been approached by an envoy from King Ferrante I of Naples, with a request that his illegitimate ten-year-old son, Alonzo of Aragon, should become engaged to James's own illegitimate young daughter Carla, a request to which he had given serious considera- tion, naively thinking that an alliance with Naples might prove a useful counterbalance to Venetian influence. In fact, it was evident that Naples still retained designs on Cyprus. Second, and equally suspect, was James II's deposed sister Charlotte and her husband Louis of Savoy, who were still plotting to regain their throne, seeking the powerful backing of the pope and Milan.

On 28 August 1473 Caterina gave birth to a son, who was quickly baptised in Famagusta Cathedral, where he was publicly proclaimed as the future James III. The infant proved sickly from birth, and Caterina devoted herself to ensuring that he survived what had always been the most dangerous months in a child's life, aided by her personal physician who was in attend- ance at all times. In order to protect Caterina, and Cyprus, the Venetian Senate ordered Captain-General Mocenigo to renew his patrol of Cypriot waters with increased vigilance. But the threat, when it came, was from the land. The islanders, growing tired of increasing Venetian control over their officials, launched a coup, led by the Archbishop of Nicosia, Louis Fabregues, and supported by the treacherous Rizzo di Marino. In the early hours of 13 November the conspirators and a band of their supporters were secretly let into the royal palace at Famagusta and burst into the queen's apartments, where they slashed to death her physician and her chamberlain as the queen protected her baby in terror.

The conspirators then raged through the other rooms of the royal apartments, where they discovered Andrea Cornaro and his son, who were both hacked to death, their naked bodies thrown from an upper window into the moat below (where they were to be devoured by scavenging dogs). Only now did the hidden purpose of the plot emerge. It had not been entirely prompted by the anti-Venetian feelings of the indigenous population, but had mainly been encouraged by King Ferrante I of Naples. Archbishop Fabregues and Rizzo di Marino now threatened Caterina, forcing her to consent to the engagement of James II's illegitimate daughter Carla to King Ferrante I's illegitimate son Alonzo of Aragon, at the same time recognising Alonzo as the legitimate heir.to the throne of Cyprus, thus effectively disinheriting her own son and allowing Cyprus to pass from the Venetian sphere of influence into the hands of Naples. The archbishop now demanded that Caterina hand over to him the royal seal and took over as de facto ruler of Cyprus, at the same time making sure that his rule at least seemed to be sanctioned by Caterina, who was always made to appear at his side in public. Her cooperation was ensured by the fact that the infant James III was taken from her and placed under the care of her quasi-mother-in-law, the fearsome Marietta *comomutena*.

When news of the coup reached Venice, the Senate decided that the time for diplomacy was over. Captain-General Mocenigo was despatched with a fleet of galleys with orders to restore Queen Caterina to her rightful role as ruler of Cyprus. As soon as the Venetian fleet arrived off Famagusta, Archbishop Fabregues fled for Naples and Rizzo di Marino managed to escape to Egypt. Others who had held positions in the archbishop's admin- istration were less fortunate. Whether they had been rewarded for actively supporting the coup, or were simply local administrators (of Greek or Venetian origin) who had merely remained at their posts, they were removed from office, disgraced and in many cases summarily executed.

Venice had no wish to disguise the fact that it had now assumed control over the governance of Cyprus, and two specially created counsellors were despatched to 'assist' the administration. In principle, as reigning monarch, Queen Caterina had first to approve any action advocated by the two counsellors. In practice, it was very much the other way round. All of Queen Caterina's wishes had first of all to be vetted by the two counsel- lors, who soon began issuing orders of their own in her name. Initially Caterina was appeased by the return of her infant son James III, who was removed from the care of Marietta of Patras. Marietta and James II's three children, Eugene, John and Carla, were then transported to a closed convent in Padua 'for the purposes of education'. Queen Caterina was overjoyed by the return of her son, but just two days short of his first birthday, on

26 August 1474, he died under circumstances that have never plausibly been explained. Once again Caterina was distraught, and by now she had no hesitation in blaming Venice for the death of both her husband and her child. The Republic appeared determined that there should be no continuation of the royal line, yet she had sufficient political acumen to realise that her own life was probably not in danger, so long as there remained another royal pretender to the throne, in the form of James II's sister Charlotte, and the potential of a claim from Naples.

Queen Caterina now considered herself very much a Cypriot, her sympathies lying with both the Venetian gentry and the indigenous Greeks, all of whom resented the interference and virtual takeover by the Republic. Unfortunately these Cypriots did not reciprocate her feelings, now being firmly convinced that Caterina was in fact nothing more than a Venetian puppet. To all intents and purposes she was indeed just this; and to make matters worse, her despair was such that she withdrew from public view altogether, retiring to her room and refusing entry to all but her trusted lady-in-waiting, Vera de Giblet. This played into the hands of the two counsellors, who now simply took over the entire administration, without even paying lip-service to Queen Caterina. Although remaining titular head of state, she was now confined like a prisoner and denied all contact with the outside world. She was deprived of any luxuries, her room being furnished with none but the bare essentials and her meals reduced to the plainest fare.

9

The End of the Queen

IRONICALLY, A SOMEWHAT similar diminution of power was just beginning in Venice, although it had not reached, and never would reach, the privations inflicted upon Queen Caterina. The power of the doge was starting to be eroded in favour of the Council of Ten. Over the years an increasing number of restrictions would be placed upon the doge's power. Of necessity, the highest office in the Republic had always required certain restrictions, all aimed at preventing the quasi-democratic rule by the noble families from degenerating from an oligarchy to an autocracy in the hands of one or two families, or even into a dictatorship – a fear that was, as we have seen, well founded. Initial restrictions were tightened: personally the doge was not allowed to hold property outside the city, his family was forced to withdraw from all commercial activity (which could often result in a severe reduction of status for his name); whilst politically he was not permitted to open or sign any despatches without others being present. Although he may have been elected for life, and have lived in circumstances of some luxury in the Doge's Palace at the heart of the Republic's government, his role over the coming centuries would gradually become more and more ceremonial.

Venice may no longer have been ruled – or perhaps, more accurately, 'presided over' – by the doge; on the other hand, he still retained an executive role in the powerful Council of Ten, of which he was the only permanent member. The others, consisting of his six signory and three leading senators, all had to be elected, usually on an annual basis, thus ensuring that Venice could never become a collective autocracy, let alone a personal dictatorship. Other checks and balances ensured that no doge could be succeeded by a member of his family; at the same time no outgoing member of the Council of Ten could be eligible for re-election until two years after leaving office. Even so, the powerful leading families were now gaining increasing control of the city. In line with such measures taken to avoid the concentration of power, all other offices continued to be elected on a regular basis, and this was certainly the case with the two counsellors who had been appointed to rule in the name of the Republic in distant Cyprus. On their arrival in 1474, they had been accompanied by the queen's father, Marco Cornaro, who had been briefed to encourage his daughter to cooperate with the current arrangements. However, when he was ushered in to see his daughter he was horrified. Isolated, and probably in a state of recovery from a nervous breakdown, her appearance had deteriorated. The bright and spirited young girl he had known just two years previously had aged into a distressed woman, who appeared to be living in a state of poverty unthinkable for a member of such a distinguished Venetian noble family. Her face was pale, her clothes in tatters, and she was being fed on what appeared to be scraps.

Marco Cornaro persuaded his daughter to write a letter outlining the injustice and disgrace of her present role, which she had only undertaken in the service of the Republic. This he then covertly removed from her cell and, on his return to Venice, personally delivered to Pietro Mocenigo, who had now become doge, a reward for his services to the Republic in the gaining of Cyprus. However, Doge Mocenigo did little to relieve Caterina's plight, either because of his own feelings concerning the Cyprus situation or because he was prevented from doing so by the Council of Ten. Her material situation improved slightly, but her political power remained non-existent.

Paradoxically, the public perception of Queen Caterina amongst Cypriots now began to undergo a transformation. Despite de facto Venetian rule, by imprisoning Caterina the Venetians had indicated to her subjects where her sympathies lay. Consequently, the islanders now firmly regarded Caterina as their own queen. Although the Venetians continued to maintain a strong hold over the island itself, this did not deter international ambitions towards its territory in the years to come. For example, on reaching Egypt, the Sicilian Rizzo di Marino had continued to plot on behalf of the Neapolitan claim to the throne of Cyprus. After ingratiating himself with the Mameluke ruler Sultan Qaitbay, he had then travelled to Naples, returning with the seventeen-year-old Alonzo of Aragon. Rizzo di Marino's daring plan was to kidnap Carla from Padua, so that she could marry Alonzo of Aragon, thus enabling Naples to lay a direct claim to the throne of Cyprus.

However, along with its growing power, the Venetian Council of Ten was also cultivating a growing expertise in how to maintain such power. This had involved creating an ever-expanding network of spies throughout the city, a network that had soon been extended along its trading networks throughout the Mediterranean. As the meticulous court records show, thanks to such spies fewer commercial galley captains now risked secretly smuggling in luxury goods at the private request of the powerful noble patrons financing their legal cargoes. A trade that had once been widespread and had proved highly lucrative for all concerned was now liable to result in ruinous fines, the dungeons or long spells in the galleys.

Such international intelligence-gathering was soon working hand-in-hand with Venetian diplomatic representatives in foreign states and ports, and it was not long before the Council of Ten learned of Rizzo di Marino's plan. It is uncertain whether Carla herself had been informed of what was happening; what is certain is that Carla, in good health and still in her late twenties, was discovered dead in her convent cell on the morning of 24 June 1480.

This may have disposed of a potential Neapolitan claim to Cyprus, at least for the time being, but the Venetian takeover of the island remained under threat from the deposed Queen Charlotte, who was backed by the pope and other powerful anti-Venetian Italian allies. In 1472 Charlotte's husband Louis of Savoy had died at Geneva, and from then on her health began to deteriorate, largely owing to the decadent and extravagant lifestyle she pursued in Rome, where she lived under the protection of Innocent VIII. The ailing forty-four-year-old Charlotte had finally died in 1487, but not before bequeathing the sovereignty of Cyprus to the House of Savoy, so that her husband's family could continue to lay rightful claim to the island throne, which had remained an obsession ever since she had been deposed. To emphasise this point, Innocent VIII ordered that her remains be buried in the Chapel of St Andrew within St Peter's in Rome, and on her tomb was inscribed the legend *Karlota Hierusalem Cipri et Armenia Regina* ('Charlotte, Queen of Jerusalem, Cyprus and Armenia'). The claims of the Savoys would persist in the background for many years.

However, during the 1480s a more serious threat to Venetian control of the island now came from the new Ottoman sultan Bejazit II, who gave every indication of wishing to expand his empire further east along the Anatolian shoreline through the former Armenian kingdom of Cilicia and into Syria, with the ultimate aim of conquering Egypt. However, on the few occasions when the Ottoman fleet moved to invade Cyprus from its ports on the Anatolian coast just fifty miles away, it was quickly put to flight by the superior power of the Venetian galleys, which maintained a constant patrol between the northern coast of the island and the mainland. The Venetians had commenced a comprehensive strengthening of the defences around the island's coast, reinforcing the many castles that guarded the ports and employing some of the finest military engineers in Italy for this task. There has long been a legend that Leonardo da Vinci, himself a renowned military architect by this time, was amongst those who contributed to this task. Indeed, there are several indications that Leonardo's visit may be more than just a legend. The renowned Leonardo historian Jean Paul Richter acknowledges that 'between the years of 1481 and 1487 there are unexplained gaps in the chronology'. It seems likely that Leonardo travelled and even visited foreign lands. In his various notebooks there are several passages describing 'The Levant'. Some of them are recognisably second-hand information, others are indisputably imaginary, but several have an unmistakably authentic ring. A notebook in the Royal Library at Windsor explicitly describes how 'departing south from the coast of Cilicia, the beauties of the island of Cyprus hove into view'. Indicating that he may well have travelled around at least part of the island's coastal defences, he describes the many wrecks littering the northern shoreline:

How many vessels have been sunk, how many there are that have been broken on these rocks. Here you can see countless wrecked barques, many crushed on the rocks, others half covered with sand, some broken in two, with only the poop or the prow visible, while others are reduced to just a keel or ribs.

There is no questioning the vividness of this account, which is reinforced by a sketch labelled 'A Temple of Aphrodite', many of which are to be found on the island with which she is so famously associated. Moreover, Leonardo is known to have had connections with the city of Venice, especially in a military capacity, so there is a possibility that he may have helped with the reinforcement work. On the other hand, his descriptions of Cyprus make no mention of castles or defences, though it is of course possible that these are amongst his notebooks that are known to have been lost.

Despite Egypt's support for Venice, as it continued to resist Ottoman attempts on Cyprus and thus established an effective buffer zone between the Turks and their Egyptian goal, the Sultan of Egypt's attitude towards his allies remained ambivalent. He allowed Rizzo di Marino to continue living in Egypt and plotting on behalf of the Neapolitan claim to Cyprus. And in 1488 Rizzo duly hatched what, on the face of it, was an even more spectacular plan. Queen Caterina's faithful lady-in-waiting Vera de Giblet happened to be the sister of Rizzo's great friend Tristan de Giblet, who had also taken part in the failed coup led by Archbishop Fabregues. He too had managed to escape, and had eventually joined up again with Rizzo in Egypt. By means of smuggled letters from her brother, Vera was persuaded to encourage Queen Caterina to seek another husband. This proved to be an easy task, as Caterina was longing to find release from her solitary confinement, which by now had lasted well over a decade and had reduced her to a state of almost permanent depression. She confessed to Vera that above all else she longed for a husband who would be her lover, her companion and her protector. Initially Vera began heartening her mistress by reading her love sonnets; then, on the instigation of her brother Tristan, she informed Caterina that none other than Alfonzo of Aragon, the son of Ferrante I of Naples, had let it be known that he wished to have Caterina as his bride. By any standards, this appeared unlikely. Caterina was now thirty-four years old and beginning to show her age: judging from later portraits, the young fresh-faced queen was no longer in the first flush of youth and had grown a little plump. On the other hand, Alonzo of Aragon was just twenty-four years old and had continued to live in Egypt, where he had taken up residence in cosmopolitan Alexandria and now 'gave himself up to the pleasures of the town'. Despite Caterina's romantic delusions, any such arranged marriage between the Neapolitan rake and the ageing Venetian lady would have been a mainly political union.

Still, Vera de Giblet's stories of her prospective fiancé had quite won over Queen Caterina, who viewed her coming marriage with heartfelt anticipation. At last she would have someone at her side who would be able to stand up against the Venetian interference in her realm. Vera's brother now sent a letter warning her that there was a possibility the Venetians were aware of their plan. (Ironically, this may have been the information that confirmed for the Council of Ten what had until then appeared to them a preposterous rumour.) In fear of her life, Vera de Giblet fled immediately, taking ship for Rhodes, which was at the time ruled by the former Crusading order now known as the Knights of Rhodes and thus lay beyond Venetian jurisdiction. Back in Egypt, neither Rizzo di Marino nor Tristan de Giblet appeared unduly worried that the Venetians were now cogniscant of their plan. Indeed, the evidence (such as it is) indicates that they may even have decided to leave for Rhodes themselves, with the intention of making contact with the Venetian representative there, so that arrangements could be made for the marriage. Possibly with this in mind, yet maintaining a certain amount of secrecy, they hired a French barque at the more remote port of Damietta on the Nile delta, ordering the captain to make preparations for a long voyage to an unknown destination. They then set sail north-east, in the direction of Rhodes. However, after several days at sea the captain was ordered to change course and head west for Cyprus. The French barque eventually made landfall at the remote north-western tip of Cyprus, where Rizzo di Marino and Tristan de Giblet asked to be put ashore, together with their two servants, informing the captain that they would return in four days, when they would light a fire on the beach as a signal for him to send a boat to pick them up.

It has been speculated that Rizzo and Tristan were so blasé concerning their supposed mission to Rhodes that their intention was to undertake a short hunting trip, during which they would visit the famous *Fontana Amorosa* (Fountain of Love), a spring whose crystal-clear waters were said to have been blessed by the Ancient Greek goddess Aphrodite and were renowned as a love-potion. At the time it appeared far more likely that they intended to make contact with leaders of the patriotic Cypriots, both ancient Venetian gentry and indigenous Greek, who had joined the cause with the aim of putting an end to Venetian rule of their island.

The waters off northern Cyprus were constantly patrolled by Venetian naval vessels, which had already forced the Ottomans to abort more than one serious attempt to invade the island. Inevitably, the sight of a French barque sailing off the north-western coast immediately raised suspicions. The barque was approached and boarded by a Venetian galley, and its captain was interrogated under threat of being sentenced to death for spying. He quickly confessed that he had been hired by Rizzo di Marino and Tristan de Giblet and was awaiting their return. Four nights later, a fire was spotted on the beach, and the captain sent a boat to collect them. The moment they stepped aboard the barque, Rizzo and Tristan were clapped in irons by the waiting Venetians, whose galley immediately set out to transport its important prisoners to Venice. With a blend of bravado and half-truth Rizzo protested that he was acting as an envoy of Sultan Qaitbay of Egypt, but Tristan knew there could be no denying the involvement of his sister in the plot. Rather than face torture in Venice, he swallowed a phial of poison that he had secreted in a ring, and was found to be dead by the time the galley entered the Adriatic.

The galley reached Venice on 14 October 1488, and Rizzo di Marino was brought ashore in chains and escorted under armed guard to a solitary dungeon in the Doge's Palace, all the while protesting that this was a violation of his diplomatic status. As it was, papers found in Rizzo di Marino's possession gave the Council of Ten cause for thought. His close friendship with Sultan Qaitbay was well known, and Venice had every reason not to disturb its close relationship with Egypt, upon which the large majority of its oriental trade now depended. The papers found on Rizzo made the Council of Ten suspect that Sultan Qaitbay may well have known of the plot, and may have looked with favour upon a marriage between Queen Caterina and Alonzo of Aragon. This would have brought him another powerful and much-needed ally in his defence against the invading Ottomans.

The Venetians urgently needed to get to the bottom of this matter. The Council of Ten set up a four-man tribunal to try Rizzo, with permission to torture him if this became necessary to extract the truth concerning his mission. There were three traditional methods of torture at the tribunal's disposal: the thumbscrew, plucking out pieces of skin from the body with red-hot pliers, and finally the rack. The torture yielded astonishing results: Rizzo made the amazing confession that during his four days ashore in Cyprus he had made personal contact with Queen Caterina, informing her of Alonzo of Aragon's presence in Egypt and his willingness to marry her. Yet even in his extremity Rizzo insisted this was no secret plan initiated by himself and de Giblet under orders from Naples. Such a mission could only have been carried out under the auspices of Sultan Qaitbay. Rizzo was no spy: indeed, he was no mere diplomatic envoy; instead he had the status of a royal representative carrying a personal message between the monarchs of two independent countries. Likewise, he insisted that he was working in the interests of Venice as well as Naples. The torture tribunal dragged on, without reaching any final conclusion, and Rizzo was returned to his isolated dungeon. Indeed, none but the Council of Ten even spoke of his presence in Venice. The captain and crew of the galley that had brought him to Venice had been sworn to secrecy before being despatched back to sea.

The fact is, the Council of Ten remained unsure what to do with Rizzo. They knew him for the treacherous rogue he was. At the same time, they knew that until his capture he had remained in close communication with Sultan Qaitbay, and so they had to tread carefully.

Many months of deliberation followed, during which all aspects of Venetian foreign policy and commercial interest were debated in the light of the information gained from Rizzo, who meanwhile languished in the dank pestilential limbo of his secret cell. Finally, on 13 May 1489, an order was signed for Rizzo's execution: death by hanging, to be carried out within three days. Yet this was not carried out: the Council of Ten had their own devious plans. Instead, news was leaked that Rizzo had committed suicide, the implication being that this had happened after he had been taken into custody by the Venetian authorities. No other details were forthcoming: why this had happened, whether it had happened recently, precisely where or how it had happened – all remained mysterious and unknown. The Council of Ten then waited for this information to reach Egypt, so that they could judge Sultan Qaitbay's reaction. Should the sultan express outrage that his envoy had been forced to this extremity, or indeed suspect that Rizzo had been murdered on Venetian orders, then Rizzo could quietly be released and shown to be alive. Stories of his mistreatment could easily be denied, shown to be lies prompted by anti-Venetian sentiment. The Venetian administration was not known for its precipitate action in such matters. In 1491, after two long years and no significant reaction from the sultan, the Council of Ten at last considered that it was safe to execute Rizzo di Marino, who immediately demanded that, owing to his status, he wished to exercise his traditional right to be hanged publicly between the two columns on the Piazzetta outside the Doge's Palace.

The Council of Ten at once ruled against this: not only would it give the lie to the rumour of Rizzo's suicide, but it might also give him the opportunity to reveal to the watching crowd certain compromising information or even dangerous state secrets. Instead, it was decided that just as he had been detained in circumstances of the utmost secrecy, so he would be executed. At dead of night Rizzo di Marino was led from his cramped cell, devoid of any means of identification: barefoot and clad only in a full-length cloth garment, with a hood over his head. This anonymous figure was hustled into the Armoury and was stood on a wooden bench, with a rope around his neck attached to a beam. The bench was then kicked from beneath his feet and he was left to hang. By now, all others had left the room apart from a single designated witness. Should news of Rizzo's murder somehow leak out (as was so often the case in clandestine Venice, despite the utmost secrecy), the Council of Ten could deny any knowledge of what had happened, placing all blame on the hapless witness who had been designated to be present at this event, and naming him as Rizzo's murderer. When Rizzo's hooded, shrouded cadaver was cut down, it was then sewn into a sack and rowed across the darkness of the lagoon to the island of Murano. Here the monks of San Cristoforo were ordered to bury the unknown body in an unmarked grave within the confines of their enclosed monastery, and were sworn to secrecy. Such meticulous concealment ensured that the larger-than-life figure of Rizzo di Marino simply disappeared from history – to such an extent that even the sixteenth-century Cypriot scholar Flori Buston declared in his celebrated history of the island that, after leaving Egypt sometime in the late 1480s, nothing was ever again heard of Rizzo di Marino.

Back in late 1488, the fate of the leading figure in this drama had also been decided. Somehow Queen Caterina would also have to cease to exist – though not perhaps in the vicious manner planned for Rizzo. As long as she remained queen, unmarried and of child-bearing age, there remained the possibility that Cyprus would be snatched from Venice's grasp. She would have to be persuaded to abdicate; this would leave the Venetians as de facto rulers of the island, a situation that Sultan Qaitbay would certainly accept. Cyprus could then to all intents and purposes become part of the Venetian Empire, with direct rule openly imposed from Venice itself. However, what if Queen Caterina chose not to abdicate? Her antipathy towards Venice was now an open secret, yet there was no question of deposing her by force. Sultan Qaitbay would be justified in viewing as an aggressive act any direct action against the ruler of what was, after all, an Egyptian tributary state. Venetian trade to Egypt would then in all likelihood be banned, leaving this lucrative route open to her Italian rivals. At the same time the sultan would also doubtless appeal to Naples, as well as all the other Italian states that continued to resent Venice, to form an alliance to protect him from the expanding Ottomans. Venice would thus at one fell swoop be deprived of her most lucrative trade route and left in a state of dangerous isolation. It was imperative that Queen Caterina was persuaded to abdicate, and as soon as possible.

The Council of Ten decided to despatch an official diplomatic delegation led by the new captain-general, Francesco Priuli. This would travel first to Cyprus to meet Queen Caterina, and then on to Egypt to seek audience with Sultan Qaitbay. Priuli would carry with him a letter (already dictated by the Council of Ten) in which Caterina confessed to the sultan that she felt so threatened by recent events that she had begged the Venetian authorities to allow her to return to her homeland. She wished to abdicate and allow the Republic to take over responsibility for the protection of Cyprus. The Venetians had assured her that they would continue to maintain the island precisely as it had been under her reign, and would of course resume paying the annual tribute of 8,000 ducats which the sultan had so generously suspended for the previous two years. Only after Queen Caterina had signed this 'letter' and abdicated was Priuli to continue on to Egypt to present Sultan Qaitbay with what appeared to be an amicable fait accompli, which he would certainly accept.

When Captain-General Priuli landed in Cyprus on 14 January 1489 he was under no illusions as to the difficulty of his task, and in order to help persuade Queen Caterina to abdicate he had brought along with him her brother, Giorgio Cornaro. Caterina was so overcome with emotion when she first saw Giorgio after so many years that she rushed forward and embraced him. She was under the misapprehension that he had come to Cyprus to protect her. Only when they retired alone to her private chamber did he reveal the true purpose of his visit: to facilitate the plan for her abdication.

Owing to the presence of the Venetian delegation listening at the door as Giorgio attempted to persuade his sister, there remains a detailed report of their conversation, which was later included in a diplomatic despatch back to Venice. The conversation was emotional and continued for some time, raging back and forth; yet its salient points are easily outlined. In his attempt to win her over to the Venetian plan, Giorgio opened by appealing to his sister's patriotism. But Caterina had now been sole ruling monarch of Cyprus for sixteen years, since the murder of her beloved husband, and for very obvious reasons now regarded herself as Cypriot rather than Venetian. She declared that she had no intention of abdicating voluntarily, and pleaded with her brother, 'Are not my lords of Venice content to have their island when I am dead, that they would deprive me thus of what my husband left me?' Giorgio persisted: if she abdicated, the Venetians had promised to reward her with a far less dangerous domain of her own. She would be granted her own large estate on the mainland, where she could hold court free from constraint; she could live in tranquillity and happiness, just as she wished, under the full protection of her country, which would reward her with a generous stipend commensurate with the magisterial services she had undertaken. Indeed, she would be able to live like a queen as she had never been able to live before. Yet still Caterina remained adamant.

It was at this point that Giorgio was forced to confront his sister with the ugly reality of the situation – for her, for Cyprus and even for himself.

The waters around the coast were filled with Venetian ships, which would not hesitate to take over the island. And there was worse. With tears in his eyes, Giorgio pleaded with Caterina: the very honour of the Cornaro family was at stake. If she did not abdicate, the authorities had threatened that their ancient and noble family would be ruined. Her beloved father would be disgraced, and the entire family deprived not only of its wealth, but also its status and good name. A tradition of honour that had been built up over the centuries – one that included not only a doge but also many other holders of the highest offices in the city – would vanish from Venetian society. The power of the Council of Ten had now grown to such an extent that it was quite capable of enforcing such a decision, which would be to all extents and purposes incontestable. Venice may have remained a republic in name, but this was becoming increasingly limited to a 'democratic' oligarchy, which spoke through the voice of the Council of Ten. Caterina, queen though she may have been, was well aware of this and certainly understood the truth of her brother's warning. This was no bluff.

Caterina may now have regarded herself as a Cypriot rather than a Venetian, but she still remained a Cornaro. She loved her family, especially her father Marco, who had voyaged to see her in Cyprus during her time of virtual imprisonment. After all he had done to try and help her, she could not have borne to see him disgraced. She heard out her brother Giorgio's arguments. Then, raising her voice so that those she knew had their ears pressed to the door of her chamber could hear her clearly, she replied to her brother, 'If this is your opinion, then I respect it. This is also my opinion, and I will follow your advice.'

Caterina dutifully signed the letter of abdication that had been dictated back in Venice by the Council of Ten, whereupon the Lusignan flag that had flown from Famagusta Castle more or less continuously for nearly 300 years was formally lowered.* In its place the crimson flag with the golden

---

* Over the years variations of this flag developed, but it retained essentially an orange, white and blue motif quartered to represent the territories claimed by the Lusignan family line. In the top left-hand corner was the star of Jerusalem, and each of the other three quarters contained a crowned lion rampant – representing Armenia, Cyprus and Lusignan itself (in western France).

lion of San Marco was run up to a fanfare and a barrage of cannon – a ceremony that was to be repeated throughout the island. Caterina's letter was then conveyed by Captain-General Priuli to Sultan Qaitbay in Egypt, where he accepted its contents without demur. The formality of Venice being officially recognised as ruler of his vassal state was now complete.

The Venetians were well aware of the way the local population viewed what had happened. In an attempt to alleviate their unpopularity (and yet at the same time reinforce the finality of what had taken place), they sent ex-Queen Caterina on a carefully staged and monitored tour of the island, so that she could take leave of her subjects. The gathered crowds listened in sadness as their former queen read out the speech that had been prepared for her, reassuring them that their fate now lay in safe hands.

On 14 March 1489, Caterina took ship at Famagusta to sail for Venice. The shore was lined by a vast crowd of her former subjects, and many are said to have waded into the sea to bid her farewell. Just over two months later, probably having put in at Rhodes, Caterina's galley and her protective flotilla arrived at the Lido on 5 June, where she was greeted with an armada fit for a queen and escorted aboard the *Bucintoro* by no less than Doge Barbarigo himself.

The procession that accompanied Caterina in the *Bucintoro* to the city was unprecedented in splendour, even in Venetian history. The blue-grey waters of the lagoon were filled with galleys, gondolas, merchantmen and craft of all kinds, while crowds lined the quaysides. Caterina was seated beside the doge on the raised poop deck at the stern of the *Bucintoro* and, according to some reports, her throne was elevated even higher than that of the doge himself, on account of her royal status. The Republic of Venice was welcoming its queen. The hypocrisy of the Venetian authorities, along with the unwitting collaboration of the citizenry, had now reached its apotheosis. In a special ceremony conducted at San Marco, Caterina Cornaro formally handed over the golden crown of Cyprus for the guardianship of the Republic. Despite being browbeaten and forced to abdicate, she was informed by the authorities that she would still be allowed to remain Queen of Cyprus, Jerusalem and Armenia and should continue to use this as her title. At the same time she would be granted by the

Republic of Venice her own private kingdom, the small hill town of Asolo, together with its surrounding territory of mulberry groves, vineyards and wooded hills, which lay just thirty miles north-west of Venice itself, in the hinterland known as the Veneto. She would also be granted sufficient funds to maintain herself in a manner befitting the royalty of a small kingdom. On her arrival there she was greeted rapturously by all her 4,000 subjects.

Queen Caterina immediately made plans for a palace to be built for her, called significantly *Il Barco* (the ship), as if she were still on a voyage that might one day carry her back across the sea to Cyprus. Here she would maintain her own court, which she staffed according to her own particular taste, with the entourage that had been allowed to follow her into exile from Cyprus. These included her favourite personal female attendant, a black former slave who originated from Nubia; the pet parrots that so amused her; a small collection of monkeys; some peacocks; and her dwarf jester, who knew how to amuse and enliven her during her not-infrequent periods of depression. Yet Caterina's court was more than just a whimsical collection of exotica; it also reflected the considerable intellectual powers that she had continued to develop since her education in Venice. She had also cultivated a wide variety of cultural interests. Indeed, the court of Queen Caterina at Asolo was soon gaining such a reputation that it began attracting artists, philosophers and poets of the newly burgeoning Renaissance, which was now beginning to spread throughout Italy.

Despite the political difficulties posed by Caterina's persistent widespread popularity amongst the people of the Republic (and its far-flung empire in Cyprus), she was permitted to visit Venice, but only on special occasions. Thus she kept in contact with her family, especially her favourite brother Giorgio, who as a reward for persuading his sister to abdicate had been awarded by the doge with the highly prestigious honour of being made a *Cavalierato di Stola d'Oro* (Knight of the Golden Sash). The Council of Ten also personally invited Queen Caterina to Venice during the severe winter of 1491, when the Grand Canal froze hard and a jousting contest was held in her honour. This was evidently a covert experiment that proved satisfactory to the Council of Ten, for Caterina was later asked to preside as hostess over the festivities when Eleanor, Duchess of Ferrara, arrived on a state visit. Ferrara may have had a duke and duchess, but Venice could trump them with a queen. Yet, as ever with the Council of Ten, there was more than met the eye here: Queen Caterina's presence was much more than civil one-upmanship. Eleanor of Aragon was the daughter of King Ferrante I of Naples, who still harboured dynastic ambitions with regard to Cyprus, and Venice wished to make it clear that the island still had a queen, whom they could produce as the official monarch. Such double-think was now very much a part of Venetian power diplomacy.

Caterina was still only in her mid-thirties, and wished to forget the tragedies that had befallen her; likewise, she was determined to put behind her the grim atmosphere of her court in Cyprus, its air poisoned by suspicion and competing interests. At Asolo she ensured that her court was staffed with handsome courtiers and beautiful young ladies-in-waiting. In the evenings, poets and musicians performed amidst the fragrant palace gardens, whose layout and planting she had personally supervised. The Venetian scholar and poet Pietro Bembo was particularly attracted to Asolo. Twenty-nine years old in 1499 and at the height of his imaginative powers, he thrived amidst this cultural ambience. He would go on to become one of the most distinguished intellectuals of his age, and one of his finest works would be *Gli Asolani* (The People of Asolano), a philosophical discourse on love between three young beaux and three girls, set in the gardens of *Il Barco*. This was written in the manner and style of Petrarch, and was intended to evoke the atmosphere of the years he had spent visiting this idyllic spot. Indeed, such was the popularity of *Gli Asolani* that it even gave rise to a new verb in the Italian language: *asolare*, meaning 'to enjoy oneself in a pleasant aimless fashion'. It was this work that also led the great Jacob Burckhardt to compare the court depicted by 'Pietro Bembo at the castle of Asolo' with 'the ideal society'.

Yet the reality had a much darker side. The 'kingdom of Asolo' was in no way independent of the Venetian territory that encompassed it, and a close eye was kept on its queen by the appointment of former Captain-General Francesco Priuli as ambassador to her court. Moreover, Venice maintained the fiction that Queen Caterina was still the sovereign ruler of Cyprus, getting the Cypriot ambassador to Venice to make regular visits to Asolo in accordance with diplomatic protocol, to pay his respects to his monarch. On these visits he would be accompanied by his aide, a good-looking twenty-year-old Cypriot called Demetrios, who came from Nicosia. According to two Asolo chroniclers cited by Caterina's biographer, Leto Severis, Demetrios fell in love with Caterina, who gave some appearance of reciprocating his feelings. One evening he made so bold as to approach Queen Caterina as she was sitting alone in her palace garden. Here he fell to his knees and confessed his love for her. She did nothing to discourage him: on the contrary, she agreed to a tryst in the gardens the following evening. However, as she approached their agreed meeting place, which was bathed in moonlight, she saw two shadowy figures suddenly leap out and attack Demetrios. At the very same moment ambassador Priuli materialised beside her and 'in a cruel voice' informed her: 'The punishment of the [Council of] Ten is inexorable. Tomorrow Demetrios will be found dead in the forest and everyone will think that it is the work of thieves.' As if to reinforce this message, he then added, 'And you, Caterina, do not forget that the Council of Ten is keeping watch and exacts punishment.' Others have suggested that this 'Demetrios' may not have had amorous intentions at all, but may in fact have been an undercover agent conveying messages from Caterina's network of loyal supporters in Cyprus.

Mention is also made of visits from the ousted ruler of Rimini, the twenty-five-year-old Pandolfo IV Malatesta (known as 'Pandolfaccio' – that is, the bad Pandolfo), who was living in exile at the heavily fortified and moated castle in Citadella, just ten miles down the road. This had been given to Malatesta by the Venetian authorities (who had long-term territorial ambitions for Rimini that were not utterly dissimilar to those they had entertained for Cyprus). Malatesta was a particularly unsavoury character, who had ruled the small Adriatic coastal city state of Rimini as a tyrant, cowing his subjects and exercising his sexual rapacity at will on his young female subjects. (It was his failed rape attempt on a popular local beauty that had caused his people to revolt, only for him to be reinstated by the Venetians, though three years later he had been chased out of Rimini by the even more notorious Cesare Borgia.) A rumour had been spread that the reasons for Malatesta's frequent visits to Queen Caterina's court at Asolo were that he lusted after one of Caterina's young ladies-in-waiting called Fiameca, yet curiously this appears to have been a cover story for his desire for the older Caterina. However, word of Malatesta's visits to Asolo (whatever their motive) soon reached the

Council of Ten, and his visits to Asolo abruptly ceased. The Venetians were taking no chances: there was to be no heir to the Lusignan line, which they intended would come to an end with the childless Caterina.

Now isolated at Asolo, Caterina continued to live in some style at her Renaissance court; but none of the other poets, musicians or painters proved to be of the calibre of Bembo, either in ability or personality, and when he departed, the cultural life of *Il Barco* descended into provincial mediocrity, and Caterina soon began to tire of this vapid life. However, there were the occasional exceptions: sometime during the early 1500s the renowned Venetian artist Gentile Bellini visited Asolo and painted Caterina's portrait, complete with a modest bejewelled crown. This is no flattering depiction, and the transformation in Caterina's appearance is dramatic. The sensitive, intelligent fourteen-year-old girl painted by Titian was no more; indeed, all trace of the more mature *'bella donna'* noted by the diarist Sanudo on her return from Cyprus some eleven years previously had vanished for ever. Bellini's painting depicts a plump, plain middle-aged matron in a distinctly subdued dress, her intelligent subtlety of expression blunted into sullen obduracy by her years of tragedy and mistreatment.

Caterina would continue living at Asolo until 1509, when the Veneto stood under threat from the north by the Holy Roman Emperor, Maximilian I, who had joined the powerful anti-Venetian alliance created by Pope Julius II, known as the League of Cambrai – whose aim was to drive Venice from the mainland. Queen Caterina fled with her court for the safety of Venice, and in February 1509 was permitted by the Council of Ten to take up residence at the palazzo of her favouite brother, Giorgio Cornaro, whose supreme diplomatic skills in the service of the city had led to him being regarded as one of the most distinguished citizens of the Republic.

In June 1509 Maximilian's army duly invaded the Veneto, occupying Asolo. A month later the Venetian army defended their territory at a site close to *Il Barco* and won a victory that forced the imperial troops to withdraw. The retreating soldiers avenged themselves by setting fire to *Il Barco*, gutting the interior of the building.* Now homeless, Caterina was

---

* Some of the building and its loggia of delicate Renaissance pillars survived the conflagration and remain standing in a rather forlorn state to this day.

permitted to remain in Venice, and was even allowed to move freely about the city. So transformed was this plainly clothed, bulky middle-aged woman that few passing citizens on the streets recognised their former favourite, for whom they had turned out in their thousands. The destruction of her palace had been the last straw in her long line of disappointments. Early in July 1510 she took to her bed with stomach pains. Her condition quickly deteriorated, and she died days later at the age of fifty-six.

In keeping with the cruel charade that had been imposed upon Queen Caterina by the Venetian authorities, the Council of Ten decided that their distinguished fellow citizen should be accorded a royal funeral, a uniquely contradictory event in the Republic's long history of glories and hypocrisies. By now, word had spread through Venice that 'the Queen of Cyprus is dead', and vast crowds turned out to watch her funeral, where the leading mourner was Doge Leonardo Loredan (though some sources claim that the doge was not able to attend the funeral, and that his place was taken instead by Caterina's nemesis, Francesco Priuli). Amongst the long procession of dignitaries following Caterina's coffin were the Signoria, all other members of the Council of Ten and the heads of the noble families of the city. The procession was accorded the honour of a bridge of boats across the Grand Canal. In a final grotesque touch, the actual crown of Cyprus, which Caterina had been made to surrender in San Marco on her arrival, was placed upon her coffin as it was carried to the church of San Cassiano, the traditional burial place of the Cornaro family. As if to add insult to injury, her simple marble tombstone was formally engraved in Latin with the inscription *Catharinae Corneliae, Cypri, Hierosolymorum ac Armeniae Reginae Cineres* [*sic*]. The emptiness of these titles was now utterly complete. And so, even in death Caterina came to epitomise the characteristic Venetian parable – the image of the individual manipulated and sacrificed in the interest of the Republic's political gain.

Coda: More than three centuries later the story of the Queen of Cyprus would inspire Donizetti's opera *Caterina Cornaro*. This is set in Venice and Cyprus amidst the atmosphere of passion, intrigue and deception that surrounded Caterina's early years as queen, though the composer's highly

10

'Lost in a day what had taken eight hundred years to gain'

THE REPULSED INVASION of the Veneto by Maximilian I, which had driven Queen Caterina from her court at Asolo, had merely been the first prong of a concerted attack on Venice by the League of Cambrai. In assembling this alliance, Pope Julius II ('the warrior pope') had exerted his formidable powers of persuasion, with the result that for varying lengths of time this alliance would include major powers throughout Europe, including Spain, France and the Holy Roman Empire, with even England and Scotland being persuaded to join. The aim of Julius II was nothing less than the conquest of all Venice's mainland territories. Not only had Venice taken over territory south of the Alps from the Adriatic to the environs of Milan, but it now appeared poised to absorb the small city states of the Adriatic hinterland to the south in the Romagna, which were officially papal territory. Not for nothing had the Venetians allied themselves with the likes of Pandolfo IV Malatesta; indeed, in 1503 they even connived in Malatesta's unsuccessful attempt to retake Rimini. If the Papal States of the Romagna fell into Venetian hands, this would not only be a personal humiliation for Julius II – a man not given to humility – but it would establish Venice's commanding role in Italy, and there was no telling where this might end.

The second prong of the League of Cambrai's attack was launched in Lombardy, when its assembled forces under King Louis XII of France crossed the Adda River into Venetian territory in April 1509. In preparation for this inevitable attack Venice had assembled a large mercenary army under the joint command of the Orsini cousins – Bartolomeo d'Alviano and Niccolò Pitigliano – two of the most accomplished *condottieri* in Italy. The Orsini were given orders to avoid direct conflict with the invading forces, restricting themselves to picking off detachments in tactical skirmishes. Unfortunately Alviano disagreed with this strategy. On 14 May he was confronted by a large force of French soldiers and crack Swiss mercenaries, which had advanced three miles from the Adda River into Venetian territory as far as the village of Agnadello. Instead of beating a tactical retreat, Alviano decided to attack, sending word to the nearby other half of the Venetian forces led by his cousin, telling them to come to his aid at once.

As battle commenced, Alviano's forces had the advantage of being on a hillside above a vineyard, and opened fire with all their artillery. The French cavalry at once charged towards the Venetian cannon, but were impeded in their advance by the lines of vines and irrigation ditches in the vineyard. In the midst of this action there was a downpour, and the rain caused the charging French and Swiss soldiers to become bogged down in deep mud. With the support of reinforcements, now would have been the time for the Venetian force to charge down the firmer slope and hack down those few French cavalrymen emerging from the vineyard, while at the same time continuing to subject the main body of the enemy to an overwhelming artillery barrage. But word arrived back from Pitigliano telling Alviano to avoid all contact with the enemy, while his cousin continued to march his army south. Despite this blow, Alviano still held the advantage and refused to withdraw his troops, persisting with his attack. Ironically, it was now that Alviano found himself plunged into the very situation that the Venetians had sought to avoid. Unexpectedly King Louis XII appeared on the scene with the main army; meanwhile a detachment of the original French forces had moved without being detected to the other side of the hill, in preparation for a surprise attack on Alviano's men from the rear. Alviano now found himself facing attack on three sides. Grimly he watched as his cavalry fled through the closing gap in the encircling enemy forces. All the remaining Venetian forces could do was stand and fight their ground as best they could, which they did heroically for three hours. During the course of this fierce hand-to-hand combat Alviano was slashed across the face and taken prisoner. Others were not so lucky: more than 4,000 of his men were slaughtered, and another 2,000 wounded.

During this era few ever survived serious battlefield injuries, and the wounded were usually left to die on the field where they fell. After the battle, soldiers of the victorious army would search for any senior enemy officers who were still alive, rescuing them for the ransom they could demand from their family. After this the bodies of the dead, as well as those of the howling and groaning non-walking wounded, were subjected to human scavengers, who emerged as if from nowhere to search for valuables, cutting off fingers to obtain rings, slashing open the outfits of the mercenary soldiers to discover any hidden trinkets or coins which they themselves had taken as booty on some previous battlefield. Morning would see the arrival of animal scavengers, such as ravens and wild dogs, which would tear without discrimination into the flesh of the dead and defenceless. In this timeless ritual, as old as battle itself, the starving peasantry and feral animals that inhabited the territory ravaged by the warring armies found their recompense.

News of this bloody defeat reached Pitigliani's forces that evening, and overnight most of his mercenaries simply melted away in the darkness. The defeat at Agnadello was possibly the worst in Venetian history, and such were its catastrophic effects that Louis XII and the army of the League were able to take possession of all but the bare coastal remnant of the Venetian mainland territories. As Machiavelli put it so memorably three years later: 'Venice lost in a single day what had taken eight hundred years of effort to gain.'* With this defeat, *La Serenissima* passed the zenith of her greatness.

Meanwhile the Republic's eastern-Mediterranean maritime empire, which it had indeed taken almost 800 years to gain, was under threat from the westward land expansion of the Ottoman Empire. However, Venice now

---

* It has been pointed out that this quote from *The Prince* (Chapter 12) is of course a wild exaggeration where Venice's mainland territories are concerned. As we have seen, the larger part of these territories constituted a comparatively recent acquisition. It is usually understood that Machiavelli was in fact identifying the European territory as the significant part of the Venetian Empire, whose overall territories had in fact been acquired over the city's 800-year history.

held Cyprus, which was the key to the trade routes with Egypt and the Levant – which most importantly centred on Alexandria and Beirut. Even so, a more significant threat to Venice's primary oriental trade in spices and luxury goods from the Orient had appeared from a totally unforeseen quarter.

The pioneering exploration of the west-African coastline in 1456 by the Venetian Alvise Cadamosto, under the sponsorship of the Portuguese, had soon been extended by his patrons on their own account. By 1488 the Portuguese navigator Bartolomeu Dias had rounded the Cape of Good Hope, and ten years later Vasco da Gama reached India; by 1509 the Portuguese had reached as far as the Malacca Strait that led from the Indian Ocean towards the Pacific, and seven years later they arrived off the Canton River in southern China. By the second decade of the sixteenth century a sea trading route between Portugal and the Orient had become well established.

At first the Venetians were complacent with regard to this development, as these new routes involved sailing such vast distances across dangerous oceans. (Vasco da Gama's trip to India and back was in fact longer than a voyage around the globe – though not quite as long as Ferdinand Magellan's first accidental circumnavigation, which lasted from 1519 to 1522.) What the Venetians had not realised was that this method of trading represented nothing less than a commercial revolution. The sea voyage to the Orient may have been more than twice as long as the Silk Route to China, but it soon became clear that it had the great commercial advantage of being much less expensive. Overland caravan traders had to pay levies on their goods at the border of every sovereign territory that they traversed; sea traders bargained for their goods at the source, bringing home considerably cheaper merchandise.

Although the Venetians were slow to appreciate this problem, their eventual answer harked back to the intrepid spirit of an earlier outward-looking age of exploration and expansion. The rulers of this city of canals conceived the bold idea of building a canal across the Suez isthmus to link the Mediterranean with the Red Sea. In fact, this idea may not have been quite as innovative as it initially appears, for a shallow link had been dug between the Nile delta and the Red Sea during classical times. Evidence of this canal may well have been provided by the Renaissance resurgence of interest in classical documents, which had been transported to Europe in large numbers by priests fleeing Constantinople in the time preceding its fall. At any rate, the Venetians began negotiations with Egypt's ruling Mamelukes regarding this project. But it was not to be.

In 1512 the Ottoman sultan Bejazit II had been succeeded by his son, known as Selim the Grim, who had revitalised his father's eastern expansionist ambitions. In 1516 the Ottomans launched a military campaign east into Syria, and a year later conquered Egypt, where Selim I (as he is more formally known) personally accepted the emblems of the Egyptian caliphate, the sword and mantle of the prophet Mohammed.*

While these Ottoman conquests spelled the death of the proposed canal, they did not put an end to Venetian trade with the Levant and Egypt, except during the intermittent periods of war between the Republic and the expanding Turkish Empire. However, the Venetians no longer enjoyed privileged trading rights, like the virtual monopoly guaranteed to them by the Mamelukes. Instead, from now on they had to compete with other European traders, especially their Italian rivals, the Genoese and the Florentines. The Venetians also suffered other trading setbacks during this period. Along with the Genoese, they had traded directly with the Turkish mainland, most notably in the highly profitable alum market. This comparatively rare mineral was mined at Phocaea on the Gulf of Izmir, and was used in the glass-making and tanning industries; but, more importantly, it also served as a fixative for dyes in the cloth trade, making it the most valuable bulk commodity on the international market, despite the substantial customs dues demanded by the Ottoman authorities. Then alum was discovered closer to home at Tolfa in the papal territory north of Rome, and when mining revealed extensive deposits of high-grade mineral, Pope Pius II sought to establish a monopoly by banning all Christian states from trading in alum with the infidel Ottomans, on the grounds that the customs duties paid in the course of this trade were subsidising the Ottoman armies that threatened Christendom. At the same time, a papal decree established a considerably increased price for the sale of alum.

---

* These can be seen to this day at the Topkapi Palace, the former residence of the Ottoman sultans, in Istanbul.

The Venetians and the Genoese, for their part, simply ignored this ban, undercut the papal price and set about establishing their trade as far afield as Bruges and England. Yet this was but one positive development. The fact remained that the Republic found itself under increasing threat. Stripped of all but the last remnants of its mainland territories after the disastrous defeat at the Battle of Agnadello, its eastern trade now stood under the shadow of the expanding Ottoman Empire and the threat posed by the new route around the Cape of Good Hope opened up by Portuguese traders. Yet faced with the possibility of ruin, Venice blossomed as never before; indeed, all the indications are that the Republic was now entering a golden age of art and culture. Venice was at last realising, in its own characteristic way, the full potential of the Renaissance. This might seem incongruous, at a time when the Republic was so exposed, yet such contradiction is far from unique in the history of city states. The emergence of Athens as the cultural exemplar of the classical Greek world – the city of Socrates, Plato and Aristotle – occurred alongside defeat by Sparta and later the Macedonians. External threat (along with a tradition of quasi-democratic freedoms, allied to material and cultural richness) would seem to be an essential ingredient in such exceptional creativity.

As the Renaissance pioneer Petrarch had observed, Venice had initially remained resistant to many of the new attitudes and ideas, as well as much of the culture, of the Renaissance. As subtly distinct culturally as it was geographically from the rest of Italy, Venice had over the centuries developed its own unique version of medieval Gothic – in the form of a Greco-Venetian style that is perhaps best epitomised by the basilica of San Marco, with its Gothic façade and Romanesque bas-relief topped by Byzantine domes and intricate spires. Although early Renaissance works such as Verrocchio's equestrian statue of Colleoni had appeared in Venice, these remained the exception rather than the rule. And, indicatively, Colleoni's statue had been conceived by a Florentine sculptor.

However, by the early 1500s a transformation was taking place on the Venetian cultural scene. This is best illustrated by the painter Gentile Bellini and his younger brother Giovanni. As we have seen, around 1480 Gentile

Bellini had been chosen to represent Venetian art at the court of Mehmet II in Constantinople. Although influenced by Byzantine painters, his work already exhibited much of the clarity of vision, and humanity, that characterised Renaissance art. And on his return he would paint the somewhat frumpish portrait of Caterina Cornaro. But by now his work was out of fashion, and his reputation had been eclipsed by that of his younger brother Giovanni, whose vivid use of colour, realism and depiction of emotion had inspired a revolution in Venetian artistic taste.

Giovanni Bellini was one of the first Venetian artists who wholeheartedly embraced the Renaissance style. He also pioneered the use of oil paint, which would revolutionise art. This replaced tempera (colour pigment mixed with a water-soluble medium such as egg white), which in order to achieve its gentle effects had to be applied in layers that dried quickly, requiring a speed of technique and judgement that was difficult to master. Oil paint, on the other hand, took much longer to dry, enabling its pigments to be blended more easily, while its plasticity and thickness enabled the artist to reproduce more easily the texture of his subject, as well as imbuing the paintings with a hitherto-unseen depth and richness of colour compared with the characteristically paler hues of tempera. This facilitated subtlety of brushwork and other techniques: Bellini is even known to have used his fingertips to blend colours and soften the effect of light.

All this would manifest itself in the sheer artistry of the ensuing generation of painters, who would lead Venetian painting into the High Renaissance. Both Giorgione and Titian are known to have worked during their youth in Giovanni Bellini's studio, where they almost certainly learned how to use oil from their master. However, Bellini's attitude with regard to his subjects would prove too tentative for both these ambitious young men, who soon quit his studio on account of what they deemed his restrictive attitude. Giorgione, whose real name was Giorgio Barbarelli, was the younger of the two apprentices. He was born around 1477 at Castelfranco on the mainland some twenty-five miles north-west of Venice. He appears to have been from a peasant family, but quickly revealed a natural grace and charm that belied his origins. He developed into a tall, strikingly good-looking young man. According to Vasari:

He was brought up in Venice and took unceasing delight in the joys of love; and the sound of the lute gave him marvellous pleasure, so that in his day he played and sang so divinely that he was often employed for that purpose at various musical assemblies and gatherings of noble persons.

Little of a precise nature is known about the life of Giorgione, who in his time was usually known in his home city by the Venetian variant of Zorzo; and though he became something of a legendary figure during his brief thirty-three years of life, he seems not to have been in the least egotistical. For the most part he did not even sign his prolific output of accomplished paintings, which has led to considerable controversy over the identity of a number of works attributed to him.

One work that is unmistakably attributed to Giorgione, and is regarded by many as the most characteristic of his genius, is *The Tempest*, which was painted sometime around 1507. Regarded by some as the first genuine landscape painting as such in European art, it portrays the enigmatic figure of a soldier gazing across a stream at a naked woman suckling a child. But these two figures only occupy the foreground at the lower edges of the canvas. The scene as a whole is given a sense of foreboding by the looming dark clouds and flash of lightning that dominate the sky above what appear to be the buildings of an abandoned city in the background. Some have interpreted this painting as representing Adam and Eve cast out of Paradise (the empty city), with the storm and lightning representing God's wrath at their Original Sin (made manifest in the form of the suckling child). However, as with many of Giorgione's works, no definitive interpretation can be given. The scene is essentially enigmatic, leaving the individual elements to be studied for their own sake, with each contributing to the overall sense of mystery. The lasting vivacity and influence of this painting, containing as it does the image of a man dressed in everyday clothes juxtaposed with a naked female figure seated on grass, can be seen in Edouard Manet's *Déjeuner sur l'herbe* (The Luncheon on the Grass), which shocked audiences when it was painted some five centuries later.

In the last year of his life Giorgione began a work called *The Three Philosophers*, depicting three men standing in a grove before a cavern. Once

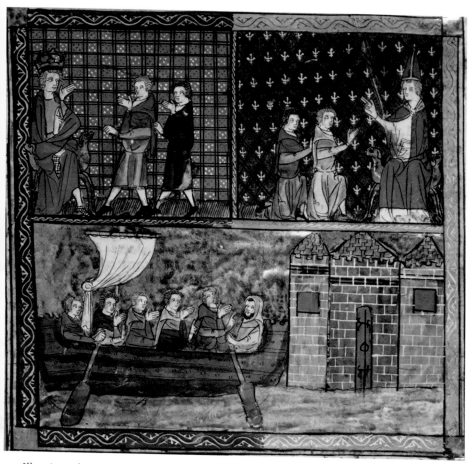

Illuminated manuscript of Marco Polo's first voyage, showing Emperor Baldwin II of Constantinople bidding Marco Polo and his father farewell, a blessing by the Patriarch, and the explorers entering the Black Sea (1333).

A Venetian plague doctor
in his protective mask
(Jan van Grevenbroeck,
early nineteenth century).

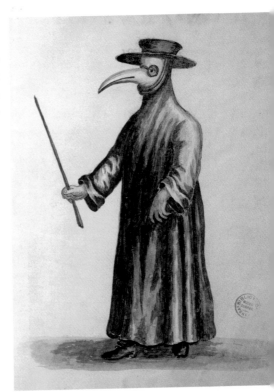

Detail of *The Miracle at Rialto Bridge*
by Carpaccio, showing the old
wooden structure with its drawbridges
which could be raised to allow
tall-masted ships to pass through to
the Rialto landing stage (1494).

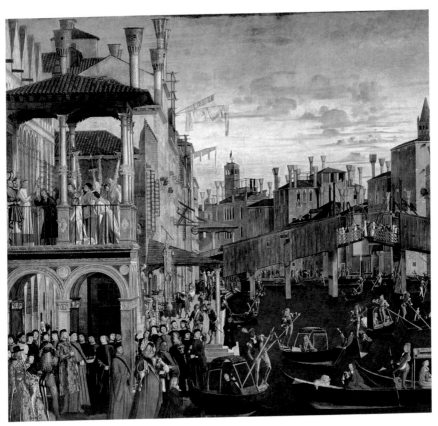

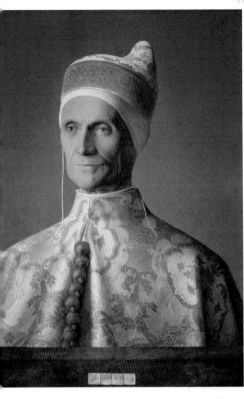

Doge Loredan by Giovanni Bellini, capturing the austere majesty of the ruling doge in all his finery (1501).

Gentile Bellini's portrait of the Ottoman sultan Mehmet II, the conqueror of Constantinople (1480).

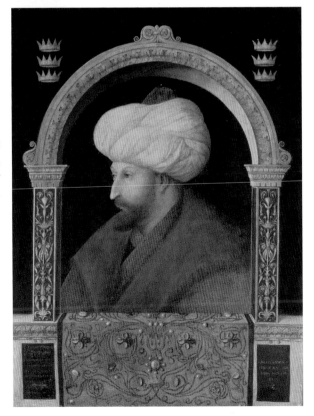

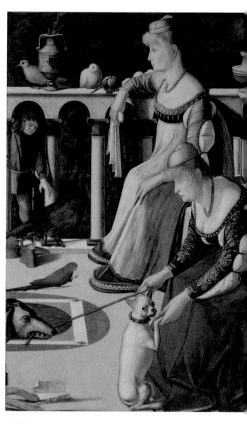

Two Venetian Courtesans by Carpaccio (*c.*1490). Some experts now suggest that this may depict two aristocratic wives waiting for their husbands to return from hunting.

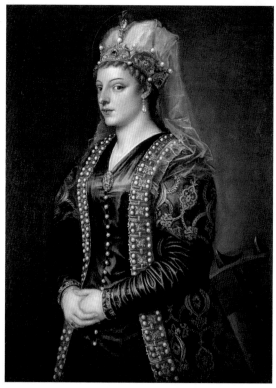

The painting by Titian of the young Caterina Cornaro, Queen of Cyprus, dressed as St Catherine of Alexandria (*c.*1542).

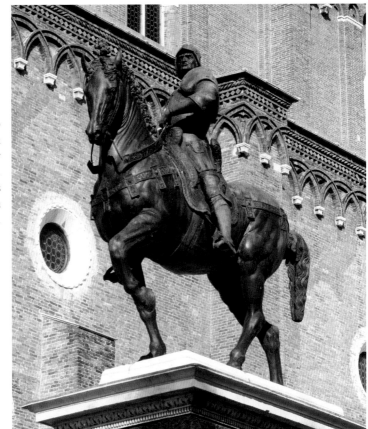

The monument to the great Venetian ndottiere Colleoni by Verrocchio (1490). At the time it was he greatest equestrian statue cast in bronze.

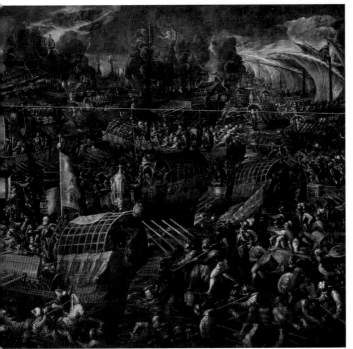

The Battle of Lepanto by Vicentino, which hangs in the Doge's Palace (1603).

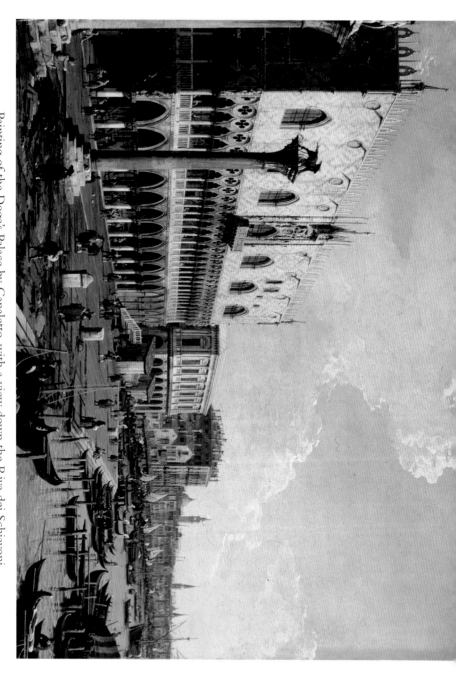

Painting of the Doge's Palace by Canaletto, with a view down the Riva dei Schiavoni (late 1730s). To the left are the two columns of the Piazzetta.

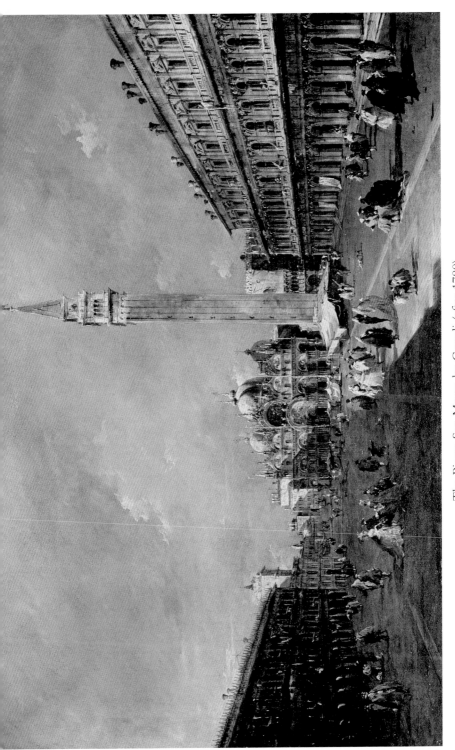

The Piazza San Marco by Guardi (after 1780).
He ended up selling his paintings to passing tourists here.

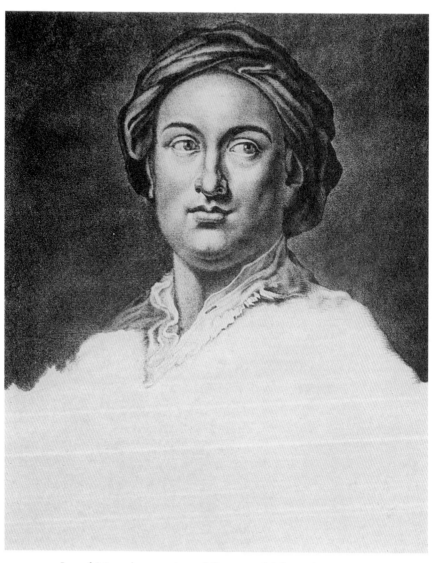

Ismael Mengs's engraving of Casanova (eighteenth century).

again the enigmatic quality of this work lends itself to a number of interpretations. Some have seen it as the Three Wise Men standing at the
entrance to the grotto wherein lies the infant Jesus; others have seen it as
indeed portraying three philosophers, all standing before the cave where,
according to Plato, unilluminated humanity busied itself watching the play
of a shadow world, whilst only the philosophers who disengaged themselves
from such chimeras could see the outside light of the ideal world of eternal
truth. Another intriguing philosophical interpretation identifies the three
figures as representing three historical stages of human development. The
stern old grey-bearded man, who appears to be holding a tablet and is
somewhat marginalised at the right of the painting, represents medieval
thought with its reliance upon interpretation of the ancient texts, which
are treated as if they are set in stone. The man in the middle wearing a
turban represents the Moslem world, from which emerged so many of the
long-forgotten European classical works – which in turn inspired the
Renaissance, represented by the seated young man gazing speculatively into
the distance as he looks up from the manuscript in his hand. Such an
interpretation represents an understanding of what precisely was taking
place in the Renaissance – a self-knowledge that remains exceptional in
the eras of human thought. There is some evidence that Giorgione died,
probably of the plague, before he could complete this work, and that it
was finished for him by his friend Titian.

Titian had been born Tiziano Vecelli, sometime during the late 1480s,
in the picturesque lakeside town of Cadore at the foot of the Alpine pass
some sixty miles north of Venice. According to Vasari, 'Because he was
seen to have a lively spirit and keen intelligence, at the age of ten he was sent
to Venice to live with his uncle, who soon perceived that he had a gift for
painting and placed him in the studio of Giovanni Bellini.' In his early
twenties Titian developed a supreme technical ability, influenced by both
Giovanni Bellini and, later, Giorgione. As a result the authorities would
later entrust him with the prestigious task of completing the series of
paintings left unfinished by Bellini in the hall of the Great Council in the
Doge's Palace. When the Fondaco dei Tedeschi was rebuilt, after having
burned down in 1505, Titian was commissioned, alongside Giorgione, with
decorating the façade of this prestigious centre of foreign commerce. Upon

the deaths of Giorgione and Bellini, Titian would emerge as the acknowledged master of Venetian art, having developed an individual style of his
own, which took full advantage of the new possibilities of colour opened
up by the use of oils. It is known that he further developed Bellini's technique of using his fingers to smear the oil paint over the surface of his
works, to the point of creating a three-dimensional effect. By means of
this method, as well as by employing forthright brushstrokes, Titian
pioneered the use of impasto (from the Italian for 'dough', 'mixture' or
'paste'), which vitalised the artist's ability to convey the effect of light,
lend an expressiveness to scenes or add reality to images (as, for instance,
in conveying the folds in a gown or highlighting jewels).

Such was the length of Titian's life and his transcendent mastery of his
medium that soon he would be receiving commissions from all over Europe.
Leading citizens now proudly displayed the works of the city's artists on
their walls, while the council chambers and churches were decorated with
flamboyant historical and biblical scenes. Meanwhile the outer walls of
palaces along the Grand Canal were decorated with frescoes and filigree
mouldings; and the façade of the Ca d'Oro was even embellished with
gold leaf, along with rare pigments such as ultramarine and vermilion. For
those who gathered in the Doge's Palace, did business in the Rialto or
were rowed along the Grand Canal, this was indeed a golden city – one
of the great wonders of Europe.

In keeping with the more pragmatic commercial aspect of the Venetian
ethos, the city had by this time also established itself as the leading centre
of book-printing in Italy. The German Johannes Gutenberg had invented
the movable-type printing press around 1439. Prior to this, books had
circulated only in manuscript form, with all copies needing to be hand-written,
a painstaking and time-consuming process that led to frequent errors and
obscurities in the text. The invention of printing, and the subsequent
dissemination of knowledge, would prove the great generating force of the
Renaissance, with printing presses soon spreading through Germany and
then across the Alps to Italy. In 1469 the first printing press was established
in Venice. Within a decade there were no fewer than twenty-two printing
establishments in the city, and by 1500 some 150 printing houses were in

business, producing nearly 4,000 editions. Initially these were mainly of works in Latin (for scholars) and Italian (for the more general educated reading public); but given Venice's international links it is no surprise that the city's presses were soon producing works in languages as wide-ranging as Serbo-Croat, Greek, Hebrew, Armenian and even Arabic – spreading Venice's fame as a publishing centre far and wide. Indeed, this was one of the main reasons why Leonardo da Vinci visited the city in 1500. He was accompanied by his close friend, the monk Luca Pacioli, who wished to have printed his recently completed manuscript *De divina proportione*, a work on mathematical and artistic proportions. Pacioli had persuaded Leonardo to illustrate this work with a series of beautiful and meticulous drawings representing three-dimensional regular geometric solids, such as the dodeca-hedron (with twelve faces) and the icosahedron (with twenty faces). Copies of these works would be made with the new copper-plate engraving tech-nique, which used acid to fix the image on the sheet of metal. This would reproduce geometric images with a much finer line than was possible using the traditional woodcut, and was an indication of the advanced printing skills now being developed in Venice.

The best-known printer in Venice during this period was Aldus Manutius, who would be responsible for creating the typeface known today as *italic*, which is said to have been based on the hand-writing of Petrarch. Initially, this type was not used for emphasis, as it is today, but purely for its commercial value; Manutius patented his new type on account of its narrow-ness and forward slant, which enabled the printer to include more words on the page and thus reduce production costs. In certain ways printing remained a fairly haphazard business, and Manutius, along with his grandson, would be instrumental in establishing a standard form of punc-tuation. His press was also responsible for producing the first octavo-sized volumes, designed so that the reader could carry them about with him in a shoulder bag or large coat pocket.

Manutius specialised in reproducing classical texts from Ancient Greece. This was no small task, given the comparative complexities of the Greek alphabet, and to overcome this difficulty he assembled a team of expert typesetters from Crete. His famous emblem, which he included on the frontispiece of works emanating from his Aldine Press (after Aldus), consisted of a dolphin and anchor, said to embody the speed and firmness that characterised his printing, a device which continued to be used by the modern publisher Doubleday, with others using variations on this theme.

Not all works issuing from Venetian printers were quite so elevated as those produced by the Aldine Press, which though widely distributed in their octavo editions would eventually reduce Manutius to ruin. Others published scurrilous pamphlets, works of erotica, topical satirical verse, and so forth. These were in part the forerunners of modern newspapers, and it was this milieu that would produce Pietro Aretino, recognised by many as the first journalist.

However, Aretino was in many ways much more than the first journalist. He was born in 1492, the illegitimate son of a cobbler in the Florentine town of Arezzo (from which his name derives). By his own account he seems to have received a piecemeal education; however, his native wit and natural inclination towards the subversive soon marked him out, and as a result he was probably banished from Arezzo at an early age. After wandering about northern Italy he ended up in Rome at around the age of twenty, possessed of little else but a precociously developed talent as a verbal prankster. He seems to have been a volatile but likeable character, given to outrageous boasting and scandalous gossip. Such talents drew him into the circle surrounding the painter Raphael, who (along with a rich banker) became Aretino's patron and protector. Raphael was at the time employed by the chubby and extravagant Pope Leo X, who set the tone of his rule by exclaiming upon being elected, 'We have the papacy, so now let us enjoy ourselves.'

Leo X would play a crucial but unexpected role in Aretino's life. Amongst his many foibles, the pope had a particular affection for his pet, an albino elephant called Hanno, which had been transported from India and given to him as a present by the King of Portugal. When Hanno died in 1516, after being fed a laxative laced with gold in an attempt to cure him of constipation, Leo X was deeply upset and composed an epitaph for his pet, to which he paid far more attention than to his faithful flock. Raphael was commissioned to paint a fresco of Hanno, and Leo X added the epitaph:

> What Nature has taken in death,
> Has been restored by Raphael to life.

Such sentimentality proved too much for Aretino, who wrote a satirical pamphlet entitled:

> The Last Will and Testament
> Of Hannibal the Elephant.

This poked fun at many of the leading figures in Rome, including Leo X himself. Aretino's satire caught the public mood, and overnight he became famous. But such renown brought few rewards and considerable danger, requiring the protection of his patrons amongst the rich and powerful. These soon included Cardinal Giulio de' Medici, a fellow Florentine, who happened to be Leo X's cousin. Despite such close connections to the Church, these sophisticated admirers were highly appreciative of Aretino, who boasted of himself, 'Born in a foundlings' hospital, but with the soul of a king'. His poems and satirical works ran the whole gamut from libellous lampoon to unashamed pornography. Dating from this period are his sixteen *Sonetti Lussuriosi* (Lust Sonnets), each written to accompany a drawing of a different sexual position. And such were the power and range of Aretino's satire that the great contemporary poet Ludovico Ariosto, who was then living in Rome, called him admiringly 'the scourge of princes'. In the end, such works inevitably forced him to flee Rome and seek patronage elsewhere. He excused his hurried departure, explaining in a letter to Cardinal de' Medici how 'due to a sudden aberration he has fallen in love with a female cook and temporarily switched from boys to girls'. Aretino's complex, combative, outrageous personality was driven as much by the conflicts of his bisexuality as by inborn resentment resulting from his illegitimacy.

When Cardinal Giulio de' Medici followed in his cousin's footsteps to become Pope Clement VII, Aretino returned to Rome. However, his days of being 'the Rabelais of Rome', as Burckhardt called him, were by now numbered. Although he dutifully continued to satirise and ridicule Julian VII's enemies and those who had voted against him in the papal elections, the intimidation against him became more serious. After a series of death-threats, he once more fled Rome, ending up in Venice in 1527.

Venice remained a staunchly anti-papal city, and under its protection Aretino continued to pillory the hypocrisy of the mighty figures of Rome, as well as turning his attention to the leading lights of Venetian society. Although Rome had succeeded Florence as the centre of the Renaissance, mainly owing to the massive spending on art and architecture by successive popes, Venice had become very much the cosmopolitan capital of Italy, one that would attract such eminent northern European intellectuals as Dürer, Erasmus and Montaigne. It was the city of this era that Shakespeare would use as the setting for *Othello* and *The Merchant of Venice*, and it was here that Aretino was to spend his glory years.

In Venice he was once again drawn into the company of a great artist, this time Titian. Aretino thrived amidst the sophisticated, intellectual, well-connected circle that centred around Titian's studio. Besides Titian, he also became a close friend of the architect Jacopo Sansovino, who was at the height of his fame. Sansovino would commemorate this triumvirate of friendship by depicting their three heads on the fine bronze door he was commissioned to create for the Sacristy of San Marco. At the same time Titian would paint a superb portrait of Aretino, depicting a lean, energetic, surprisingly youthful figure in pensive pose, as if quietly contemplating some further enormity. Such was the man who would boast in a letter 'the doge is my father'.

Despite Aretino's irreverence, and the atmosphere of scandal surrounding his works, he was now regarded as a leading literary figure. Although he could write in neither Latin nor Greek, his use of vernacular Italian did much to encourage popular reading in this language. The output of this 'secretary to the entire world' (his own self-description) was prodigious, including comedies, dialogues and satires, which came hot off the thriving Venetian presses to find avid audiences throughout Italy and beyond. Of similar merit to his literary output, and similar in popularity to his racy pamphlets, was his prodigious output of letters – several volumes of which, despite their personal nature, were published in Venice during his lifetime. These missives are filled with all manner of gossip, outrageous observations concerning well-known figures and unorthodox comments. Writing to

congratulate a well-known Venetian physician who claimed to have found
a remedy for the pox, he could not help but ask, 'Yet what will happen
now? Those who previously abstained from coupling out of fear will surely
lose all their inhibitions, and then where will we be?' In one letter he even
boasted, 'kings and emperors now reply to my letters'. And amazingly, this
was true. Such was the delight his letters caused that his list of correspondents ranged from Pope Clement VII to King Henry VIII of England,
from King Francis I of France to the Holy Roman Emperor Charles V,
the latter pair of rivals being the most powerful rulers in Europe (each
of whom rejoiced in Aretino's observations concerning the other). His
letters were by turn satire, libel, blackmail and dripping unctuous flattery
– for which his aristocratic correspondents often richly rewarded him
(perhaps in part through relief at not being pilloried themselves). These
letters also provide a vivid picture of his age, including a timeless image
of the city in which Aretino lived. In one he describes a scene such as
would be painted by Canaletto some two centuries later:

> With my arms resting on my window sill I began to gaze out over
> the marvellous spectacle of the Grand Canal lined with innumerable
> barges, all packed with spectators delighting in the regatta as two
> competing gondolas manned by brave oarsmen raced past the cheering
> humanity cramming the banks, the Rialto Bridge and the Ca' da
> Mosto.

And he even goes on to anticipate J.M.W. Turner's depiction of misty
Venetian light, describing:

> buildings which at first seemed as insubstantial as stage sets, though
> they were made of real stone . . . the very air which in some places
> appeared so limpid and pure, at others dissolved into murky dullness
> . . . looming clouds stretching from the rooftops to the horizon,
> buildings which flared with flames in the sun's fire, while others
> glowed like semi-molten lead . . . I cried out, 'Where art thou, Titian?'
> If only you could have painted the scene I am describing, you would
> have stupefied all who witnessed your art.

During Aretino's later years, Titian would paint another portrait of his beloved friend. This shows the mature Aretino in all his glory – the glory to which he had perhaps always aspired, though it took the insight of a great artist to realise this in all its fullness. Titian depicts the considerable bulk of a heavily bearded middle-aged figure dressed up in a resplendent scarlet robe and gold chain – here is Aretino *in excelsis*. The bastard from Arezzo now regards himself as the equal of any man – and with some justification. Yet despite his renown he was never a rich man, and his presence was little better than tolerated by the authorities of the city in which he spent his maturity (or what little of this quality he acquired over the years). In Venice, writers and artists still remained confined to the demimonde. They might on occasion have mixed with the nobility, even have been commissioned by them, but they were not admitted to the social rank of such exalted company. And Aretino was not one to forget this. Indeed, it probably sharpened the quill of the man who claimed that he lived 'by the sweat of his ink'. At the same time, he was not one to forget those less fortunate than himself. He was renowned for his generosity, and it was said that he never sat down to his Easter dinner without entertaining eighteen street urchins at his table. Aretino finally died in 1556, at the age of sixty-four. According to one report, 'his death was caused by his falling off his chair when convulsed with laughter at an abominable story'. Even if apocryphal, this would seem to be apt.

II

Discoveries of the Mind

A S WELL AS being a cultural centre, the Venetian Republic would now also begin to attract attention as one of the great European centres of learning and research. This was largely due to the University of Padua on the nearby mainland. The university here was one of the oldest in Europe, having been founded as early as 1222. Its subsequent list of students and faculty would include a roll call of great scientific figures – ranging from Copernicus to Galileo, from the Englishman William Harvey, who discovered the circulation of the blood, to the Flemish-born Andreas Vesalius, the founder of modern anatomy. The medical school at Padua was particularly renowned, and it was here that the twenty-year-old Polish canon Nicolaus Copernicus came to study in 1501. Copernicus had long been fascinated by the night sky, and had attended extracurricular lectures on mathematical astronomy at the University of Cracow, where he first studied in detail the complex movement of the planets around the Earth as described by the Ptolemaic view of the universe. When he came to Italy as a student, he witnessed a lunar eclipse in Bologna in 1500.

It has been claimed, with some justification, that Copernicus' first ideas concerning a solar system, with the Earth and the other planets revolving around the sun, crystallised during his medical studies at Padua. As part of his course he was expected to attend lectures on astrology, for it was believed that the movement of the stars had a direct effect on the overall health and 'humours' of a patient. The leading authorities on this subject remained the Arabic astrologers, who were among the first in recent history to cast serious doubts on the Ptolemaic system. Copernicus' interest in humanism also led him to study the ancient Greek philosophers, translations of whose works were now becoming much more widely available through the printing presses of Venice. In particular, he seems to have learned of the works of Aristarchus of Samos, who used the sun's shadow to calculate a remarkably accurate figure for the distance of the sun from the Earth. Aristarchus was also known to have speculated that the Earth revolved around the sun. Copernicus would take his ideas back to his homeland when he returned in 1503 to take up his clerical posting in the remote province of Warmia in eastern Poland. Here his misgivings concerning the Ptolemaic system continued to deepen, despite the fact that this was the orthodox teaching of the Church and the questioning of such matters was heresy. In correspondence with former student friends in Italy, he began speaking of 'defects' in the Ptolemaic system, admitting, 'I often considered whether there could perhaps be found a more reasonable arrangement . . . in which everything would move uniformly about its proper center [sic], as the rule of absolute motion requires.'

But the young canon remained cautious. Only in his later years would he set down his definitive conclusions in a work entitled *De revolutionibus orbium coelestium* (On the Revolution of the Heavenly Spheres), which firmly placed the sun at the centre of its own planetary system. However, not until he was lying on his deathbed in 1543 would Copernicus allow his revolutionary work to be published. This would literally change the world for ever, and would go on to spark great controversy within the Catholic Church. Even the Protestant leader Martin Luther poured scorn on the idea: 'This fool wishes to overturn the whole science of astronomy. Does not the Holy Bible tell us that Joshua commanded the sun to stand still, and not the earth?' Just under half a century later Copernicus' work would be read by Galileo, who would become a convinced advocate of heliocentric astronomy, before being appointed professor of mathematics at Padua, thus bringing Copernicus' idea full circle.

Just six years after Copernicus left Padua in 1503, the city would be overrun by the forces of the Holy Roman Emperor Maximilian I and the League of Cambrai, causing the university to be shut down. Though the imperial troops only occupied the city for a few weeks, teaching would not resume here until 1517. Amongst the first influx of new students was a young man known as Tartaglia, who would later take up residence in

Venice, where he would make an algebraic discovery that would involve him in the greatest mathematical controversy of his age.

The man known to history as Tartaglia was born Niccolò Fontana in 1500 at Brescia, fifty miles east of Milan (though this was part of Venetian territory at the time). His father was a despatch rider, travelling on horse-back across country to neighbouring towns to deliver mail; but in 1506 he was murdered by robbers, plunging his already-poor family into near-destitution. Worse was to follow in 1512 when Brescia was sacked and pillaged by the invading troops of the French king Louis XII, who had arrived in Italy to support the League of Cambrai against Venice. During the sack more than 45,000 citizens of Brescia were put to the sword by the rioting foreign soldiery. In the course of this mayhem the twelve-year-old Tartaglia, along with his mother and brothers, managed to take sanctuary in the local cathedral, but to no avail. A French soldier slashed Tartaglia across the head with his sword, leaving him for dead. In fact, the blow had only severed his jaw and palate. His mother found him alive, and over the coming month nursed him back to health. But the shock and the wound ensured that the young boy would never fully recover the power of speech – hence his nickname Tartaglia, which means 'the stammerer'. After this he would never shave, growing a beard to camouflage his frightful scars.

As a result of this distressing setback Tartaglia would spend most of his time at home, where he developed an interest in mathematics. Consequently his mother sought out and found a patron for her exceptional son, who took him to study in Padua and then Venice. But as Tartaglia's talent blossomed, and he began outstripping all those around him, this had a detrimental effect on his character, causing him to overcompensate for his lowly origins and ugly appearance by becoming unbearably proud and arrogant. On his return to Brescia he soon fell out with his patron, and around the age of seventeen he left home to teach mathematics in Verona. He is known to have been desperately poor during the ensuing decade or so; despite this, he seems to have got married and had a family sometime in his early thirties. Then in 1534 he moved to Venice, where he quickly began attracting a reputation for brilliance by defeating a number of renowned mathematicians in the public contests that were becoming so popular. These were a development from the philosophical disputations held by medieval theologians, the intellectual equivalent of the jousting tournaments between knights. One of the basic rules was that no contestant should submit to his opponent a problem that he could not himself solve. Victory was a means to advancement for the exceptionally skilled in a hierarchical society; even so, the work Tartaglia gained as a mathematics teacher and tutor to the sons of noble families brought him only a modest income.

Tartaglia was soon making significant contributions to his field. One of his first achievements was to translate Euclid's *Elements* into Italian. Prior to this, Euclid's work had only been available in Latin translations taken from badly corrupted Arabic sources, rendering parts of the text incomprehensible. Tartaglia's work revived the study of this formative text, which would prove an inspiring influence on Galileo, leading him to conclude that 'the book of the world is written in the language of mathematics'. Tartaglia was also the first to understand that cannonballs travel in a trajectory when fired from a gun. (Previously, in accord with Aristotle's thinking, it had been assumed that the cannonball travelled in a straight line, and then simply dropped straight down out of the sky when its momentum was spent.) This enabled Tartaglia to calculate precisely the angle at which to fire a cannonball, if it was to follow a certain trajectory and hit a particular spot. He would publish a book giving tables of angles and target distances, thus hugely improving the accuracy of cannon fire.

However, his major achievement was to discover a general formula for solving cubic algebraic equations (that is, those that contain an unknown to the power of three, or x^3 as we would write it*). The solution of the cubic had become the major mathematical challenge of the age: many sought it, while others simply despaired. When Luca Pacioli had published his masterwork *Summa* in 1494, a work that was said to contain all the mathematical knowledge known to that date, he had offered the opinion that no one would ever find a general solution for cubic equations. Unlike equations involving a simple unknown such as x, or even x^2, cubic

* I have used the simplified modern notation here, which Tartaglia would not have used. At the time, even those who studied algebra had a different name, calling themselves 'cossists' — after the Italian word *cosa*, meaning 'thing', this being the name they gave to the unknown quantity (which we would call x).

equations involving x^3 were simply too complex for there to be a general formula that would give a solution. Yet soon after moving to Venice, Tartaglia managed to prove Pacioli wrong and came up with a solution to the cubic. However, news soon reached him that a young mathematician by the name of Antonio Fior had also discovered a method for solving cubic equations. In the prime of his manhood, Fior was even more arrogant than Tartaglia had been, and he reckoned that the uneducated Tartaglia was merely bluffing in an attempt to enhance his reputation. With the aim of achieving an even greater reputation for himself, he challenged Tartaglia to a mathematical duel.

In fact, Fior had not himself discovered a method for solving the cubic. This had been passed on to him sometime earlier by his teacher, Scipione del Ferro, who had decided on his deathbed that he did not wish the secret he had discovered to die with him. During this period mathematicians were not in the habit of publishing their original discoveries. On the contrary, they were in the habit of keeping them to themselves. These were the methods they could use to overcome their opponents at public mathematical contests, thus gaining them prestige, and on occasion leading to academic posts. However, the method passed on by del Ferro to his eager pupil, Fior, did in fact only solve a certain type of cubic equation. As it happens, we now know that Tartaglia too had only discovered a method for solving one type of cubic equation – and this was the very same method that had previously been discovered by del Ferro.

Preparations were soon under way for the great mathematical contest between Tartaglia and Fior. This was to be held on 20 February 1535 at the University of Bologna, where it was expected to attract a large crowd of mathematicians and aficionados to see this great problem resolved once and for all. Each contestant was to submit a list of thirty cubic equations for his opponent to solve using his own method; according to the rules of such competitions, no one could set a problem that he himself was unable to solve.

It was estimated that each contestant would take at least forty days to work his way through the list he had been given, during which time the contest was liable to seesaw either way in an exciting fashion. At the end of the allotted time, the contestant who had correctly solved the most problems would be declared the winner. The prize for winning the contest was characteristically medieval – the loser would have to pay for a feast to be enjoyed by the winner and thirty of his friends. The real prize would of course be the renown accruing to the winner, who would become famous in universities and courts all over Europe for having discovered the finest solution to this problem, which had defeated all-comers.

However, as the day of the contest approached, Tartaglia became more and more nervous, suspecting that perhaps Fior had in his possession methods for solving every type of cubic equation. Racking his brains, Tartaglia set to work night and day in an effort to discover a method for solving all cubic equations. Just before dawn on 13 February, seven days before the contest was due to begin in Ferrara, Tartaglia at last discovered the answer. By manipulating the different types of cubic equation and making a number of ingenious substitutions, he was able to transform the different types of cubic equation into the very type for which he had a solution.

The day of the contest arrived, and the two contestants duly presented themselves at Bologna University before the assembled authorities and onlookers, including many members of Venetian society who had travelled to see honour done to their city. Each contestant in turn presented his list of thirty problems to the authorities. Fior's list included a number of difficult problems – one involving a transaction with a Jewish moneylender, another concerned with the price of a sapphire – each of which could be reduced to a cubic equation. Unfortunately all the equations set by Fior were of the one type of cubic equation that he knew how to solve. Tartaglia's list, on the other hand, contained individual problems involving all types of cubic equation, the large majority of which Fior had no idea how to solve. The result was a crushing victory for Tartaglia, who managed to solve all thirty of the equations put to him in just two hours, leaving Fior humiliated and struggling to come up with a single answer. Tartaglia graciously declined to accept the thirty meals that were his due, and set off in triumph back to Venice.

But, unbeknown to Tartaglia, this was just the beginning. Word spread through Italy of his great triumph, soon reaching Milan and the ear of Girolamo Cardano, who was possibly the most brilliant and certainly the most unscrupulous mathematician of the age. Cardano would later write to Tartaglia asking permission to include his solution of the cubic in a book he was writing on methods of calculation. He assured Tartaglia that he would credit him as the sole discoverer of this new method, which Tartaglia had ensured still remained known only to himself. But Tartaglia refused to be drawn, replying that he intended to publish his secret in a book of his own.

Girolamo Cardano had been born at Pavia, just outside Milan, in 1501. He was the illegitimate son of a young widow and a distinguished lawyer in Milan called Fazio Cardano, who was sufficiently adept at mathematics to have been consulted by Leonardo da Vinci on difficulties that he was having with certain geometric problems. Even in his youth, Cardano seems to have been a difficult character, and it was with some reluctance that his father sent him abroad to the Venetian Republic to study medicine at the University of Padua. Here his father's misgivings were confirmed: Cardano proved an exceptional student, yet his arrogance knew no bounds. As a student he even put himself up for election as the university rector, winning the post because no one else could afford the expensive entertaining that was part of the job. He expected to finance this by gambling, but to no avail. As if this were not enough, his ensuing behaviour proved so obnoxious that, despite his evident brilliance, the authorities were only persuaded to grant their ex-rector his doctorate after a third vote. His reputation preceded him and, when he arrived back in Milan, the College of Physicians refused to grant him permission to practise locally. In the end he had to return to a village outside Padua, where he practised for five years as a lowly country doctor. Despite such setbacks, Cardano would go on to achieve an international reputation, to the point where he even treated European royalty. Even more astonishing was the fact that he simultaneously gained a supreme facility in mathematics. Yet for Cardano this was to prove no abstract pursuit, and he was soon using his mathematical abilities to great advantage in gambling, a pastime to which he became addicted, to the point where he boasted in his autobiography, 'Not a day went past on which I did not gamble.' His pioneering understanding of probability theory, which was a century ahead of its time, enabled him to know in advance when the odds were in his favour and place his bets accordingly – though this did not stop him from cheating, when he deemed it necessary. On top of these vices he had many others, which may be gleaned from his disarmingly frank autobiography. Despite such revelations, he still claimed in this work: 'I have but one ingrained and outstanding fault – the habit I have of saying things which I know will upset people. I am fully aware of the effect of this, but persist in it regardless of all the enemies it creates for me.'

Besides being a boastful liar, he was also devoid of conscience. In 1534 his father managed to secure for him a post as a mathematics lecturer in Milan. Even so, this did not prevent him from gambling away all his possessions, including his wife's jewellery, so that he ended up in the poorhouse the following year – the very year of Tartaglia's triumph in Bologna.

Cardano bided his time, and it was not until three years later that he wrote to Tartaglia, offering to publish his solution in the work that he was writing. This was intended as a rival to Pacioli's *Summa*, no less, and included an entire chapter listing Pacioli's mistakes. Despite Tartaglia's persistent rejections, Cardano would not be put off and continued to pester him. In 1539 he even went so far as to send the bookseller Zuan Antonio da Bassano as an intermediary, suggesting to him that if he could not wheedle the secret out of Tartaglia, he should ask him for the list of thirty questions that Fior had submitted to him at the contest in Bologna, as well as Tartaglia's thirty correct answers. Cardano suspected that he might be able to gain a clue from these questions and answers, which would enable him to solve the problem of the cubic for himself. Tartaglia was well aware of this, and remained adamant. Finally, Cardano appeared to admit defeat and issued a friendly invitation to Tartaglia to visit him in Milan, suggesting that he might be able to advance Tartaglia's career. Although Tartaglia was well respected as a mathematician in Venice, his earnings as a teacher of this subject remained meagre; as a result he accepted Cardano's offer with alacrity, and in 1539 travelled to Milan to meet his colleague.

Here Cardano soon revealed his hand: if Tartaglia was willing to confide to him the secret of the cubic, he was willing to introduce him to Alfonso d'Avalos, the governor of Milan, who happened to be a friend of his. D'Avalos would certainly be interested in the discoveries that Tartaglia had made on how to increase the accuracy of cannon fire, and was liable to offer him a well-paid post as a military adviser. After giving some thought to the matter, Tartaglia warily agreed to tell him the secret of the cubic, but only after he had made Cardano take the following solemn oath:

I swear to you on the Sacred Gospel and on my faith as a man of honour not only never to publish your discovery, if you reveal it to me, but also promise on my faith as a Christian only to note this down in code, so that even after my death no one will be able to understand it.

Cardano duly swore the oath, and Tartaglia wrote down for him the twenty-four-line poem that he had composed to memorise the secret of how to solve the three types of cubic equation. The words unfolded in all their enigmatic glory, like some magic spell:

When the lonely cube on one side you have found,
With the other terms being together bound:
. . . two numbers multiplied, swift as a bird,
Reveal the simple answer of one third . . .

Ending triumphantly:

These things I did discover before all others
In fifteen hundred and thirty-four
In the city girt by the Adriatic shore.

Cardano duly penned a letter of introduction to d'Avalos. At this point it becomes unclear precisely what happened. The two main contemporary sources, both written down many years after the event, were each heavily biased: one was written by Tartaglia himself, the other by Cardano's pupil Ludovico Ferrari, who claimed to have been present (he almost certainly was not). Tartaglia knew that d'Avalos was not in Milan, but was visiting the fortifications at Vigevano, fifteen miles away on the banks of the River Ticino; so he set off with Cardano's letter of recommendation. However, on the way he seems to have come to the conclusion that he had somehow been tricked by Cardano, and thereupon turned his horse back to Venice. His only comfort was that Cardano was sworn to secrecy.

But Cardano was not a man so easily bound. He began pondering: how had a distinctly mediocre mathematician such as Fior discovered how to solve the cubic, a problem that had defeated the finest minds of the age? The obvious answer appeared to be that he had learned it from his talented master, Scipione del Ferro. In 1543 Cardano travelled to Bologna, where he visited the man who had been entrusted with del Ferro's notebooks and mathematical papers. Amongst these Cardano soon found the formula for solving the cubic. Evidently del Ferro had discovered this first. Cardano returned to Milan and included the formula in his book *Ars Magna*, which he published the following year.

When Tartaglia discovered what had happened, he was furious. He angrily accused Cardano of betraying his oath, but Cardano pointed out that his oath only concerned Tartaglia's discovery, which he had now learned was not entirely original; del Ferro's discovery pre-dated his by some years, and this was the formula that he had included in *Ars Magna*. Tartaglia in fact had only himself to blame — if only he had published his method of solving the cubic, instead of keeping it to himself, none of this would have occurred. As it was, Cardano had triumphed over him, albeit in a most underhand manner. Tartaglia would never really get over this defeat, and would die an embittered impecunious old man in Venice in 1557.

12

The Loss of Cyprus

EANWHILE VENICE ALSO found itself facing some difficulty where money was concerned – a crisis that was only avoided by some swift and astute financial manipulation. The Republic's monetary policy had continued to rely heavily upon silver, whilst maintaining a Gold Standard to keep its currency in line with other European currencies. This fixed the gold ducat as worth 124 silver *soldi di piccoli* (literally 'little coins'). The soldi were considerably smaller than ducats and, in terms of actual precious metal, silver in fact remained the more valuable of the two – a situation reinforced by the fact that gold was more plentiful throughout Europe. This suited the Republic's finances while there was more gold on the markets, and while Venice still had access to silver from the East. All this began to change after the Spanish conquest of Mexico in 1521, when silver began to flow into Europe from the New World. This flow became a torrent with the discovery by the Spanish in 1545 of the Potosi 'Silver Mountain' in Peru, which would soon be accounting for more than half the silver mined throughout the world. Consequently the price of silver plummeted in Europe against that of gold. As a result, the Venetian authorities took the drastic step of transferring the Republic's finances to a Silver Standard – though still at the rate of 124 silver soldi to the gold ducat. This bold move brought a great reward for the authorities, enabling them to pay off the public debt with the official currency, which was now the vastly cheaper silver soldi. Bond-holders, and others who had bought quantities of the public debt, had little choice but to accept this payment. The government had benefited at the expense of its many investors; but, as ever, the interests of the Republic always overrode those of individual citizens.

And never was this more so than when the Republic was confronted with the prospect of war. Venice still faced a potential threat from the powers of Europe as well as from the expanding Ottoman Empire. Caught between a rock and a hard place, the Republic persisted in its policy of appeasement towards the Turkish sultan, Suleiman the Magnificent, while at the same time irritating the European powers by refusing to support any aggressive moves against the Turks. This situation was epitomised in 1535 when Venice antagonised the Holy Roman Emperor, Charles V, by its unwillingness to support his imperial fleet, under the command of the Genoese admiral Giovanni Andrea Doria (great-nephew of Andrea Doria), when it embarked to seize Tunis, which stood in the path of Ottoman expansion along the North African coastline.

However, the policy of appeasing the Turks was to prove terribly flawed when, two years later, Suleiman the Magnificent decided it was time to declare war on Venice: he had simply been biding his time. In August 1537 the Ottoman fleet appeared off the Venetian island of Corfu, under the command of the formidable Khaireddin Barbarossa, a Greek-born former pirate. Corfu guarded the entrance to the Adriatic, and this move directly threatened not only Venice, but also the kingdom of Naples, just a hundred miles across the water, which was part of the European empire ruled by Charles V. Venice appealed to Charles V and the European powers for help, but received no reply. Even more ominously, the imperial fleet under Giovanni Andrea Doria, which happened to be sailing through nearby waters, simply turned tail and set course for Genoa. Doria explained that he could not possibly put into battle without direct orders from Charles V. It was evident that he had not forgotten Venice's lack of support two years previously, and that the Genoese still saw Venice as their real enemy.

Barbarossa landed on Corfu, laying waste the agricultural estates of the Venetian landowners and shipping 20,000 Corfiots off into slavery. But he could not break down the resistance of the 4,000 Venetian soldiers in the Old Citadel overlooking Corfu Town, whose high, thick walls were defended by 700 cannon. Reluctantly Barbarossa withdrew and sailed across the strait to the Italian mainland, where he unleashed his wrath on the coastal population of Calabria. This move prompted the newly elected Pope Paul III to call for a Holy League against the Turks. In 1438 this was duly joined

by Charles V, the Venetians and the Genoese. The combined fleet of the
Holy League under the leadership of Giovanni Andrea Doria now assembled
off Corfu, with more than 300 ships. This included the pride of the
Venetian navy, a huge new galleon with a high prow and rounded bows,
whose gun-ports bristled with cannon, but which had not yet been proven
in battle.

On 28 September 1538 this fleet confronted Barbarossa's force of 120
vessels off the north-eastern Greek coast at Preveza.* Precisely what took
place, and why, during the ensuing battle remains a matter of dispute.
Expecting Doria to follow them into battle, the Venetian galleys and galleon
sailed forward to meet the Turkish warships that Barbarossa had cunningly
lined up along the coast, backed by the cannon on the walls of the fortress
of Actium. The Venetians engaged with the Turkish galleys, which succeeded
in surrounding the becalmed galleon, but were easily held off by the
galleon's superior fire power. However, this was the only good news for the
Venetian forces. Doria held back and refused to support the Venetians.
According to one version, he was attempting to entice the Turkish vessels
beyond the cover of the cannon lining the Actium fortress walls. Other
sources point to evidence that Doria was under orders from Charles V not
to support the Venetians, 'unless victory was certain'.

Either way, the result was an overwhelming defeat for the fleet of the
Holy League, but most of all for the Venetians, who suffered the sinking
of seven galleys, with more than three times that number of vessels captured
and several thousand men taken prisoner. Doria's losses were minimal by
comparison, and he managed to lead most of his fleet to escape in hurried
disarray.

Victory at the Battle of Preveza left Barbarossa in virtual control of
the entire Mediterranean. The following year he would capture almost all
the remaining Venetian and European outposts in the Aegean, and then
return to occupy the Ionian islands at the mouth of the Adriatic. And the
year after that Venice was forced to sign a humiliating treaty with Suleiman

* Coincidentally these happened to be the same waters where Mark Antony had fought the
Battle of Actium in 31 BC, when his desertion by the fleet of his lover Cleopatra had resulted
in his defeat.

the Magnificent, agreeing to pay him 300,000 ducats for the privilege of peace.

The Ottoman navy and their Barbary allies now posed a continual threat to the southern underbelly of Europe, preying at will over the Mediterranean and beyond. At various times Barbarossa had occupied Capri and took Nice, and once even had the effrontery to put his fleet in at Toulon for the winter. Meanwhile unwary fishing boats were constantly attacked way up the Adriatic, and Barbary raiders would soon be putting ashore as far afield as south-west England, taking villagers for galley slaves or to be sold as harem girls in the markets of Algiers and Tripoli.

Suleiman the Magnificent soon began plans for a seaborne invasion of Europe. But in 1566, ending a forty-six-year reign that had seen the Ottoman Empire enter its golden age, he died and was succeeded by his son Selim the Sot, his offspring by a Ruthenian* former slave girl who had risen through the harem to become his favourite. Owing to Sultan Selim's preoccupation with drunken orgies, the effective power was wielded by his father's Bosnian Grand Vizier† Mehmed Sokollu, who continued with Suleiman the Magnificent's expansionist policy, with mixed results – an ambitious invasion across the Black Sea against the southern Russian territory of Ivan the Terrible came to naught when the Ottoman fleet was destroyed in a storm. Despite this setback, in the summer of 1570 another Ottoman fleet launched an invasion of Cyprus, dramatically breaking the peace between the Republic and the Ottoman Empire that had lasted for a quarter of a century.

But despite this treaty, the Venetians had for some time harboured their suspicions concerning Ottoman intentions. On the night of 13 September 1569 there had been an extraordinary midnight explosion at the Arsenale, followed by a fire that had spread beyond the walls and destroyed the entire district to the east of the shipyards, reducing houses, churches and a large convent to a smouldering ruin, before it was brought under control. Ottoman sabotage was suspected, but despite intensive enquiries by the

---

* The Ruthenians were an Eastern Slavic people who occupied much of Western Russia and the Ukraine.
† The sultan's chief minister.

Council of Ten no evidence came to light. Things had come to a head with a number of aggressive incidents in Constantinople against Venetian traders, including the confiscation of trading galleys. At the same time Grand Vizier Sokollu had summoned the Venetian *bailo* to his presence and informed him that, as Cyprus had once been a fiefdom of the Mameluke rulers of Egypt, the island was in fact historically part of the Ottoman Empire now that the Turks ruled Egypt. The Venetians recognised this spurious claim for the threat it was, and immediately pursued the well-trodden path of appealing to all Christian powers for assistance, stressing the seriousness of the situation. If Venice stood under threat, this jeopardised the whole of Europe.

Meanwhile the Ottoman subjugation of Cyprus continued apace. The invasion itself had begun as early as 1 July 1570, when an Ottoman fleet appeared off the coast. This consisted of 350 ships and an army of 200,000 men under the command of Lala Mustafa Pasha. (Even months later, the intelligence reaching the allied Christian fleet had continued to underestimate the Ottoman fleet. Had the two fleets engaged, the humiliation and destruction of Doria's disorganised fleet would have been inevitable. As it was, they lived to fight another day: an accident that was to prove of no little consequence.)

To test the lie of the land, the Ottomans initially launched a raiding party on Limassol, where they sacked the port and a nearby monastery before being driven back by the modest local force of the Venetian commander, Nicolò Dandolo. Mustafa had then sailed along the coast, where owing to Dandolo's lack of experience and indecision he had been allowed to land his entire force at Larnaca, some thirty miles to the east. Victory appeared to be a formality, and Mustafa sent ahead a blind Greek monk captured at Limassol as an emissary to the capital, Nicosia. Mustafa's note demanded that the Venetian authorities surrender the island forthwith, whereupon the Ottomans would be willing to sign a treaty returning to the previous conditions of peace that had prevailed for a quarter of a century between the Republic and the Empire.

No reply was forthcoming, and Mustafa set forth with his invasion force, arriving at Nicosia on 24 July. The city and its surrounding ground were encircled by nine miles of formidable medieval walls, within which was a force of around 20,000 well-armed soldiers, including 500 cavalry and more than 1,000 arquebuses*, all under the command of Dandolo. Unfortunately this force was too small to defend the entire wall at once, its soldiers were too ill trained to effect any rapid deployment and were for the most part comically ill suited to the task at hand (when the infantrymen discharged their arquebuses, the explosions set alight their beards). Despite these drawbacks the defenders of Nicosia managed to resist wave after wave of Turkish assaults, which continued through the intense heat of August, when temperatures frequently rose to 100°F (38°C).

Meanwhile Venice's self-serving alarmist argument – that an alliance of Christian powers was required to halt the march of the Turks – met with a mixed reception. Maximilian II invoked his treaty with the Ottomans, while others presented less plausible excuses. However, in the end Pope Pius V and Philip II of Spain agreed to send a fleet of fifty armed vessels under the command, once more, of Giovanni Andrea Doria. This was due to meet up with the Venetian fleet of just under 150 warships at Zara on the Dalmatian coast. The Christian fleet would now number more than 200 ships, and they estimated that the Ottoman fleet consisted of fewer than 150 ships – the advantage clearly lay with the alliance. But under secret instructions from Philip II, Admiral Doria bided his time at Sicily. After further delays and 'misunderstandings' the combined fleets did not actually meet up until they reached Crete on 1 September. Further obstructive tactics by Admiral Doria meant that it was not until 17 September that the allied fleet eventually set sail for Cyprus. This was to prove a deadly delay.

By the first week of September, Turkish reinforcements had arrived on Cyprus from the mainland, and joined the siege of Nicosia. On 9 September, Mustafa launched his fifteenth assault on the city walls, and at last broke through. Dandolo and his loyal supporters made a final stand at the commander's palace, before he realised that further resistance was useless. Dandolo emerged at the top of the palace steps in his scarlet robes of office in order to surrender, whereupon an Ottoman officer simply decapitated him on the spot. There followed the customary three days of rape

* An early form of musket fired by gunpowder, which discharged a metal ball or scatter-shot.

and pillage.* In this case, local refinements included impaling, mass rape of the young of both sexes, as well as the desecration of Christian churches and holy relics.

When news of the fall of Nicosia reached the allied fleet it simply disintegrated, with the different parties making their separate ways home, thus allowing Mustafa to continue his pillaging unhindered. Over the centuries the strategic position of Cyprus meant that its capital city had accumulated a vast collection of Byzantine and Holy Land treasure, as well as a cornucopia of valuables in the form of gold, silver and jewels. After organising the trans-shipment of booty, Mustafa summoned his troops to order and marched them towards Famagusta on the east coast, leaving behind a sizeable garrison. He was concerned that he had little time to act decisively before the arrival of a large Venetian relief force, which would inevitably be followed by further Christian forces from western Europe.

The customary offer of surrender was sent ahead to the Venetian commander of Famagusta, Marcantonio Bragadin, accompanied by the persuasive gift of Dandolo's head in a basin. Unlike Niocosia, the walls of Famagusta were all but impregnable, and its 8,000 defenders were led by a brave and able commander. Bragadin refused to surrender, and Famagusta was soon completely surrounded, from both land and sea, by a large Turkish force, which was reinforced by further contingents arriving from the mainland. Even so, Bragadin had high hopes that a Venetian relief force would soon arrive.

The siege of Famagusta began in earnest on 17 September. Autumn passed into winter, and still no Venetian fleet appeared. Then spring came and went. By midsummer 1571 food and ammunition were running out. Not a donkey or cat remained in the city, and by now only 500 able-bodied men remained in a fit state to defend the city and the citizens were imploring Bragadin to surrender. Hoping that if he surrendered voluntarily he might circumvent the harsh penalty meted out by the rules of war, on 18 August Bragadin sent envoys to Mustafa, who agreed to peace, allowing

---

* According to the prevailing rules of war, the commander of a besieged city was initially given the opportunity to surrender. If he refused, in the event of the besieging forces breaking into the city their soldiers were permitted to wreak three days of uncontrolled vengeance on those within.

the Venetians astonishingly magnanimous terms. All Venetians would be permitted to disembark for Crete, along with any Greeks or indigenous Cypriots who wished to accompany them. Any of the latter who chose to remain in Cyprus would be permitted to return to their property and livelihood. Mustafa's treaty was guaranteed by the great seal of Sultan Selim, no less, and was accompanied by a personal letter from Mustafa to Bragadin, warmly commending him on the gallantry and courage with which he had defended his city.

The soldiers of the garrison, followed by the local inhabitants who had chosen to leave, were permitted to march out of Famagusta with flags flying as the church bells of the city rang out behind them. When all had embarked safely upon Turkish ships offshore, Bragadin donned his robes of office and, together with his leading officers, went to visit Mustafa in his tent, apparently with the intention of formally handing over the keys of the city. Here he was accorded a courteous reception. However, during the course of the conversation between Mustafa and Bragadin something about the Venetian commander's manner evidently antagonised Mustafa. He suddenly demanded to know what security was being given to ensure that he returned the Turkish ships he was taking to Crete. Bragadin replied that he gave his word of honour. Mustafa scorned this, saying that he required a rather more tangible guarantee, and suggesting that he was given hostages. Bragadin refused this demand, which appeared to impugn his honour. Whereupon Mustafa's face is said to have clouded with anger: he began accusing Bragadin of mistreating Turkish prisoners and breaking the conditions of the peace treaty, all the while working himself up into an uncontrollable rage. Then without warning he leapt to his feet, pulled out his dagger and sliced off Bragadin's ear, at the same time ordering a Turkish bodyguard to cut off his other ear and chop off his nose. Yelling to his guards, Mustafa ordered them to seize and kill Bragadin's accompanying officers, who were at once slashed to pieces.

Soldiers in Mustafa's camp were then ordered to round up all the Christians they could find, behead them and bring their heads to his tent. Soon a pyramid consisting of some 350 heads is said to have been piled up before him. By now word had spread amongst the Turkish ranks of what was taking place and, overcome by a mass hysteria of bloodlust, they rushed into the city to begin murdering its inhabitants. According to one report, at this point Mustafa came to his senses and immediately sent orders forbidding his troops from entering the walls of Famagusta on pain of death. But it was too late – his screaming soldiers had already launched upon an unstoppable orgy of rape, looting and slaughter.

Despite regaining his composure, Mustafa appears nonetheless to have been intent on further inflicting his anger upon Bragadin. After several days of torture, Bragadin was subjected to a grotesque ceremony of public humiliation. First he was dragged around the walls of the city, then tied up and hoisted in a chair to the yardarm of the Turkish flagship, where he was subjected to the jeers and insults of the Turkish sailors. He was then dragged to the main square, where before Mustafa, his gathered soldiery and a crowd of cowed Venetian and Cypriot captives his naked body was tied to a pillar, where according to a contemporary report he was 'brutally flayed alive by a Jewish hangman – a spectacle of hideous and unparalleled barbarity'. Reports of this grim ritual (albeit Venetian reports) speak of Bragadin's composure under torture, and how he continued to call upon Christ to save him and forgive his enemies right up to the moment of his death. The last of his skin was then removed from his lifeless body and stuffed with straw; afterwards this was placed astride a cow and paraded through the streets. Later this hideous dummy was hauled to the masthead of a Turkish galley and carried off in triumph to Constantinople, where it was graciously presented to Sultan Selim.

This story has an all-but-incredible coda, whose truth would appear to be confirmed by recently uncovered evidence. According to one version of this story, some years earlier Bragadin had organised the payment of a ransom for the release of an Italian from Verona who had been taken prisoner by the Turks. Upon hearing what had happened to Bragadin, this man had sworn to do all he could to redeem Bragadin's fate. Nine years later, after a peace treaty had been signed between Venice and the Ottoman Empire, he travelled to Constantinople, where he learned that Bragadin's skin was kept as a trophy in the Turkish Arsenal. Either by ingenuity or bribery, or both, he contrived to steal the skin and carried it back to Venice, where he presented it to Bragadin's family. (The other version of this story has the skin being removed by one Girolamo Polidoro, a survivor of the siege of Famagusta.) According to the nineteenth-century American writer and popular historian of Italy, Francis Marion Crawford, 'It is related that the skin was found soft as silk and was easily folded into a small space; it is preserved in the church of San Giovanni e Paolo.' In 1961 the lead casket reputed to hold Bragadin's skin was opened and found to contain several remnant scraps of tanned human skin.

As these stories suggest, the siege of Famagusta and the fate of Bragadin would enter the folklore of *La Serenissima*: here was the exemplar of Venetian resistance and honour betrayed – though perhaps more significant was the fact that these twin events unquestionably marked the end of Venice's glorious imperial period and the beginning of a lengthy twilight.

Part Three
The Long Decline

13

The Battle of Lepanto

FOLLOWING THE DEBACLE of the Holy League's attempt to relieve Cyprus from Ottoman aggression, there was no avoiding the serious nature of the threat now facing western Europe. Either the Holy League prevailed, or all was lost. Pope Pius V decided to act decisively, and persuaded Philip II of Spain of the need to cooperate with Venice. Giovanni Andrea Doria was replaced, and Philip II appointed his illegitimate half-brother, the dashing twenty-six-year-old Don Juan of Austria, as captain-general of the fleet of the Holy League, with the assurance that the opinions of the newly appointed Venetian commander Sebastiano Venier and the papal commander Marcantonio Colonna would be taken into account in all major decisions. Filled with a new resolve, the 250 ships of the Holy League fleet assembled off Sicily at the port of Messina (just as Famagusta was surrendering). The formidable task facing Don Juan was to search out and engage the Turkish fleet, and he set sail for the entrance to the Adriatic, where the Turks were known to be operating.

It was now that news reached the commander of the Ottoman fleet, Ali Pasha, that Famagusta had fallen. And when this was followed quickly by intelligence that the Venetian fleet under Venier had sailed for Messina, Ali Pasha decided to sail at once for the Adriatic, at the head of which stood a defenceless Venice. He began by launching attacks on Corfu and the Dalmatian coast. However, when he heard of the approach of the combined Holy League fleet, he decided against possibly being cut off in the Adriatic and withdrew to the safe anchorage of Lepanto (modern Nafpaktos), on the north shore at the entrance to the Gulf of Corinth. On 4 October 1571, when the Holy League fleet put in at Kefalonia, they learned of the fall of Famagusta and the outrage on Bragadin, uniting the allies in widespread anger. However, differences between the allies remained, and the same day there was a volatile incident on Venier's galley when a Spanish liaison officer and his men insulted some Venetian sailors, resulting in drawn swords and a fight during which some men were killed. Venier immediately arrested the Spaniards and had them hanged from the mast-head. News of this incident so enraged Don Juan that he ordered Venier's arrest. Fortunately, cooler minds prevailed before any harm could be done, and the order was not despatched. Had Venier been arrested, the alliance would certainly have collapsed on the spot, with the 100 Venetian galleys refusing to participate in any further action. Ironically, it may well have been Giovanni Andrea Doria who was responsible for averting this catastrophe. Philip II had allowed Doria to join the Spanish contingent, with secret orders for him to keep an eye on the impulsive Don Juan, making sure that he did not recklessly jeopardise the Spanish fleet.

Don Juan now set sail south, determined to confront the Ottoman fleet, arriving off Lepanto on 6 October. The sight of the Holy League fleet offshore had a galvanising effect on Ali Pasha. Both fleets were of similar size, but Ali Pasha was convinced that the Ottoman fleet had the advantage. The Turks had remained undefeated since the Battle of Preveza, more than thirty years previously. Here was his chance to gain glory by destroying the Holy League fleet, leaving the way open for an Ottoman invasion of Europe. The scene was set for the most decisive naval battle in western history since the Battle of Actium, which had taken place 1,600 years previously just fifty miles to the north.

As dawn broke on 7 October it was seen that Ali Pasha had arranged his fleet in a long crescent extending from the northern shore out into the waters at the entrance to the gulf, thus ensuring that he could not easily be outflanked. As the two fleets rowed in line towards one another, Don Juan had two galleons towed ahead of his fleet; his intention was that the gunfire from their cannon would interrupt the Ottoman line of advance. This tactic succeeded well beyond his estimation when it was seen that the Ottoman captains mistook the galleons for unarmed supply vessels, and several galleys broke line to move in for the kill. The two galleons opened fire and more than half a dozen Ottoman galleys were sunk, to say nothing of the consequent confusion arising from the break in their line as they manoeuvred around the galleon.

Just before 11 a.m. the two lines began coming together, first in the north where the Turkish galleys closed with the left wing of the Holy League fleet. This was the Venetian contingent of more than 100 galleys, and fierce fighting broke out as the two lines rammed and engaged, the combatants leaping onto the enemy's decks, swords clanging against scimitars above a howl of cries, with the occasional detonation and cloud of smoke from cannon fire. Gradually the Venetians managed to force the Ottoman vessels back against the shore. In the shallow waters before the beaches the Turkish soldiers began abandoning their galleys and scrambling ashore, only to be pursued by the Venetians. The Turkish retreat quickly degenerated into flight, as the soldiers tried to escape across the salt flats for the safety of the hills, while being cut down by the pursuing Venetians.

The fighting between the central sections of the two lines of galleys was fiercer. These squadrons were commanded by Ali Pasha and Don Juan respectively, with the two commanders visible amidst the thicket of hand-to-hand fighting and the blast of arquebuses. After an hour or so of desperate combat, Ali Pasha's bodyguard of 400 highly trained Janissaries had managed to fight their way aboard Don Juan's flagship, the *Real* (Royal), only to be repulsed, before another wave made it aboard. This too was eventually driven back, and the Spanish soldiers now scrambled forward onto the Ottoman flagship, the *Sultana* (named after the sultan's wife). Here, amidst the confusion of yells and savage fighting, Ali Pasha was hit on the head by a cannonball, knocking him to the ground dead. Don Juan ordered his body to be carried aboard the *Real*, but the joyous Spanish soldiers hacked off his head and jammed it onto a pike, waving it in the air for all to see as they yelled encouragement to their comrades. The Turks, seeing their commander dead and their flagship taken, began retreating across the decks of their galleys, fleeing as best they could.

Meanwhile the southern wing of the Holy League fleet was in trouble. This was under the command of Giovanni Andrea Doria, who had found his sixty galleys outnumbered by the approaching 100 Ottoman galleys. Fearing that he was about to be outflanked, he contravened his explicit orders and separated his wing from the main body of Don Juan's fleet, rowing his galleys south to counter any outflanking manoeuvre. The Turkish commander, Uluch Ali, immediately exploited this blunder, switching the direction of his galleys with the intention of passing inside, through the gap in the line of the Holy League fleet. This would leave him free to attack the exposed rear of the allied line. Uluch Ali's galleys were soon cutting through the galleys straggling at the edge of Don Juan's exposed central line. A squadron of sixteen galleys, which had been held in reserve behind the main line of the Holy League fleet, surged forward to stem Uluch Ali's advance and were soon engaged in fierce fighting. But to no avail: the Turkish galleys swept through, leaving the Christian galleys cut to pieces, drifting in the water, manned only by dead oarsmen, their decks littered with slaughtered soldiery.

At this stage, the victorious Don Juan was able to disengage his galleys from the fighting and come to the rescue. Uluch Ali saw that he was outnumbered and cut off, abandoning his intention to attack the rear of the Holy League fleet. With all speed he began making his way north towards the shelter of the islands off the coast, where he made good his escape from the battle.

This was the last of the Turkish resistance, and when the Turkish galleys in the main line saw what had happened they turned tail, heading back towards Lepanto. Within five hours the battle had been won by Don Juan's Holy League fleet, and Europe was saved. The loss of life amongst the Christian ranks had been heavy, but the Ottomans had suffered a devastating slaughter. Amongst the Holy League fleet probably 7,500 men died, with many wounded (amongst these, on one of the Spanish galleys, was the twenty-four-year-old Miguel de Cervantes, the future author of *Don Quixote*, who would remember the battle as the greatest experience of his life). The Holy League fleet lost fifty galleys, whilst the Ottoman losses included more than 200 vessels; probably around 30,000 Turks died and nearly 7,000 were taken prisoner. At the same time, the Holy League soldiers were able to free as many as 15,000 mostly Christian slaves from the Turkish galleys. News of the victory at Lepanto did not reach Venice until 18 October, some days after news of the fall of Famagusta and the outrages perpetrated on Bragadin. Within an hour the city had put aside its atmosphere of mourning, humiliation and fear, launching with gusto into celebrations inspired as much by relief as by joy. The church bells rang out over the rooftops, the crowds crammed into the piazza before the Doge's Palace, and as night fell the people danced with abandon amidst streets and buildings illuminated by thousands of trembling candles.

Yet what precisely had this victory achieved? Uluch Ali had eventually made it back to Constantinople with half his galleys intact, and these would become the core of a new Ottoman fleet that was constructed in record time. When the Venetians sent emissaries to Constantinople to negotiate a new peace in 1573, Grand Vizier Sokollu told them, 'In wresting Cyprus from you we deprived you of an arm; in defeating our fleet you have only shaved our beard.' Of the Republic's larger possessions in the eastern Mediterranean, only Crete now remained, with Venice no longer controlling any trade routes to the Levant; whilst in the western Mediterranean the Ottoman navy and its Barbary allies continued to menace European shipping – as late as 1575 Cervantes would be captured by Barbary pirates on his way home to Spain, and would be carried back to Algiers to spend five years as a slave. Despite this ongoing menace, the victory at Lepanto did establish an important precedent. This can be seen in the funeral oration that had been delivered at San Marco to honour those who had died in the battle: 'They have taught us by their example that the Turks are not insuperable, as we had previously believed them to be.' This crucial psychological point, along with the very fact that the European powers could muster a fleet, put an end to the possibility of a full-scale Ottoman invasion. Europe would remain a Christian continent.

Despite the decline of its eastern trade, for a while Venice continued to prosper as never before. Islands such as Crete and Corfu remained a valued source of income, while once again the reopened alum trade with the Anatolian mainland flourished. Consequently the city's population would go on rising until it reached an all-time peak of 190,000 in 1575, when it was the plague rather than economic forces that brought about its reduction. The public debt may have been reduced at a stroke by the conversion to the Silver Standard, but those amongst the wealthy who continued to hold long-term bonds in the public debt still received more in interest on these bonds than they paid in income tax; the rich got richer, also receiving income from their mainland estates. The mainland territory of the Veneto was now stabilised, and income from cities such as Padua, Vicenza and Treviso contributed to keep taxes low in Venice itself.

The rich queued up to have their portraits painted by the likes of Titian, who had now reached such eminence in his old age that, in recognition of his services to the Republic, he had been elevated to the nobility and his family name was inscribed in the Golden Book. Titian would finally die at around ninety years of age during the plague outbreak of 1576. He had achieved such fame and riches that he received the doubtful honour of having his house ransacked by thieves after his death. During this grim time when inns and shops were closed and the streets were deserted, there were frequent outbreaks of civil disorder as the downtrodden poor took out their spite on those who had benefited so disproportionately during the years of prosperity. The inhibitions of others were cast aside as the belief prevailed that the plague outbreak marked the long-delayed end of the world – expected by many at the one-and-a-half millenium in 1500. Venice had not suffered an affliction like this since the Black Death more than two centuries previously. All those who could, fled to their estates on the mainland, whilst those suffering from the plague were shipped across the Lagoon to the Lazaretto islands.* These were soon so overflowing with the afflicted and the dying that sufferers were then housed in disused galleons anchored nearby. These spots were said to have witnessed pitiful scenes, with desperate inmates screaming in their extremity beneath make-shift shelters on the small islands, while others threw themselves from the high decks of the galleons, and many called pitifully to passing fishing boats to rescue them. A continual pall of smoke hung over the entire Lazaretto islands from the burning of the dead bodies. In all, 51,000 citizens of the city and the lagoon islands (well over a quarter of the population) are known to have died in the outbreak, which began in the winter of 1575

---

* In the early fifteenth century the small island of Santa Maria di Nazareth in the Lagoon was established as an isolated lodging for travellers arriving from ports known to be affected with the plague. Here they would be detained for forty days (giving rise to the name 'quarantine'). The island was known locally as Nazaretto, but when it was also used for isolating those suffering from leprosy it became known as Lazaretto (after Lazarus, the beggar whom Christ cured of leprosy). The general name Lazaretto stems from this island. Later, when the quarantine area was extended to the neighbouring island, the two islands became known as Lazaretto Vecchio (old) and Lazaretto Nuovo.

and disappeared as mysteriously as it had arrived in the early months of 1577.

Titian's death left his rival Tintoretto as the city's acknowledged leading artist, along with Veronese. Tintoretto had been born Jacopo Comin in Brescia on 29 September 1518. His father was a dyer by trade; hence Jacopo's nickname 'Tintoretto', which means little son of the tinter (or dyer). Tintoretto quickly demonstrated a precocious talent, using his father's dye to paint on the walls of his workshop. When he was fifteen his father took him to Venice to become an apprentice in Titian's studio. But after ten days the master despatched his pupil back home. Such was Tintoretto's expressive independence of style that Titian recognised that he would never accept the discipline of being his pupil, one of whose duties was to finish the paintings of his master. Tintoretto's artistic style was matched by his dramatic temperament, which would further alienate him from Titian when he returned to Venice. However, Titian was generous enough to recognise his growing talent, a recognition that brought Tintoretto his first commissions. Despite these, during his early years he suffered from some financial hardship, whilst continuing to teach himself how to master the necessary technique. During these years he ambitiously advertised his studio with a notice proclaiming that his paintings had 'the design of Michelangelo and the colour of Titian'. Yet still he received insufficient work. At the age of twenty-eight he desperately offered to paint two large works on religious subjects for the church of Madonna dell'Orto for no other recompense than the cost of the materials, in order to advertise his talent. This was beginning to develop through his study of Michelangelo, his attendance at dissections in the medical schools, and his habit of making wax models of the figures grouped in his paintings. This gave them a three-dimensional appearance amidst the perspective background, for which he often used dark tones to emphasise the drama of his scenes. The subjects of his paintings for the Madonna dell'Orto were the Worship of the Golden Calf and the Last Judgement, theatrical settings which accorded with his style to such effect that they were quickly recognised as the works of a new master.

Soon afterwards Tintoretto was commissioned to paint a portrait of the satirist Aretino. In order to impress upon his untameable sitter who was to be master of the situation, Tintoretto is famously said to have measured up Aretino using a pistol – a hint that Aretino quickly understood. The subsequent portrait was recognised as showing a deep understanding of Aretino's nature.

Tintoretto was by now receiving civic commissions for works in San Marco, an accolade that elevated him to the company of Venice's finest artists, past and present. But some of his finest work, along with master-pieces by Giovanni Bellini, Titian and Veronese, would be destroyed in 1577 by a fire that gutted many of San Marco's major council chambers — to such an extent that parts of the administration were forced to move temporarily to the Arsenale. Tintoretto and Veronese would be able to paint replacement works, but those by Bellini and Titian were lost for ever.

While Titian had become an honoured and very well-rewarded cultural ambassador for Venice, travelling far afield to paint the portraits of kings and queens, an emperor and a pope, Tintoretto would never leave Venetian territory, indeed seldom straying beyond the often claustrophobic confines of the city itself. His character remained throughout his life a not uncommon Venetian blend of spiritual otherworldliness and unscrupulous ambition. He made a habit of asking for little or no payment for a commis-sioned work, other than to cover his costs; yet he would go out of his way to ensure by any means that he obtained the commission in the first place. In 1560 he was asked to bid, along with several other distinguished artists including Veronese, for a commission to paint the ceiling of the school of San Rocco. Each of the competitors was asked to submit their drawings and designs for judgement. Instead, Tintoretto quietly measured the space to be covered by the painting, hastily painted a canvas of the same size with a speed and expertise such as only he could accomplish, then secretly had the painting put in place and covered over. When the day of the competition arrived and he was asked to submit his design, he simply pulled back the cover to reveal his finished painting in place. The judges, to say nothing of his competitors, were furious, remonstrating that he was only meant to submit a design for the painting. To which he replied that this was his method of designing a painting and he knew no other way – for a design was surely intended to show the ultimate effect of the painting.

Such methods made him many enemies, but all were forced to admire the sheer artistry of his work, which retained its spectacular flourishes and the dimmed realism of its atmospheric colouring throughout his life. And even in old age, he still could not resist combining this brilliance with his underhand methods of obtaining work. Such unscrupulousness would be epitomised in the commissioning and execution of his final masterpiece, *Paradise*. The painting itself would be a towering work filled with all manner of ethereal and exemplary figures swirling through the clouded heavens beneath the haloed figure of Christ *in excelsis*. Yet the manner in which Tintoretto won this important commission was somewhat less exalted: he virtually blackmailed various influential senators, telling them how he prayed night and day that he could gain this commission, believing it would allow him one day to enter paradise. Two years after completing this work, Tintoretto would die at the age of seventy-six, when he would be buried in the church of Madonna dell'Orto, where he had painted the paintings that first brought him to wider public notice.

14

Women of Venice

THE MODELS USED by Venetian artists such as Titian and Tintoretto for their sumptuous nudes would usually have been courtesans, or sometimes prostitutes. As the ambassador of Ferrara noted with regard to Titian, 'I suspect that the girls whom he often paints in different poses arouse his desires, which he then satisfies more than his limited strength permits.' No respectable woman would have been permitted to pose in such a fashion.

In a city of otherwise somewhat strict morality, there were a surprising number of courtesans and prostitutes. Paradoxically, this was because the morality, especially that imposed upon women, *was* strict during this period. Young women were preserved as virgins until they were married, usually well before they were twenty; these young women, as well as wives, were closely chaperoned when they left their homes. This left a large number of young men, who usually did not get married until at least their late twenties, with considerable sexual energy to expend. Owing to the authorities' fear of homosexuality, prostitution was covertly encouraged, though strictly regulated, so that it brought in a tidy sum to the Republic's exchequer. Prostitutes were confined to certain streets and were required to sit at their windows with their breasts exposed. It appears the authorities soon became more concerned with revenue than regulation, for a shocked English visitor during this time estimated that there were around 20,000 prostitutes working in the city, 'whereof many are esteemed so loose, that they are said to open their quivers to every arrow'. While this description would seem to be symptomatic of the profession, outrage may well have caused him to exaggerate their number – local sources suggest a figure closer to 15,000. Even so, this would have accounted for more than one in five of the entire female population. Not for nothing was Venice a city of sailors; and as word of its unique beauty, artistic treasures and reputed libertinism spread over Europe, it also began to attract a stream of cultured and dissipated visitors. During 'the folly and madness' of the pre-Lenten Carnival, when the revellers of both sexes wore masks, prostitutes were able to escape the districts to which they were normally confined. And they also customarily took part in other typically Venetian events. At the regatta – which Aretino had so vividly described, and Canaletto would so colourfully depict – there was traditionally a women's race where the prostitutes competed standing bare-breasted, rowing in two-oared gondolas, cheered on with gusto by the crowds lining the quaysides. But there was no such place on the public stage for respectable women.

When young women married, they were expected to bring with them a handsome dowry. Many noble families were unable to afford these dowries for more than one or two of their daughters. This meant that a large number of women of good families were left unmarried. These were for the most part encouraged, or forced, to forswear the world, become nuns and enter convents. The extent of this practice can be seen in the fact that by 1481 there were 2,500 nuns in the city. These were confined in some fifty convents – one-third of which were on remote islands in the lagoon. Many of the nuns confined in these institutions felt no calling, and as a result tales of desperate unhappiness and promiscuity abounded. Perhaps inevitably, Aretino wrote a scurrilous book entitled *The Secret Life of Nuns*, which contained much graphic and hilarious description of the titillating antics within a convent. The reality was rather more desperate and sad, as can be seen from the case of Laura Querini, whose story would be repeated in many variations, and in many convents.

Laura took her vows in 1584 at the age of fifteen in the convent of San Zaccaria, whose sisters included many from amongst the most noble families in Venice, as indeed she was. The convent itself was in the heart of the city, backing onto a canal that led off the busy Riva degli Schiavoni just a stone's throw away. This location, around the corner from San Marco, must have made it even more difficult for the nuns, who would have heard all the daily commerce and cries of the city beyond their incarcerating walls. However, although they could never leave the convent, the rule for the nuns within it appears to have been quite relaxed, though in a characteristically Venetian fashion. A woman who regularly visited the monastery, by the name of Donna Cipriana, was in the habit of introducing Laura to male 'friends', and during her twenties and thirties Laura would form several 'friendships' with visiting young men. Although these meetings were secret, they were conducted in the convent parlour, suggesting the connivance of someone within the monastery. However, nothing particularly untoward appears to have taken place at these meetings. Laura would later claim, 'I never did anything wicked, that is, I never lost my virginity.' But as she approached her forties, Laura evidently found the whispers, fondlings and kisses in the parlour increasingly inadequate.

When Laura was thirty-nine, Donna Cipriana introduced her to a nineteen-year-old young man whom she came to call Zuanne Cocco. As she confessed, 'I fell in love with him, and I induced him to fall in love with me.' She even paid Donna Cipriana to bring her magic potions, so that she could cast a spell on Zuanne, inducing him to make love with her. But Zuanne remained cautious: having sex with a nun could result in the death penalty. So Laura hatched a desperate and daring plan. Together with a fellow nun she called Sister Zaccaria, she began digging a wall in a storeroom that backed onto the canal, using a piece of iron pulled from the grille on her cell window. For more than a month Laura and Sister Zaccaria continued digging away at the stone wall – which proved to be six stones deep – before finally they made a hole through it that overlooked the waters of the canal. They disguised the hole on the canal side by pushing a large stone into place and blocking the gaps at the edge of the stone with terracotta. The hole in the storeroom wall they apparently covered with black and white lime.

Laura's determination evidently overcame Zuanne's reluctance. He set out one night, accompanied by his cousin (who was intended as Sister Zaccaria's reward for her part in the plot), and together the two of them made their way by boat along the canal, put a plank across from the boat to the hole and clambered into the convent. According to Laura, 'they stayed with us for two or three hours, while they had intercourse with us'. After this first visit, Zuanne returned alone and concealed himself in the storeroom for some ten to twelve days. During this time Laura brought him food, but also diligently made a point of being seen by the other nuns in the communal places within the convent, 'and then when everyone was asleep, I went alone to be with him'.

Yet despite all Laura's precautions, news of her secret trysts somehow leaked out and was passed on to the authorities, who set about putting her on trial, threatening her with torture if she did not reveal every detail of her dalliance. The preceding quotations from Laura are all taken from her eventual trial, at which she was forced to reveal the true identity of the young men she had called Zuanne Cocco and his cousin Zorzi. These were Andrea Foscarini and Alvise Zorzi, both scions of distinguished noble families (each of which would boast a doge). However, as soon as Andrea and Alvise had got wind of Laura's coming trial they had fled. In their absence they would be sentenced to twenty years' exile from the city and all the territories of Venice, with the stipulation that if ever they set foot in the Republic during their exile they would be sentenced to death. In the course of the trial it came out that Laura and Sister Zaccaria had been assisted in their plot by a servant woman called Antonia and her husband Zulian, who worked as a carpenter at the Arsenale. They had acted as go-betweens, and Zulian had used his boat to collect Andrea Foscarini and Zorzi. For their comparatively minor part in the plot, Antonia and Zulian were given extremely harsh sentences, presumably to deter others who might be tempted to accept payment for such services. Zulian was condemned to serve eight years as a galley slave in the Republic's navy – with the proviso that if he was physically unable to complete this term he would receive eight years in gaol and have his right hand cut off. His wife was sentenced to be publicly flogged through the streets the quarter-mile from San Marco to the Rialto – an ordeal that would certainly have inflicted on her seriously debilitating injuries and incurred such disgrace as to have rendered her a social outcast (as indicated in the further proviso that if henceforth she ventured again into a convent or convent church, she would have her nose and ears cut off).

This trial, which took place in 1614, caused a great scandal, along with widespread gossip, made all the more piquant by the fact that the convent of San Zaccaria was known to contain daughters of the most noble families.

The precise fate of Laura and Sister Zaccaria remains unknown. As they were both nuns they could not have been sentenced by the secular court, and would have been placed in the hands of the Patriarch of Venice. According to records in the Vatican, the Patriarch sent to Rome a plea for their absolution, almost certainly at the instigation of the powerful Querini family, so it seems that they may well have escaped further punishment. Yet the final word should perhaps be left with the Cambridge historian Mary Laven, whose *Virgins of Venice* includes this and many other examples of life in Venetian convents: 'For these two women, a life sentence within the walls of San Zaccaria was probably punishment enough.'

The nearest that Venetian women came to any degree of self-fulfilment and independence was perhaps in the life of the courtesan, though this way of life was beset by its own risks. The courtesan occupied an ambiguous niche in society. The 'honest' courtesan was certainly far from being a common prostitute, despite the fact that she expected to be paid for her sexual favours. She was frequently a figure of some repute, attracting artistically talented and intellectual young men (and some not so young) to the social gatherings she hosted. Here conversation was often witty, intelligent or poetic – fulfilling a genuine need, for these aspects of social life were not usually found at home amidst the domesticity of family life, in the corridors of power at the Doge's Palace or amidst the businessmen who gathered at the Rialto. Courtesans were often 'sponsored' by rich and powerful figures, but usually came to rely upon the generosity of their several admirers. As such, jealousies were frequent; and this certainly contributed to the risk of the courtesan's life. Without a powerful figure lurking in the background, one false move could easily bring about her downfall and ruin. And even with such protection, the prospect of ruin was ever-present – in the form of fading looks, pregnancy or sexual diseases, most notably syphilis. This hideous disease had spread throughout Italy during the last decade of the fifteenth century, and from then on was a constant threat to sexual libertines of both sexes. Where prostitutes were concerned, syphilis was taken as an occupational hazard, for both the women and their clients. Painful and quackish 'cures' abounded – with treatments ranging from poisonous mercury to harmless (and useless) 'charms' such as garlic. Prostitutes would continue working until disfigurement and other hideous ailments rendered this impossible. With courtesans, the effect was more genteel, but equally vicious. A hint of this disease, in whispered gossip or a jealous satirical poem, and a courtesan's clientele of admirers could vanish overnight. Few patrons were of sufficient compassion to support a courtesan when her health and charms had gone. And yet the finest of the courtesans were figures of genuine distinction.

Amongst these was Veronica Franco, who was born in Venice in 1546. Her family belonged to the merchant class, though her mother before her had been an 'honest' courtesan, and coached her in the skills, charms and intellectual accomplishments that were required if she wished to establish herself as a courtesan, or gain a good marriage. Initially, Veronica succeeded in the latter sphere, and in her teenage years was married to a prosperous physician called Paolo Panizza. But this did not last, and they were soon separated. Around this time, Veronica gave birth to the first of her three surviving children, though she later insisted that Paolo was not the father. By the age of nineteen she had established herself as a courtesan, her name appearing alongside that of her mother in *Il Catalogo di tutte le principal et più honorate cortigiane di Venizia* (The Catalogue of All the Main and Less Honoured Courtesans of Venice), which was published in 1565. This listed the names, along with an indication of the addresses and fees charged by known courtesans in the city. Veronica is listed as living in the Santa Maria Formosa district, charging '2 scudi' and with 'her mother as go-between.'* *Il Catalogo* would have been for under-the-counter circulation in certain bookshops, being purchased by locals and acting as a guide for visiting tourists. The first general guidebook to the city, *Venetia, città nobilissima*, would be published sixteen years later in 1581

Within nine years Veronica Franco would be the most celebrated courtesan in the city. There is a portrait of her, almost certainly by Tintoretto, which depicts someone of striking rather than traditionally beautiful features, with the gaze of a self-possessed woman of some character and

---

* The modesty of Veronica's fee has led some to suspect that *Il Catologo* also had a certain mischievous satirical intent. This is indeed possible, given that amongst the 210 courtesans listed, several charged five times more than this amount, and one Paula Filacanevo charged as much as 30 scudi. On the other hand, it has been argued that the coinage referred to in Veronica's case could have been silver scudi, which were each of only slightly less value than a gold ducat.

seriousness. It is not difficult to imagine her as the talented poet and letter-writer that she was by now becoming, to such an extent that she was a welcome guest at the literary salon presided over by Domenico Venier,* and was soon exchanging love-poems with his young relative, the poet Marco Venier.

In 1574 the French king Henry III made a celebrated visit to Venice, when the city went out of its way to impress upon the twenty-three-year-old monarch its worthiness as an ally in the dangerous power game now being played out in Europe between France, Spain and the Holy Roman Empire. Not only was Henry shown the most advanced technology of the Republic (the galley miraculously constructed in the Arsenale in the time it took him to dine) and its cultural achievements (having his portrait painted by Tintoretto), but he was also encouraged to sample the delights for which the city had now achieved renown throughout Europe. One evening, his royal finery disguised beneath a cloak, he managed to slip out of a side-door to a waiting gondola. Here he was taken on a journey through the canals, probably by the poet Marco Venier, and secretly deliv-ered to the house of Veronica Franco. Here, in the words of Veronica, he arrived 'like Jupiter descending from heaven to my humble roof. Afterwards she would write him a letter and two sonnets, expressing her 'immense desire' for him. When he left, Henry had taken with him a small coloured enamel portrait of her, which she had given him 'in exchange for the lively image that you have bequeathed to the centre of my heart'. Veronica would never forget this royal visit – as an overwhelming personal experience, as well as for the ultimate social honour it bestowed upon her.

The following year she would publish the first of her two books of poems, *Terze Rima*. This consists of twenty-five poems, though only seventeen of them are hers. Others are by Marco Venier and another, unnamed, male author. Veronica's own poems give all manner of insights into her life and her understanding of herself as a woman. She explicitly challenges the time-honoured idealised woman so beloved of Dante and Petrarch. Instead, she proclaims her sexual expertise, claiming that it is enough to satisfy any man's

---

* A close relative of Sebastiano Venier, the Venetian hero at Lepanto, who would be elected doge in 1570, the third in this distinguished family to be honoured with the post.

desires. At the same time she also gives glimpses into her daily life and preoccupations, which appear to have been similar to those of many bourgeois Venetian women of the period: she sits for her portrait, plays the lute, prepares for a dinner party with her friends, and so forth. These poems contain numerous classical allusions, especially to the works of Ovid and Catullus, echoing many of their joys and agonies in the game of love.

But we also have a glimpse of the more difficult side of Veronica's life. At the literary salon in the Ca' Venier she made an enemy of Marco's cousin Maffio Venier, an overambitious ne'er-do-well who lived beyond his means and was dissatisfied with the minor diplomatic postings that he only achieved through his family name (and he may well have increased his income by passing on state secrets as a spy). Jealous of her talents and the adoration accorded her at the Ca' Venier salon, Maffio wrote a number of satirical poems about her in the Venetian dialect, and circulated them amongst fellow poets. In them he lashes out at everything his jealous mind can concoct about Veronica – her perceived social-climbing, her inflated reputation as a poet and an intellectual, but above all her perceived beauty. Indeed, there is more than a suggestion that she may have turned down his impecunious sexual advances. He lambasts her ('an infamous bastard born beneath the stairs'), claiming that she puts on airs and calls herself *principessa* (princess), while holding a *corte* (court), which is in reality no more than *una stalla* (a stable). In another poem he descends to grotesque exaggeration and lies, hinting that she might have syphilis:

> Your head is a sea of pustules,
> Your face all covered in wrinkles,
> And your eyes bulge and roll
> As if exorcising your soul.
> Your tits hang so low
> That you can use them to row
> When you're fucking about on a boat.

In one of her poems in *Terza Rima*, Veronica defends herself with dignity, rebutting Maffio's profanities by pointing out what they reveal about their author. By descending to such diatribes, he simply drags himself down into the mud. In other poems she takes it upon herself to defend all defenceless courtesans against such hatred, castigating those men who insist upon placing women on pedestals, attempting to transform them into some idealised virginal beauty – only to tear them down again when they do not live up to this impossible state, blaming them for all the decadence which they saw as corrupting Venetian society.

In the very year that *Terza Rima* was published, Venice would be struck by the plague. By now Veronica Franco was living in a sizeable house in some comfort, supporting her three surviving illegitimate children, as well as her family and servants. But as panic swept through the city, and all who could fled for the mainland, she too decided to leave – taking only such valuables as she could carry, so that she could support herself and her family until they returned. However, word of her flight quickly spread, and her house was soon broken into, with looters making off with all her remaining treasures. Two years later she would return, all but penniless.

The thirty-one-year-old Veronica would set about re-establishing herself, with the support of the ageing Domenico Venier. In 1580 she published her second book, *Letteri familiari a diversi* (Informal Letters to Various People), which would contain her letter to Henry III amongst others, and the two sonnets that she had addressed to him. But despite this attempt to raise her social standing, her jealous enemies were now beginning to gang up on her. Later in the same year she was hauled before the Venetian Inquisition on a charge of witchcraft or, more specifically, performing 'magical incantations'. (In the popular imagination, courtesans were frequently seen as casting a spell over their rich lovers.) These charges were eventually dropped, almost certainly due to the behind-the-scenes influence of Domenico Venier; but the social stigma remained. Just two years later Domenico Venier died, leaving the fading Veronica devoid of protection or financial support. The woman who just eight years previously had been deemed fit for a king was now reduced to poverty and disgrace. She would spend her last years all but forgotten, living in the slum district where many destitute courtesans and former prostitutes took refuge during their final years. In 1591 she died, aged just forty-five.

✳   ✳   ✳

Such was the usual fate of Venetians who did not adhere to the strict rules of marriage and sexual fidelity. A glorious exception to this rule came in the case of Bianca Capello, who was born in Venice in 1548. Both her mother and her father came from distinguished noble families, and Bianca grew up amidst circumstances of some privilege, blossoming at an early age into a flame-haired woman of considerable beauty and intelligence. However, at the early age of fifteen she fell in love with a twenty-four-year-old Florentine clerk called Petro Bonaventuri, who worked at the Florentine Salviati bank, whose Venetian branch lay directly across the canal from the Palazzo Capello. When the young couple eloped to Florence in November 1563, this caused a sensation in Venice. Her outraged father lodged a complaint with the Council of Ten, and the affair gave rise to a diplomatic incident when the Florentine ruler Grand Duke Cosimo de' Medici refused to allow Bianca to be taken back to Venice. The Council of Ten replied by declaring her an outlaw.

In Florence, Bianca was quickly married to Bonaventuri and in July 1564 gave birth to a girl, who was christened Pellegrina. However, the impulsive Bianca was by now beginning to regret her marriage, as she was forced to live with Bonaventuri's impecunious family, where instead of being allowed to read books and play music she was expected to perform what she looked upon as servants' tasks about the house.

The presence of a young Venetian aristocrat of radiant beauty living in a lowly commoner's house caused widespread public interest in Florence, and it was not long before she came to the notice of the twenty-three-year-old Francesco de' Medici, the eldest son of the Grand Duke. According to a contemporary source, Francesco was 'a man of quiet thoughts . . . and a melancholy disposition'. But besides being somewhat impenetrable and spending long hours in his laboratory practising alchemy, he was also an avid womaniser. At the time he was married to Johanna of Austria, but this marriage had been arranged for dynastic reasons and had not blossomed into a love-match. Johanna remained homesick, and Francesco continued to womanise. He soon contrived to seduce Bianca, and to the annoyance of his father established her as his mistress, giving the cuckolded Pietro Bonaventuri a compensatory post at court, where he soon began to exploit his own philandering tendencies. All this had not endeared Bianca to the Florentine people, and she quickly realised the vulnerability of her position. All she could rely upon was the not-altogether-trustworthy love of Francesco de' Medici.

In 1572 her husband Bonaventuri was set upon and stabbed to death in a back-alley, ostensibly for having an affair with another man's wife, but possibly on orders from Francesco de' Medici. Bianca was now free, but felt even more exposed. Two years later Grand Duke Cosimo I died, and his son succeeded him as Grand Duke Francesco I. Bianca's fears were somewhat allayed when Francesco installed her in a palazzo literally around the corner from the Grand Ducal residence in the Pitti Palace, and also built her a superb country residence, called Villa Pratolino, whose gardens were replete with artificial waterfalls and grottoes. Francesco spent an increasing amount of time at Villa Pratolino, neglecting his duties, but to Bianca's delight he now publicly acknowledged her as his mistress. The humiliated Johanna of Austria isolated herself in her apartments in the vast Pitti Palace and took consolation in religion. She had by now produced six daughters, and Francesco I was becoming increasingly concerned that she would not produce a male heir.

Bianca saw an opportunity and hatched a daring plot. When Francesco I was forced to return to Florence on state business, she remained behind feigning illness. Eventually she announced that she was pregnant and gave 'birth', producing a male child which she passed off as her own. Francesco I was overjoyed, and the son was christened Antonio de' Medici – though it soon became clear to Bianca that her scheme had only partially succeeded. Although Francesco appeared to regard Antonio as his heir, in the eyes of the other members of the Medici family, who regarded Bianca with disdain and suspicion, this illegitimate child could not succeed to the title. This view was held with some vehemence by Francesco's younger brother, Cardinal Ferdinando de' Medici, who saw himself as the legitimate heir. However, in 1577 Bianca's illusions were utterly shattered by the unexpected news that Johanna of Austria had given birth to a son, who was christened Filippo de' Medici. At last Francesco I had an undisputed male heir and the people of Florence gave way to wild rejoicing.

Yet this did not last long. The following year Johanna of Austria died, falling downstairs at the Pitti Palace whilst heavily pregnant, an accident that aroused considerable suspicion. Two months later Francesco I secretly married Bianca, and the following year he announced that he would marry her publicly in a great ceremony to be conducted in Florence. Now that Bianca was to become the next Grand Duchess, she seized the opportunity to affect a reconciliation with her family and her native city. Francesco was persuaded to write to the doge requesting that friendly relations between the two states be sealed by the appointment of his future wife to the befitting honour of Daughter of the Republic (of Venice). This placed the authorities in something of a quandary. The Capello family, amongst the most noble in Venice, had been grossly insulted by the previous Grand Duke when he had refused to return their daughter, and this same daughter remained an outlaw. However, as ever in Venice pragmatism (or hypocrisy) overruled all other considerations. For their part, the Capello family quickly forgot the earlier insult as it was superseded by the honour of having one of its members become a Grand Duchess. Meanwhile the Senate, having received a letter from the future Grand Duchess promising that she would use her position to work in the interests of Venice, immediately decided to grant Francesco's wishes: the outlawed Bianca Capello was designated a Daughter of the Republic, and for good measure her father and brother were both granted the distinguished title *cavaliere* and assigned to the illustrious delegation being sent to represent Venice at the wedding in Florence. Once again the actions of the individual were deemed as nothing beside the interests of the Republic. Bianca Capello was now a foreign-policy asset, no less.

The new Grand Duchess would keep her promise, with the alliance between Florence and Venice growing stronger over the years. Yet the one event that would have united this alliance in blood was not to be. Although Francesco I's heir by Johanna of Austria died at the age of five in 1582, Bianca was unable to produce her own legitimate heir to the Grand Duchy. In desperation she tried once more to effect a false pregnancy, but to no avail. Cardinal Ferdinando and the other disapproving members of the Medici family hovered in the wings, waiting for the succession. And the following year they were rewarded.

In the autumn of 1587 Francesco and Bianca retired to one of the Medici villas in the countryside ten miles west of Florence. Here they were visited by Cardinal Ferdinando, and some days later both Francesco and Bianca were struck down with a violent illness, which Cardinal Ferdinando claimed had been caused by overindulging in rich food in Francesco's case, and grief in his wife's case. Their illnesses rapidly worsened, and on 19 October Francesco died, with Bianca dying twelve hours later. Francesco I was forty-six, and Bianca just thirty-nine. In order to allay any suspicions against him, Cardinal Ferdinando at once ordered an autopsy to be carried out. This revealed no evidence of poison, and the new Grand Duke Ferdinando I was exonerated; it was generally believed that Francesco and Bianca had died of malaria. In the first decade of the twenty-first century Francesco I's tomb was opened in the course of two forensic examinations: one of these found evidence of the malaria parasite, another found unmistakable evidence of arsenic poisoning.

Bianca Capello had not been buried alongside her husband in the Medici tombs. On the orders of Grand Duke Ferdinando I her body was wrapped in a cloth and spirited away to the anonymity of a common grave behind the nearby church of Santa Maria on the edge of the woods. He also ordered that all evidence of Bianca's residence in the ducal palace, such as portraits and family crests, be removed and replaced by those of Johanna of Austria. There were also instructions that there should be no public mourning in Florence, and in accord with his feelings the Council of Ten agreed to a similar lack of observance in Venice. This craven behaviour was despised by the citizens of Venice, where her family crest remains to this day on the Palazzo Capello, in which she had grown up and, as a fifteen-year-old, had dared to follow the love that would transform her life.

15

The Jews of Venice

No WORK ON the spirit of Venice would be complete without a
description of yet another section of the population that suffered
from undue discrimination: namely, the Jews. The ghetto of
Venice was established as the enclosed Jewish residential district in 1516.*
This was the original ghetto, from which all others derive their name, and
it is said to stem from the Italian word *getto*, the name given to the slag
left over from metal-casting, as this had previously been the location of a
foundry casting cannons for the Arsenale. The original ghetto, known as
the Ghetto Nuovo, was limited to an island surrounded by canals in the
northern Canareggio district of the city; this could only be reached by
two drawbridges. (Later, in 1541, it would be extended south-west to the
anomalously named Ghetto Vecchio [Old Ghetto], in order to accommodate
the influx of Romanian and Levantine Jews who had become so useful to
Venice's eastern trade.)

Jews were only permitted to leave the ghetto when the daybreak bell
began tolling from the Campanile in the Piazza San Marco, just over a
mile away, and were required to return before sunset when the drawbridges
were raised and guards were posted. As the ghetto became more crowded,

---

* This was in line with other confined areas established for communities of foreigners resident
in the city. As early as 1314 German traders had been confined at night to the warehouse-cum-
residence of the Fondaco dei Tedeschi. And in the 1570s the community of Turkish traders
would petition for their own confined residential quarters. As we have seen, such residential
restrictions on foreigners had long been accepted as normal practice for the Venetians and the
Genoese in Constantinople – both under Byzantine and Ottoman rule. Indeed, such enclosed
quarters were accepted as commonplace in trading cities throughout the eastern-Mediterranean
region – for both the control and the protection of their foreign inhabitants.

the houses were built ever higher; and by 1590 it contained a population of some 2,500 men, women and children, with buildings rising as high as seven storeys in order to accommodate them all. Fable has it that one house became so tall that from its roof one could glimpse the sea, some three miles distant, which is conceivably true, as initially the land around the ghetto contained scattered low houses amidst gardens and vegetable plots, the only substantial buildings being two nearby convents. The houses at the edges of the ghetto were not allowed windows looking out, and thus presented a cliff face of brick walls to the outside world.

Relations between the Jews and the citizens of Venice had fluctuated over the centuries since their first arrival, which may well have been as early as the eleventh century. Periods of tolerance were punctuated by outbreaks of persecution against the 'Christ-killers', especially during periods of danger, plague or civil unrest. The official attitude towards the Jews always contained an unsettling element of ambivalence. They were seen as foreigners – doubly so, on account of there being German Jews, Iberian Jews, Levantine Jews, and so forth. As the ghetto historian Riccardo Calimani put it, 'the Jews' language, religious observances, customs, dress and food were a mystery'. Jews were required to wear a yellow badge, though exemptions were granted for doctors – the only profession they were permitted to practise outside the ghetto, apart from moneylending and pawnbroking. However, many Jews disguised or hid their badges in order to pass themselves off as Christians, a practice that was frequently overlooked by the authorities. On the other hand, any Jew found having sexual relations with a native Venetian woman, including a prostitute, would be sentenced to have his testicles cut off.

It is of course no surprise that Venice housed the first ghetto. This most pragmatic of cities understood that, owing to the Christian ban on usury, the presence of the Jews as moneylenders was a necessity in promoting commercial enterprise, especially in the financing of maritime ventures by those attempting to establish themselves in this business. Indeed, in order to obtain residence Jews were *required* to lend money at interest – though they would frequently be subjected to swingeing taxes. While many of the other citizens of Venice retained elements of peasant life – growing vegetables on their plots on the edges of the city, fishing in the lagoon, travelling to country markets on the mainland to buy wine or grain – the Jews were completely urbanised. They were not permitted to own land, their travel was restricted, and their precarious situation inclined them to preserve their fortune in the form of easily concealed and transportable currency or promissory notes. Within the ghetto the Jews developed rich cultures of their own, as varied as their different languages and the different synagogues within which each foreign group worshipped. According to Calimani, 'The Hebrew language, spoken with many different accents, may well have been the only element common to the different groups in the ghetto.' Amongst themselves the Ashkenazi Jews used varieties of Yiddish, with combinations of Hebrew and many different types of German dialect; whilst the Sephardic Jews used Ladino, a Judaeo-Spanish combination.* Over time, those who did business in Venice quickly became practised in rudimentary Italian, 'until they all eventually absorbed the sing-song cadence of the Venetian dialect'.

The coexistence and coming together of Jewish indigenous mores and Venetian culture (itself a blend of Italian and Byzantine sources) would prove a forcing ground for a number of remarkable figures. One of the earliest of these was the larger-than-life figure of Leon da Modena (Judah Aryeh mi-Modena), a rabbi who became renowned as a poet, scholar, part-time iconoclast and full-time gambler. Da Modena was born in Venice in 1571 of a distinguished family of French Jews: his grandfather, a noted physician, had been knighted by the Holy Roman Emperor Charles V. Young Leon was brought up in prosperous circumstances and quickly showed exceptional mental powers allied to the emotional instability of genius. By the age of twelve he had translated the first canto of Ariosto's *Orlando Furioso* into Hebrew, and a couple of years later completed an exemplary dialogue against gambling, a work intended to dissuade his two elder stepbrothers from this vice. Yet within a short time he too had become addicted to gambling, a flaw that he ascribed to the astrological sign under

---

* In its isolation from its Spanish roots, this language would preserve over the centuries the precise enunciation of its sixteenth-century Spanish elements – so much so that in the first half of the twentieth century Spanish literary scholars took to visiting Ladino communities in Venice and Corfu in order to acquaint themselves with the Spanish that Cervantes would have spoken.

which he had been born. By now the family fortune had been lost, owing largely to a ruinous dispute in which his father had become involved with a Ferrarese nobleman. In 1591, at the age of nineteen, Leon was married to his cousin Rachel, and two years later, after a period of intensive study, he became a rabbi. But his quest for knowledge was not limited to religious matters, or even orthodox intellectual studies. As he would later confess, 'even if I have not been able to learn any more than a man who attempts to drink all the water in the sea, I have never hindered my intellect from seeking to understand anything I wished'. This included the books of heretics and unbelievers, sorcery, magic and even what he regarded as the profound theological understanding acquired by other religions. But all this was not undertaken indiscriminately: his search was for the truth, justice and the distinction between good and evil – even if such researches did mean investigating the banned, the forbidden and the sacrilegious.

This was evidently not a man who studied with the aim of gaining himself a respectable position in society. Even so, Leon's preaching soon began attracting such attention that his audiences included leading figures from all sections of the ghetto. And as word spread, his public orations were even attended by Christian priests and distinguished nobles from outside the ghetto. A combination of factors appears to have contributed to his appeal. These included the sheer brilliance of his intellect, his astonishing depth of learning and the power of his arguments against cant and empty ritual in the practice of any religion, as well as the poetic force of his language – all this combined with a charismatic element in his unstable genius. He also wrote voluminously, especially essays and poetry, which soon found him gaining admission to the leading literary salons in Venice. The charismatic element in his character also made him a superb teacher, and after gaining a reputation within the ghetto he was soon in demand amongst the nobility in Venice, who had a tradition of continuing to receive instruction in intellectual matters throughout their life.

All this should have made Leon a rich, successful and admired figure, but this was not the case. The flaws in his character ensured this. His energetic pursuit of learning was accompanied by an equally energetic pursuit of gambling, in all its forms, from cards and chess to simple coin-tossing, which he continued to pursue on a heroic scale – matched only by his similarly brilliant contemporary, the mathematician Cardano. And this was not the only similarity between these two highly gifted mavericks: just like Cardano, Leon would also in his later years write a remarkably frank autobiography in which he spared few detrimental details of his life – especially with regard to gambling. As he confessed at one point, 'the devil mocked me and harmed me not a little for I lost 100 ducats'. This was no mean sum: equivalent to the annual income of a middle-ranking civil servant in the administration. Yet worse was soon to follow. He then mentions losing 300 ducats, followed by a period of intense study and teaching in order to pay off his debts, only to be followed by another disastrous bout that lost him 300 ducats. This was a full-blown addiction from which he could not be cured by astrology, religious practice, magic or will-power (all of which he studied in some detail). The ineradicable underside of his obsessive thirst for learning was an obsessive attraction to risk-taking. As a result of his gambling he soon became so unreliable and disreputable that his lucrative teaching and preaching engagements dried up and he was forced to take on any work he could find. And this he did with characteristic gusto. It says much for his enthusiasm (and unpredictability) that he worked at more than two dozen different professions. These ranged from interpreter to bookseller, from alchemist's assistant to public storyteller, being also at various times 'a merchant, rabbi, musician, matchmaker and manufacturer of amulets'. Despite his misdemeanours he remained proud to be a rabbi, and the ghetto's religious authorities never forbade him from using this title.

His family life was tragic, although his instability without doubt contributed to this sorrowful state of affairs. Over the coming years several of his daughters are known to have died, and his sons seem to have acquired some of their father's less positive characteristics. One was murdered in a gang brawl, another poisoned, another ran away to sea, whilst yet another simply took ship to Brazil, never to be seen again. Only his eldest son Marco (sometimes known as Mordecai) seems to have acquired a measure of Leon's talent, becoming his father's favourite. Despite this (or perhaps because of it), Marco fled to Vienna in 1609 at the age of eighteen. However, six years later he returned, having acquired an extensive knowledge and expertise in the practice of alchemy. He soon persuaded his father to set up a small laboratory in the Old Ghetto, where the two of them set to work on the time-honoured alchemical quest to turn base metals into gold. This did not go quite according to plan, but eventually achieved a lesser success when they apparently managed to transmute nine ounces of lead and one of silver into ten ounces of pure silver. Writing of this achievement Leon claimed, 'Twice I myself have seen this happen, and I myself and no other sold the silver after having assayed it in the crucible.' Whoever bought this 'silver' appears to have been quite satisfied with his purchase, and Leon was convinced that his financial worries were at last at an end. According to Riccardo Calimani, 'He was convinced that he had found an inexhaustible source of wealth, which he estimated would bring in a thousand ducats a year.'

Not only did this not come to pass, but it soon became evident that Marco's many hours spent labouring day and night amidst the arsenic fumes and noxious chemicals of their alchemists' den had poisoned his health. After two years of increasing decrepitude and haemorrhages, Marco died at the age of twenty-six. Later, the son who had run away to sea returned to Venice, but the captain of the ship refused to allow him ashore without the payment of a large ransom to cover debts that he had incurred 'in the East'. It comes as little surprise that some years later Leon's wife Rachel went insane and would remain so for the rest of her life.

Meanwhile Leon's literary output continued apace, its volume, controversy and ingenuity undimmed by his passing years. In 1631, when Leon was sixty, the leaders of the Jewish communities in the ghetto issued an edict against gambling of any sort, with excommunication being the punishment for transgressors. Whereupon Leon summoned his considerable scholarship to refute this edict, pointing out that it did not concur with biblical teaching, and that the authorities themselves were breaking the Law by issuing such an edict without consulting the entire community. More pertinently, he argued that gambling was frequently expected of Jews when they encountered Venetian noblemen in the course of their business, such meetings often taking place in gambling houses. Indeed, such an edict could easily lead to the ruin of the Jewish community. And so forth . . . Leon's arguments won the day, and he was thus able to continue along the road to ruin.

He had in fact long been an expert on the interaction between the Jewish and Christian communities. As early as 1616 he had been commissioned by the English ambassador to produce a work entitled *Historia de' Riti Hebraici vita e oservanza*, describing the history of Jewish religious rites, life and observances. Because this manuscript was intended as a private personal gift from the ambassador to King James I of England, Leon felt safe to embark upon his description with some enthusiasm, at the same time adding a number of derogatory remarks about the Inquisition, whose malign influence was now reaching its climax in Rome. His later, somewhat feeble justification for this incautious lapse was 'because this work was a manuscript that was not to have been read by anyone connected with Papal influence'. After all, the Church of England had now been entirely independent of the Roman Catholic Church for more than eighty years.

Leon would live to rue his cavalier attitude towards the Inquisition, when word reached Venice that without either his knowledge or his permission an edition of his manuscript had been published in Paris. On hearing this news Leon became extremely frightened: 'Because of this I felt ill, tore my beard and was numb and dispirited for I knew that, when this book reached Rome, it would harm all Jews.' Indeed, he was not the only one to realise this: his few friends avoided all contact with him and he was regarded as an outcast in the ghetto. No one wished to be associated with this heretic who was liable to be burned at the stake.

Fortunately for Leon, the French publisher had tactfully deleted Leon's derogatory remarks about the Inquisition and had even gone so far as to dedicate the work to 'the noble ambassador of the French King who had come to live in Rome'. This had been a lucky escape. Leon was able to cease tearing at his beard, and when the (edited) Venetian edition eventually appeared in 1638 he was persuaded by his friends amongst the ghetto authorities to preface his now-blameless manuscript with a cryptic, but nonetheless suspicious apology that, 'In writing [this work] I truly forgot I was Jewish, imagining myself to be a mere neutral narrator.'

Despite such difficulties, Leon's *Historia de' Riti Hebraici* was to prove influential in an entirely unforeseen way. Prior to its arrival, English knowledge of the Jews and their practices was practically non-existent. Evidence of this is noticeable in Shakespeare's *Merchant of Venice*, which appeared some sixteen years before Leon wrote his work. Uncharacteristically, although Shakespeare gives glimpses of an intimate knowledge of Venice (almost certainly gained from an English student who had studied at Padua), any references to Jewish religious practice – to which a realistic Shylock would have made frequent allusion – are to all intents and purposes absent. When characterising Shylock as a Jew, for once Shakespeare literally did not know what he was talking about. However, such ignorance was soon to be dispelled. Leon's work so impressed King James I that he had copies made of the manuscript, and these were well received in England, leading to a more liberal interest in the Jews and their faith, despite the fact that they remained banned from the country. In part as a result of Leon's *Historia de' Riti Hebraici*, some Puritan thinkers in England came to regard Jewish society as a successful working blend of civil and religious laws upon which they should model their own society. Indeed, when Oliver Cromwell took over England after 1649 and wished to establish a theocratic republic, he was said to have sent emissaries to the Jews of Antwerp and Venice for advice on this matter.

Although Leon's bold remarks in the *Historia* had caused him considerable danger, his appetite for theological controversy remained undiminished. Even before the trouble with the Roman Inquisition had been resolved he had launched into a number of attacks on certain aspects of Judaism and Talmudic interpretation, which only served to make him further enemies amongst the religious authorities in the ghetto. In the main, he attacked Talmudic interpretation that insisted upon the letter of the law, rather than its spirit – which, in his opinion, was frequently relevant only to earlier times and earlier places in Jewish history. He insisted that many rituals and dietary laws should either be simplified or abrogated altogether. Although the ghetto authorities hardly welcomed such attacks, and indeed did their best to refute them, they continued to regard Leon with astonishing leniency, taking no direct action against him. He was lucky: just twenty years later in Amsterdam the philosopher Baruch Spinoza would be excommunicated – bell, book and candle – and cast out from the Jewish community for proposing similarly heterodox theological ideas. The fact is that Jewish thought was entering a time of controversy and uncertainty – which some, such as the Venetian Jews, thought it best to ignore, whilst those less sure of their position amongst the Christian community sought to eradicate.

An indication of the conflict within Jewish thinking at this time can be seen in the case of the notorious Sabbatai Zevi, whose teachings would spread like wildfire through the Venetian ghetto. Zevi was born in 1626 in Smyrna (modern-day Izmir, in Turkey), and after becoming inordinately attracted towards the mystical variant of Judaism known as the Kabbala, at the age of twenty-two he proclaimed himself to be the Messiah (in the eyes of the Jews, Jesus Christ had been a false messiah). This coincided with a widespread belief amongst Jews that the coming of the Messiah predicted in the Bible was now due, and as a result Zevi soon attracted a widespread following amongst Jewish communities throughout the Levant. Not content with this, he despatched his main disciple, Nathan of Gaza, to Venice, where his preaching caused huge controversy – alienating almost all the rabbis, yet stirring a passionate following in their congregations, especially amongst the poorer Jews. This version of Messianism, which came to be known as Sabbateanism after its founder, soon reached epidemic proportions, its message spreading to Jews throughout Europe, who had been waiting so long for the appearance of the 'anointed one', the Jewish king descended from the royal line of David who would lead them back to the Land of Israel to build a new Temple at Jerusalem and usher in an era of peace on Earth.

Yet this was not to be. After falling foul of the Ottoman authorities, Zevi was taken to Constantinople to be seen by the sultan. Here, to the horror of his followers, he was persuaded to convert to Islam. Surprisingly this did not lead to the immediate downfall of Sabbateanism, but the movement would never fully recover from this apostasy, and not long afterwards Sabbatai Zevi himself faded into obscurity. He is thought to have died in 1676 in Albania, where he had been exiled by the sultan.

Ironically, although Leon da Modena had died in 1648, the very year in which Zevi had proclaimed himself the Messiah, it was Leon's theological writings against the Kabbala that would prove a bulwark against Zevi's influence in Venice. In a situation unique throughout Europe, young Venetian Jews had been permitted to study at the University of Padua, where they were in no way segregated and attended lectures in medicine;

away from the restrictions of the ghetto, many of these students had become ardent devotees of the Kabbala as propagated by Zevi. When Leon da Modena had heard of this, he had been horrified that such clear-thinking young students in the science of medicine had been seduced into what he saw as metaphysical mysticism, and had taken it upon himself to demonstrate to them the error of their ways. Leon's rebuttal of the Kabbala had been typically sensational – characterising it as fraudulent, and backing his claims with a blend of profound interpretation and inspired intuition (or guesswork). The beliefs of the Kabbala were founded upon the Zohar, a collection of works written in an 'eccentric style of Aramaic', and said to date from the same Old Testament era as the Book of Ezra, around the second or third century BC. Evidence of the Zohar had first appeared in Europe in Spain during the thirteenth century, when it had been published by the rabbi Moses of Leon. Rushing in where angels feared to tread, Leon da Modena had made so bold as to suggest that the Zohar was really a forgery, which had been assembled by Moses of Leon himself, thus accounting for its faulty Aramaic. This had caused a sensation that had divided the Venetian Jewish community, with some abandoning Kabbalistic practice as a result, whilst others pointed out that Leon had no actual proof to back up his claim, apart from a blend of obscure scholarship and speculation.* However, the doubts raised by Leon da Modena were to prove sufficient to combat Sabbatai Zevi's Messianism, and the influence of Sabbateanism soon faded.

All this indicates a profound difference between the Italian Christian and Jewish intellectual traditions of the period, especially with regard to original thinking and religion.† While Christianity adhered to a strict orthodoxy, maintained by the power of the Roman Church and such institutions as the Inquisition, the Jewish community was in an intellectual ferment, producing such figures as Leon da Modena, who would inspire a legacy of Jewish thought.

---

* Modern scholarship has gone a long way towards confirming Leon's thesis.
† Outside Italy, in northern Europe, the Reformation had begun to release thinkers from the strictures of a moribund intellectual orthodoxy, whilst within Italy the power of the Counter-Reformation launched by the Church had only served to put a halt to such speculation.

16

Deepening Decline

DESPITE THE LOSS of Cyprus, and Ottoman control of the eastern Mediterranean coastal cities from Greece to North Africa, Venice still held Crete and remained the leading western European commercial power in the region. From its zenith in around 1500, Venice had settled into a gentle decline throughout the ensuing century, as Spain prospered immensely from its New World trade and Portugal profited from the luxuries transported from the Orient around the Cape of Good Hope. This decline in Venice's fortunes would accelerate slightly with the coming of the 1700s – though these years remained a period of economic stagnation, rather than actual ruin. Over its long years of prosperity, Venice had built up considerable wealth, and this would not easily be dissipated by its canny businesslike citizens, who not only continued to participate in financing trading ventures ranging from the Americas to the East Indies, but at the same time reaped incomes from their mainland estates.

However, over the earlier years of Venice's decline a significant social division would gradually open up, leaving the commercial activity of the Republic lacking in that vital spark of enterprise and innovation that had served it so well in the former times of its pre-eminence. By 1610 a noble speaker in the Senate would find himself lamenting to his fellow members that 'commerce now lacks capital. The nobility takes no more part in trade; all its resources are tied up in funds or in real property, and expended either on house property or on amusements in the city.' The egalitarian attitude towards making money, which had once so distinguished the Republic, giving it the edge over its rivals, had given way to snobbery: the nobility now considered commerce to be beneath them. This would have a catastrophic effect on many noble families. Whilst the more-distinguished richer families, with their great estates, investments and incomes from their government positions, would grow richer still, the vast majority of noble families would be gradually taxed into poverty. This would bring about a political struggle that would result in a profound transformation of the Republic's democratic oligarchy. A majority of the nobles in the Great Council would soon number amongst the impoverished families, giving them considerable power. But the rich and powerful families now engineered a constitutional change by which far more of the effective executive power of government was transferred from the unwieldy Great Council to the more efficient Council of Ten. This certainly improved the effectiveness of the Republic's government, but it meant that an important check on the ruling power of the Council of Ten had been diminished. It also severely limited the democratic nature of the Republic's government. This had never been widespread at the best of times, but at least many people had believed that they had a say in power, be it ever so indirect. Such belief now vanished.

What had taken place in the oligarchy of noble families also had its effect amongst the population at large. While many prospered, many more were reduced to penury, a distressing tendency that had its effects in all manner of different fields – from tourism to emigration, from civic pride to personal honesty. Court reports and contemporary accounts indicate that gambling, petty thievery, prostitution and even murder all increased. Ignorant tourists became fair game; and knives, formerly worn almost as symbolic ornament, were more readily used for muggings and were drawn to settle disputes. But for draconian measures introduced by the Council of Ten, the city's reputation as a place of cultured pleasure and leisurely decadence might well have suffered, damaging the tourist trade, which now provided an important source of income to all levels of society.

Despite such strictures, Venice's decline should be regarded as relative in the overall scheme of things. While other European powers – from England and Holland to Spain and Portugal, along with France and Austria – continued to rise, Venice remained static.

A feel for Venice during this period can be gleaned from the regular despatches of Sir Henry Wotton, the English ambassador during the first two decades of the 1600s. This was the man who famously wrote: 'An ambassador is an honest man, sent to lie abroad for the good of his country.' And where better to acquire this skill than amongst the intrigues of Venetian society. According to his biographer, Logan Pearsall Smith, paraphrasing Wotton's somewhat verbose despatches:

> Venice, with its hundreds of churches, monasteries, and gardens, with its ten thousand gondolas, and with the great concourse in its *piazze* and streets, of men from all nations of Europe and the East, was regarded as the home of pomp and pleasure, and the most admired city of the world . . . In spite of the decline of Venetian power, the wealth and display of the noble families had gone on increasing; great palaces had been recently built, or were in the process of erection, and the ceremonies of the Church and State, the processions and pageants, which dazzled contemporary visitors, and still shine for us in the productions of Venetian art, had grown in magnificence and pomp.

He continues with a most telling image: 'Venice now lies like a sea-shell on the shores of the Adriatic, deserted by the organism that once inhabited it.'

Even though it was now a political backwater, Venice could not escape the growing power struggle that was building up in Europe with the emergence of Protestantism in the German and Czech lands, a development that was on the point of plunging the entire continent into violent conflict. To complicate matters further, Italy too was the scene of growing tension between two major external European powers. Spain, which now held Naples and Milan, confronted Austria, which stood poised north of the Alps, already held northern Dalmatia and was opposed to the powerful Pope Paul V. It became increasingly clear that whoever gained control over independent Venice would hold the balance of power over the entire Italian peninsula.

The tension reached boiling point in 1618, when Venice was gripped with hysteria over the so-called 'Spanish Plot'. The Republic had recently despatched a mercenary army to drive inland the Uskoks, the people of the northern-Dalmatian coastal region, who (with the encouragement of their Austrian masters) had begun preying on Venetian shipping. When this victorious army had returned to Venice, the unemployed mercenaries – the so-called *bravi* – had taken to roaming the streets brawling, drinking and whoring. To this volatile mix had been added a large number of naval mercenaries who had recently taken part in a victorious seaborne campaign to drive from the Adriatic a fleet despatched by the Duke of Osuna, the Spanish viceroy of Naples.

The Duke of Osuna, seemingly furious that his plans to take Venice had been thwarted, then decided to hatch a bold and highly original plan to accomplish his aim. In the spring of 1618 he sent a coded despatch to the Spanish ambassador in Venice, the aristocratic Marquis of Bedmar, who was already regarded by the authorities with some suspicion. In the words of John Julius Norwich, the marquis's embassy was 'the busiest centre of intrigue in the whole of Venice, its basements, anterooms and corridors teeming with sinister slouch-hatted figures whispering together in groups while they awaited audiences with the ambassador'.

The Duke of Osuna's despatch instructed the Marquis of Bedmar secretly to hire all the *bravi* and unemployed naval mercenaries roaming the streets of the city and employ them in a plan to storm and seize the Doge's Palace, thus instituting a *coup d'état*. This would be supported by a force of several hundred fully trained Spanish soldiers, who would be infiltrated into the city in disguise. The likelihood of such a plan remaining secret, let alone coming together in any coordinated fashion, was remote from the start. Yet ironically its failure came about through religious differences, which were all but irrelevant to the issue at hand. A Protestant French mercenary officer by the name of Balthasar Juven, who decided that he had no wish to see the power of Catholic Spain increase, betrayed the Spanish Plot to the Council of Ten. To overcome the plot, the Council of Ten knew that it had to act at once. Two *bravi* were immediately seized and hanged, their bodies left dangling by a single leg on gallows erected between the two columns of the Molo, the traditional public humiliation for traitors, a practice that had in fact fallen into abeyance over recent years. As intended, this spectacle created a sensation: the city was gripped with hysteria and the rumours had soon reached every district. Word spread amongst the *bravi* that their secret plot had been betrayed; they were quickly rounded up, incarcerated and put to torture. Out of their confused and conflicting confessions the truth in all its haphazard ineptitude was soon revealed. The ringleaders, along with around 300 *bravi*, were executed – though no action could be taken against the Marquis of Bedmar, owing to his diplomatic status and aristocratic rank (which included a number of powerful family connections in Italy that Venice could ill afford to antagonise). However, the publicising of the plot proved a propaganda coup, embarrassment enough for the Duke of Osuna, and the whole affair was condemned by Sir Henry Wotton in the strongest possible terms as 'the foulest and fearfullest thing that hath come to light since the foundation of the city'.

This is strong language to describe what would on the surface appear to have been a fairly inept minor plot (even if its intentions were of the most serious nature). Indeed, this conspiracy may not have been quite all that it seemed. Certain mysterious elements were never fully cleared up. According to plans extracted by torture from a few sources, the Duke of Osuna intended to sail his fleet to within sight of the Lido, where he would land a Neapolitan force under his own command. Such a move would have been impossible without the cooperation of the Venetian authorities, and many suspect there was a plot-within-the-plot, to which only a few of the most powerful in the city were privy. According to this version, the Venetians had cooperated with Osuna, who was scheming to rid Naples of Spanish domination and bring the whole of southern Italy into the Venetian sphere of influence. Such a powerful alliance would soon have united the whole of Italy, re-establishing the Italians as a major power in Europe, a dream that had persisted since the glory days of the Roman Empire. A united Italy would thus have been able to resist Spain, France, Austria and the threat of the Ottoman Empire, possibly even laying the foundations for a re-emergence of power not seen since classical times.*

Convincing evidence of such a scheme-within-a-scheme in the so-called

---

* All this is by no means as far-fetched as it may sound, and was certainly in the air at the time. This was the motive that had driven no less a figure than Machiavelli to compose his ruthless political instruction-manual *The Prince*, which had first been published in 1532 and was now established as one of the most widely read works in Italy.

'Spanish Plot' is admittedly fragmentary and unreliable. However, one telltale fact remains: in the course of eradicating the plot after its premature discovery, the Venetian authorities went to great lengths to murder anyone Spanish, Neapolitan or Venetian who was known to have had contact with Osuna. As for Osuna himself, he remained silent on the matter – neither denying nor confirming the rumours that quickly passed through the courts of Italy. And besides, from now on he would have more pressing matters to consider. For 1618 saw the outbreak in Europe of the catastrophic Thirty Years War.

What began as a religious conflict within the Holy Roman Empire between Catholics and Protestants would eventually involve the major powers in Europe, such as Spain, France, the Holy Roman Empire, Denmark, Sweden, the Netherlands, Bohemia and Italy itself. Venice naturally sided against Spain, but apart from a couple of defeats whose effects were nullified elsewhere, managed for the most part to remain on the sidelines. Much like England, it was aided in this by astute diplomacy and its fortunate geographical location on the periphery of Europe. The result of the Thirty Years War was the commercial, agricultural and social destruction of large swathes of northern Europe, the bankruptcy of nations and an unprecedented loss of life. Whole regions were reduced to barren overgrown fields infested with carrion and scavengers, entire villages were simply obliterated from the map, and provincial cities reduced to ghost towns. Civil order disappeared, and bands of desperate brigands roamed the countryside.

Europe was left exhausted, and the beneficial advances following upon the Renaissance were halted – though by this stage Renaissance humanist ideas were too firmly entrenched in European civilisation to disappear altogether. (After all, they had played a major role in sparking the Thirty Years War in the first place.) However, the Enlightenment, which might naturally have evolved out of the late Renaissance, was set back by many decades, and in some cases by almost a century.

Following the spread of slaughter and war came pestilence and the bubonic plague. And from this Venice did not escape. In the summer of 1630 the plague swept across Lombardy, spread largely by invading *Landsknechte*

(German mercenaries) besieging Mantua some sixty miles to the west. In July it reached Venice: during the summer heat the fetid canals and putrid detritus were at their worst, which only contributed to the widespread fear of this disease, whose means of contagion remained unknown, but was certainly thought to be spread by malodorous and unhygienic conditions. This was the time when the Venetian 'plague doctors' would don their distinctive outfit, which was invented in the previous century but only came into widespread use sometime later. This guise consisted of a cowled wax-covered black robe impregnated with aromatic oils and herbs. Beneath the hooded head their faces were rendered eerily inexpressive by large, round, rimmed glasses (intended to prevent the disease from entering the body through their eyes); the rest of his face was covered by a white mask, from which protruded a grotesque, long beaklike nose whose nostrils were protected by gauze (intended to filter the air). Such sinister figures were able to offer little by way of succour to the afflicted and served mainly to stigmatise the stricken abodes – from palazzi to slum tenements – that they were seen to enter. This outfit distinguished the doctors from other members of the population, enabling them free passage between districts of contagion and those that had remained free of the disease, though needless to say their very appearance was enough to spread terror. During the first months of the 1630 outbreak no fewer than 24,000 are known to have fled the city for the mainland.

The population of Venice had in fact never fully recovered from the plague of 1575–7, which had carried off Tintoretto and reduced the population by more than a quarter from its zenith of 190,000. By 1630 the population had gradually increased to almost 150,000, but over the ensuing sixteen months of plague it would be reduced by one-third of that number. According to the records, two years after the plague had abated in October 1631 the city population stood at only just over 102,000, reduced to the level it had been at two centuries previously, prior to its rise to imperial greatness.

Relations between Venice and the Ottoman Empire had been healed in the years since the Battle of Lepanto in 1571. One factor contributing to this uneasy alliance was the mutual development between Venice and the Ottoman Empire of their lucrative maritime trade. Venice remained the leading trading partner with the Ottoman Empire, despite increasing inroads into the eastern-Mediterranean market by the French, the Dutch and even the English. However, perhaps the main reason for the improvement in Ottoman–Venetian relations during these years was the unexpected influence of a Venetian woman who became known as Safiye.

Safiye had been born Sofia Baffo in 1550 on the strategic Venetian island of Corfu, where her father, the scion of a respected noble family in Venice, had been appointed governor. During the early 1560s, on a trip home to her family, the ship on which she was travelling had been attacked by Corsair pirates and she had been taken prisoner. Such a prize – a beautiful, educated young European virgin of a noble family – had quickly been sold to the harem of the sultan's son, Murad, in Constantinople. Here she had given birth to a son in 1566. Eight years later, in 1574, Murad had ascended to the sultanate as Murad III, with Safiye becoming his first wife and Bash Kadin (Chief Woman of the Harem).* Making use of this powerful position, Safiye had skilfully and stealthily undermined the pervasive influence of Murad III's mother, Nur Banu, who had effectively run the empire in league with the Grand Vizier. Safiye had then used her dominating influence over Murad to ensure good relations between Venice and Constantinople. When Murad III died in 1595 she had moved swiftly and ruthlessly to protect her power, having eighteen of her husband's nineteen sons strangled.† This had left the way open for Safiye's own weak-willed son to succeed as Sultan Mehmet III, and she would rule as

---

* Strictly speaking, during this period the sultan did not formally marry the concubines of the harem who produced his children; however, the hierarchy of the harem was such that the favoured women who produced male heirs were, to all intents and purposes, regarded as wives, with the Bash Kadin being the senior and most influential wife. The only woman senior to her was the Valide Sultan, literally 'Mother of the Sultan'.
† Such seemingly vicious slaughter was not quite as wanton as might at first appear. In preceding generations it had often been the practice for an ascending sultan's brothers and half-brothers to be slain, in order to preempt any attempted coup. Later, such male heirs would be confined to the 'Golden Cage' in the harem, where they would take no part in politics and have no occupation other than to entertain the concubines and young boys with whom they shared their quarters. Eventually the one chosen to become sultan would be released, while his brothers and half-brothers would be strangled in the traditional manner with a silken cord. Such captivity, and its ever-attendant insecurity, would result in several cases of mental instability amongst ascending sultans.

Valide Sultan, though in this instance her power was more akin to that of regent.

During this period, relations with Venice had continued for the most part to be diplomatically cordial. Yet, in the interests of commerce, Safiye had also maintained relations with Venice's rivals. She had even written to Queen Elizabeth I of England, who sent her a modern horse-drawn carriage, in which Safiye took to driving about Constantinople to inspect her city. It was during this period that she instigated the construction of the last great classical mosque, the Yeni Cami, which to this day dominates the southern shore of the Golden Horn overlooking Galata Bridge: the full name of this architectural masterpiece is Yeni Valide Cami (New Mosque of the Valide Sultan); likewise the Malika Safiya mosque in Cairo is named after this Venetian matriarch of the Ottoman Empire.

However, over the years Safiye had made several powerful enemies, and in 1602 she herself was strangled in the harem at the behest of a rival faction.* The following year her son Mehmet III died, and Venice now lost its favoured status amongst the Ottoman allies, with relations soon beginning to deteriorate. Although the two nations remained mutually dependent upon their maritime trade, their ships now intermittently clashed in the shipping lanes, and on occasion both sides resorted to outright piracy. By the early decades of the seventeenth century Venetian trading agents in Constantinople were down to single figures, though admittedly Smyrna had now eclipsed the Ottoman capital as Venice's main trading port in the north-eastern Mediterranean, and neither of these compared with the likes of Alexandria, Aleppo or Beirut.

Since the Ottomans had taken Cyprus in 1571 they had begun to view the Venetian island of Crete as the last remaining obstacle to their domination of the eastern Mediterranean. Here was a danger that lay at the heart of the trading routes within their empire and would always pose a potential threat as long as it remained in Venetian hands. Inevitably as relations between Venice and Constantinople became increasingly fractious, it was not long before an incident sparked a full-scale war over this issue. Ironically,

---

* Despite her death, Safiye's legacy would live on. All subsequent sultans of the Ottoman Empire would be direct descendants of this remarkable Venetian woman.

the incident in question had nothing to do with the Venetians, and was in fact provoked by the Knights of St John, whose habit of indiscriminate raids on merchant shipping had long incurred Venetian animosity.

The 600-year-old Knights of St John, originally a crusading order, had been driven from their base in Rhodes by Suleiman the Magnificent in 1522, eventually making their headquarters in Malta, where in 1565 they had resisted the most determined efforts by Suleiman to dislodge them. From this time on, they had existed largely as naval mercenaries and pirates. In late September 1644, a flotilla of half a dozen ships under the flag of St John happened across a poorly protected galleon travelling from Constantinople to Alexandria, transporting a select group of pilgrims on their way to the annual Haj in Mecca. Amongst its passengers were the Cadi of Mecca,* fifty Greek slaves, and thirty members of the sultan's harem, including his favourite wife. The galleon, along with its passengers, was taken captive by the Knights, who then sailed west, calling in at southern Crete to take on provisions and release the Greek slaves. News of this incident soon reached Constantinople.

The new sultan was now Ibrahim I, the great-grandson of the Venetian Safiye. Ibrahim had emerged by the customary process after spending many years in the Gold Cage. Unfortunately, this experience had left him so mentally unstable that he had soon become known, with good reason, as Ibrahim the Mad. Upon hearing the news of what had happened to his favourite wife and the members of his harem, he flew into a state of uncontrollable anger.† In response to this outrage by the Knights of St John, Ibrahim ordered the immediate slaughter of all Christians throughout the Ottoman Empire. This would have eliminated a considerable number of Greeks, Serbians, Albanians, Georgians, Armenians, Syrians, Copts, and so forth, many of whom provided the commercial lifeblood of their local communities; indeed, conservative estimates indicate that this could have

* Chief judge of sharia law, appointed by the sultan.
† Sultan Ibrahim I's feelings for his harem, with whom he was in the habit of spending his days frolicking in a marble pool on a terrace overlooking the Golden Horn, were particularly volatile. According to contemporary sources, when he suspected that one of the members of his harem had been unfaithful to him, he ordered all 280 of them to be tied up in sacks weighted with stones and thrown into the Bosphorus.

involved anything up to a half million souls, and would have wreaked havoc on the economic life and political stability of the empire. In the event, Sultan Ibrahim's Grand Vizier 'reinterpreted' this ruinous order, but would later pay for such bravery with his life. (During his eight-year reign Ibrahim would be in the habit of promoting, and then executing, Grand Viziers on an all-but-annual basis, though he would eventually be strangled at the behest of his final appointment to this post.)

In a more considered response to the act of piracy, the Grand Vizier ordered the assembling of a vast fleet in the Bosphorus. By the time this set sail on the last day of April 1645 it consisted of more than 400 ships carrying possibly as many as 100,000 troops. It was naturally assumed that this fleet was destined for the Knights of St John's headquarters in Malta, but the Venetian *bailo* in Constantinople sent a despatch to Venice warning that he had received intelligence that the Turkish fleet was in fact bound for Crete. His suspicions were dismissed when it was learned that the Turkish fleet had sailed past Crete, and in June had put in for supplies and ammunition at the south-western Peloponnese port of Navarino (modern Pylos).

When news reached the new Pope Innocent X in Rome that this huge Ottoman fleet was sailing west, he immediately suspected that the Turks were planning a full-scale invasion of Italy. Acting decisively, he summoned Naples, Tuscany and Venice to join with the papal forces and form a joint fleet to repel the Turks. All agreed, and moves to assemble this naval force began at once.

After two weeks at Navarino, the Turkish fleet again set sail; but no sooner had it sailed over the horizon than it reversed its course, sailing east for Crete, where it arrived on 25 June, landing an army on the beaches to the west of Canea (modern Hania), the city controlling the west of the island. Within days, the port of Canea was blockaded and the Turkish army had begun digging in around the walls in preparation for a siege. When news of this surprise move reached Rome and Venice, the combined fleet set sail with all speed for Crete, picking up reinforcements on the way. Eventually the allied fleet numbered more than thirty galleons and seventy galleys, a well-trained and well-equipped fighting force whose skill would easily have matched that of the cumbersome Ottoman fleet.

However, by the time the allied fleet arrived off Crete, it learned that Canea had surrendered on 25 August, and the Turkish army had begun its march eastwards along the coast towards Candia (modern Heraklion). In September the Venetian fleet, supported by its allies, attempted to retake Canea by surprise attack, but were driven back by a storm. During a second surprise attack the allied ships were dispersed by another storm, and in a familiar development the papal and Neapolitan contingents decided to return home rather than ride out the winter in such a vulnerable situation. The ships of the Venetian fleet were now left on their own in dangerous waters to defend their colony as best they could. Fortunately the Turkish forces soon found themselves in similar disarray when their commanders were summoned to Constantinople to face a charge of transporting back insufficient booty, on which charge they were summarily executed. Not until July 1647, when the new Turkish commanders were in place, did the Ottoman army begin its siege of Candia.

Yet Venetian ships were soon managing to elude the Turkish blockade of the harbour and keep supplied the 15,000 or so who had taken refuge within the city. Safe behind the city's formidable walls, the inhabitants had sufficient provisions and ammunition to resist a prolonged siege. Both the Venetians and the Turks realised that the key to Crete lay in who held Candia, but the Venetians understood that they simply did not have sufficient manpower to fight a land war against the Ottoman army, which was soon being reinforced with further troops transported from the Anatolian mainland, as well as by many indigenous Cretan Greeks, who resented the injustices inflicted upon them by their Venetian colonisers. On the other hand, the Venetians well understood that even with their depleted fleet they held the advantage where naval superiority was concerned. If they conducted a prolonged and daring naval campaign, this might well swing the war in their favour.

In pursuance of this policy various Turkish ports along the southern Dalmatian coast were bombarded and overrun. This was followed by some unexpectedly successful attacks in the Aegean. Finally, in 1648 the Venetians succeeded in blockading the Dardanelles, thus severing the Ottoman capital's main naval link with the rest of its Empire. When news of this reached Constantinople it caused widespread public alarm and civil disorder.

Consequently, Ibrahim I was deposed and murdered, to be succeeded by his six-year-old son, who became Mehmet IV. Inevitably, even at this early age Mehmet's sanity also came under suspicion – and with some justification. A few days after his birth his father had flown into a rage with his mother, wrenched the infant from her arms and hurled him into a deep cistern in the Topkapi Palace. In the nick of time Mehmet had been rescued by harem servants, but in the course of this incident his head had suffered a serious blow, and afterwards he had retained a permanently scarred dent in his skull. Fortunately this proved to have affected only his outer skull, leaving his mental faculties intact and able to develop to full sanity, apart presumably from certain unavoidable psychological scars.

The ascent to the sultanate of the young Mehmet IV was followed by a power struggle between his mother, the Valide Sultan, Grand Vizier Sofu Mehmet and the commanders of the sultan's crack household guard, the Janissaries. These divisions were echoed throughout the Ottoman Empire, and led to a weakening of the Turkish forces in Crete – though despite Venetian naval dominance, supplies continued to reach the invading army who were able to persist with the siege of Candia.

In 1649 Venice approached Constantinople with the aim of securing a peace treaty; but negotiations came to an abrupt halt when the Ottomans insisted upon the surrender of Crete. With Ottoman rule in disarray, and Venice barely able to finance a war, though neither side was willing to give in, hostilities would continue intermittently through the ensuing decades. In 1656 the Venetians won a great victory at the Battle of the Dardanelles, inflicting on the Ottoman fleet a defeat such as it had not suffered since Lepanto. The following year Captain-General Lazzaro Mocenigo penetrated the Ottoman defences, sailed across the Sea of Marmara and led his squadron of twelve ships right up to the walls of Constantinople. Unfortunately, his ship was then struck by a cannonball from artillery on the walls: this ignited the ship's magazine and Mocenigo was killed in the ensuing explosion. Persuaded that any further attempt to inflict damage on the city, let alone take it, was futile, the Venetian squadron then sailed back across the Sea of Marmara.

Meanwhile, although the Turkish forces now virtually controlled most of Crete, the siege of Candia dragged on and on. As the years passed this siege became a cause célèbre in Europe, especially in France, with dashing young noblemen voyaging to Crete on various minor crusades to fight the infidel and relieve Candia. Such adventures were regarded as strictly unofficial by the French authorities, for French trade in the eastern Mediterranean was benefiting greatly from the lack of Venetian competition and they had no wish to upset the Ottoman authorities. In 1668 Louis XIV himself unofficially despatched a force of 5,000 men to relieve Candia, which had by now been under siege for some twenty years. When this too ended in failure, the Venetians finally realised that they could not afford to prosecute such a ruinous war any longer, and the following year agreed to a peace treaty in which they were humiliatingly forced to concede all the major Ottoman requests. After more than four and a half centuries of occupation, Venice's oldest major colony in the eastern Mediterranean was surrendered, though the Republic did manage to retain various minor possessions in the Aegean for use as trading ports.

This treaty and the lack of any formally combined opposition enabled the Ottoman Empire to begin expanding once more, west out of Hungary into central Europe, and in 1683, after an absence of more than a century and a half, the Turks were once more at the gates of Vienna. While the Austrians put up desperate resistance, managing to fight off the Ottoman army thanks to the sudden intervention of Polish-Lithuanian forces, Pope Innocent XI rapidly organised yet another Holy League. This consisted of the Holy Roman Empire, the Polish-Lithuanian Commonwealth and Venice, which were joined two years later by Russia. Confident in the support of such powerful allies, the Venetians now launched a major new campaign in Greece. At sea, their replenished fleet was commanded by Francesco Morosoni, who had held out so valiantly during the final years at Candia. At the same time a land campaign was launched by the Venetian army under the command of the Swedish mercenary general Count Otto Wilhelm von Königsmarck.

Over the coming years Königsmarck would manage to retake from the Ottomans large tracts of the Peloponnese, including such strategic former Venetian ports as Coron and Nauplia. Meanwhile Morosoni was achieving considerable success in the Aegean, as well as aiding the Venetian land forces. However, it was in September 1687 that Morosoni left his most lasting mark, when he laid siege to Athens and one of his mortars scored a direct hit on the Parthenon, which the Ottomans had been using as their gunpowder magazine. The ensuing explosion blew off the roof of the building and damaged several pillars, leaving Ancient Greece's greatest monument in the ruined state, which it remains to this day.

After another decade or so of intermittent warfare, the Ottoman forces were all but exhausted and sued for peace, which was finally signed at Karlowitz (Karlovci in modern Serbia) in February 1699. This confirmed the Hapsburg Holy Roman Empire as the dominant power in central Europe. Venice had now retaken a portion of its lost territory and once again had an eastern empire, yet this illusion of imperial greatness was but an echo of an era that was now past. The regained colonies in the Peloponnese and the Aegean would remain vulnerable to any resurgence of Ottoman power, and back in Europe the Republic was seen as subservient to the domination of the Hapsburg rulers of the Holy Roman Empire, which occupied the territory to the north and clearly had designs on northern Italy. Meanwhile the Hapsburg port of Trieste, just fifty miles to the east of Venice, was beginning to develop as a major trading competitor both in the Adriatic and further east, in such ports as Constantinople, Smyrna and Alexandria.

Surprisingly, a number of pragmatic Venetian merchants had managed to continue limited trading with the Ottoman Empire throughout the long war against the Turks. This was achieved mostly under the auspices of Armenian and Jewish merchants who were citizens of the Ottoman Empire, but also had family connections with their respective communities in Venice. These agents would arrange the import and export of goods on foreign ships, such as those flying the French or even the English flag. Inevitably, this placed Venetian trade at a considerable disadvantage with its international competitors, but enabled it to continue nonetheless, supplying such items as silk, glassware and expensive cloth (often destined for the sultan's court), usually in exchange for cotton and hides. Venice also continued to play a role in the lucrative trade through Smyrna of currants and figs, apart from the intervals when this trade fell under a general ban.

Despite the war, Venetian interests at Ottoman ports were still handled by a Venetian agent (often the former consul or *bailo*), who vainly did his best to prevent Venetian property, warehouses and factories from being seized. The holding of such office certainly required exceptional social skills, as well as many local contacts, and one of the most remarkable men to hold such a difficult post was the Venetian consul at Smyrna, Francesco Lupazzoli.

Lupazzoli had been born as early as 1587 at Casale Monferrato, a small Lombardy town on the banks of the River Po. He took his name from his father's nickname, *Lupa soli* (lone wolf), Lupazzoli being the Venetian variant. The indications are that Lupazzoli senior was a Venetian of gentleman rank (namely, respectable, but not of a noble family) who was employed at the court of the Duke of Mantua. Initially young Francesco was drawn to study for the Church, but feeling unable to commit himself immediately to a life of celibacy, obedience and lack of worldly possessions, he decided beforehand to join a mission to Constantinople despatched by Urban VIII in 1624. The ship carrying the papal mission set sail from the east coast of Italy, probably calling in at Sicily and later Crete, before heading north into the Aegean. When it arrived at the eastern-Aegean island of Chios, Lupazzoli decided to leave the mission and remain behind. Here he married a Greek girl called Angiola, who bore him a son in 1626. Over the coming years, Angiola would bear him a further seven children before she died. The 'lone wolf' then married a second wife called Orieta, with whom he would father a further six children.

Possibly driven by the need to support his ever-growing family, Lupazzoli now turned to writing. During his voyage from Italy on the papal mission he had kept a travel diary, in which he had recorded detailed descriptions of the places he saw, complete with drawings of the islands visited, the local costumes and ancient monuments. This he now proceeded to expand into a full-scale manuscript covering forty-two closely written and illustrated pages, comprehensively describing all the islands of the Aegean, as well as Sicily and the Lipari islands, the whole of Crete, and even areas through the Sea of Marmara as far as Constantinople, most of which he could not possibly have visited. Internal evidence from the hand-written manuscript (which is in the British Library) indicates that Lupazzoli took considerable trouble over this work and the necessary further research that it required. He evidently relied upon extensive, and mostly accurate, hearsay knowledge in describing, and drawing maps of, the many places that he had not seen. The frontispiece of his manuscript is entitled *Isolario dell' Arcipelago et altri luoghi particola* (Islands of the Achipelago [the contemporary name for the Aegean] and other particular sites) and describes it as 'made in the year 1638 in Chios'. It seems that this was a second, fair copy – the first and only other extant version remains in Chios to this day. Lupazzoli's painstakingly copied manuscript was probably written with the intention of taking (or sending) it back to Venice, where the publication of such an exotic *Isolario* was liable to become fashionable reading and earn its writer a good sum of money – or at least enough to help provide for himself, his wife and his fourteen children. Such a scheme was far from being wishful thinking. It is worth remembering that the first tourist guide to Venice had been published just over fifty years previously, and widespread publication of the first general travel guides was only just beginning – though more as an entertaining novelty genre intended to educate and stimulate the imagination of the reader than to be used as an aid to actual travel. Lupazzoli was evidently hoping to cash in on this trend.

However, for some reason his money-making venture fell through. When war broke out between Venice and the Ottoman Empire in 1644, he moved with his family to the nearby mainland port of Smyrna and took on the hazardous task of acting as Venetian agent. To ensure him a modicum of diplomatic protection, he was attached to the Dutch consulate as a chancellor. Inevitably, trading was difficult, even with the use of Armenians as go-betweens and goods transported under foreign flags, especially when the war dragged on into its second decade. In the early 1660s Lupazzoli's second wife Orieta died, and in 1665 at the age of seventy-eight he decided to marry for the third time, choosing as his wife one of his slaves, called Anna, who soon gave birth to yet another child. When the war finally came to an end in 1669, Lupazzoli was appointed Venetian consul, in recognition of his services to the Republic. This was a great honour, as such a post was all but invariably awarded to a member of a noble family. Seeing himself as a man of some achievement, Lupazzoli now began to demand the respect that he considered to be his due. In the consular service there was a strict protocol with respect to seniority, and the freshly appointed eighty-two-year-old Lupazzoli caused an immediate stir by insisting that

– on account of his age, his long-term residency in Smyrna and the importance of the Republic he represented – he should be regarded as the senior consul in Smyrna. This claim was treated with derision by the senior French consul and his Dutch, English and Genoese consular colleagues, who had held their positions for many years throughout the war, while Lupazzoli had been no more than a mere agent, reduced to involving himself in all manner of murky business deals.

To make matters worse, Venetian trade through Smyrna remained at a low ebb, which meant that back in Venice his posting was regarded as of little importance, a fact that was reflected in his meagre salary. Normally a noble appointee would have been able to supplement his income with the aid of his family wealth; Lupazzoli, on the other hand, found that he was barely able to provide for his vast family, to which had now been added numerous grandchildren, a succession of dependent former in-laws and the like. As for keeping up the appearances required of his office, this was becoming all but insupportable – at least in the material sense. However, where maintaining dignity was concerned, he would not be outdone: his dealings with the French consul, who still insisted upon claiming diplomatic seniority, became increasingly acrimonious.

In 1671 Lupazzoli's third wife Anna died, having added four more children to his progeny. Within a year he had married his pregnant fourth wife, a servant from Chios called Maria. After giving birth to a second child, she too died, in 1674. Undaunted, the 'lone wolf' now married his fifth wife, a local woman from Smyrna who provided him with four children. The last of these was a daughter born in 1682, by which time her father had reached the venerable age of ninety-five.

A year later the Ottoman Empire once more declared war on Venice, along with its allies in the Holy League, and once again Lupazzoli was reduced to the status of mere agent, though by now trade between Smyrna and Venice had dwindled to the point where there were only a couple of Venetian traders left. This state of affairs was quickly resolved when he was banished from the city as an enemy subject. After the Peace of Karlowitz was finally signed in 1699, the doughty 112-year-old Lupazzoli returned to take up his official post as consul, and once more he was forced to endure the seniority of the French consul, who had remained in place throughout the war. (Louis XIV had maintained his duplicitous policy of covertly offering sympathy to his European neighbours whilst maintaining peace with the Ottomans.) Although Lupazzoli gamely kept up appearances, while seemingly remaining as fit and healthy as ever, it had now been seventeen years since his fifth wife had produced a child, and two years later his age finally began to catch up with him. The following year, in 1702, he eventually died at the age of 115.

Despite their differences, the French consul had evidently been intrigued by the exceptional qualities of his former adversary, for he now commissioned the writing of a biography of Lupazzoli. This task was given to Lupazzoli's son Bartolomeo, who had followed his father's original calling and become a priest. The French consul was eager to discover any features that might have contributed to Lupazzoli's amazing longevity and his equally amazing sexual potency. Father Bartolomeo duly followed his brief, and revealed that his father's secret appeared to lie in his abstemious behaviour (in all but one department): 'His diet consisted of fruit, bread, and water, supplemented by an occasional bowl of soup or a few slices of unseasoned roast meat.' To replenish his thirst in this hot clime, he seems to have drunk only water: 'He had never touched wine, brandy, coffee, or sherbert, nor milk since he was weaned. He did not take snuff or tobacco.' Such was the regimen that was evidently responsible for his longevity, his five marriages and his twenty-four children. However, in the words of the Oxford historian Sonia P. Anderson, 'Nor was this the end of the tale. Father Bartolomeo had to report that besides his legitimate offspring, the "lone wolf" of Smyrna was responsible for 105 bastards.'

17

An Intellectual Revolution

B Y THE MID-SEVENTEENTH century the Grand Tour was becoming a required feature to round off the education of wealthy young English gentlemen, as well as aristocratic young noblemen from countries throughout Europe. And Venice, renowned for the beauty of its unique location as much as its relaxed attitude towards gambling and prostitution, soon became a welcome break after the cultural rigours of Florence and the religious requirements of Rome. Meanwhile at the University of Padua, a new liberalism was infiltrating the world of ideas. The calibre of teachers here was continuing to attract intellectually gifted students from all over Europe. As we have seen, at the start of the sixteenth century, Copernicus had travelled here all the way from Poland, and may well have found at Padua the inspiration for his heliocentric universe. A century later, the young Englishman William Harvey would arrive to study medicine under Hieronymus Fabricius, who was renowned throughout Europe for his pioneering work on anatomy, especially with regard to developing our understanding of the foetus.

Fabricius himself had studied at Padua under the pioneering anatomist Gabriele Fallopius, after whom the Fallopian tube was named. He was also the first to propose the use of condoms – made from pigs' intestines – to combat the spread of syphilis. And prior to Fallopius the chair of medicine at Padua had been occupied by the great Flemish physician Andreas Vesalius, whose work on anatomy released medicine from the stifling 'authority' of Galen. Much as Aristotle had been regarded as the last word on everything from biology to philosophy throughout the medieval era, and Ptolemy's view of the Earth as the centre of the universe had been similarly sacrosanct, Galen's view of medicine had since classical Roman times been regarded as unquestionable, especially with regard to anatomy, despite the fact that much of his anatomical knowledge had been gained from dissecting the cadavers of dogs, pigs and goats. In the renaissance of the arts and the humanities there had been a rebirth of classical knowledge, which had led to the questioning and casting aside of the old medieval certainties; now, with the emerging scientific renaissance, it was this very classical knowledge, with all its hindering flaws and mistakes, that would be questioned and cast aside.

Whilst the twenty-three-year-old Harvey was attending anatomy demonstrations by Fabricius he learned that his master had discovered there were valves in the walls of the veins. Fabricius' ingenious explanation for this was that the valves prevented all the blood in the veins from sinking to the lower half of the body. Harvey became increasingly sceptical of this explanation, but could produce no other answer. According to Galen, the blood in the veins was created by the liver. Half of this flowed through the branching system of veins, where it was eventually 'consumed' by the body. The other half flowed to the heart, where it passed through the central wall so that in the other half of the heart it could absorb air from the lungs and become arterial blood. From here it travelled through the branching system of arteries, where it too was 'consumed' by the body. This lost blood was continuously being replenished by the liver.

Harvey's pondering on the purpose of the valves discovered by Fabricius led him to realise that the blood was not 'consumed' by the body, but in fact circulated around it. At the ends of the arterial system it passed through minuscule capillaries into the ends of the veins, allowing it to continue to flow towards the heart (and being prevented from flowing away from the heart by the valves that Fabricius had discovered). In fact, the heart acted as a pump, forcing the blood to keep circulating through this system.

The seeds of this idea were discovered by Harvey in Padua, though it would be more than twenty-five years before he published in London his revolutionary work *De motu cordis* (Concerning the Motion of the Heart), which is now regarded as the founding work of modern physiology. This subject is concerned with how the body works, rather than what it consists of, which is the main concern of anatomy. Nevertheless, Harvey's work would not have been possible without the latest discoveries in anatomy. The succession of great medical figures at Padua had not only broken the stranglehold imposed by Galen's faulty descriptions, but had led to a completely new understanding of how we think about the body.

Although Fabricius had nothing but praise for his brilliant young English student, it appears that Harvey was not an easy man to get along with. And ideas were not the only thing he would bring back with him from Padua, when he returned to England in 1602. In the Venetian Republic at the turn of the seventeenth century it was the habit of a young man to wear a dagger. This was not only a display of self-protection, but could also be used as a handy weapon when one became involved in any violent dispute, a frequent occurrence amongst the hot-headed young men of the period. Harvey's contemporary and friend, the biographer John Aubrey, mentions how Harvey retained this Italian custom when he returned to England, claiming that he was 'very cholerique [that is, quick-tempered] and . . . would be too apt to draw his dagger upon every slight occasion'. Harvey's habit would persist into his old age, long after the custom for wearing such weapons had fallen out of fashion in England with the passing of the Elizabethan age. And it appears that this habit gave his presence an unsettling air, owing to 'his trick of fingering the pommel while he talked'.

The notorious exception to Venice's reputation as a haven of liberal behaviour and ideas occurred around the same time as Harvey's years at Padua, and concerned the case of Giordano Bruno, who arrived at Padua believing that at least in the Republic of Venice it would be safe to express his new scientific ideas. Bruno had been born just outside Naples in 1548, and at the age of seventeen entered a Dominican monastery to study for the priesthood. However, his intellectual curiosity soon led him to read subjects far beyond orthodox theology, such as astronomy, alchemy and humanism, in all of which he developed original ideas of his own. In astronomy, Bruno came to the conclusion that the sun was the centre of our planetary system, and that the universe was infinite, with each star being a sun at the centre of its own planetary system. (Copernicus had published his heliocentric theory in 1543, but this remained unknown to

Bruno, whose speculative ideas regarding the universe went far beyond those of his predecessor.) In contrast to such far-sighted scientific ideas, Bruno also delved into the distinctly unscientific realms of hermetic secrets and the mysticism attached to alchemy. Meanwhile in the course of his study of humanism he read Erasmus, whose ideas led him to adopt the Arian heresy, which declared that Christ had been human and not divine. Bruno was a bold and outspoken character and made no secret of his ideas. Consequently in 1576 he found himself facing a charge of heresy. This was a very serious matter: if found guilty, he could well have been burned at the stake. Bruno acted swiftly: casting off his robes and donning secular clothes, he fled Naples and made his way north in this disguise, eluding those despatched by the clerical court to apprehend him. Even so, his trial went ahead and he was excommunicated *in absentia*. Afterwards, a dossier concerning Bruno and his activities was forwarded to the Roman Inquisition.

Not surprisingly, Bruno ended up in Venice, from where he travelled to Padua, in the hope of finding a teaching post. Here he was persuaded by some fellow Dominicans that his chances of employment would be considerably enhanced if he once more donned Dominican robes, but despite this he was unable to obtain an appointment, and for the next seven years he wandered Europe, publishing his ideas and entering into debates with theologians and leading thinkers in such intellectual centres as Geneva, Lyons and Paris.

In 1583 he arrived in England, where he would remain for two years. At one stage he took up residence at Oxford. Here his arrogant and sarcastic manner of debate, to say nothing of his heretical blend of scientific, humanistic and hermetic ideas, made him few friends. Indeed, a twenty-two-year-old don named George Abbot (who would later rise to become Archbishop of Canterbury) ridiculed him for holding 'the opinion of Copernicus that the earth did go round, and the heavens did stand still, whereas in truth it was his own head which rather did run round, and his brains did not stand still'.

Further travels followed, and there is a suspicion that at some stage he may have supplemented his meagre income by acting as a spy, passing on rather more mundane ideas than those expressed in his frequent and varied works, which ranged over a variety of exotic and novel topics, including one on a new memory system that he had invented. 1591 found him attempting to sell his works at the Frankfurt Book Fair.* Here he was befriended by a Venetian nobleman named Zuan Mocenigo, of the distinguished family who had for centuries been providing the city with admirals, diplomats and doges. Mocenigo was deeply interested in Bruno's new system for improving the memory, and invited him to come and stay at his palazzo in Venice so that he could personally tutor him in how to use this system. By now Bruno was forty-three years old: he was beginning to tire of his continual travelling and longed to return to his native Italy. Surely his troubles with the Church would have been forgotten? Anyway, he would be quite safe in Venice. Furthermore, he had heard that the chair in mathematics had fallen vacant at Padua. Bruno prevaricated over Mocenigo's offer, indicating that he would travel first to Padua, where he arrived in the late summer of 1591. He foresaw himself using Padua as a base where he would be free to propagate his theories and at the same time deliver lectures incorporating his constant flow of original ideas, attracting students and acolytes from all over Europe. However, it soon became clear to Bruno that he was not going to be offered a post at Padua, so he travelled on to Venice to take up Mocenigo's offer. Mocenigo immediately put him up at the family palazzo, one of the finest in Venice, the Ca' Grande on the Grand Canal. The intellectuals of Venice were delighted to discover that this major European thinker had come to live in their midst, and they flocked to the Ca' Grande to discover his latest ideas.

Over the years these had developed, but they remained as original and controversial as ever. As indeed they remain to this day. In the scientific sphere he adopted a strictly materialistic approach: he now proposed that everything in the world was made up of tiny indestructible atoms, of different shapes and sizes to account for the variety of material objects. Yet at the same time he persisted in his utterly contradictory magical-mystical ideas. It is difficult to see how Bruno could possibly have believed genuinely in both of these world-views at the same time. Here was a man

---

*This annual event was already nearly 150 years old, having started soon after Johannes Gutenberg set up his first printing press at nearby Mainz. Apart from periodic breaks during times of war and plague, it has continued for more than half a millennium since then.

who seemed to stand with one foot firmly planted in the medieval world of the past (and remnant hermetic ideas from even earlier), while the other stood firmly in the Renaissance world and the enlightened scientific future that it seemed to be heralding. Bruno was well aware of this glaring contradiction, yet he maintained that in some inexplicable way his occult beliefs and his genuine science had a 'point of union'. Perhaps the best illustration of this — even if it is in no way a convincing explanation — is to be found in his ideas about the solar system. Bruno was convinced that the Earth and the planets revolved around the sun, yet at the same time he also believed that the solar system was a mystical-magical symbol of the cosmos.

Such ideas inevitably became the talk of intellectual Venice. However, Mocenigo soon began to grow jealous of all the brilliant men who called at his palazzo, but were only interested in talking with Bruno. It appears that Mocenigo was no giant of an intellect, but he had his pretentions, and he had been hoping that Bruno's memory system might gain him entrée into the intellectual circles of Venice. At any rate, from the outset Mocenigo found difficulty in mastering even the basic principles of Bruno's memory system. This he blamed on his teacher. Relations between the resentful aristocrat and his arrogant tutor soon began to deteriorate, to the point where Bruno informed his host that he had decided to break off his teaching and return to Frankfurt to publish a new book that he had written. Outraged at Bruno's perceived ingratitude, Mocenigo accused him of being a charlatan, claiming that his so-called memory system, which he found impossible to comprehend, was nothing more than a fraud. Mocenigo was determined not to let Bruno leave Venice and reported him to the city's Inquisition for holding heretical views.

Bruno was now put on trial, and proceeded to defend himself against the none-too-pressing questions of his inquisitors. It appeared that he would probably escape with a reprimand and be allowed to go on his way. Although Bruno had travelled the courts of Europe and in the course of this must have encountered many of the finest portraitists, there are in fact no surviving portraits of him. The only descriptions we have stem from his trial in Venice. Like the man and his ideas, these are appropriately incompatible. The clerk of the court described him as middle-aged, of medium build, with a chestnut-coloured beard. On the other hand, a local bookseller called Ciotto who was summoned as a witness described him as short and thin, with a black beard. Many remarked on how Bruno spoke with great speed and flamboyant gestures, in the manner of southern Italians; others, who had attended his lectures, emphasised his earnest and deliberate manner of speech, which was accompanied by such concentration as to make him appear absent-minded, unselfconscious and oblivious to all but what he was saying.

Either way, Bruno adopted a prudent tactical approach to his trial, which was conducted in the Hall of the Council of Ten in the Doge's Palace. Right from the start Bruno decided to concede that in the course of his teaching he had perhaps committed certain minor doctrinal errors. Yet these were all concerned with his scientific ideas, and thus could surely not be seen as serious theological errors. Apart from this, he believed utterly in the message of Christ and in no way contradicted the teachings of the Church. This was an undeniably disingenuous approach, prompted perhaps by his characteristic arrogance. The 'minor errors' that he appeared so willing to recant were nothing less than his original scientific ideas – his heliocentric theory, the infinity of solar systems in the universe, and atomism. Likewise, where his religious beliefs were concerned, he chose to overlook his belief in the dark arts of alchemy, hermeticism and magic, all of which were based on utterly heretical beliefs. However, Bruno was convinced that the Venetian Inquisition was not deeply concerned and was merely going through the motions.

And such would probably have been the case. But word soon came through that the Roman Inquisition had been informed of Bruno's trial, and they insisted that the Venetians despatch their prisoner to them at once. This was a much more serious matter. The Roman Inquisition was a powerful force in the Counter-Reformation, which had been launched almost half a century previously to combat the influence of Protestantism and exterminate any other unorthodox religious ideas. On top of this, Bruno still had charges of heresy to face, dating from sixteen years previously when he had fled from his monastery in Naples – meanwhile his cause had hardly been assisted by his travels about Europe attempting to convert Catholics and Protestants alike to his scientific and metaphysical ideas.

There is evidence that it was Mocenigo who tipped off the Roman Inquisition about Bruno's trial in Venice. Indeed, there is more than a suspicion that Mocenigo had been playing an extremely devious role from the outset of his relationship with Bruno. Mocenigo made no secret of the fact that he had links with the Venetian Inquisition – with his family connections it is unlikely to have been otherwise. Less evident was the fact that he also had connections with some members of the Roman Inquisition. In the opinion of his biographer, Michael White, 'It was these men who encouraged Mocenigo to forge a relationship with Bruno with the deliberate intention of trapping the philosopher.'

Initially, it seems, the Venetian Inquisition was reluctant to surrender its prisoner to the more vindictive court in Rome. However, pressure was soon brought to bear upon the Republic: Bruno was not even Venetian, and besides he still faced a charge of heresy in Rome. By retaining Bruno in their custody, treating him leniently and perhaps even letting him escape back across the Alps, Venice would be guilty of a dangerous act of defiance against Rome. The Venetian authorities soon caved in. Here, if needed, was further evidence of Venice's decline. The Republic was no longer a proud imperial power, with possessions all over the eastern Mediterranean, or even a major ruler over much of northern Italy. Those days were over: Venice was now a marginal provincial power, keen to retain whatever friends it could find in order to protect its independence. The Republic had no wish to make an unnecessary enemy of Rome. In February 1593 Bruno was unceremoniously surrendered to the papal authorities, clapped in irons and transported to Rome. Here he was taken to the notorious dungeons of the Castel Sant' Angelo, the papal fortress in the Vatican.

Even at this juncture Bruno was not unduly worried. Clement VIII, a man known for his liberal views, had been elected pope in January 1592 and had already given evidence of his broad-mindedness by consulting on matters of doctrine with Francesco Patrizi, an occultist who had published his own 'new philosophy', which included both Christian and hermetic ideas. Bruno felt sure that if he could but gain an audience with the pope he would soon be able to persuade him of the validity of his ideas and their effectiveness in combating the attractiveness of the simpler spirituality embraced by the Protestants. But such meetings were not so easy to arrange. The papal Curia was an intricate balance of opposing hierarchies and power structures, held together by all manner of intricate protocol, which the pope interfered with at his peril. In order to rule effectively, a pope was frequently forced to make compromises with the demands of these disparate elements. In Bruno's case, the Roman Inquisition made sure that any contact between the pope and Bruno was out of the question – there was to be no repeat of the Patrizi affair.

Bruno was kept in the dungeons and eventually brought to trial. As was often the case in Rome, this dragged on for years, with Bruno becoming increasingly confident that his views would prevail over the objections put forward by prosecutors who were simply no match for his superior intellect. No longer did he admit, as he had in Venice, that he had committed minor errors: boldly he began insisting upon the veracity of all his scientific and hermetic claims. His inquisitors put forward orthodox, but otherwise ineffectual, objections.

By now Clement VIII was becoming increasingly disturbed at the mockery that Bruno appeared to be making of the Inquisition, and consulted on the matter with his senior adviser, Roberto Bellarmino (usually known by his English equivalent Robert Bellarmine). The fifty-seven-year-old Bellarmine was a Jesuit, a man of considerable intellect and strict orthodoxy who had been a professor of theology for some twenty years. Clement VIII soon came to a decision. In 1599 Bruno's trial was placed in the charge of Bellarmine, who had been appointed a cardinal for the purpose. (Strict protocol had to be observed: as a Jesuit, Bellarmine would not otherwise have been able to preside over a court of the Inquisition, which was an institution of the Dominicans.)

After years of futile bickering, Bruno's trial now began to move more swiftly. When confronting Cardinal Bellarmine, he hoist himself on his own petard. His self-confident claims for his scientific and hermetic beliefs were quickly demonstrated to be heresy by Bellarmine. Bruno was found guilty and condemned to be burned at the stake. On 19 February 1600, as Bruno was led out towards the unlit pyre of kindling wood in the Campo di Fiore (Field of Flowers), it was noticed by the crowd that his mouth had been stuffed with a gag and his lips bound with a leather strap.* There was to be no possibility of him proclaiming his ideas in public before the flames reduced his mind to silence and his body to ashes. The Inquisition was taking no chances: in order to preserve one true faith of the Catholic Church, *all* new ideas had to be silenced.

The man who succeeded in obtaining the chair of mathematics at Padua the year after Bruno had been turned down for the post was Galileo Galilei, who is seen by many as the founder of the modern scientific era. He had been born in Pisa, on the west coast of Tuscany, in February 1564. His father was a highly skilled lutenist, who had in fact studied musical theory in Venice; however, he would never achieve the success he deserved, owing to his rebellious character. Like father, like son. Galileo grew to be a bumptious, self-confident youth, with a shock of flaming red hair, whose obvious extrovert charms concealed a rather more complex temperament. At the age of seventeen he returned to Pisa to study medicine at the university, but soon rebelled against the stale medieval curriculum and began embracing the humanistic Renaissance ideas that were themselves now beginning to emerge from the shadow of classical learning into the light of modern reality. The spirit of originality that in its different ways had inspired Copernicus, and would inspire Bruno and Harvey, was very much in the air. Glaring mistakes were being discovered in the science of Aristotle and Galen; a new science was being born that studied the workings of the world rather than the authority of the ancients.

At the age of twenty-one Galileo left Pisa without having gained a degree, and for the next few years precariously supported himself in Florence and Siena by tutoring – at one point even giving lessons to Cosimo de' Medici, the young son of Grand Duke Ferdinand II, the ruler of Florence. Whilst in Florence, Galileo came under the influence of the Medici court mathematician Ostilio Ricci, a man of some brilliance, who quickly recognised a fellow spirit and encouraged Galileo to pursue the study of mathematics, a subject that had long fascinated him. Indeed, Galileo soon made such

---

* According to White, Bruno's silence was ensured by more vicious means: 'A long metal spike was thrust through Bruno's left cheek pinning his tongue . . . Then another spike was rammed vertically through his lips.'

progress in this field that he managed to obtain the chair in mathematics at his old university in Pisa. According to legend, it was here that he publicly disproved Aristotle's theory that heavier bodies fall more quickly to the ground than lighter ones, by dropping objects of differing weights from the top of the Leaning Tower of Pisa and showing that both reached the ground simultaneously. Whether or not this incident actually took place, its brazenness and scientific intent were characteristic, making Galileo a great favourite with the students, amongst whom he enjoyed the boisterous life of the taverns. Such scandalous behaviour, as well as Galileo's openly contemptuous regard for his more orthodox academic colleagues, meant that in 1592 his contract was not renewed.

It was now, at the age of twenty-eight, that he applied for the vacant chair of mathematics at Padua and was accepted for the post that had eluded Bruno. From a purely intellectual point of view, the authorities had made an astute choice: Galileo's ideas were not allied to any anomalous metaphysical hermeticism. Unlike Bruno, who speculated on the nature of the world around him, Galileo experimented. This meant that his science was permeated with exactitude. He confidently pronounced, 'The book of the world is written in mathematics.' Likewise, he insisted that the way forward in science lay in 'measuring what is measurable, and rendering measurable what is at present not so.' Yet with a dangerous arrogance similar to that of Bruno, he was not afraid of expressing himself on matters of theology: 'I do not feel obliged to believe that the same God who endowed us with sense, reason and intellect intended us to forgo their use.' Here too he was contemptuous of fellow academics who clung to outmoded medieval ideas, especially 'the foremost philosophers of this university, who refuse, with the obstinacy of bloated adders, to see the truth of my ideas'.

Fortunately Padua retained its intellectual freedom – despite the Bruno debacle, which was soon to move to Rome and its grisly climax. Although the university curriculum required Galileo to lecture on such orthodox topics as the Ptolemaic universe and Aristotelian science (which decreed that everything was made up of a mixture of earth, air, fire and water), he also was able to give private lectures explaining his more modern scientific ideas. Not all of these were original – Galileo was not above 'improving' on the ideas of others and claiming them for himself. Yet such was his genius that this activity invariably rose above the level of mere plagiarism. Thus, in line with what Tartaglia had discovered some fifty years previously, Galileo too contradicted Aristotle's belief that cannonballs travelled in straight lines, maintaining that their trajectory did in fact follow the course of a parabola. Yet where Tartaglia had only written of this discovery, producing a handbook of tables, Galileo went a significant step further, producing a hinged mechanical range-finder, which could be placed in the mouth of a cannon to determine the angle to which its barrel should be raised in order for its trajectory to reach a certain range. This was the device that he would sell to armies all over Europe, and in this way make his fortune. Unfortunately, the unsatisfactory state of the current patent law was such that competitors were soon manufacturing their own cheap versions of Galileo's range-finder and undercutting his market. Undaunted, Galileo would continue over the years creating a number of other inventions and ingenious devices – ranging from the first modern thermometer to instructions on how to reinforce ancient battlements so as to withstand the latest artillery. These too were soon copied, and riches continued to elude Galileo.

Making a fortune would become a lasting preoccupation with Galileo. However, he was not naturally given to the quest for fame and fortune, and this was largely thrust upon him by his financial circumstances. Although his professorial salary at Padua was far from meagre, it was not enough to support his continuing extravagant lifestyle and the financial burdens that had now been forced upon him.

In 1591 Galileo's father had died, leaving his large family in dire financial straits. He now had to provide for six brothers and sisters, as well as an elderly complaining mother, none of whom he could even travel to see. During his earlier years as a tutor in Florence, his extravagances in the taverns and elsewhere had left such a trail of unpaid bills that his mother had written to warn him not to visit Florence as his creditors were now 'threatening to have you clapped in irons as soon as you set foot in the city'.

On top of this, Galileo now had a family of his own in Padua. He had taken up with a twenty-two-year-old local woman called Marina Gamba, known equally for her striking beauty and her volatile temperament. This proved a fine match for Galileo's own character, and Marina would eventually produce two daughters and a son by Galileo – though he never married her.

Despite his busy life supporting two families, and performing his professorial duties as a public and private lecturer whilst constantly searching for some invention that would make his fortune, Galileo also found time to advance his theoretical ideas. During his early years at Padua he had quickly come to the conclusion that the Copernican heliocentric view of the universe was correct, and had begun corresponding with the astronomer Johannes Kepler in Prague, who was at the time calculating the elliptical orbits of the planets about the sun. However, even the ebullient Galileo felt it best to refrain from publishing his Copernican views in the light of Bruno's fate in Rome.

In the summer of 1609 news reached Venice of a sensational new type of perspicillum that had been invented in Holland. Previously a perspicillum had consisted of a lens or a pair of glasses, but this new instrument was said to be made up of two lenses arranged in a single tube and enabled a distant object to appear close up, enlarging its image by as much as three times that seen by the naked eye. When Galileo heard of this instrument, 'by which a man two miles away can be distinctly seen', it immediately sparked his scientific curiosity. Without even seeing one, he quickly grasped the optical principle upon which it was based and began constructing a perspicillum of his own. As ever he improved on this purloined idea, and after a number of experimental versions produced an instrument capable of almost three times the power of the orginal. Here, surely, was the invention that would guarantee his future. But this time, guided by astute Venetian friends, Galileo curbed his financial ambitions and took the unprecedented step of offering his invention to the Venetian authorities for free. Accompanied by a number of senior senators, Galileo climbed the stairs to the top of the Campanile and demonstrated his new instrument, so that they were able 'to observe at sea sails and vessels so far away that, coming under full sail to port, two hours and more were required before they could be seen without my spyglass'. He further claimed that his instrument could 'represent an object which is for example fifty miles away as large and near as if it were but five'. The defensive uses of such an instrument for a city like Venice were obvious: there would be no further surprise attacks from the sea.

The Senate voted to accept Galileo's gift, and gratefully awarded him an immediate grant of 500 ducats, as well as doubling his university salary to more than 1,000 ducats a year for life. Fortunately the headstrong Galileo had heeded the advice of his friends: by selling manufactured examples of his perspicillum he could never have earned such a sum, especially since he had no patent on the idea. Within no time instrument-makers all over Europe were producing what two years later came to be known as a telescope,* which Galileo now insisted he had invented. When presented with incontrovertible evidence to the contrary, his reply was characteristically robust: 'Any idiot can discover such a thing by accident. I was the one who discovered it by reason, which requires genuine originality.'

Within months of his original 'invention' Galileo had improved upon his telescope so that it magnified the original object twenty times. But this was only the beginning. Though he was certainly not the first to raise a telescope to the night sky, he was the first to understand the full significance of what he was seeing. Indeed, he was hardly exaggerating when he now referred to himself as 'the new Columbus'. His drawing of what he saw would cause a revolution in science and transform humanity's entire understanding of the world and our place in it. Galileo's drawings of the moon showed that it was not a perfect sphere, as it was described according to the dictates of Aristotelianism. Instead, it was another world, in many ways resembling our own, complete with volcanic craters and mountains, which cast shadows across its sunlit surface. And when he turned his telescope to the Milky Way, instead of a diaphanous haze it became transformed into a vast rash of stars extending through the heavens. There were even stars that were not visible to the naked eye, completely disproving Aristotle's claim that there could be no such thing. Galileo went on to observe, and record in remarkably accurate drawings, four moon-like satellites of Jupiter, sunspots which darkened and then disappeared from the surface of the sun, as well as the 'phases of Venus', which showed that this planet waxed and waned like the moon. This could only have taken place if Venus orbited the sun. Here was incontrovertible evidence for the solar system, utterly disproving the Ptolemaic model.

* From the Greek *tele* meaning 'distant' and *skopos* 'to see'.

Galileo quickly wrote up his findings, and in 1610 published them in a short work called *Sidereus Nuncius* (The Starry Messenger). Later that same year he received word from Florence, from his former pupil Cosimo de' Medici, who had recently succeeded as Grand Duke of Tuscany. Grand Duke Cosimo II formally invited Galileo to accept the well-paid post of 'first philosopher and mathematician' at his court. Galileo was elated by this opportunity, and late in 1610 left Venice for his native Tuscany. He is known to have taken his two daughters with him and to have placed them in the San Matteo convent at Arcetri in the hills a mile south of Florence. By means of letters he would remain in constant contact with his favourite eldest daughter Virginia, who certainly inherited at least some of her father's intellect. Their mother, Marina Gamba, and his four-year-old son were left behind in Venice; it was long thought that Galileo had provided her with sufficient money for a dowry, which she used to get married, but it now appears that she was probably in ill health and too debilitated to travel such a distance, for she died two years later.

Galileo would live to regret leaving the protection of Venice. In 1615 a decree was issued in Rome declaring that the Copernican theory was heretical, and banning his work, as well as several other works, including one by Kepler. No work by Galileo was banned, but he received a private warning from Cardinal Bellarmine, who just fifteen years previously had condemned Bruno to be burned at the stake. Galileo would rashly ignore this warning and, despite the efforts of Grand Duke Cosimo II to protect him, in 1633 the sixty-nine-year-old Galileo was summoned to Rome to face the Inquisition. Fearing Bruno's fate, Galileo publicly retracted his view that the Earth moved around the sun, though at the same time he is said to have been unable to refrain from muttering to himself, 'And yet it does move.' He was now banned from disseminating any of his scientific views and condemned to house arrest. He chose to stay in a villa in Arcetri, in order to be near his daughter in her convent, but was heart-broken when she died of dysentery in 1634, within a year of his return. The ageing Galileo lived on in Arcetri, surreptitiously continuing with his work even as his sight began to fail, until he died blind at the age of seventy-seven in 1642.

News of Galileo's trial, his confinement and his eventual demise would all have been followed closely in Venice. A direct consequence of the liberal climate maintained by the Republic was that the people of Venice were becoming increasingly informed on all manner of matters. Sir Henry Wotton stigmatised the dissemination of 'news' as 'the very disease of this city'. When reports of events reached Venice, they would be publicly read out before an assembled crowd of citizens, each of whom was expected to pay a coin called a *gazzetta* for the privilege. And news reported by these means was not only confined to such matters as war, disasters and Galileo's appearance before the Roman Inquisition. People were equally interested in, and willing to pay for, all manner of the latest information: Galileo's discoveries of the wonders of an entirely new universe were also reported in this fashion. When the world's first newspaper was produced in Venice sometime around 1630 it was known as the *Gazzetta*.* Although there are other claims to this 'first', the *Gazzetta* was perhaps the earliest publication to appear regularly, usually on a weekly basis; it was printed on a large sheet, which could be folded so as to produce four pages of news.

Ironically, this liberalising and insatiable thirst for news of all kinds also had its repressive underside. Gossip flourished in the narrow streets of the city, secrets from overheard conversations quickly circulated, and within this comparatively close-knit community everyone kept an eye on everyone else. Inevitably this fuelled a collective paranoia about spying, which was put to effective use by the Council of Ten in the interests of public order, detecting plots against the government and any suspicious activities by agents acting for foreign powers. As had been seen in the 'Spanish Plot' of 1610, fears of spying were certainly justified, and throughout the following century the city would continue to attract foreign spies, even in the most unlikely of guises. Thus in 1625 the French philosopher René Descartes would spend a month or so in the city, acting as a spy for the Jesuits. And three-quarters of a century later the German philosopher and polymath Gottfried Leibniz would make two visits to Venice of a similar

---

* Despite the fact that Aretino is called 'the first journalist', he did not write for a newspaper. Instead, his libellous rumours, scurrilous poems and satires were distributed in the form of printed handbills and pamphlets.

18

'The Seat of Music'

I T COMES AS no surprise that a city of such fluidity and limpid reflection should also be a city of music. The gondoliers were not the only ones known for their spontaneous singing as they worked. In the market places the vendors sang out praises (and prices) of their fresh vegetables, fish and meat. Many early visitors from northern Europe commented on how the sound of musical instruments and singing flowed from open windows into the streets and alleyways, while groups of musicians roamed the streets playing for money. Even a public reading of the news was liable to be preceded by a song, intended to draw the attention of the *gazzetta*-paying onlookers. Meanwhile the skill and commercial acumen of the city's many publishers ensured that printed music was readily available, and during the sixteenth century the city's skilled instrument-makers played their role in ensuring that the violin, the lute and other stringed instruments evolved into the classical shapes we know today. Indeed, some Venetians even came to regard their violin-makers on a par with those from Cremona, the Lombardy city that was home to the Stradivari family. It is no wonder that the first 1581 guidebook to Venice even went so far as to call it *la sede de musica* (the seat of music).

Yet there can be no doubt as to Venice's major musical accomplishment – namely in the pioneering and development of opera, though curiously this musical form so associated with Venice was in fact invented in Florence – and coincidentally it was Galileo's father, Vincenzo Galilei, who would play a leading role in this. He and a circle of friends who played music together found themselves becoming increasingly frustrated by the medieval restrictions imposed by polyphony, which required voices to sing in counterpoint against each other. They wished to see music too undergo a renaissance, breaking free of church polyphony and returning to its classical roots. They attempted to revive Greek tragedy, which was known to have been accompanied by music that has since been lost. It was the writing of music to accompany Greek tragedy that gave birth to opera – with a single-voice recitative, in part invented by Vincenzo Galilei, being used to draw together the narrative between aria and chorus. The earliest extant opera is *Euridice*, composed by Galilei's friend Jacopo Peri, which was performed in Florence in 1600.

Opera quickly became all the rage, but nowhere more so than in Venice. It is no anachronism to claim, as many have, that this was the first 'pop' music, the great leveller of its day. Opera had something for the entire audience: instrumental expertise, virtuoso singing, catchy melodies, passion and high drama, star performers and scandalous costumes – it was all there and at prices to suit all. As such, it appealed to all classes, and its rapturous reception in republican Venice is not surprising. As early as 1637 the city built its first public opera house – the Teatro Tron, near the Rialto. By the end of the century Venice had become the undisputed capital of opera in Europe, with more than ten full-sized opera houses, and perhaps another half-dozen more intimate venues, as well as no fewer than four conservatoires where young musicians and singers trained. But it was not only the performers themselves who contributed to this pre-eminence. As evidenced in the production lines of the Arsenale, this was a city of highly skilled engineers, and when they turned their attentions to the mechanics of stage management they were soon producing awe-inspiring scenery as well as sensational effects – a succession of which could speedily be manoeuvred into place behind the curtains between scenes. This produced a thrilling spectacle to delight the eye as well as the ear.

Despite Venice's triumph in this field, its audiences were not always as appreciative as their city's reputation had led many visitors to expect. The many boxes that ringed the upper tiers of the opera houses were the preserve of noble families, who purchased them outright and thus came to regard them as their personal property. Thus many came to use their family box as another living room, an extension of their palazzi, often attending the theatre many nights a week regardless of the opera being performed. Guests were entertained to food and drink, and conversation would continue throughout the performance, while noble friends often made the rounds of other boxes. Meanwhile, below in the stalls, the lesser strata of Venetian society would continue to gossip, giggle and even play cards throughout the performance on stage. According to the writer Peter Ackroyd, 'The noise of their chatter was compared to a bush filled with birds.' The lower orders were permitted to wear hats in the theatre to protect them from the rain of refuse from above, as the nobles spat out their fishbones and fruit pips, and tossed their gnawed chicken bones over the balconies of their boxes.

As gondoliers had transported their charges to the opera, and were expected to wait until the performance was over to take them back, they were granted free entry to the opera house, providing a welcome service for the management by filling up unoccupied seats at less popular performances, or simply cramming along the walls and crouching in the aisles at more popular shows. At the end of the opera they would be particularly vociferous towards the singers, with competing groups stamping and shouting 'Bravo!' for their favourites, or setting up a deafening chorus of catcalls, whistles and jeers to greet their opponents' favourite, an inept performer or one who for some reason attracted their opprobrium. Different groups were frequently bribed by interested parties to jeer or boo, sometimes even being encouraged to interrupt the performance to express their feelings at the entrance of a particular singer.

Venetian opera came into its own during this period and would produce a succession of operatic composers. The finest of the earlier wave was undoubtedly Claudio Monteverdi, whose operas and madrigals carried over from the early Renaissance polyphony to elaborately ornamental flourishes of the baroque period.* This is epitomised by his opera *L'Orfeo*, which he wrote in 1617 at the age of forty. One of the earliest operas, it was based on the Greek myth of Orpheus, who descends into the Underworld and after charming the gods with his music, is allowed to lead his dead bride

---

* The word 'baroque', which especially characterised both the music and the architecture of the period, takes its name from the Portugese word *barroco*, meaning 'an irregularly shaped pearl'. In music, it preceded the classical period.

Eurydice back to the upper world, but fatally disobeys them by turning back to look at her. This of course echoes the story of Peri's earliest opera *Euridice*, but in Monteverdi's version both the musical and narrative line are more fully developed, making this in many ways the first completely realised example of operatic form – to such an extent, and with such success, that *L'Orfeo* remains in the repertoire to this day.

In 1613 Monteverdi moved to Venice, where he became conductor of the orchestra at the basilica of San Marco. Although he had married in earlier life, by this time his wife had died and his children had grown up and married, so in 1632 he joined the priesthood. This may well have been prompted by his survival of the 1630 plague, which is known to have killed almost one-third of the population. Despite Monteverdi taking up holy orders, 1642 would see the staging of what many experts regard as his most technically accomplished opera *L'incoronazione di Poppea* (The Coronation of Poppea), which is based upon the most unholy subject of the Roman emperor Nero and his mistress. Indeed, it was famously decribed by the music critic Bernard Holland as 'the story of virtue punished and greed rewarded'. Such inversion of morality is transcended by Monteverdi's skill in incorporating elements of tragedy, romance and even comedy, as well as by a portrayal of realistic character in some psychological depth.

Amazingly, Monteverdi accomplished all this when he was in his seventies, a decade that marked some of his most creative years, as well as the peak of his widespread fame. Possibly through the sheer effort of producing such work during his late years, his earlier abrasiveness is said to have developed into the full-blown crotchetiness of old age. The following year he revisited his birthplace in Cremona and then travelled on to Mantua, the scene of his earliest triumphs, before returning (in the words of Tasso), 'Like a swan, feeling the fatal hour is near, approaches . . . Venice, the Queen of all waters'. He would die in Venice in November 1643 at the age of seventy-seven.

Less than half a century later would see the birth of the greatest of all Venetian composers, Antonio Vivaldi, on 4 March 1678. It was said that on the day of his birth Venice was shaken by an earthquake, and that in response his mother promised God that her son would be dedicated to the priesthood. His father, on the other hand, had been a barber who abandoned his trade to become a musician. His first appointment as a professional violinist was with the orchestra that played in the basilica of San Marco at a salary of fifteen ducats a year. However, this soon rose to twenty-five ducats when it became clear that he had sufficient talent to perform solos. It appears that the young Vivaldi was expertly taught the violin by his father from an early age, and soon began showing such exceptional talent and originality that his father even began instructing him in the art of composition. Despite the prospect of a promising career in music, his mother seems to have insisted upon the fulfilment of her promise to God, and Antonio trained for the priesthood, eventually being ordained at the age of twenty-five in 1703.

Even so, it soon became clear that he was unable (or unwilling) to fulfil all his priestly duties. He had to give up performing mass because he was so often unable to finish administering the service as he suffered from *strettezza di petto* (literally 'tightness of the chest'). Several interpretations have been put upon this complaint. Some assert that since his youth Vivaldi had suffered from bronchial asthma, with its suggestion of psychological stress induced by a suppressed unwillingness to enter the priesthood. Others see this ailment as angina pectoris. Another suggestion, in keeping with the more individualistic view of all artists that was beginning to emerge during this period, has him suspended from saying mass because he was in the habit of becoming preoccupied and wandering off into the sacristy to jot down a snatch of music that had occurred to him.

In the same year as he was ordained Vivaldi was appointed to the post of violin teacher at the Ospedale della Pietà, the large orphanage on the Riva degli Schiavoni overlooking the open water close to the house where Petrarch had lived. This institution took in abandoned children: here young boys were taught a trade before being despatched into the outside world, while girls received a more standard female education before taking up their duties as skivvies or servants. Girls who showed talent were permitted to stay on as members of the Ospedale's choir or orchestra. In time, Vivaldi would become director of this choir, as well as the composer of its music and a virtuoso musician in its orchestra. Even in a city where musical competition was fierce indeed, the public performances of this choir achieved a high reputation under the direction of '*il prete rosso*' ('the red priest'), as he came to be known on account of his red hair. The girls performed in rising galleries behind wrought-iron grilles, their voices emerging as if from the building itself or the upper air, achieving a sublime beauty. During performances the canal outside the building would be clogged with gondolas as their passengers listened to the sheer beauty of the girls' voices floating out over the water. Vivaldi was soon expected to produce a new piece of work for each feast day, but as his output increased, so did its quality. Besides sacred vocal music, he now also produced cantatas and concertos. He well understood the brilliance of his music, and was ambitious to have it appreciated. However, his early forays into the outside world of music made little impression: Venice had a jealously guarded hierarchy of composers, and no mere orphanage priest was going find a place here without difficulty. At the same time, relations with the board of the Ospedale became strained, partly owing to jealousies, and partly it would seem because of certain eccentricities in Vivaldi's character. It is difficult to pin down the precise nature of these eccentricities; his portraits suggest a slight capriciousness, and he may well have exhibited some oddities of manner. His persistent asthma, the possible effects of an autistic nature, a weakened physique overstrained by excessive work – all these have been suggested. Even the reports of his behaviour seem contradictory: there are some reports of him being solitary, spending hours lost in the isolation of his room amidst scattered sheets of music, constantly composing. He may have been in poor health, yet others speak of his boundless energy, endlessly coaching the girls' choir in their new pieces, and of the strain caused by the amazing dexterity of his virtuoso violin-playing. Many remarked on his piety; others on his ambitious nature.

In 1711 Vivaldi travelled to Brescia with his father to assist in a production of his music at a religious festival. Two years later he set up as an impresario, running a small theatre where his works and those of others could be produced. He would later describe himself as '*un franco intraprenditore*' (an unashamed businessman, an out-and-out entrepreneur). Perhaps only in Venice could such activity have lived in unhypocritical unity with priestly piety. Although to begin with his commercial activities met with only mediocre success, he would in time hone his skills. By now the board of the Ospedale had realised the error of their ways, and Vivaldi had been allowed to return to his post on a permanent basis. Even so he now began to travel more frequently, and for longer periods of time, playing his work in Rome, Milan, and even staying at the court of Mantua for three years. In Venice his music was subjected to the constant vicissitudes of fashion, that one would expect of such a rich and varied musical scene, but elsewhere his music proved more lastingly appreciated. It was whilst occupying the post of maestro di cappella at Mantua that he was inspired to write the four violin concertos for which he is best-known today – namely, *Le quattro stagioni* (The Four Seasons).

Such a work could never have been written had he remained in Venice. The four concertos, each of which depicts a different season, relate closely to the countryside around Mantua. They are also each accompanied by a sonnet, presumed to have been written by Vivaldi himself, giving an indication of what the music is describing – along with a few more precise instructions in the score, such as 'the dog barking'. This is programme music of the clearest and most evocative kind, yet it is also so much more than this in its expressive musicality – it can be enjoyed just as well without any knowledge of the 'programme'. In the opening concerto, 'Spring', there is the sound of birdsong (with the calls of the different birds quite clearly distinguishable), the murmur of water in the flowing brook. A gentle breeze is followed by lightning and thunder; and later comes the sound of bagpipes, with nymphs and shepherds dancing. 'Summer' includes the unmistakable call of the cuckoo, the languor of heat and the buzz of swarms of insects. 'Autumn' depicts a bacchanal as the peasants celebrate the end of the harvest, and later a hunting scene; while 'Winter' portrays snow and ice and freezing wind, then a cosy scene inside before a warm fire.

The Four Seasons would be published in 1723, and this, along with several similar virtuoso pieces, would gain Vivaldi a reputation throughout Europe. (Louis XV is said to have been particularly keen on 'Spring', and would insist upon it being played, regardless of inappropriate circumstances.) Despite such widespread renown, Vivaldi's initial attempts to break into the lucrative opera market proved unsuccessful. Ironically, his first operatic success was *Nerone fatto Cesare* (Nero Made Caesar), a work to which he only contributed some of the music. The plot involved a woman falling in love with a woman dressed as a man, hardly the kind of work one expects to be associated with a pious priest. Indeed, *Nerone* was initially banned by the Venetian censors, and was only allowed to be performed after certain cuts had been made. Despite this dubious beginning, Vivaldi would go on to establish himself in the operatic field, from now on producing a steady stream of operas – some successful, others less so. Towards the end of his life he would speak of himself as 'having composed 94 operas', which was seen as something of an exaggeration, since after his death only fifty operas were found. Even so, this was a prodigious output, especially in the light of all the other choral and instrumental work he produced.

In 1726 the sixteen-year-old mezzo-soprano Anna Girò sang the leading role in Vivaldi's opera *Dorilla*. Although the range and strength of her voice were far from exceptional, her presence on stage was electric and her acting both passionate and controlled. From now on she became Vivaldi's leading singer, travelling as part of his entourage when he took his work abroad *'in moltissime città d'Europa'* ('in cities throughout Europe'). Inevitably the forty-eight-year-old Vivaldi was suspected of becoming romantically involved with Anna, an accusation that he always denied – though in somewhat evasive fashion on occasion, especially when pressed on the matter by her middle-aged half-sister. Anna Girò would remain Vivaldi's leading operatic singer for some eleven years – until, out of the blue, in 1737 the Archbishop of Verona issued a decree forbidding Vivaldi from visiting the city to stage his opera. Two reasons were given: Vivaldi was not performing his duties as a priest by performing mass, and he was embroiled in an *amicizia* (affair). Sometime after this Anna appears to have joined another operatic company performing in Graz in Austria.

Still Vivaldi continued to pour out his operas at an astounding rate, sometimes composing faster than the copyists could take down his dictation. In the margin of one of his operas there is even the inscription *'fatta in 5 giorni'* ('completed in five days'). Yet once again with quantity came quality: his works were increasingly progressive, constantly developing the form in style and content.

Yet Vivaldi's ambitions seem to have remained somehow unfulfilled. He felt that he was not fully appreciated in Venice. Perhaps it was the money. The indications are that he was given to capricious extravagance: being as prolific with his money as he was with his talent. A contemporary source, writing at the end of his life, would claim that he 'earned at one time more than fifty thousand ducats'. This is a colossal sum – yet he seems to have saved nothing. Details of his extravagance are lost: they would appear to have been associated with generosity of spirit as well as love of display. They probably included disastrous business ventures in his role as an impresario, but they do not appear to have involved dissipated habits. He must certainly have run up bills, for he was short of money on numerous occasions. He became notorious for not publishing his works, finding that he could sell his original manuscripts for much more to wealthy tourists. According to the English visitor Edward Holdsworth, 'he finds a good market because he expects a guinea for every piece'.

In 1730, writing from Venice, Vivaldi would claim, 'I lack nothing here for perfect happiness'; yet by the end of the decade he appeared to want to abandon his native city. In the course of his travels through Europe, Vivaldi had encountered the Holy Roman Emperor Charles VI, who had been highly impressed with his music and had taken a personal liking to 'the red priest'. In 1728, when Charles VI had visited Trieste to oversee the enlargement of powerful Austria's only port (a development viewed with some concern in Venice), Vivaldi had been included in a 200-strong delegation despatched to greet the emperor. Contemporary evidence suggests that Charles VI singled out his friend, 'giving him a great deal of money and a gold chain . . . and knighted him'. The emperor then insisted that the newly created Cavaliere Vivaldi should stay with him, and it was said that 'he talked more with [Vivaldi] in two weeks than he had with his ministers in two years'.

Some ten years later, following Vivaldi's parting from Anna Girò and in the midst of his disillusionment with Venice, Charles VI sent word inviting Vivaldi to Vienna, giving him to understand that he would be able to stage his operas at the Kärntnertortheater. Sometime in mid-May 1740 Vivaldi took his leave of the Ospedale della Pietà and set off for Vienna. On the way he called in at Graz, where he seems to have met Anna Girò, perhaps promising her further work. Within months of Vivaldi arriving in

Vienna, Charles VI died, whereupon it appears that Vivaldi's offered appointment fell into abeyance. Stranded in a foreign city, with little or no money, he took cheap lodgings in the dwelling of a saddle-maker's widow. And here, in poverty and forgotten, he suffered from an 'internal inflammation'. This proved fatal, and he died on 28 July 1741, his body being carried off to a common grave in the 'poor sinners' burial ground' belonging to the nearby city hospital.

Vivaldi's plunge into obscurity at the end of his life was echoed by the fate of his work, and even the details of his life itself. His cavalier disregard for his manuscripts meant that most of them were scattered and lost. Astonishingly, for well over a hundred years little was known of his work other than a few violin concertos, and even the earlier recognition of Vivaldi's genius by the great Johann Sebastian Bach proved of no avail. As early as 1710 Bach had begun transcribing a series of Vivaldi's concertos for performance on harpsichord or organ. However, when curious later scholars tried to track down the orginal concertos no trace could be found.

Then in 1860 a large cache of Vivaldi's original manuscripts was discovered 'in a music cabinet of the Catholic Hofkirche in Dresden'. All the indications were that they had remained undisturbed here for more than a century. Even so, contemporary musicologists remained unimpressed: the German conductor Wilhelm von Wasielewski described Vivaldi's concertos (including *The Four Seasons*) as 'the Italian composer's thin and lifeless skeleton'. Vivaldi was dismissed as 'a scribbler in the worst sense of the word . . . constantly producing works devoid of substance and meaning'. Since then, several further discoveries of Vivaldi manuscripts have been made, ranging from a trove of more than a hundred concertos and twelve operas in a remote monastery in Piedmont in 1926 to a few manuscripts that turned up in Manchester Central Library in the 1970s. It is now clear that Vivaldi was far from exaggerating when he claimed to have composed ninety-four operas, for we now know that he did in fact compose more than a hundred. In all, he is (to date) known to have also composed some 500 instrumental works, to say nothing of another 200 cantatas, choral works, and so forth.

The 1920s discovery in Italy resulted in a certain revival of interest in Vivaldi, but the true renaissance of his work did not occur until the years following the Second World War, when it was interpreted in all its freshness and virtuosity by such chamber orchestras as La Scuola Veneziana. Vivaldi had at last returned to his native city, one of the most apt and characteristic of all the artistic ornaments of *La Serenissima*.

However, an opera still required one vital ingredient beyond music and singers, an opera house and an unruly audience. At the outset it needed a librettist, and eighteenth-century Venice teemed with good, bad and very bad writers of operatic drama, most of whom were highly unoriginal. Classical, mythical and fairytale adaptations abounded: the old stories pulled in the audiences, and the impresarios preferred it that way. This was as true of the best librettists as it was as of those who merely passed themselves off as experienced stage craftsmen (whose reputation was invariably of the highest, yet in some other city).

The leading writers were frequently dramatists in their own right, and this was certainly true of Venice's leading librettist of the period, Carlo Goldoni, who collaborated with Vivaldi several times – despite his opinion that the red priest was 'an excellent violinist and middling composer'. Goldoni has even left us a description of a meeting with his mediocre collaborator, though this is a largely stereotypical caricature. The entire episode consists of Goldoni astonishing a sceptical Vivaldi by rewriting an entire eight-verse aria in record time, so that Vivaldi ends up casting aside his breviary in amazement, crying out with joy and heaping lavish praise upon Goldoni's superb skill: 'Ah . . . here is an unusual man, here is an excellent poet. Read this aria. This gentleman has done it right here without hedging and in less than quarter of an hour.'

Unexpectedly there is more than a little truth in Vivaldi's (alleged) words. Goldoni was almost as prodigious, and talented after his own fashion, as the composer himself. Carlo Goldoni had also been born in Venice, though almost thirty years after Vivaldi, in 1707. Like Vivaldi, he had childhood problems concerning his vocation. Goldoni's father wished him to qualify as a lawyer, which was not what Goldoni had in mind at all. Instead of studying, he wrote poems and comic sketches, and participated in a number of comical escapades himself, to the extent that he was expelled from school and ran away a number of times. However, his father prevailed and he qualified in law at Padua in 1732, returning to Venice to practise. But after two years he could bear it no longer, and ran off with a roaming troupe of *commedia dell'arte* players, for whom he wrote tragicomic sketches. A year later he was back in Venice, where he achieved his first success in November 1734 with *Belisario*. Such was the effect on the audience of this work that 'The play was listened to with a silence which was extraordinary, indeed almost unheard of in Italian theatres.' He would achieve his first success as a librettist the following year with *Aristide*, for which Vivaldi almost certainly provided the music – though for some reason both librettist and composer appeared under somewhat unconvincing pseudonyms (Goldoni as Calindo Grolo, and Vivaldi as Lotario Vandini). Vivaldi's reason may well have been financial, while Goldoni may by then already have been under contract to a rival company. In 1734 he is known to have joined the prestigous Imer company, to which he would remained attached over the next ten years – the genial young actor enjoying the favours of several of the actresses. Amongst the female leads was an attractive young widow called Zanetta Casanova, mother of the celebrated lover, Giacomo. Not all of Goldoni's affairs brought him happiness, and when he was eventually driven to extremes of jealousy by a particularly fickle leading lady named Elisabetta Passalacqua, he took his revenge by maliciously casting her in his original version of the old *commedia dell'arte* classic *Don Giovanni*. Passalacqua was said to have played the part with such superb contempt that the audience soon understood what had happened and the play became an immediate *succès de scandale*.

During these years the Imer company frequently went on tour, playing the cities of northern Italy, and not long after the *Don Giovanni* affair Carlo Goldoni would meet his future wife Nicoletta Conio, the daughter of a notary, in Genoa. Carlo and Nicoletta would be married within a matter of weeks, before the company left the city. According to the Italian historian Indro Montanelli, 'Nicoletta Conio was not only pretty and in possession of a fair-sized dowry, but she also showed understanding, patience and devotion when it was necessary (and God knows it was necessary often enough) to put up with the infidelity of a lay-about like him.' Despite this harsh judgement, Carlo and Nicoletta would remain together for fifty years of seemingly happy marriage, which according to Goldoni was not marred by either 'domestic quarrels or inflamed temper'. At the end of his life he would pay her the generous, if somewhat disingenuous compliment of claiming that 'she was and always has been my only consolation'.

During Goldini's ten years with the Imer company his talents would quickly develop, the 'lay-about' producing a constant stream of librettos and dramas. From penning farces and adapting hackneyed *commedia dell'arte* stories, he progressed to contriving his own delightful brand of comedy involving realistic characters. These were increasingly set in recognisable Venetian locales, portraying the foibles, sadnesses and passing joys of local family life amongst the growing middle classes. This may not have been great literature, but it made for excellent theatre – both entertaining and moving the audiences, who recognised themselves. This was the poetry of domestic life, maintaining the dignity of common people as they underwent life's perennial upsets. The audiences loved seeing these dramas, which poked gentle fun at the idiosyncrasies of their everyday existence. There was no overblown farce, or hideous tragedy, or licentiousness: Venetian audiences did not appreciate such matters when they referred to themselves. Impresarios, writers and even actors understood this. A visitor describes how on one occasion, when it became evident that a husband onstage was about to kill his wife with a sword, the audience cried out with one voice for him to stop. At this point the actor playing the husband stepped to the front of the stage and addressed the audience, apologising and reassuring them that the scene would in fact have a happy ending.

Not content with the reputation of his lighter comedies, Goldoni now set about trying to gain a reputation in *opera seria*, the more melodramatic and serious form. This proved disastrous, both artistically and financially, and by 1743 he found himself so heavily in debt that he and Nicoletta left Venice and he abandoned writing altogether, setting up practice as a lawyer in Tuscany.

Four years later, at the age of forty, he would return to his native city. He now set about writing further Venetian comedies, his mature style developing these well-observed dramas to the point where they were unrivalled throughout Italy. His Venetian audiences were ecstatic. And in between times he produced a series of libretti for *opera buffa* (the traditional, rather more exaggerated form of comic opera). By this time his creativity was at its height, as was his work-rate. He took on all that he was offered:

by the start of the 1750–1 season he had promised to write no fewer than sixteen new comedies, all of which were duly delivered on time. Not surprisingly, his popularity created much jealousy amongst his rivals, many of whom were also highly talented – though lacking the sure-handedness and subtlety of Goldoni. One of these was the aristocratic Carlo Gozzi, who resented Goldoni's even-handed description of the Venetian social scene, complaining, 'He has often made true noblemen the mirror of all that is iniquitous and absurd, and he has made the common people a model of all virtues.' In Gozzi's view, such work also displayed a lack of imagination and grace. (Gozzi's own work consisted of wildly imaginative flights, involving fairies and the supernatural, though admittedly this was often tempered by satiric intent – his best-known work being *The Love of Three Oranges*.) Goldoni's other main rival on the Venetian scene was Giuseppe Baretti, who was incensed when the great Voltaire wrote a letter to Goldoni expressing his effusive admiration: 'your name is already immortal'. Naturally Goldoni made sure that the contents of this letter became known to his rivals. Baretti was beside himself with rage: first he claimed that the letter was a forgery, then he contradicted himself by declaring, 'Voltaire has no right to judge things written in Italian.'

Venice may have been 'the seat of opera', but in many other respects the city had, by the second half of the eighteenth century, become a provincial backwater compared with the capital cities of the great powers that now controlled the destiny of Europe. And Goldoni was well aware of this. It was time for him to leave what his biographer Timothy Holme characterised as 'the dainty powdered and prattling world of Venice where corruption and decay were so lovingly disguised with silks and perfumes'. The attention of Voltaire made Goldoni realise that it was possible for him to achieve fame and fortune in the greatest cultural city of them all, namely Paris. In May 1762 the fifty-five-year-old Goldoni and his wife left Venice, taking a leisurely four months to reach their destination. Here, after some initial difficulties, he began to achieve a modicum of success, writing in French, which he spoke fluently, though with a pronounced Italian accent. His work was put on at the Comédie-Française, and King Louis XV invited him to Versailles, where he became a royal tutor and was given a state pension. But Goldoni no longer worked so hard, preferring instead to enjoy the delights of Europe's most sophisticated society. Instead of cups of Venetian coffee driving him on to work night and day, he drank chocolate and played cards, letting it be known that 'I almost always accept invitations to lunch'. But not to dinner: he still felt the need to write, and started his memoirs. He died in France in 1793, just a few days short of his ninety-sixth birthday.

Once, the likes of Marco Polo had left Venice to explore the outermost limits of the known world, and beyond, in an attempt to expand the Republic's trading empire. Now its leading artists were forced to leave the city and seek their fortune elsewhere, in the great capitals of Europe, amongst which Venice no longer numbered. Vivaldi had gone to Vienna, Goldoni and others to Paris; even Goldoni's great rival, Baretti, eventually left for London, where he became a popular member of Dr Johnson's circle. Such was the city's continuing decline.

Part Four

Dissolution and Fall

19

The Last Days

THE 1699 TREATY of Karlowitz had effectively marked the end of Ottoman territorial ambitions with regard to the heart of eastern Europe, but the elements of the 'empire' that Venice regained in the Aegean and the Peloponnese under the terms of the treaty were another matter. In Turkish eyes, such possessions would always represent a threat, though for fifteen years nothing was done about this. However, when the Venetians intercepted a Turkish ship in the Adriatic, the Ottoman Empire used this as a pretext to declare war against Venice in December 1714. This belated attempt to assert Ottoman domination was organised by Grand Vizier Damat Ali, who now effectively wielded the power of Sultan Ahmed III. In 1715, in a well-prepared two-pronged attack, the Turkish fleet sailed south to attack Venetian coastal strongholds in the Aegean, the Peloponnese and other outposts, while an Ottoman army marched south through Thessaly (northern mainland Greece) into the central Peloponnese. The Venetian forces in the region proved unprepared, undermanned, ill-equipped and unwilling to fight. (Bernardo Balbi, the Venetian commander of the Aegean island of Tinos, even went so far as to surrender before the Turkish fleet had arrived; a deed for which he would be lucky not to be sentenced to death on his arrival back in Venice, instead being gaoled for life.)

During the summer of 1715 the Turkish forces swept all before them, taking all Venetian possessions in the Aegean, overrunning the Peloponnese and even taking Venice's last remaining outposts in Crete at Souda Bay and Spinalonga. Emboldened by this success, Damat Ali launched Turkish forces north through the Balkans and west towards the Venetian Ionian islands, where Corfu guarded the entrance to the Adriatic. Though the Venetian authorities had initially been slow to act, they now speedily appointed the great German mercenary general Matthias von der Schulenburg as military governor of Corfu, where he immediately set about building up the defences of the island's formidable fortress. However, when the Ottoman fleet arrived off Corfu on 5 July, ready to disembark a 33,000-strong invasion force, the promised reinforcements had yet to arrive from Venice. Schulenburg decided against trying to defend the island and tactically withdrew to the fortress of Corfu Town, organising the local inhabitants as support for the inadequate Venetian garrison. The island was quickly overrun, apart from the fortress itself. Here the invaders encamped beneath the walls, preparing to wait through the hot months of summer for what promised to be a long, but ultimately successful siege.

At this stage the war took an unexpected turn. The Turkish advances in the Balkans had prompted the Holy Roman Emperor Charles VI, ruler of Austria, to form an alliance with Venice. In August, news reached the Turks besieging Corfu that the Imperial Army, under its commander Prince Eugene of Savoy, had won an overwhelming victory at the Battle of Peterwardein (modern Petrovaradin, on the Danube fifty miles north-west of Belgrade). The Turkish commander at Corfu now realised there was no time for an extensive siege. If the fortress was not taken quickly, he was liable to be attacked from the rear, or simply cut off. In the early hours of 18 August, under cover of darkness, the Ottoman forces launched a surprise all-out attack on the fortress.

Woken by the screeches of the charging Turks, Schulenburg rushed to take charge of the defences, which were soon being defended by the entire population – including bearded orthodox priests, women in peasant dress and even children. The Greeks and Venetians were soon driven back from the outer defences, but managed to hold out behind the solid high walls of the inner bastion, despite heavy artillery fire. After six hours of fighting Schulenburg decided to take the initiative. At the head of 800 chosen men, he slipped out of a small side-gate in the walls and quickly outflanked the Turkish line, before launching a surprise attack from the rear. In the ensuing confusion the Turks fled in disarray, abandoning their guns as they tried to get back to their own lines. More than 2,000 of them were cut down by Schulenburg and his men.

Later that day the Turkish commander withdrew his lines in order to recoup his forces in preparation for a further more powerful assault that would overrun the walls. But that night a violent storm broke, with high winds and torrential rain. The tents of the Turkish camp were blown away in the wind, the trenches filled with water and the encampment was reduced to a quagmire. Meanwhile the offshore Ottoman fleet was blown from its moorings, and in the resulting chaos ships rammed into each other, splitting their hulls and sinking.

Next morning, when the winds abated, the defenders in the fortress spied sails making their way up the channel between Corfu and the mainland. This was the allied Hapsburg fleet sailing to the relief of the beleaguered fortress. When Schulenburg sent out a patrol to reconnoitre outside the walls, they found the shattered army camp deserted. The Turks had fled, leaving the remnants of their tents, their artillery, provisions and equipment, and even a number of wounded. They soon learned that the Turkish besiegers had been picked up by the few remaining ships of the Ottoman fleet, which had set sail for the open sea on a stiff easterly breeze with a flotilla of allied ships in pursuit. In all, the Turks had lost 15,000 men in the course of the seven-week siege. Never again would Turkish warships venture into the Adriatic.

When the victorious Schulenburg finally made it back to Venice, the grateful Great Council presented him a bejewelled ceremonial sword and a pension of 5,000 ducats for life. So touched was Schulenburg that in 1718, at the age of fifty-seven, he took up residence in the Palazzo Loredan on the Grand Canal, living out his retirement in Venice. Here he proved himself to be an art collector of considerable taste, assembling a fine collection that included works by Raphael and Giorgione. At the same time he also supported a number of contemporary artists, as well as enjoying a reputation as a convivial host.

After Corfu, the tide of the war turned against the Turks. With Venetian confidence restored, the Republic assembled twenty-seven ships off the Ionian islands and sailed for the Dardanelles with Admiral Ludovico Flangini in command. On 12 June 1717 Flangini encountered a Turkish fleet of forty-two ships near Mount Athos in northern Greece. Fighting continued for four days and nights, with the fleets manoeuvring for advantage under the clear moonlight. On 16 June, Flangini was shot by a Turkish archer, but insisted upon being carried up to the poop deck of his ship, from where he was able to witness, in his dying moments, the victory of the Venetian fleet.

Flangini was succeeded by Andrea Pisani, who the following month linked up with the papal and Portugese fleets. On 19 July this allied fleet encountered a Turkish fleet of fifty ships off Cape Matapan, south-west of the Peloponnese. The ensuing hard-fought battle was indecisive, but the Turkish fleet eventually withdrew after losing fourteen ships, while the allies lost but three. By now the Ottoman forces were being forced into retreat by Prince Eugene in the Balkans, as well as by the resurgent Venetians and their allies in Greek waters. The Venetians were poised to take back the Peloponnese; but before they could act, news came through that the Turks had agreed a peace with the Austrians. The Venetians were furious at being thwarted.

The actual peace negotiations were held in May 1718 at Passarowitz (modern Pozarevac, thirty miles south-east of Belgrade), and the Venetian delegation arrived in no mood for compromise, determined to reclaim all the territories of the empire they had lost in the early stages of the war. The head of the Venetian delegation was the sixty-four-year-old Carlo Ruzzini, a man of wide diplomatic experience, who had represented the Republic at the negotiations nineteen years previously, which had resulted in the Peace of Karlowitz. However, Ruzzini was quickly made to realise that Venetian wishes now counted for little on the international scene, even though the Republic had played such a leading role in the fight against the Turks. The Austrians had their own agenda: they wished for a speedy conclusion to the negotiations so that they would be free to pursue their own military objectives in Europe. For six long hours Ruzzini argued the Venetian case: the restoration of the Peloponnese, the return of Tinos and Aegean ports, as well as the re-establishment of the strategic Cretan outposts at Souda Bay and Spinalonga. But no one was listening. When the treaty was signed, Venice was lucky to be given Cythera (the southernmost of the Ionian islands), some strategic ports along the eastern Adriatic coast and a number of fortresses to defend the Dalmatian hinterland. Ruzzini returned to Venice humiliated, though he was not blamed for this loss of face. Instead, he was rewarded with the appointment of ambassador to the Ottoman court, and during his last years he would be appointed doge, before his death at the age of seventy-eight in 1735.

Venice still retained an empire, but this was now reduced to a size that had not been seen since the early fourteenth century. On the other hand, this was the final delineation of Venetian overseas territory: an empire that would remain intact through the ensuing eighty years. Venice may have been reduced to a minor power on the international scene, but its skilful diplomacy would prevent it from becoming dragged into the struggles between the major European powers throughout much of the rest of the century. Indeed, during its long, gradual decline Venice would achieve a stability that had often eluded the city during the days of its greatness. Such stability ensured that it now earned much of its living from tourism rather than as a leading commercial power. Trade continued as before, but elsewhere the commercial powerhouses of Europe were empire-building on a global scale and embarking upon an era of industrial revolution that would far outstrip the technological marvels of the Arsenale, which had once been one of the wonders of the Western world.

The beauty of the canals and the palazzi, the abundance of courtesans and prostitutes, the opera and so many fine works of art, as well as the joys of gambling, were now the main attractions of the city. Carnival, with its fancy-dress balls and public revelry conducted behind the anonymity of masks permitting all manner of blatant promiscuity, proved such an attraction that it was extended from the weeks between Christmas and Lent to a period of five whole months. Rich tourists on the Grand Tour were able to take full advantage of the much-vaunted liberty of Venice, even if they had to be protected from the avarice and thievery of its citizens by an increasingly repressive Council of Ten. Spies were everywhere, reporting on everything from the latest gossip of the Rialto and the rumours in the coffee houses to the tittle-tattle of the gambling rooms. Yet tourists knew they were perfectly safe so long as they did not step out of line. Indeed, many found excitement in the 'bit of intrigue, even of danger' lurking in 'the curious and murky quarters' that lay behind the historic attractions of the city.

However, when the controversial French political writer Montesquieu visited Venice in 1728, he could not resist the temptation to make a study of the city's constitution and political life. According to a contemporary commentator, 'he wrote much and inquired more'. When informed that his activities had come to the attention of the Council of Ten, who had ordered his arrest, he immediately attempted to flee the city on a boat for the mainland. Yet as he did so, 'he saw several gondolas approaching, and row round his veffel: terror feized him, and in his panic he collected all his papers which contained his Observations on Venice, and cast them into the sea.' Later Montesquieu learned that he had been the victim of a practical joke. Even so, such an anecdote is illustrative of the pervasive fear inspired by the Council of Ten's spies.

The coffee houses that had sprung up in Venice to purvey this exotic Levantine beverage amidst informal social circumstances had, from the outset, proved popular with locals and visitors alike. The Venetians first encountered coffee in Constantinople, where it had arrived in the late sixteenth century; by 1638 it was being commercially imported into the Republic, and soon after this the first *caffè* opened. In the words of the *Encyclopaedia Brittanica*, in contrast to the tavern, the coffee house provided 'a much-needed focus for the social activities of the sober'. So popular did these prove that a century or so later the city had nearly 200 coffee houses, with no fewer than thirty-five of them located in the arcades of the Piazza San Marco. The most famous of these, the Caffè Florian, had opened in 1720; it would later be described by an English visitor as consisting 'of some half dozen very small rooms, almost to be called cells'. Similar 'cells' were to be found in all public establishments in Venice, a development imposed by the Council of Ten to prevent populous gatherings that might give rise to political discussion, though from the outset coffee houses became favoured as places for gathering news (political or otherwise), with copies of the *Gazzetta* and similar early newspapers being sold over the counter. The professions, artists and other like-minded groups each tended to favour chosen coffee houses for their own particular purposes; thus Casanova is known to have favoured the Caffè Florian because it was the first establishment to permit the entry of women.

Another popular gathering place of the period was the gambling establishment, which for similar political reasons was at this time frequently located in a small house, or *casino* in Venetian. As we have seen from the lives of figures such as Leon da Modena, gambling had for centuries been an obsession with citizens of the Republic: dealing with the risks involved in maritime commercial ventures, when one was liable to lose everything in case of shipwreck, meant that gambling was in their blood. Well understanding this predisposition, the authorities had originally banned all public gambling, though they were well aware that this activity continued in private houses, as well as in nefarious semi-private games organised in various dens. (The inveterate gambler and mathematician Cardano describes in his autobiography an incident in such a house. Whilst in the process of losing all his money, Cardano noticed that his opponent had marked the cards. Whereupon he leapt up, slashed his opponent across the face with his dagger and grabbed the money. Outwitting his host's spear-wielding servants, he fled into the night-shrouded maze of streets, eventually falling into a canal . . .)*

The advent of public gambling in Venice is largely due to the architect Nicolò Barattieri, who as early as 1181 was responsible for building the first bridge across the Grand Canal, a pontoon construction that was to be the forerunner of the present Rialto Bridge. Barattieri was a man of great ingenuity, combined with a very Venetian eye to the main chance, and some years later offered to solve a problem that had for some time been bothering the doge and the Signoria. Almost a hundred years previously two large columns had been shipped in from Constantinople as spoils of war. (Originally there were three columns, but one of them fell into the sea as it was being unloaded.) The two granite columns proved so heavy and unwieldy that no one could work out how to haul them upright, and for almost a century they simply lay abandoned on the quayside of the Molo. It was now that Barattieri offered his services, assuring the doge that he had devised a scheme that could raise the pillars upright. This involved a sailor's technique known as 'watering the rope'. Barattieri ordered a heavy pivot of stone to be placed against the foot of the pillar, then he attached the head of the column by means of a hemp rope to a strong

---

* It is interesting to note that Cardano may well have been rector of the University of Padua at the time.

upright post. Next the hemp rope was doused with water, causing its diameter to expand and its length to decrease, thus raising the head of the column a few inches from the ground so that a wedge could be placed beneath it. This was repeated with increasingly short lengths of rope until gradually, to the delight of the increasing crowds of onlookers, the column was raised.

Barattieri had asked for no payment, but instead requested that if he succeeded he should be allowed to set up a public gaming table between the two pillars. This proved a huge success, earning him a large income. However, this spot between the two pillars soon came to be regarded as a place of ill fortune by more than just unlucky gamblers, when it was chosen as the site for public hangings.*

In the ensuing centuries gambling fever swept Venice, affecting all classes. Nobles set up gambling tables in their palazzi, as did the courtesans in their salons, while street corners hosted vicious games for more modest stakes. Regular edicts issued by the authorities banned gambling in taverns, courtyards, barber shops, on gondolas and even on canal bridges (favoured on account of the good vantage point they gave to lookouts). Such vain attempts to stamp out gambling only served to indicate the widespread nature of the contagion. Even the courtyards and corridors of the Doge's Palace were not immune, and there large bets would be placed on the results of elections to public office, up to and including that of doge.

In the sixteenth century the authorities had given in to the inevitable, issuing licences for *ridotti* or *casini*, usually small, well-decorated sets of rooms with gaming tables, often including a side-chamber – known as a 'room of sighs' – where unlucky gamblers could retire to rue their losses. Not content with gathering revenue from the licensing of *ridotti*, in 1638 the authorities opened their own state-sponsored Ridotto, which is generally recognised as the first full-scale casino in Europe, on which all later versions would be modelled. Such was the popularity of the Ridotto that

---

* In years to come, the condemned man would be hanged with his back to the water, thus ensuring that the last thing he saw was the Torre dell'Orologio (the Clock Tower, across the Piazzetta) marking the time of his death. This custom gave rise to the seemingly innocuous, but in fact chilling Venetian threat: '*Te fasso vedar mi che ora che ze!*' (I'll show you what time it is).

other lesser casinos soon followed. An English visitor would remark of these establishments, 'The crowd is so great that very often one can hardly pass from one Room to another, nevertheless the silence here observ'd is much greater than that in Churches.'

The Ridotto itself remained the most prestigious of all the gambling establishments, occupying an entire wing of the Palazzo San Moisè,* just a hundred yards west of the Piazza San Marco. This four-storey building had a grand, long entrance hall the size of a ballroom, which became a popular meeting place. Further inside there were dining rooms, with the different gaming rooms located upstairs. Theoretically, as a public institution of the Republic, the Ridotto was open to all; but the high stakes required at the tables and a rigid dress code ensured that it was frequented mainly by nobles and the like. Entry was granted only to those in formal dress, with men expected to wear black three-cornered hats and women fashionable full-length gowns. Gamblers had to wear white masks, with some women wearing smaller black masks, adding a distinct frisson to card games such as basetta, which involved high winnings and high losses, and the poker-like faro, whose participants came to the tables to *puntare* (bet), and were thus the original 'punters'. The clientele of the Ridotto consisted of a heady mix of nobles – old and young, rich or in 'reduced circumstances', sometimes accompanied by their fashionably dressed wives – as well as raffish professional sharks, courtesans and young English bucks.

The most famous of all the gamblers to be seen at the Ridotto was undoubtedly the Scotsman John Law, who around the start of the eighteenth century gambled with unrivalled sums of money, frequently with spectacular success. Law was that far-from-unique combination of financial genius, con-man and escapee from disaster. The earliest disaster from which he escaped was at the age of twenty-one, when he killed a man in a duel in London and was sentenced to be hanged at Tyburn. Spirited out of gaol, he took ship to the Netherlands, an exploit that was aided by Elizabeth Villiers, William III's mistress (women played a key supporting role in

---

* Literally, the Palace of St Moses. The Venetians adhered to the Byzantine tradition of canonising the leading figures and prophets of the Old Testament.

many of Law's exploits). From now on, Law would be forced to live off his wits, a circumstance that led to the full psychological development of his three exceptional talents – as a thinker of remarkable penetration and foresight, as a mathematical gambler par excellence and as a similarly skilled womaniser. In this way he visited – and then quickly moved on from – the gaming tables, boudoirs and financial exchanges of Amsterdam, Geneva, Turin and Venice, the last of which he first visited during the final years of the seventeenth century. Here his success at the Ridotto was matched only by his amatory skills, leaving in his wake a procession of broken hearts and outraged husbands. But Law was so much more than a pioneer Casanova. According to his contemporary memoirist, the 'Scots gentleman' W. Gray:

He constantly went to the Rialto [where] he observed the course of exchange all the world over, the manner of discounting bills at the bank, the vast usefulness of paper credit, how gladly people parted with their money for paper, and how the profits accrued to the proprietors from this paper.

Over the coming years Law would acquire an aristocratic English mistress, Lady Catherine Knowles (or Knollys), with whom he would have two children, and he would at same time develop the idea of 'paper credit' into the modern concept of an alternative currency for higher denominations, in the form of publicly exchangeable paper money.

With the expertise of a confident man, in 1715 Law finally managed to persuade the roué Regent of France, Philippe II, Duc d'Orléans, to allow him to put his paper-money idea into practice on the vast but stagnant French economy. Philippe had more enjoyable things to do than busy himself with arcane economic matters, and simply handed over to Law the financial affairs of the country, including the French colonies, as well as allowing him to hatch a scheme for the development of French North America (so-called Louisiana, which in fact extended north into the entire Midwest). The Mississippi Scheme, as it came to be known, was created in order to mine the vast quantities of gold widely supposed to lie along the banks of the Mississippi and in the hinterland French territory. The public was encouraged to invest in this potential goldmine by purchasing a special offer of shares that were released onto the market. At the same time the French economy, which had ground to a halt through a lack of solid currency and massive debts, was revived by the introduction of large quantities of paper money. This was backed by a minimal amount of 'real' money, as well as the enormous profits that Law confidently expected would soon be flowing in from the Mississippi Scheme, whose shares quickly shot up in price. In order to facilitate all this financial and economic activity, in 1716 Law was allowed to set up what became the Banque Générale, the first French central bank, with control of the currency. To balance this pyramid of enterprises would require, over the next few years, financial gambling on an extraordinary scale, not seen before or since.*

Expert opinion is still divided as to whether Law was, in the opinion of the great twentieth-century economist Joseph Schumpeter, 'in the front rank of monetarists of all time' or simply a superlative con-man whose fraudulent activities led him into waters way beyond his depth. He was certainly ahead of his time, leaving his pioneering scheme exposed to the flaws inherent in paper currency (many of which remain to this day); and all the evidence concurs that he did not set aside any secret personal profit from his scheme. When the Banque Générale eventually collapsed in 1720, bringing down with it the paper money, the Mississippi Scheme and all the rest, many were ruined. On the other hand, the massive debts that had clogged up the French nation's economy simply vanished in a whirl of worthless paper notes. All the same, Law was lucky to escape with his life, fleeing the country dressed as a woman – though unavoidably he was forced to leave behind his beloved Lady Catherine.

He ended up in Venice in the mid-1720s, back living once more off his wits and his winnings at the tables in the Ridotto. Law was by now famous throughout Europe: never before had the gambling of one man – not even royalty, not even an aristocrat – bankrupted the coffers of a major European nation. Back at his old haunt, he began to gamble on a more modest scale,

* In terms of contemporary monetary proportion (and possibly value), the amounts involved were at least on a par with the amounts gambled in the 2007–8 financial crisis. Finance ministers, and even individual financiers, have frequently gambled on a national scale: Law was gambling on an international, imperial scale.

gradually building up his assets. Yet he was unable to resist cashing in on his celebrity. He would sit behind a table, at his elbow a pile of coins worth 10,000 gold pistoles.* Law knew that many tourists, especially from France or England, would not be able to resist the temptation to gamble with him, so that they could boast of this fact when they returned home. He extended an open invitation to all-comers: for an outlay of one golden pistole, he was willing to gamble his entire 10,000, if his opponent could roll six dice and get each one to come up a six. Well worth a bet, they thought, even at odds of 10,000:1 — and one by one the extra gold pistoles came rolling in. (Law was well aware that the real odds were in fact an even more unlikely 46,656:1.)

This side-show provided him with a small but regular income, which he augmented many times over at the tables with his astute gambling. A lightning-quick mathematical mind, particularly with regard to probability theory, as well as an all-but-flawless memory, remained his main assets. These had survived the colossal responsibilities and mental pressure of his years in Paris, which had by all accounts several times brought him to the brink of complete nervous collapse. But now, once again, he knew that he was just playing the odds. It was during this period that Montesquieu made his visit to Venice. Previously, Montesquieu had been so incensed by what Law had done to his country that he had written a bitter satire, characterising Law as the son of Aeolius, the god of wind, travelling over the world accompanied by the blind god of chance and an inflated bladder. But when he actually encountered Law, Montesquieu could not help but be impressed, recognising that Law was 'more in love with his ideas than his money . . . his mind occupied with projects, his head filled with calculations'. He still believed in the concept of paper money, and remained convinced that — introduced under the right circumstances — his project would succeed: there was still a future for it. Others were less impressed, recognising that the immense strain had taken its toll. The handsome womaniser was now but a shadow

---

* Several different types of gold pistole were in circulation during this period, minted anywhere from Spain to Hungary, most of which had different values. It is safe to assume that the value of the coins at Law's elbow was probably around 10,000 ducats. Indeed, the English sources who recorded this scene may even have mistaken the ducats for pistoles in the first place.

of his former self, his features haggard, racked by an increasingly disfiguring tic.

The end was not long in coming. One frigid night, towards the end of February 1729, as Law was returning home on a gondola through the dark misty canals, he was taken ill. Over the coming weeks his weakened frame succumbed to pneumonia. The French ambassador, the Comte de Gergy, and Colonel Elizeus Burges, the British Resident (senior diplomatic representative), were both frequent visitors to his bedside. Law was known to have been working on a book setting forth his monetary ideas, and both men wanted to gain possession of this document the moment he died. The French had no wish for the secrets of the 1729 financial debacle to become public knowledge; while the British had their own opposite motives. At the same time, both men suspected that at the height of Law's power in France he must have secretly stashed away a vast fortune, and were keen to discover where this was hidden. But neither Burges nor Gergy would succeed in their aims. On 21 March 1729 John Law died at the age of just fifty-four, taking with him any secrets that might have definitively damned or exonerated him in the eyes of history.

During Law's last years, he appeared to lose faith in the permanent value of currency, preferring instead to invest his surplus winnings in paintings. Here too he was ahead of his time, impervious to the ridicule of Burges: 'No man alive believes that his pictures when they come to be sold will bring half the money they cost him.' During the course of his few years in Venice, Law accumulated a collection containing some 500 paintings, including works by Titian, Tintoretto, Holbein, Michelangelo and even Leonardo. There is a suspicion that some of these were secretly despatched from Paris by his 'wife', Lady Catherine Knowles, before they could be seized by the authorities. Even so, Law is certainly known to have bought works by artists who were alive and working in Venice during his time there. And the greatest of these was undoubtedly the young Tiepolo, who in the latter half of the 1720s began to produce his first masterpieces.

Gianbattista Tiepolo was born in Venice in 1696, in the working-class Castello district close to the Arsenale. He was the sixth child of a local sea captain. However, the Tiepolo family had a long and illustrious history, including a thirteenth-century ancestor who was Duke of Crete and was later doge for an exceptional twenty years. Despite such former glories, Tiepolo's father was no longer of noble rank. Around the age of fourteen, the young Tiepolo was apprenticed to the studio of Gregorio Lazzarini, an accomplished but ultimately undistinguished artist who was much influenced by Veronese. Tiepolo would absorb this influence, yet his major influences came from outside Lazzarini's studio, with his style taking on baroque and even rococo flourishes. His exceptional talent was immediately apparent, exhibiting an entirely original sense of energy and spectacle. From the beginning he appeared to draw in light and paint rather than outline, and as a result his works took on a blaze of colour and tone.

The quality of Tiepolo's work set him apart, but there also seems to have been an element of psychological 'apartness' in his character. He bore an illustrious name, yet he was not a member of the ruling class, while his talents set him apart from the people amongst whom he had grown up. Furthermore he had never known his father, who had died just a year after his birth, and there would always remain in his work an element of display that acted like a mask to protect, or distract from, a sense of inner emptiness. In 1719, at the age of twenty-three, he married the sister of the painter Francesco Guardi, and they would eventually have nine children, yet it seems that he was not in the habit of taking his family with him when he went to work abroad, often for years at a time. Even so, two of his sons would be sufficiently inspired by the example of their father to become painters themselves.

Shortly after his marriage Tiepolo would paint his first masterpieces, a cycle of vast paintings to decorate the large reception hall of the Ca' Dolfin, a palazzo on the Grand Canal near the Rialto Bridge, and he then went on to paint a series of spectacular frescoed ceilings. It quickly became apparent that he had found his medium. Fresco enabled him to transform ceilings into luminescent sky where brilliant mythological figures floated amidst clouds and architectural structures, seen from below in complex and often differing, yet always convincing perspectives. Yet these were all achieved with a lightness and brilliance that harked back to the traditions of an earlier Renasissance.

Tiepolo's fame quickly spread, and he began travelling Italy to fulfil commissions. His style, in the eyes of many experts, represented the last great flourishing of the Italian Renaissance, and Tiepolo was soon in demand all over Europe. Here was yet another creative spirit who felt drawn to leave his native city in order to fulfil his talent in exile. He spent the years 1750–3 in Würzburg in Germany, and although he returned to Venice to fulfil commissions from as far afield as Poland and Russia, he still spent much time away from home travelling the mainland.

Yet despite Tiepolo's international appeal, in many ways his art was Venetian through and through. His technique of building up his figures with colour upon colour echoed that of Giorgione, while his theatricality and flesh tones were reminiscent of Titian and Tintoretto. But his work also very much reflected the Venice of his own time. This was an art which delighted in spectacle, which chose above all else to dazzle and delight with its sheer brilliance. It was an art whose essential qualities lay in its surface. There was no straining after meaning or profundity. Its figures may have been fully realised and even recognisable in their individuality, but they had little in the way of psychological depth. The dazzling spatial effect of his ceilings, which frequently spilled out of their stucco frames, were sufficient to induce vertigo in the spectator below. They evoked wonder, rather than inspiring contemplation. Like the city itself, they were a carnival of colour and form played out against a background of almost unbelievable beauty.

In 1761 Tiepolo travelled to Madrid, where he was commissioned by Charles III to cover the ceiling of the throne room with frescoes depicting in mythological form the glories of Spain when it had dominated the globe as an imperial power. The arrival of the sixty-four-year-old Tiepolo would incur the jealousy of the thirty-three-year-old German-born painter Anton Raphael Mengs, who was already established as a court painter. But the conflict between the remote Tiepolo and the learned and earnest Mengs was more than just personal. The young Mengs was a champion of the up-and-coming neoclassical school, whose restraint and austerity of style were in marked contrast to the flamboyance of Tiepolo. A year later, following the cold early months of 1770, Tiepolo suddenly collapsed and died. He was buried in Madrid, far from Venice and his family. In his native city, and indeed across Europe, many recognised his death as the end of an artistic era. The Renaissance was long past, and Venice's tradition of great artists who extended its political influence was now over. Such surface display and brilliance were no longer fashionable: the power-centres of Europe required a more realistic art to mirror their increasingly modern and enlightened world. Tiepolo's mythological gods in the sky were to be replaced by the more realistic down-to-earth humanity to be found in the likes of Mengs' neoclassical works.

And in Venice the human figure all but disappeared, becoming a mere cipher amidst the meticulous beauty of the city itself, as depicted by its finest copyist, Giovanni Antonio Canal, better known as Canaletto. Here was an artist who reflected his city as no other, an artist who was all but created by his market – the rich tourists who wished to take home a souvenir of their visit to the most delight-filled city they had ever seen.

Canaletto was born in Venice in 1697, the year after Tiepolo. His father Bernard Canal was also a painter (hence his son Giovanni being given the diminutive of the family name). The young Canaletto would receive his initial training in his father's studio, which specialised in painting theatrical scenery for opera – a form that in many ways echoed the style that Canaletto himself would raise to the highest level. Sometime in his early twenties Canaletto travelled to Rome, where he was particularly struck by the street scenes (which were in certain ways an evident novelty to a Venetian). This inspired in him an interest in painting urban landscape, and on his return to Venice he began producing scenes of life in the streets of his own city. Initially these tended towards depictions of ordinary back-street, back-canal life – such as his early masterpiece *The Stonemason's Yard*, painted between 1726 and 1730. This includes several small but realistic figures, as well as sheets hanging out to dry from the windows and a general sense of the shabbiness that characterised the more typical life lived by ordinary citizens behind the tourist façade. In such scenes his paintings became a symphony of muted colours, with precise renderings of peeling stucco walls and shabby balconies, and glimpses of the familiar towers and spires far away across the rooftops beneath faded skies. At this early stage it was the play and juxtaposition of surfaces that he sought to convey, as much as the image itself.

At the same time, he also began producing pictures of the better-known sights and grand events for which the city was famous. Typical of these was his 1732 work *The Return of the Bucintoro to the Molo on Ascension Day*, with the great golden hulk of the doge's barge, along with the Doge's Palace, the Campanile and Sansovino's Library in the background, all conveyed with meticulous attention to detail, forming a play of different textures. As one critic put it, 'He paints with such accuracy and cunning that the eye is deceived and truly believes it is reality it sees, not a painting.' However, as Canaletto's biographer J.G. Links perceptively observed of the artist's work at this juncture, 'They were pictures painted in Venice, rather than pictures of Venice; pictorial quality always took precedence over topographical accuracy.' The emphasis on precise verisimilitude came later, though even then Canaletto frequently 'remodelled' the scenes for proportional effect.

Canaletto's paintings soon began to attract the attention of rich buyers, mostly tourists, and he quickly outshone his established competitors who supplied this lucrative market. However, when it came to the actual sale of his works there were often difficulties. By all accounts Canaletto was not an easy man to get along with. He would remain a bachelor, and continued to live in the modest family apartment where he had been born. Although his creative output was high, even higher demand meant that delivery was not always certain; on occasion he would accept advances for commissions he could not fulfil on time, requiring a third party to sort out the consequent misunderstandings. He was soon commissioned to produce works for the agent Owen McSwiney, a gregarious Irishman based in London, who wrote of Canaletto:

The fellow is whimsical, and vary's and his prices, every day: and he that has Mind to have any of his Work, must not seem to be too fond of it, for he'l be y^e. worse treated for it, both in the price, & in the painting too.

He has more work that he can doe, in any reasonable time, and well.

McSwiney may have been an amiable character, yet unfortunately for Canaletto he developed the habit of going bankrupt. It was thus lucky that around this time Canaletto came into personal contact with the Englishman Joseph Smith, who resided in Venice for many decades. Smith was a collector-cum-artists'-agent, who purchased all manner of *objets d'art* and bric-a-brac for himself, as well as buying up paintings for trans-shipment to London, where they would be sold on to wealthy clients, many of whom had passed through Venice on their Grand Tour. Smith was not a pleasant man, being regarded by those who met him as a bumptious, egotistical snob – one contemporary even going so far as to describe him as 'literally eaten up with vanity'. But although he may have been essentially self-serving in his dealings, Smith was also a man of perceptive taste and business acumen, all of which worked to Canaletto's advantage.

It was now that Canaletto began adapting his style to something approaching a production method, although in the hands of such a skilled artist this seldom worked to his detriment. Figures may have been reduced to mere stylised occupants of their urban landscape, and the water of the canals to an opaque opalescent surface decorated with repetitive caricature wavelets, but the stone, stucco and façades of the city retained a masterly detail and perspective. This was certainly recognised by his competitors, who paid Canaletto the tribute of flooding the market with poor forgeries of his work.

Then suddenly the bottom fell out of the market, as Europe descended into war and the flood of English and other tourists dried up. In 1740 Charles VI, the Emperor of Austria, died without an immediate male heir, having stipulated that his daughter Maria Theresa should ascend to the imperial throne. By this stage the Hapsburg Austrian Empire straggled over vast territories of central Europe, from Translyvania (part of modern Romania) in the south-east to Silesia (part of modern Poland) in the north-west, as well as the Duchy of Milan and other territories in northern Italy. Frederick the Great of Prussia decided to use the accession of Maria Theresa as an excuse for marching into Silesia, thus beginning the War of the Austrian Succession; and in 1744 France, which supported Prussia, declared war on Britain. Despite suffering heavy defeats during the war, the Austrians managed to retain their northern-Italian territories. For the time being, Venice remained protected by its powerful northern ally.

Canaletto continued to eke out a living during the early years of the war, but when Britain entered the fray it became evident that his career in Venice was over. By now Joseph Smith had been appointed British consul, having characteristically recommended himself to the Foreign Office in London as a 'middling genius'. Despite the international situation, Smith still did his best to promote Canaletto's ailing career; and when the Campanile was struck by lightning on 23 April 1745, Smith regarded it as a promising omen. This was St George's Day, that of the patron saint of England, and Smith decided that Canaletto should try his luck in England. He then arranged (through contact with McSwiney) for Canaletto to travel to London, where a number of lucrative commissions were set up in advance.

Canaletto arrived in 1746 in England, where he would remain for the next nine years. This proved something of a disaster. Although he would paint some fine scenes, mainly of London and its environs, his clients became disappointed with his treatment of the dull English light and the sheer size of the city. They still expected the translucent qualities and immediacy of his Venetian scenes. This appears to have plunged Canaletto into a form of depression that caused his abilities to deteriorate. What had previously been artfully stylised now degenerated into uninspired copies. The plain banality of Westminster Bridge and the Lord Mayor's barge were as nothing beside the grace of the Rialto Bridge and the gilded magnificence of the *Bucintoro*. Indeed, things reached such a pitch that Canaletto was accused of being an imposter, and was forced to submit to the humiliation of a public demonstration of his abilities. During a lull in the European wars in 1755 the fifty-eight-year-old Canaletto returned to Venice for good.* In 1763 he was elected to the recently formed Venetian Academy (having been turned down just a few months previously). He continued painting, often working from old sketches that he had made years previously, often repeating popular scenes. The glory days were over, and he is said to have lived a life of some austerity, finally dying in 1768 in the very apartment where he had been born seventy years previously.

By now, Canaletto's pupil Francesco Guardi had taken over his mantle

---

* There is evidence that he may have made at least one brief trip to his native city during the previous nine years.

as the painter of Venice, but this was no longer such a great honour and certainly did not promise riches. On the contrary: according to Links, 'Guardi was known to have been so poor that he had bought defective canvases and used wretched priming and, to save time, very oily colours.' Worse still was to come: in the last years of his life Guardi was even reduced to selling his canvases in the Piazza San Marco, at a spot by the Campanile and the Doge's Palace. Here he would set up his easel so that spectators could watch him drawing sketches and painting small landscapes for sale as souvenirs.

A Venetian writer who would travel even further afield than Canaletto was Lorenzo Da Ponte, who will be renowned for ever for his operatic collaboration with Mozart. Amongst the picaresque details of Da Ponte's life and oft-changing fortunes, his Venetian origins (and escapades) are sometimes overlooked. In fact, Da Ponte was very much a man who reflected the time and place in which he spent the first thirty years of his life. He was born in 1749 in the Venetian mainland territory some forty miles north of the city at Ceneda (now known as Vittorio Veneto), the son of a local tanner. Both his father and his mother (who would die in childbirth when he was five) were Jewish, but in this small provincial town they suffered fewer restrictions than their compatriots in Venice. Even so, they were far from fully integrated, having to return at night to their tiny ghetto in the old quarter, with the men being required to wear red berets and the women red headscarves when they travelled. According to Da Ponte's not-always-reliable memoirs written in his later years, even as a child 'I had a lively manner and a ready wit, but most of all I had an insatiable curiosity and wished to know everything, which soon gained me a reputation for a great memory and exceptional ability.' His father hired a tutor, but one day his father unexpectedly entered the room:

> to find the schoolmaster, a peasant's son who had exchanged the ox and plough for the teacher's ferule, yet retained the boorish demeanour of his birth . . . clouting me about the head with his clenched fist for making a mistake in a Latin lesson. My father seized the teacher by the hair and dragged him around the room, before flinging him

downstairs, followed by inkwell, pens and Latin primer. And for the next few years there was no more talk in our house of Latin.

Even so, Da Ponte discovered a collection of forgotten books in the attic, and seems to have spent his time reading and rereading these. Amongst them was a book of poems by the Rome-born lyric poet and librettist Pietro Metastasio, who had achieved fame in Vienna where he was Poet Laureate to the imperial court. Da Ponte was enchanted by Metastasio's work, claiming 'It produced in me precisely the same feeling as music.' He would soon begin attempting poetry of his own.

When he was fourteen the family converted to Roman Catholicism, whereupon he shed his Jewish name, Emanuele Conegliano, taking on the name of the priest who baptised him, Monsignor Lorenzo Da Ponte, Bishop of Ceneda. However, the real reason for this conversion was so that his forty-one-year-old father could marry a local sixteen-year-old Christian girl. Only two years younger than his stepmother, Da Ponte quickly felt the need to leave home, hinting suggestively, 'I foresaw what the consequences of such an unbalanced marriage would be.' He entered the local seminary to obtain an education, but this also involved training to become a priest and he was ordained in 1773. The psychological pointers from his childhood did not augur well for his choice of vocation.

After he was assigned to a teaching post at a seminary in Treviso, he took the opportunity of making trips to Venice. Here he called at book-shops and visited one of the early coffee houses that were springing up in the city: the Caffè Menagazzo, often called the Caffè dei Letterati, where writers such as Carlo Gozzi and his brother Gasparo, the leading critic, would gather. It may have been here that Da Ponte made friends with another famous Venetian who also had literary ambitions, but had already achieved his Europe-wide fame in another sphere, namely Giacomo Casanova. And it was now that Da Ponte's life began to take on a remark-able resemblance to that of his new friend. The tall, slim priest with the distinguished features and aquiline nose, who did not always wear his robes when in town, soon began attracting amorous attention. During the weeks of Carnival he entered into the spirit of the occasion, donning a mask – and quickly found himself becoming embroiled in a series of sexual adventures with a number of women, often under circumstances resembling a French farce. No one seemed to mind that he was a priest, nor did the good-looking young man of the cloth seem to care that many of the women with whom he became involved were married. At one point, he fell in love with Angiola Tiepolo, a member of the ancient noble family, though the branch to which she belonged no longer had any money. He described her as 'one of the most beautiful and one of the most neurotic women in the city'. The latter point he learned to his cost — despite being in love, Da Ponte still found time for other affairs, which provoked Angiola to fits of jealousy. Only now did he learn that her behaviour had driven her first husband to flee their marriage and take refuge by becoming a priest. Angiola's jealous rages knew no bounds. At one point she hurled a heavy inkstand at him, damaging his hand so that he was unable to write for a month; on another she came at him with a knife and tried to stab him; and on a number of occasions she resorted to hiding his clothes so that he could not leave the house.

Yet in the end he always had to return to Treviso and resume his teaching post at the seminary. Here he eventually decided to forswear love and concentrate instead on his literary endeavours. Even so, his long days amidst the provincial boredom of Treviso soon began driving him to distraction. One of his duties at the seminary was to compose a series of Latin and Italian poems to be recited by his pupils before the bishop at the local festival. Mediocrity and pious sentiments were the expected order of the day, but Da Ponte unwisely gave way to his true inspiration, writing a series of verses celebrating a life of freedom from the oppression of ordered society:

> I long to live and sing
> Without envying even a king,
> Yet the law pummels my head
> Making me earn my daily bread.

This was 1776: the American colonies had declared their independence from the British; meanwhile in France, Rousseau's inflammatory ideas on the 'natural freedom of life', coupled with Voltaire's demands for civil liberties, were fomenting talk of revolution. Such ideas were anathema to the ossified oligarchy of Venice and the heavy hand of the Catholic Church. Unfortunately for Da Ponte, the festive recital by his pupils was attended not only by the bishop, but also by the local chief magistrate. Both religion and the Law were outraged.

The twenty-seven-year-old Da Ponte affected indifference to the ensuing scandal, which quickly spread to Venice. Soon the city was split on the issue – the literati championed Da Ponte's noble cause, while the authorities were determined that he should be punished. Da Ponte's case was taken to the Senate, where he was defended by Gasparo Gozzi no less, who ironically had once held the post of state censor, yet now insisted that Da Ponte 'was a young man of talent, who should be encouraged'. The authorities were not convinced, and Da Ponte was publicly reprimanded, stripped of his post at the seminary in Treviso and forbidden for life from holding any teaching post within the Republic of Venice.

Seemingly undaunted, he now embarked upon an even more scandalous period in his life. He took up residence in Venice and was appointed priest at the church of San Luca, in the crowded district north of the Piazza San Marco. Da Ponte found accommodation in a nearby lodging house, and here he fell for the second great love of his life, a duplicitous and disreputable woman named Anzoletta Bellaudi, who was also married.* This time the boot was on the other foot, and it was Da Ponte who was driven to bouts of extreme jealousy by the behaviour of his beloved, who not only still lived in the same house as her husband, but was also notorious for her wanton adventures. According to Da Ponte's biographer, Sheila Hodges, 'marriage did not stop her from taking lovers, and even in church she was observed to be engaged in mutual fondling of the most intimate kind with any young man who caught her fancy'. Meanwhile her husband was conducting an affair with a local girl, and took to placing his secret messages to her in the hands of the trustworthy young priest living in his house.

Although Da Ponte was now living a life that would not have been out

---

* Anzoletta is the Venetian version of her first name. This is frequently written as Angioletta, but I have retained the dialect spelling to distinguish her from Angiola Tiepolo.

of place in an *opera buffa*, he had yet to try his hand as a librettist. He still concentrated on poetry, and although he remained clearly influenced by Metastasio, Goldoni and Carlo Gozzi, he was gradually beginning to forge a voice of his own, developing a rare facility for extemporising witty verse, yet at the same time writing more serious poems that expressed his liberal political views. It was now that he became a close friend of Caterino Mazzola, possibly through their mutual friend Casanova. Mazzola was just four years older than Da Ponte, and he was already beginning to establish himself as a librettist; indeed, they may even have discussed opera plots at the Caffè dei Letterati.

Da Ponte was still besotted with Anzoletta Bellaudi, but nevertheless resorted to his old ways, making several amorous conquests, who resented his continuing close attachment to her. This came to a head when three of Da Ponte's lovers set upon Anzoletta with knives, and her life was only saved by Da Ponte's swift intervention. As his life became ever more liberal, so did the ideas that he expressed in his poetry:

> Always remember the Republic
> Belongs only to the public,
> To everyone
> And to no one.
> It is a man's right to call
> For justice for one and all.

This was dangerously subversive. Yet the authorities were well aware that in the prevailing political climate prosecuting Da Ponte for expressing such views would only stir up a hornets' nest. The influence of Rousseau and Voltaire had led many intellectuals to espouse such views, to which the authorities preferred to turn a blind eye. Da Ponte would have to be silenced by other means and, given his lifestyle, these were not difficult to find. Someone (almost certainly a relative of Anzoletta, who was related to the chief prosecutor's chef) was persuaded to lodge a secret denunciation of Da Ponte for immoral behaviour.

In June 1779 Da Ponte was charged under the prohibition forbidding *mala vita* (basically, a debauched life), with specific reference to the section dealing with *rapito di donna honesta* (abducting a respectable woman). Once again he displayed a curious indifference to his trial, not even bothering to turn up as the court proceedings ground on through the long, hot months of summer. However, he must have belatedly realised the serious-ness of his position, since before he could be found guilty he slipped out of Venice. In his absence the Council of Ten sentenced Da Ponte to fifteen years in exile, and if he was discovered anywhere in the Republic during this period he would be 'imprisoned in a dungeon without light for seven years'.

Da Ponte eventually made his way to Dresden, where his friend Mazzola was achieving great success as a librettist. Here Mazzola took him on as his assistant, and Da Ponte quickly found that his talents were superbly suited to the writing of operas. However, his other talents also remained very much to the fore, culminating in a typical episode concerning a painter whom he had befriended. Having seduced the painter's two daughters, who both wanted to marry him, he confessed to their mother that he was unable to choose between them, 'and if it were not against the law, I would have asked both of them to marry me'. Having explained his dilemma, he then made an attempt to seduce the mother. Enter the outraged husband . . . Da Ponte descided it was time he left Dresden, and departed for Vienna. As a farewell gift his loyal friend Mazzola gave him a letter of introduc-tion to the leading court composer, Antonio Salieri, who happened to have been born in Venice, but had left at the age of nineteen.

Da Ponte arrived in Vienna in late 1781, where he was overjoyed to be introduced to his hero Metastasio and to meet up again with his old friend Casanova. Salieri employed Da Ponte as a librettist, and after an initial setback they soon achieved such success that he came to the attention of Mozart. Who was better equipped to write the libretti for *Don Giovanni*, *The Marriage of Figaro* and *Così fan tutti* (loosely, 'everyone does it' – a justi-fication that Da Ponte himself may well have used on occasion). Like his Venetian compatriots Vivaldi and Goldoni, Da Ponte would achieve prolific creativity at his peak. In his memoirs he claimed that whilst writing *Don Giovanni* he was also simultaneously writing two full-length operas for other composers. In his own words, 'I went on working for twelve hours every day, with brief intervals, for two months without a pause. A bottle of

Tokay on my right, my inkwell in the middle and a box of Seville snuff on my left.' When he required anything else, he would ring a bell for his landlady's daughter: 'A beautiful young girl of sixteen (whom I would have liked to love simply as a daughter, but . . .).'*

For ten years he would remain in Vienna. At one point he was congratulated by the emperor Joseph II on his work; at another he survived poison, which had been given to him by a jealous lover. In 1790 he was finally banished from Vienna, perhaps for privately circulating a satire on the new emperor, Leopold II, or possibly as a result of court intrigue. Da Ponte would blame Salieri, whom he claimed had now become his enemy.

There followed years of wandering and various adventures. Yet the days of amorous dalliance came to an end two years later, when the forty-three-year-old Da Ponte travelled to Trieste, where he fell in love with and married a young Englishwoman called Nancy Grahl (whose Jewish parents had also converted to Christianity). An unlikely but enthusiastic convert to married life, Da Ponte continued to work as a librettist with diminishing success, staying in Paris, Holland and then London, where he and his family were soon penniless. Da Ponte wrote despairingly to his friend Casanova, who helpfully suggested that Da Ponte should recoup his fortunes by selling Nancy's favours. Da Ponte drew the line at this, and eventually, on the point of being arrested for debt, took ship for America – having prudently despatched Nancy ahead of him with their four children. Here he would live out his last years, variously becoming a grocer in Philadelphia, writing his memoirs and becoming a professor of Italian in New York, before losing his savings investing in an Italian opera house. Even so, he would live to see *Don Giovanni* performed in New York for the first time, before dying there in 1838 at the age of eighty-nine. Like his friend and collaborator Mozart, who had died forty-seven years previously, Da Ponte was buried in an unmarked grave.

By now the Europe that Da Ponte had known was utterly changed. The forces of liberty, which he had previously championed, had once more triumphed. Six years after America had gained independence from Britain, the people of France rose up and overthrew the rule of Louis XVI, who

---

* The ellipsis is Da Ponte's.

would be sent to the guillotine. No king or ruler in Europe now felt safe from his downtrodden subjects. In an effort to overcome the revolution, attacks were launched on France from all sides, and elsewhere repression became the order of the day. Once again Europe was in turmoil. Though Venice would remain geographically and politically on the margins of all this, the tourist trade dried up – this time causing considerable economic hardship and unrest. The Council of Ten tightened its grip even further, and its spies were everywhere. Meanwhile the revolution in France prevailed, and as its armies defended its territory a charismatic young military genius called Napoleon Bonaparte rose through the ranks.

20

The Very End

URING THE LONG years of Venice's decline artists of the calibre of Vivaldi, Goldoni and Tiepolo had left to seek their fortune in exile. Now the city was reduced to exporting the likes of Da Ponte and his notorious friend Casanova.

Giacomo Casanova de Seingalt had been born in April 1725 – he was not originally of noble birth, his 'de Seingalt' title being his own creation. His mother, Zanetta, was an actress (who, as we have seen, would later tour in the same troupe as Goldoni); at the age of sixteen she had eloped with an actor-dancer named Gaetano Casanova. The following year she would produce her first son, Giacomo, whose real father was almost certainly Michele Grimani, a man of noble family who owned the San Samuele theatre where Gaetano and Zanetta had been performing. Zanetta soon went on tour abroad and achieved considerable success in Dresden, then in London, where in 1727 she had a second son, this time by the Prince of Wales, who ascended to the throne that same year as George II. Meanwhile young Giacomo was brought up by his maternal grandmother. According to Casanova's memoirs,* at this period in his life, 'I was very weak, ate practically nothing, was unable to concentrate on anything, and looked like an idiot . . . I had difficulty breathing and always kept my mouth open.' In an effort to cure him of his ailments, which included a 'constant nosebleed', his grandmother took him on a gondola to the island

---

* Originally written in French as *L'Historie de ma vie* (History of My Life), this entertaining if somewhat repetitive description of Casanova's life and multifarious seductions (real and imagined) stretches to a dozen volumes.

of Murano, where they visited the 'hovel' of a local witch: 'She was an old woman sitting on a straw-filled mattress who had a black cat in her arms and five or six more around her.'

At the age of nine he would be boarded out in Padua with a priest, the Abbé Gozzi. From the outset, Casanova displayed astonishing abilities: according to his own testimony, he learned to read and write within a month. He began reading theology books in the abbé's library, but one day came across a 'forbidden' book, which he appears to have enjoyed, despite his young age. At eleven he fell in love with the abbé's fourteen-year-old sister Bettina, who 'little by little kindled in my heart the first sparks of a feeling which was later to become my ruling passion'. The abbé had designated Bettina to look after Casanova, and in the morning she would come to wash him before he got up, 'telling me that she did not have time to wait for me to get dressed'. She would:

> wash my face and neck and chest, and then give my body further caresses which I knew must have been innocent even though they excited me . . . One day, sitting beside me on the bed, she told me that my body was beginning to grow and demonstrated this to me with her own hands, arousing a feeling in me which would not stop until it exceeded all limit and surpassed itself.

And with this Casanova was launched upon his 'ruling passion'. A year later he enrolled at the University of Padua, where he studied philosophy, law, mathematics and chemistry – the last-named awakening in him an interest in alchemy and the occult sciences. He read widely, including works on the Kabbala and magic, as well as taking a keen interest in medicine (which he later regretted having not taken as his main subject). All this was accompanied by a steady diet of erotic literature. Like any other student he caroused in the taverns, but surprisingly did not accompany his fellow students to the bordello. Instead he appears to have become something of a chaste, precocious dandy who developed 'a longing for literary fame'. However, he did develop a taste for gambling, which would become a lifelong preoccupation. But despite his fine mathematical talent, he frequently miscalculated the odds, incurring heavy losses. After he completed his studies in 1739, his grandmother paid off his debts and summoned him back to Venice. Here she insisted that he take minor orders in preparation for becoming a lawyer (a common practice at the time).

Possibly through the influence of his real father (who remained a shadowy influence) Casanova now acquired as a patron the seventy-six-year-old senator Alvise Malpiero, who in his time had achieved a somewhat dubious name for himself by acquiring (and being able to afford) twenty mistresses, whilst simultaneously gaining a reputation for being a homosexual. It was at Malpiero's palazzo on the Grand Canal that Casanova learned the manners required in upper-class society – a schooling in the flourishes of charm and ingratiation for which he had a natural talent.

And it was now, at the age of sixteen, that Casanova had his first bonafide sexual experience. According to his memoirs, this was achieved in suitably impressive circumstances, when he succeeded in seducing (or was seduced by, it is difficult to distinguish) two sisters of aristocratic family, the sixteen-year-old Nanetta and the fifteen-year-old Marta. All three would appear to have been virgins when they got into bed together, but found their mutual deflowering so exhilarating that they 'spent the rest of the night in ever varied skirmishes'. Casanova's memoirs, written in his later years, contain many exaggerations and even palpable falsehoods; on the other hand, many of his most implausible and unlikely escapades almost certainly took place, having about them an idiosyncratic and psychological ring of truth. Casanova may have been a fabulist, but he also lived a fabulous life. And the story of his first full sexual experience with the two sisters (members of the noble Savorgnan family, which Casanova tactfully omits to mention) appears utterly credible, especially given the moral example set by their elders in the Venice of the period.

Having launched the career of his 'ruling passion' there was now no holding back on Casanova's behalf. In quick succession he was angrily dismissed from the Malpieri palazzo after being discovered in a compromising embrace with a young girl who was intended for his host's delectation; and he was also dismissed from his seminary for being found in bed with a young boy. On the latter occasion Casanova seems to have been innocent – though in the years to come he would not be so prudish as to deny himself the occasional homosexual adventure. As his memoirs make clear,

Casanova was to be omnivorous in his sexual exploits: women, men, sisters (separately and together), mothers and daughters (ditto), women disguised as castrati, undisguised castrati, *ménages à trois*, *ménages à quatre*, and so on – all were welcome.

At the same time he found occasion to pursue his other two callings, which he also claimed to follow with a passion – namely, literature and gambling. With regards to the former, his talent was in its infancy during these early years, though he was already showing signs of being an accomplished poet. However, his gambling was another matter. His favourite game was faro, which depended upon the turn of the card, where the odds were usually almost even, and for this he used his own gambling system, which was a variation on the Martingale method. In its simplest form, this involves doubling your next bet each time you lose – an apparently plausible process that often results in winnings, but does eventually prove ruinous, as Casanova was to discover time and time again. In 1743, after his expulsion from the seminary, he tried to earn a living at the Ridotto and other casinos, but soon found himself in such deep debt that he was imprisoned in the fortress of Sant'Andrea on an island in the lagoon. Probably through the background influence of his natural father, he was soon released, and departed from Venice to take up an appointment as a secretary in the employment of the Church. He ended up in Rome as secretary to Cardinal Acquaviva, the Spanish ambassador to the Holy See. In the course of this work Casanova had an audience with the worldly Pope Benedict XIV, who was so charmed by his wit and learning that he invited Casanova to visit him regularly in the Vatican. At the same time Casanova had his first encounter with a pretty young castrato whom he initially mistook for a girl, but who offered to spend the night with him 'either as a boy or a girl, whichever I chose'. Uncharacteristically, Casanova turned down this offer.

At first Cardinal Acquaviva was highly impressed by his talented eighteen-year-old secretary, even employing him to write love-poems to one of his long string of amatory conquests, a certain 'Marchesa G'. Indeed, Casanova performed this task so well that the cardinal felt obliged to insert a few faults in his verses, in case the marchesa thought them too accomplished to be the cardinal's own work. Perhaps inevitably, Casanova was soon dismissed from his post, for the unlikely misdemeanour of enabling his French tutor's daughter to elope with another man (though not until he had made his own unsuccessful attempt on her virtue). He could be altruistic as well as unlucky.

There now followed long years of travelling, during which he would pass through cities from Constantinople to St Petersburg, and all capitals in between, with occasional return visits to Venice. During the ensuing decades he pursued his three ruling passions with varying success. His gambling was at best modestly successful, more often than not ending in disaster. His literary pursuits met with passing success: his first play was put on in Dresden to some critical acclaim, he translated *The Iliad*, edited magazines, kept up his interest in the occult, was elected to the distinguished Arcadian Academy in Rome, and almost certainly collaborated with Da Ponte and Mozart on *Don Giovanni*. Meanwhile he obsessively indulged in the pursuit for which his name had become a byword. What drove this obsession, which at times took on the proportions of a full-scale addiction?

Psychologists have pointed to the behaviour of his mother. And to the absence of a father – both that of his shadowy natural father and that of the man whose name he took on, who was frequently away touring with his mother and died when Casanova was eight. Others suggest that whilst he was with his grandmother he was the centre of attention amidst a company of worshipping women, and that he merely sought to prolong this paradisiacal situation into adult life. Casanova's own explanation is disarmingly simple: he was constantly falling in (and out of) love – and there is no doubting the compelling force and capriciousness of his serial infatuations, hinting at some form of deep emotional instability. Whatever the explanation, there is no denying that Casanova's 'affairs' certainly numbered well into three figures. There are also some compelling external reasons for his behaviour. The eighteenth century was a notoriously promiscuous era, and nowhere more so than Venice. The all but non-existent sexual morality in the city in which Casanova grew up must surely have played a significant role in encouraging his behaviour, which can only have been boosted by the confidence that his many early conquests assuredly gave him. Later he was certainly aided by the fact that his reputation preceded him. This led him to increasingly bold and multifarious escapades – perhaps the most monstrous of which would involve an affair with his own seventeen-year-old illegitimate daughter, which resulted in her giving birth to a boy who was both his son and his grandson.

Gambling, spying, editing, fighting duels, avoiding assassination attempts, practising magic, self-administering medicines for the inevitable succession of sexual diseases that he contracted, spells in gaol, as well as banishment from a string of major European cities (including Madrid, Vienna, Florence, Turin and Barcelona) and personal banishment from France by Louis XV – all these give an indication of the occupational hazards that his compulsion led him to endure. But there were also high moments (quite apart from those of a sexual nature). In the course of his travels he met many of the leading figures of his age: Louis XV, popes Benedict XIV and Clement XIII (who was so impressed that he invested Casanova as a Knight of the Golden Spur, a papal order of chivalry, no less), Rousseau, Voltaire, Madame Pompadour, Frederick the Great of Prussia (whose offer of employment he turned down), Catherine the Great of Russia (whom he advised to reform the Russian calendar, to bring it into line with that operating in Europe) . . . and so it went on.

However, Casanova's most celebrated exploit, for which he would become famous throughout Europe, was neither amatory nor took place abroad. In 1753 he returned to Venice, where for two years he continued with his usual behaviour in the boudoir, at his writing desk and in the casinos. In July 1755 the network of spies acting for the Council of Ten brought his behaviour to the attention of the Venetian Inquisition and he was arrested. The official charge was heresy – and there is no doubt that he did continue to practise 'the magical arts'. However, Casanova's cause cannot have been helped by the fact that he had circulated a scurrilous poem poking fun at religion, his gambling had recently ruined an influential senator, and he was having an affair with the mistress of one of the Inquisitors.

Casanova was marched off to the Doge's Palace, where he was led up to the notorious cells known as *Il Piombi* ('The Leads'), which were housed beneath the lead roofing of the palace. These cells were so low that it was impossible to stand upright; giant rats scampered over the floor and the place was infested with fleas. In winter the cells became freezing cold, while during summer the lead roof heated to such a temperature that the atmosphere was all but suffocating. Casanova was tried in his absence from court, and sentenced to five years in prison. But he was not informed of the verdict. For all he knew, when the heavy cell door slammed closed and was bolted behind him, he was liable to be detained in The Leads for the rest of his life. Such was all too often the case.

No one had ever escaped from The Leads before, but the man who had escaped from so many angry husbands, irate gamblers and even hired assassins now set about planning the impossible. This would take more than a year of careful preparation, mishaps and false alarms, until early on the evening of 31 October 1756 he was at last ready. With the aid of a sharpened iron spike, and the assistance of a disgraced monk called Marin Albi in the next cell, Casanova eventually managed to break out onto the rooftop. After clambering over the lead roofing and heaving himself precariously along gutters, overcoming crippling cramp in the process, Casanova happened by chance across a ladder left by some builders. The two of them then scrambled down and broke through a lower window, though this was still way above ground level. Once inside, they found that they were in a locked room inside the main part of the Doge's Palace, but by this stage Casanova was so exhausted that he fell asleep, being woken by Albi at around five in the morning. He now used his spike to open the door and they passed through a succession of rooms, corridors and chambers, until they found themselves confronted by a large door that proved impervious to all Casanova's efforts.

It was at this stage that Casanova noticed how his endeavours had left him 'torn and scratched from head to foot and covered with blood'. He proceeded to tidy himself up as best he could, so that if they managed to get out of the building 'he would look like a man who had attended a ball and later gone looking for a house of ill repute where he had been beaten up'. Albi looked less conspicuous in his ragged robes, and had sustained fewer injuries as he had simply followed behind Casanova after he had hacked his way and broken through the obstacles in their path. Casanova now tried opening the window of the room in which they were trapped, but they were spotted by a passer-by on the quayside below. The passer-by assumed they had mistakenly been locked in the building overnight and went to get the caretaker, who came and unlocked the door to the room where the two of them were trapped. Boldly Casanova brushed past the caretaker, leading Albi down the main stairway of the Doge's Palace, across the Piazzetta to the quayside, where they took a gondola and were eventually delivered to the mainland. Here, after several further adventures, Casanova and Albi finally made their way overland to the edge of Venetian territory, where they parted company and Casanova made good his escape.

This is but a brief summary of the actual sequence of events. The detailed description that Casanova gives of his imprisonment in The Leads and his consequent escape is one of the most exciting in literature, inspiring writers from Alexandre Dumas to Franz Kafka.* But is his story true? It has been suggested that Casanova in fact bribed his way out of The Leads. Indeed, his written account is filled with unlikely details — yet bills for the repair of the damages that Casanova and Albi caused during their daring, dangerous escape across the rooftops and through the chambers have been found in the ubiquitous Venetian archives. Casanova's account may well have contained the occasional embellishment, but astonishingly it would appear in the main to be true.

The story of his daring escape spread through Europe, and by the time he reached Paris in 1757 he was famous. Here he had a further stroke of good fortune when he became involved in setting up the first French state lottery. From this he made a fortune, but lost it in an ill-judged investment in a silk-printing factory. However, eventually — inevitably — the life of seduction (and disease), gambling, spying and hack-writing started to take its toll. His teeth began to fall out, and he suffered from diminishing sexual potency. In 1784, whilst in Vienna, he formed a friendship with Count Joseph von Waldstein, based on their shared interest in magic. Waldstein became so enamoured of Casanova's company that he offered him the post of librarian at his castle at Dux in Bohemia (now Duchcov in the Czech Republic). Fifty-nine years old, broke and all but toothless, Casanova had little choice but to accept this generous offer.

---

* Casanova's description appears in his short work *Escape from The Leads*, as well as in Volume Four, Chapters 14 and 15, in the more readily available Everyman translation of his *History of My Life*.

He now found himself living in isolation amidst the hills and woodlands of provincial Bohemia. The count soon lost interest in him and spent increasingly long periods away from home, leaving Casanova at the mercy of the hostile German major-domo and his servants. Plunged into despair, and with little else to do, in 1790 Casanova began writing his memoirs, whose twelve volumes would occupy him through the ensuing years. Alone and in failing health, he longed to return home, but by now the Venice he had known had ceased to exist.

Europe had become a different world. Following the French Revolution the continent had been plunged into the Revolutionary Wars, as an alliance supported by the Prussians and the Hapsburg Austrians attempted to reinstate the monarchy. After the execution of Louis XVI in 1793, and the death of his heir Louis XVII two years later, the forty-year-old Louis XVIII had become claimant to the throne of France; and, with the encouragement of the Hapsburg emperor Francis II, he took up residence in the safety of Verona, which was in neutral Venetian mainland territory. Though not a participant in the Revolutionary Wars, Venice remained closely allied to Hapsburg Austria, which counted much of northern Italy as its territory. During the long years of pursuing its policy of neutrality, Venice had neglected its militia, which now consisted of a comparatively small army of mainly Serbo-Croatian conscripts. The Republic thus had little alternative but to acquiesce to the presence of Louis XVIII in Verona, where the French claimant soon set up a court attracting many monarchist exiles. Meanwhile the French revolutionary government protested in the strongest possible terms, insisting that if Venice did not expel Louis XVIII and his court it would forfeit its neutral status and be regarded as an enemy. Venice, protected by the Austrian occupancy of Milan, took scant notice of this impotent threat.

Then suddenly the situation was transformed. In early April 1796 Bonaparte led the French army across the Alps into northern Italy, quickly outwitting the Austrians, forcing them into retreat. The French demanded once more that Louis XVIII be expelled from Verona or the city would no longer be regarded as neutral territory; at the same time the Austrians insisted that Venice should not comply. Faced with Bonaparte's advancing army, Venice caved in; and on 21 April, Louis XVIII departed from Verona. The emperor Francis II was outraged, and Venice now found itself under increasing threat from both sides.

In May, Bonaparte secured a major victory over the Austrians at the Battle of Lodi, where thousands of imperial troops were taken prisoner, and a few days later he marched triumphantly into Milan. By June the Austrians were under siege at Mantua, just five miles from the Venetian border. Venice's neutrality was once more threatened when Austrian troops marching south to relieve Mantua demanded permission to cross Venetian territory. The weak and ill-trained Venetian army was in no position to oppose this demand and the Republic weakly conceded. This time it was Bonaparte's turn to be outraged.

Up until now Venetian policy had been characterised by weakness. Caught between two major powers, it had dithered, seeking to appease one side and then the other. The Republic was devoid of leadership. It was as if more than seventy years of inglorious neutrality, combined with the increasingly repressive internal policy maintained by the Council of Ten and its network of informants, had crushed all trace of individuality. Da Ponte and Casanova were far from being the only free spirits to seek their fortune in Europe and the New World. With the administration characterised by the spirit of the committee, the enterprise that had once been the glory of the city had now all but vanished. Just a few years earlier one of the Republic's few successful businessmen had lamented that the city's life-blood — trade — 'is falling into final collapse. The ancient and long-held maxims and laws which created and could still create a nation's greatness have been forgotten'. As in trade, so in all other matters. Even the Council of Ten's efforts to maintain a police state were beginning to falter. Many Venetian citizens had been stirred by the French Revolution and ideas of liberty. There was even muttered talk of the overthrow of the oligarchy and the establishment of a truly democratic republic.

Doge Lodovico Manin had by this time been in office for some seven years and was in his seventies. In failing health and partially deaf, he was more inclined to spend his time in religious devotions than the affairs of the Republic, his negligence allowing the once-great Venetian fleet to dwindle to a mere 390 merchantmen. Less than three months after Manin's election, the news of the French Revolution had reached Venice, causing consternation amongst the Council of Ten – and now French revolutionary troops were camped at the Republic's borders, fewer than fifty miles from the lagoon itself. Where previously the Council of Ten and the Senate had dithered in their foreign policy, from this point on their jittery indecisiveness would lead to catastrophic blunders.

By now Bonaparte himself had marched north, pursuing the Austrians across the Alps. The Venetians were thus astonished when in the autumn of 1796 he offered them an alliance. In fact the Venetians should not have been surprised: Bonaparte was desperate to protect his overstretched army. But when his reassuring offer was put to the Senate, they voted to turn it down. It is all but impossible to think of a rational explanation for this self-destructive decision. Under the circumstances, continuing neutrality was out of the question. It has been suggested that the senators were afraid that an alliance with France would mean the spread of subversive ideas. Either way, Bonaparte immediately ordered his troops to march into Verona, in order to protect his supply lines, and there was nothing that Venice could do about it.

Six months later, two incidents would put the Venetians in a yet more precarious position. The citizens of Verona rose up against the French, and were savagely put down – again with no attempt at Venetian intervention. Shortly afterwards three French ships attempted to sail into the lagoon. As Venice remained technically neutral, strictly speaking this did not constitute an act of aggression. Indeed, it seems the French intended none. On the other hand, the French appeared to be unaware that the Council of Ten had issued an order barring all foreign ships from entering Venetian waters. As the French warships entered the lagoon, they were fired upon by Venetian defence batteries at the Sant'Andrea fort. Two of the French ships managed to turn and sail for the open sea, but the third received direct hits from the Venetian cannon fire. Its captain and a number of French sailors were killed and the ship immobilised. This was undeniably an act of war, and the French were not slow to brand it as such.

As if matters were not bad enough, Venice's ally Francis II had now entered into peace negotiations with Bonaparte. Venice found itself standing alone against the might of the French revolutionary army. Panic swept through the city as the news came in that French troops were overrunning the mainland territories, and by the end of April 1797 the revolutionary army was lining the shores of the lagoon. The island city, wall-less and defenceless, now stood within range of the French artillery.

The end was swift in coming. On 9 May, Bonaparte issued an ultimatum that boiled down to two alternatives: either Venice surrendered or it would be destroyed. The city appeared to have little option. On 12 May, the tearful seventy-two-year-old Doge Manin appeared before the Great Council and asked them to vote. By now most of its members had already disappeared from the city. The remaining 537 voted by 512 to twenty to surrender, with five abstaining, and then fled the chamber in disarray, casting off their robes so that they could slip away undetected through the crowd gathered outside in the Piazza San Marco. They had effectively voted themselves out of existence. Three days later French soldiers sailed across the lagoon and took possession of the city. They encountered no resistance. When the city and the nearby islands had been secured, 4,000 soldiers of the revolutionary army staged a parade, accompanied by brass bands, in the Piazza San Marco. The watching citizens well understood the significance of the event: this was the first time in Venice's long history that foreign troops had set foot in their city. Further humiliations marking the end of the independent Republic soon followed. Bonaparte ordered that a 'Tree of Liberty' be planted in the Piazza San Marco, beneath which the doge's *corno*, and other insignia of office, were ceremonially burned, along with a copy of the Golden Book listing all the noble families. The deposed doge and the former members of the Grand Council who had not fled the city were then made to dance around the flames, while the watching citizens were encouraged by the French soldiers to jeer at their former masters. Next it was the turn of the city itself to be dismantled. The French army began taking down the bronze horses of San Marco and removing other treasures, in preparation for their transshipment to France. The city's destruction, both political and symbolic, was now complete. The 1,000-year-old Republic of Venice was no more.

Select Bibliography

Because this is intended as a popular work I have not included endnotes with an exhaustive and meticulous list of sources for quotations and precise information, which can often extend the endmatter by as much as a quarter the length of the actual text. Instead I have indicated in the text the sources of most direct quotes and have given here a bibliographical round-up of the works that I consulted, which may prove useful for further reading.

Ackroyd, Peter, *Venice: Pure City* (London, 2009)

Anderson, R.C., *Naval Wars in the Levant 1559–1853* (Liverpool, 1952)

Anderson, Sonia P., *An English Consul in Turkey* (Oxford, 1989)

Aretino, Pietro, *Selected Letters* (London, 1976)

Barbaro, Nicolò, *Diary of the Siege of Constantinople*, trans. J.R. Jones (New York, 1969)

Barbaro, Nicolò, *Giornale dell' Assedio di Constantinopoli*, ed. E. Cornet (Vienna, 1856)

Barcham, William L., *Giambattista Tiepolo* (London, 1992)

Bembo, Pietro, *History of Venice*, 3 vols, trans. R.W. Ulery (London, 2007–9)

Benedictow, Ole J., *The Black Death 1346–1353: The Complete History* (Suffolk, 2004)

Bergreen, Laurence, *Marco Polo* (London, 2008)

Bicheno, Hugh, *Crescent and Cross: The Battle of Lepanto 1571* (London, 2004)

Bishop, Morris, *Petrarch and His World* (London, 1964)

Brown, Horatio F., *Studies in the History of Venice* (London, 1907)

Brown, Horatio F., *Venice, An Historical Sketch* (London, 1893)

Browning, Oscar, *The Life of Bartolomeo Colleoni* (Arundel, 1891)

Byrne, Joseph P., *The Black Death* (Westport, 2004)

Calimani, Riccardo, *The Ghetto of Venice* (New York, 1987)

Calimani, Riccardo, *Storie di Marrani a Venezia* (Milan, 1991)

Cardano, Girolamo, *The Book of My Life*, trans. Jean Stoner (London, 1931)

Casanova, Giacomo, *History of My Life* (London, 2006)

Cleugh, James, *The Divine Aretino* (London, 1965)

Crawford, F. Marion, *Gleanings in Venetian History*, 2 vols (London, 1905)

Curiel, Roberta, *The Ghetto of Venice* (London, 1990)

Da Ponte, Lorenzo, *Memoirs* (New York, 2000)

Drake, Stillman, *Galileo at Work* (London, 1978)

Epstein, Steven, *Genoa and the Genoese: 998–1528* (North Carolina, 1996)

Ferino-Pagden, Sylvia, *Giorgione, Mythos und Enigma* (Vienna, 2004)

Foglietta, Uberto, *The Sieges of Nicosia and Famagusta*, trans. C.B. Cobham (London, 1903)

Gabrieli, G.B., *Nicolo Tartaglia* (Siena, 1986)

Goffman, Daniel, *The Ottoman Empire* (Cambridge, 2002)

Goldoni, Carlo, *Memoirs*, trans. John Black (London, 1926)

Gould, Cecil, *The Sixteenth-Century Italian Schools* (London, 1975)

Graziani, Antonmaria, *The Sieges of Nicosia and Famagusta*, trans. R. Midgely (*sic*) (London, 1989)

Heller, Karl, *Anthony Vivaldi* (Portland, 1991)

Hibbert, Christopher, *Venice* (London, 1998)

Hodges, Sheila, *Lorenzo da Ponte* (London, 1985)

Hodgson, F.C., *Venice in the Thirteenth and Fourteenth Centuries* (London, 1910)

Holden, Anthony, *The Man who Wrote Mozart: Lorenzo da Ponte* (London, 2007)

Hollway-Calthrop, Henry, *Petrarch: His Life and Times* (London, 1907)

Holme, Timothy, *The Life and Times of Carlo Goldoni* (London, 1976)

Hunt, David, *Caterina Carnaro* (London, 1989)

Hutton, Edward, *Pietro Aretino* (London, 1922)

Il catalogo delle principlai . . . cortigiane di Venezia (republished Venice, 1956)

Imber, Colin, *The Ottoman Empire 1300–1530* (London, 2002)

Jervis, Henry, *History of the Island of Corfu* (London, 1852)

Kedar, Benjamin Z., *Merchants in Crisis: Genoese and Venetian Men of Affairs and the Fourteenth-Century Depression* (New Haven, 1976)

Kelly, John, *The Great Mortality* (London, 2004)

Kindleberger, Charles, *A Financial History of Western Europe* (London, 1984)

Lane, Frederic C., *Money and Banking in Medieval and Renaissance Venice: Vol. 1, Coins and Moneys of Account* (Baltimore, 1958)

Lane, Frederic C., *Venice, A Maritime Republic* (Baltimore, 1973)

Larner, John, *Marco Polo* (New York, 1999)

Laven, Mary, *Virgins of Venice* (London, 2002)

Leonardo da Vinci, *Notebooks*, 2 vols, ed. J.P. Richter (New York, 1970)

Links, J.G., *Canaletto* (Oxford, 1982)

Livio, Mario, *The Equation That Couldn't Be Solved* (New York, 2005)

Longworth, Philip, *The Rise and Fall of Venice* (London, 1974)

McKee, Sally, *Uncommon Dominion: Venetian Crete* (Philadelphia, 2000)

Mann, Nicholas, *Petrarch* (Oxford, 1984)

Martineau, Jane (ed.), *The Genius of Venice* (London, 1983–4)

Masters, John, *Casanova* (London, 1969)

Milton, Giles, *Paradise Lost: Smyrna* (London, 2008)

Molmenti, Pompeo, *Venice*, 6 vols (Bergamo, 1908)

Morris, Jan, *The Venetian Empire* (London, 1980)

Morris, Jan, *Venice* (London, 1960)

Mueller, Reinhold C., *Money and Banking in Medieval and Renaissance Venice: Volume 2: The Venetian Money Market* (Baltimore, 1958)

The New Cambridge Modern History: Vol. 1, The Renaissance, ed. G.R. Potter (Cambridge, 1964)

The New Grove Dictionary of Music and Musicians, ed. Stanley Sadie, 29 vols (London, 2001)

Norton, Rictor (ed.), *My Dear Boy* (San Francisco, 1998)

Norwich, John Julius, *A History of Venice* (London, 1983)

Oliphant, Margaret, *The Makers of Venice* (London, 1905)

Ore, Oystein, *Cardano, The Gambling Scholar* (New York, 1965)

Parker, Derek, *Casanova* (Stroud, 2002)

Parry, V.J., *A History of the Ottoman Empire to 1730* (Cambridge, 1976)

Pastor, Ludwig, *The History of the Popes from the Close of the Middle Ages*, 40 vols (Liechtenstein, 1968–9)

Petrarca, Francesco, *Lettere Senile*, 2 vols (Florence, 1892)

Polo, Marco, *The Book of Ser Marco Polo*, 2 vols, ed. and trans. H. Yule and H. Cordier (London, 1903)

Polo, Marco, *The Travels of Marco Polo*, trans. Ronald Latham (London, 1958)

Ramusio, Giovanni Battista, *Delle Navigationi et Viaggi*, 3 vols (Venice, 1550, 1583, 1606)

Ridolfi, Carlo, *The Life of Titian*, trans. J. and P. Bondanella (Philadelphia, 1996)

Ridolfi, Carlo, *La Vita di Giacopo Robusti detto il Tintoretto* (Venice, 1642)

Romano, Dennis, *The Likeness of Venice: A Life of Doge Francesco Foscari 1373–1457* (Yale, 2007)

Rosenthal, Margaret, *The Honest Courtesan* (Chicago, 1992)
Rowland, Ingrid, *Giordano Bruno* (Godalming, 2008)
Runciman, Steven, *The Fall of Constantinople 1453* (Cambridge, 1965)
Sabellico, Marcantonio, *De Latinae linguae reparatione* (reprinted Messina, 1999)
Sanudo, M., *Diarii* [Jan 1496–March 1533] 58 vols (Venice, 1879–1903)
Schrade, Leo, *Monteverdi: Creator of modern music* (London, 1972)
Setton, Kenneth, *The Papacy and the Levant 1204–1571* (Philadelphia, 1976)
Severis, Leto, *Ladies of Medieval Cyprus and Caterina Cornaro* (Nicosia, 1995)
Simonson, George, *Francesco Guardi* (London, 1904)
Spino, Pietro, *Historia della vita . . . Coglione* [Colleoni] (Venice, 1569)
Spuridakis, Konstantinos, *A Brief History of Cyprus* (Nicosia?, 1964)
Steegmann, Mary, *Bianca Capello* (London, 1913)
Stonor Saunders, Frances, *Hawkwood* (London, 2004)
Thayer, William Roscoe, *A Short History of Venice* (Boston, 1908)
van Gelder, G.J.H., *Eastward Bound . . . Adventures in the Middle East* [Lupazzoli] (Amsterdam, 1994)
Vasari, Giorgio, *Lives of the Artists*, trans. George Bull, 2 vols (London, 1965, 1987)
Venice: A Documentary History 1450–1630, ed. David Chambers (Oxford, 1992)
White, Michael, *The Pope and the Heretic* [Bruno], (London, 2002)

Acknowledgements

First of all I would like to thank Ellah Alfrey, formely of Jonathan Cape, who commissioned this work. My present editor at Cape, Alex Bowler, has played a more than significant role in shaping this book. His detailed and insightful suggestions have improved my original work no end, from the overall structure to the smallest historical facts.

I would also like to thank the staff and fellow researchers I encountered on my round of the various libraries and museums in Britain and Italy, some of whose suggestions proved particularly fruitful. My visits to Venice, Padua, Vienna, Paris, Crete and Istanbul over the years have all led me into contact with countless sources who have contributed to this work. As always, the staff in the Humanities 2 Reading Room of the British Library were exceptional.

Once again, no thanks can be complete without acknowledgement of all the work and encouragement provided by my agent, Julian Alexander of the LAW Agency, who for so many years now has been both a helpful and reassuring friend.

Index